D1294219

University of Michigan Publications

HISTORY AND POLITICAL SCIENCE

VOLUME XV

JOHN STUART AND THE SOUTHERN COLONIAL FRONTIER

JOHN STUART AND THE SOUTHERN COLONIAL FRONTIER

A Study of INDIAN RELATIONS, WAR, TRADE, and LAND PROBLEMS in the SOUTHERN WILDERNESS, 1754-1775

By

JOHN RICHARD ALDEN

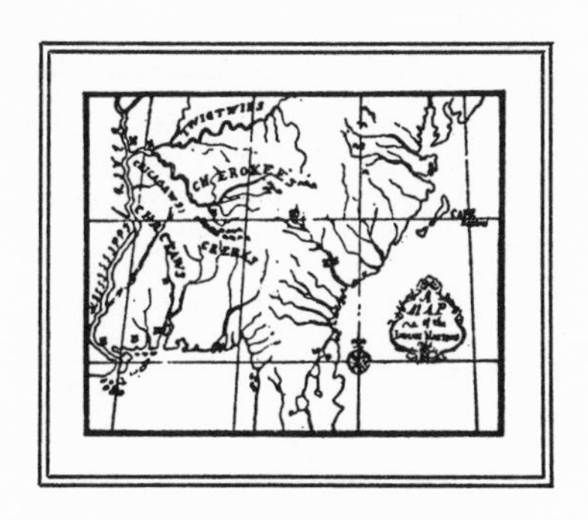

GORDIAN PRESS, INC.
NEW YORK
1966

Reprinted by Gordian Press, Inc. with
the permission of The University of Michigan 1966

Library of Congress Catalog Card No. 66-29459

Printed in U.S.A. by
EDWARDS BROTHERS, INC.
Ann Arbor, Michigan

To

PEARL ALDEN

PREFACE

IN A pioneer work on *The Southern Frontier, 1670–1732,* Verner W. Crane has given the most scholarly and complete account of an American colonial frontier, but the struggle for empire in the southern wilderness between 1732 and 1783 has not attracted the attention it deserves. I have attempted to describe that struggle (largely dominated by Indian relations) during the period 1754–75. The year 1775 was chosen as a terminus for obvious reasons. It may not be quite so clear why my narrative (after a necessarily lengthy introduction) begins in 1754. The outbreak of the French and Indian War is an important consideration. Even more compelling reasons, in the mind of the writer, lie in the facts that 1754 was a great turning point in the development of British policy regarding the old West and that the imperial offices of Indian superintendent and military commander in America were created in that year. The men who held those offices exercised large powers in the West before—and for that matter during—the American Revolution.

Good work has been done in chronicling the history of the southern frontier during the period 1732–83. Chapman C. Milling, though primarily interested in the southern Indians as Indians, has made some contribution toward a better understanding of relations between red men and white in the eighteenth century. Robert L. Meriwether, in his *Expansion of South Carolina, 1729–1765,* has described in detail the westward advance of South Carolina settlements within the chronological limits of his study. We have also had articles by Philip M. Hamer upon Anglo-French rivalry in the Cherokee country during the Seven Years' War and upon the policy of John Stuart, the British Indian superintendent, at the beginning of the Revolution. Clarence E. Carter has contributed a discussion of British policy in respect to the southern Indians during the period 1763–68; and Helen Louise Shaw, in her *British Administration of the Southern Indians, 1756–1783,* has offered a fairly extensive exposition of the financing and structural organization of the southern Indian department. Nor should it be forgotten that Clarence W. Alvord, in his *Mississippi Valley in British Politics,* and Thomas P. Abernethy, particularly in *Western Lands and the American Revo-*

lution, have described phases of the development of the southern frontier after 1763. Other writers could be mentioned. Nevertheless, many important aspects of the history of that frontier during the twenty years before the Revolution, especially the development and execution of British policy, have never been adequately analyzed. It is astonishing that John Stuart has not yet attained the dignity of a biography—astonishing even though his papers have not yet come to light. The major facts regarding the remarkable career of that romantic scion of the royal house of Scotland are included within these pages.

The materials for this study have been gathered from several parts of the United States. The present war prevented researches abroad, but there is good reason to believe that no serious lacunae have resulted, for the great bulk of the relevant documents in the British Public Record Office, the British Museum, and the Archives Nationales in Paris were available in the form of transcripts or photocopies on this side of the Atlantic, notably in the Library of Congress. It is an interesting fact that it would not have been possible to complete this work in Great Britain without recourse to American archives and libraries. The Historical Commission of South Carolina and the William L. Clements Library of the University of Michigan proved to be unusually rich in original manuscripts not available elsewhere. It has been my privilege to have free access in the William L. Clements Library to the General Thomas Gage MSS, which contain a mass of hitherto unused papers relative to frontier and Indian problems, including correspondence between General Gage and John Stuart covering the period 1763–75.

Acknowledgments for courteous helpfulness are due to Miss Mabel L. Webber, of the South Carolina Historical Society; the late Miss Louise Phelps Kellogg, of the State Historical Society of Wisconsin; Henry W. Meikle, of the National Library of Scotland; Julien C. Yonge, editor of the *Florida Historical Quarterly;* Miss Nina M. Visscher, of the Kentucky State Historical Society; Miss Mildred L. Saunders, of the Dartmouth College Library; and Kenneth G. Hamilton, assistant archivist of the Archives of the Moravian Church.

I am specially indebted for friendly services and assistance to Dr. St. George L. Sioussat and Miss Grace Gardner Griffin, of the Division of Manuscripts, Library of Congress, and to Miss Ellen Fitzsimons and the staff of the Charleston Library Society. Mr. Alexander S. Salley was exceedingly helpful in placing the resources of the Historical Commission of South Carolina at my disposal. In the

William L. Clements Library Dr. Randolph G. Adams, librarian, Miss Elizabeth Steere, associate librarian, Mr. Howard Peckham, curator of manuscripts, and Mr. Lloyd Brown, curator of maps, cheerfully put up with my presence for several years, and gave me all the assistance within their power.

I owe a heavy debt of gratitude to the University of Michigan. As holder of the Alfred H. Lloyd Memorial Fellowship of that institution for 1939–40 I was able to travel and to complete investigations without which this book would not have been possible.

Above all, my thanks must go to Dr. Verner W. Crane, professor of American history in the University of Michigan. He suggested this study early in 1936; and he watched this volume develop in seminar after seminar and in manuscript after manuscript. Of course, he is not responsible for my shortcomings.

I appreciate highly the services of the University of Michigan Press in publishing this volume. Dr. Eugene McCartney, editor of that organization, has very graciously carried through the tedious task of preparing the manuscript for the printer.

A word should be added regarding dates and capitalization. I have not converted Old Style dates into New Style, but have assumed January 1 as the beginning of every year. When citing from manuscript sources I have reduced unnecessary capitals.

John Richard Alden

Bowling Green State University
Bowling Green, Ohio

CONTENTS

CONTENTS

APPENDIXES

LIST OF MAPS

KEY TO ABBREVIATIONS

ANC—Archives Nationales, Colonies

CHJSC—Commons House Journals, South Carolina

CJSC—Council Journals, South Carolina

CO—British Public Record Office, Colonial Office

GCR—Allen D. Candler, ed., *Colonial Records of the State of Georgia;* also typescript colonial records of Georgia in Georgia State Department of Archives and History

IBSC—Indian Books of South Carolina

MPAED—Dunbar Rowland, ed., *Mississippi Provincial Archives, 1763–1766: English Dominion ....*

NCCR—William L. Saunders, ed., *The Colonial Records of North Carolina*

NYCD—E. B. O'Callaghan, ed., *Documents Relating to the Colonial History of the State of New York ....*

SCHGM—South Carolina Historical and Genealogical Magazine

WLCL—William L. Clements Library, University of Michigan

WO—British Public Record Office, War Office

NOTE

The place and the date of publication of books are given on the first citations of them in each chapter.

PART I

THE SOUTHERN FRONTIER DURING THE SEVEN YEARS' WAR

CHAPTER I

INTRODUCTION

WHAT to do about the Indian was a serious question during the entire colonial period of American history. Almost all the colonies faced the Indian question. Some dealt with it rather successfully, while others failed to progress toward a solution. William Penn and James Oglethorpe made good records when they governed respectively Pennsylvania and Georgia; at times South Carolina handled Indian affairs both efficiently and honorably. But the problem was an extraordinarily difficult one because a satisfactory formula to reconcile the ideal of justice to the Indian and the advance of white civilization could not be found. Indeed, the federal government of the United States was never able to find such a formula. Moreover, before 1754 the colonies were compelled to deal with it under far more difficult circumstances than those under which the national government labored. Since most of the colonies by their charters extended far inland, quarrels inevitably arose between province and province over the possession of the Indian trade and lands in the interior of the continent. Conflicts between governors and assemblies, in which the participants were too often swayed by private interests in land and trade, also led to confusion. And the task before the English colonies was not lightened by the efforts of the French to win the friendship and aid of the Indians. As a result, the English colonies were often on bad terms with their Indian neighbors before 1754.

Provincial inefficiency in regard to Indian affairs appeared in a blinding light when it became necessary for the colonists to defend themselves against the Indians, and especially against the French assisted by allied Indians. During the long struggle between England and France on the American continent the attitude taken by the Indians, chiefly the Creeks and Cherokees in the South and the Iroquois in the North, was of major importance, because for considerable periods the Indians held the balance of power. They were therefore an object of solicitude to the great antagonists, and it was early discovered that French methods of handling them were superior to those of the English. Whereas the French, under the careful supervision of royal governors, pursued a policy of fraternization and of gradual infiltration into the Indian country, the divided counsels of the British colonies permitted the alienation of the Indians by condoning the wholesale seizure of Indian lands and cheating by rapacious traders. The French might have gained the alliance of all the Indians between the Gulf of St. Lawrence and the Gulf of Mexico, had it not been for the fact that the English were consistently able to furnish the Indians with better trade goods at cheaper prices. But in spite of the advantage that the English held in trade many important tribes fell under French influence. It was therefore inevitable, whenever war between the two rivals approached, that London officials should seek some better method of handling Indian affairs.

At the very beginning of the Anglo-French duel the Dominion of New England was formed in order to establish imperial authority on a firmer basis in the colonies and to create centralized government in America that would offer stronger resistance to the French than disunited colonies. A major problem in defense was to secure the aid of the Five Nations, which had been pulled hither and yon by the conflicting interests of New York and New England. These diverse interests constituted a serious danger, and the appointment of Andros as governor of New York and of the New England colonies was partly caused by the need for following one efficient policy in regard to the Iroquois. Andros was successful in bringing the Iroquois into the English camp, and the French were unable to make much progress in the North while he was in power. This first attempt on the part of the home government to employ centralized authority over Indian affairs was definitely a success.[1]

Of course, later plans of British statesmen to create a centralized colonial régime would have brought unity in the conduct of Indian affairs. Thus the famous Board of Trade plan of 1721 would have vested the supreme military power and the conduct of Indian relations in a governor general.[2] However, British statesmen failed to take any action regarding this and other projects for colonial federation before 1754.[2]

Although the home government made no real attempt during the first half of the eighteenth century to secure centralized management of Indian relations in America, London officials continued to

[1] Viola Barnes, *The Dominion of New England: A Study in British Colonial Policy* (New Haven, 1923), Chapter X.

[2] Stanley M. Pargellis, *Lord Loudoun in North America* (New Haven, 1933), 8–9.

try to direct Indian policy through the royal governors. The governors were ordered to facilitate the conversion of the Indians to Christianity, although little attention was given to the instruction. As early as 1700 supplies of presents for distribution to the Indians were sent from England to the governors, and this practice continued until the closing years of the Revolution. The imperial government also sought to preserve for the inhabitants of all the colonies the opportunity to engage in the Indian trade on a basis of equality.[3] Officers of state in London likewise attempted to bring about intercolonial coöperation in dealing with the Indian problem. In 1720 the governors of South Carolina and Virginia were instructed to coöperate in regulating the Indian trade. They did consult from 1720 to 1722, and the governor of North Carolina participated in their discussions. These discussions, says Professor Crane, "marked the first halting steps toward the development of an imperial policy in the regulation of the southern fur trade." [3] In 1720 the Board of Trade instructed Governor Spotswood of Virginia to join with the governor of New York in holding a congress with the Iroquois, since both provinces had dealings with those tribes. Pennsylvania was also interested, and therefore all three provinces sent delegates to the conference, held in 1722.[4] A little later gatherings of this kind became a favorite device of the Board of Trade to secure unified Indian policy.

As the Seven Years' War approached ideas for centralizing governmental authority in the colonies were again seriously considered in London. After much discussion a long step toward securing unity in Indian policy was taken, for it was decided to place the conduct of political relations with the Indians under two superintendents appointed by the crown. After the withdrawal of the French from the continent these officials were also given for a time partial but not complete authority over the Indian trade. In fact, the governors were even permitted to interfere in the management of Indian politics until the very end of the American Revolution. Curiously enough, the superintendents, though originally appointed to counteract French efforts to win over the Indians in the Seven Years' War, played their most important rôles between 1763 and 1775 in connection with the Western problem. In the South the governors exercised almost as great influence in Indian affairs during the Seven

[3] Verner W. Crane, *The Southern Frontier, 1670–1732* (Durham, N. C., 1929), 203–4.

[4] Leonidas Dodson, *Alexander Spotswood, Governor of Colonial Virginia* (Philadelphia, 1932), 102–8.

Years' War as in the years preceding that conflict. Before entering upon a narrative of their activities it will be necessary to describe briefly the southern Indians and to offer some analysis of their relations with their white neighbors toward the middle of the eighteenth century.

The southern Indians were at that time more numerous than the Indians living north and east of the Ohio River, and their settlements were much more compact. They were, on the whole, less warlike than the Six Nations. Like the Iroquois, almost all the southern tribes possessed an organization for government which was still crude, but which was very gradually developing into a settled system. They had come to inhabit fixed homes in straggling "towns," where they lived when not hunting or on the warpath. Each town usually had one leader, recognized as such because of martial virtues, family connections, or the wisdom of experience. The headmen of the towns acting together informally or in solemn prearranged conclave constituted the ruling body of the nation. The dictates of even the grandest of national councils were not always heeded, however, for there were no means of coercing a minority except by force, the employment of which was to be avoided as likely to cause civil conflict. In spite of the fact that writers of the eighteenth century often speak of Indian kings and emperors, there were in reality no such dignitaries, unless among the Catawbas, for these terms were loosely applied to chiefs who wielded great influence in the councils of a nation.[5] Land ownership was in common, except for dwellings and garden patches in the towns. Even part of the produce of the land was placed in a common storehouse. Rude agriculture was rather extensively carried on by the women, old men, and boys.[6] Cattle, hogs, and poultry were also raised. Although the southern tribes had been self-sufficient when the white man appeared on the scene, they had gradually become more and more dependent upon him, for they began to copy the white man, especially in the use of clothing, firearms, and liquor. Once these articles had become seem-

[5] The Catawbas were apparently never numerous. By 1750 they were confined to a small area in the northern part of South Carolina. Power was therefore more easily centralized among them. Head chiefs elected by them and known by the English as kings possessed greater authority than other tribal leaders given that title. This was particularly true after 1750, when the elections were closely supervised by the governors of South Carolina, who placed their favorites in office and supported them.

[6] One authority even ventures an opinion that the great Choctaw tribe was composed of farmers rather than hunters. Bernard Romans, *A Concise Natural History of East and West Florida* (New York, 1775), 71.

ingly indispensable to them they lost their independence; when guns needed repair or replacement, when ammunition supplies were depleted, when clothing was worn out, the services of the white man were absolutely necessary. The southern Indians were hardly free of vice before the coming of the palefaces,[7] and their morale seems to have sunk rather steadily as they were brought more and more into contact with vicious traders, outcasts, escaped criminals, and runaway Negro slaves. Rum was the Indian's special curse, for, unlike most whites, the Indian drank until he had become stupefied.[8]

About 1750 there were approximately 12,000 Indian warriors in the southern nations, divided among some twenty tribes.[9] All these resided at some distance from the seacoasts of the southern English colonies, for those nations that had occupied the coastal plains at an earlier time had either been exterminated or had removed inland. One of the less important nations still existing in 1750 was that of the Natchez, who had been decimated, driven from their homes on the banks of the Mississippi, and scattered among the more powerful tribes as the result of a campaign of extermination waged against them by the French colony of Louisiana in 1729–31. For more than a generation after their expulsion the Natchez continued to cherish a dream of returning to their native country. Until the close of the eighteenth century they partly retained their tribal customs and their language, but the scattered units of the nation were gradually lost to sight. Other tribal groups which played minor rôles in the drama of Indian politics during the last generation of British rule in the southern colonies were the remnant of the Tuscaroras that

[7] See Romans, *op. cit.*, 62, 64, 70, 82.

[8] For a remarkable instance of the Indian's craving for liquor see James Adair, *History of the American Indians* (Samuel C. Williams, ed., Johnson City, Tenn., 1930), 326–28.

[9] In a compilation prepared in 1764 or 1765 John Stuart, British superintendent of Indian affairs in the southern district of North America, estimated the number of warriors under his jurisdiction at 13,941, but he included several tribes that resided on Spanish territory and two others in the Illinois country. "Stuart's List of the Indian Tribes in the Southern District of North America," General Thomas Gage MSS, William L. Clements Library. In 1773 Sir William Johnson, British superintendent for the northern Indian district, which properly included all tribes from the Hudson Bay country to the Ohio, set the number of gunmen in his department at 25,420. At least half of these belonged to tribes with which his department had no substantial connection, such as the Sioux. Johnson to Dartmouth, Oct. 22, 1773, E. B. O'Callaghan, ed., *Documents Relating to the Colonial History of the State of New York* . . . (Albany, 1856–61), VIII, 458–59. (Hereafter these volumes are cited as *NYCD*.) Johnson estimated one warrior to every five Indians. On this basis there were about 60,000 southern Indians in the third quarter of the eighteenth century, but that figure is possibly too high.

continued to inhabit the frontier of North Carolina until 1769; the Nottoways and Saponeys of southern Virginia, who were not numerous and who had become partially domesticated; the Yamassees, who had been forced to retreat into Florida after the great war to which their name was attached; the Alabamas, who had dwelt on the river of the same name and were affiliated with the Creeks before 1763, finally moving beyond the Mississippi; the "Small Tribes," a group of nations, chief of which was the Tonicas, inhabiting the eastern bank of the lower Mississippi and numbering fewer than five hundred warriors in all. Six tribal groups, the Catawbas, Cherokees, Creeks, Choctaws, Chickasaws, and the Southern Shawnees, were of such importance that they deserve brief special treatment. (For locations of the various Indian tribes and towns and a reasonably accurate contemporary sketch of the southern wilderness, see Map 1, in the pocket at the end of the book.)

In 1750 the Catawbas were unable to muster more than three hundred fighting men, but their courage and the narrow compass of their settlements on the Catawba River had enabled them to resist successfully the assaults of their enemies, notably the Iroquois, whose enmity they had earned by slaying a great Iroquois chief a generation earlier. Incessant raids by war parties from the Six Nations and from other tribes in alliance with France living across the Ohio had sorely tried the little nation, because it could ill afford to lose men. In spite of the fact that their numbers had been enlarged through accretions from other South Carolina tribes before the mid-century, the Catawbas were constantly threatened with extinction. Yet they had served as a stout bulwark protecting South Carolina from Indian invasion, and grateful South Carolina officials supported them. As a result, they were able to furnish valuable assistance in the defense of the southern frontier in the great colonial conflict between France and England then impending. However, their fertile lands had already aroused the covetousness of English settlers and speculators, and English settlements were approaching their towns at the beginning of that struggle.

The villages of the Cherokees, who could muster perhaps 2,500 gunmen,[10] were commonly classified by the English in four groups: the Lower settlements in the valleys of the Keowee and Tugaloo rivers; the Middle towns on the upper reaches of the Little Tennessee River; the Valley settlements, located just north of the Hiwassie River; and the Overhills, who occupied the lower stretches of the

[10] Contemporary estimates vary greatly. The total given is commonly found and seems to be the most accurate.

Little Tennessee. Contemporary writers frequently included the Valley towns in the term "Overhills," a usage so convenient that it is generally followed in this discussion. The Lower townsmen inevitably came into close contact with South Carolina and Georgia, while the Overhill subtribes were easily accessible to French influence before 1763 and were deeply affected by the advance of Virginia and North Carolina settlements along the Holston River after that time. More civilized than the other southern nations, the Cherokees prided themselves upon a supposed racial unity and considered themselves to be one people, although the several groups did not always act in unison, for their interests were at times in seeming conflict. Chiefs residing at the Overhill town of Choté near the Little Tennessee and known as "emperors" seem to have exercised little more power than many other leading warriors. During the first half of the century the Cherokees had come into extensive commercial relations with the English, more particularly with traders from South Carolina, and had gradually fallen largely under English influence. A treaty of amity and commerce negotiated by a famous Cherokee embassy at London in 1730 has been justly described as the cornerstone of Anglo-Cherokee relations before the Revolution.[11] Yet the French usually managed to maintain a small party in their interest.

About 1750 the lands of the Creek confederacy extended from the Alabama River on the west to the Ogeechee River on the east and included most of the Florida peninsula. The Creeks also claimed the lower part of the triangle between the Alabama and the Tombigbee rivers, but possession of that area was disputed by the Choctaws. There were actually three divisions in the confederacy after the conflict between Oglethorpe's forces and Spanish Florida, although only two, the Upper and the Lower Creeks, are frequently mentioned before the American Revolution. The Upper towns, chief of which were Mucolasses, Oakfuskie, and Tuckabatchie, were located mainly in the valleys of the Coosa and Oakfuskie rivers. The Lower towns, most important of which were Coweta and Cussita, were spread along the valleys of the Chattahoochee and Flint rivers. A third division, which was in the process of formation and which came to bear the name of Seminoles by 1770, was rapidly settling the northern part of the Florida peninsula from the Altamaha River to Appalachie Bay. Their earliest and most notable eighteenth-century settlement was one founded at Alachua, directly west of St. Augustine, by a band of Oconee Creeks who had gone into Florida as allies of Oglethorpe

[11] A scholarly account of this embassy is to be found in Crane, *op. cit.*, 276–80, 298–302.

under the leadership of the belligerent chief Cowkeeper.[12] Because the lands of the Creeks were widely extended and because their confederacy was composed of various Indian elements they were less united than the Cherokees. The Upper and Lower Creeks acknowledged each other as brethren and usually pursued the same policy, but they not uncommonly acted independently. The Seminoles, after establishing themselves in Florida, moved toward a complete separation from the other groups, which was eventually effected.[13] The nation as a whole had about 3,500 gunmen.[14] In 1764 the Upper Creeks numbered some 2,000 warriors, the Lower Creeks were hardly more than half so numerous, and the Seminoles had only a few hundred men.[15] Before 1763 the English, French, and Spanish alike strove to secure an alliance with the Creeks; each succeeded in maintaining a party in the nation, although that of the Spanish was inconsequential. The French strengthened their influence by building Fort Toulouse [16] on the east bank of the Coosa River, four miles above the junction of that stream with the Tallapoosa, in 1716, but the fort failed to counterbalance the usefulness to the Creeks of the English traders from Carolina and Georgia. The Creeks, benefiting greatly from the courtship of the three powers and realizing that an alliance with any one of them would cause an internal conflict, wisely refused to commit themselves as a nation and maintained with great success a policy of neutrality. This fact, coupled with their extensive hunting grounds, rendered the Creeks more independent than their neighbors. Because of an inherent fondness for war they were feared and distrusted by those neighbors.

The Choctaws were the most numerous of all the southern tribes, totaling some 5,000 gunmen.[17] Their villages extended from the upper reaches of the Pearl River to the Tombigbee River, but they claimed as their boundaries the Yazoo on the west, the Alabama on

[12] On the early history of the Seminoles see Stuart to Halifax, Oct. 29, 1764, Public Record Office, Colonial Office (hereafter cited as CO), 5/66. Cf. John R. Swanton, *Early History of the Creek Indians and Their Neighbors* (Washington, 1922), 180–81, 398–99. Cowkeeper's Indian name was Ahaya.

[13] The name "Seminoles" was used by the Creeks to indicate their fellows who established new homes distant from the nation and who failed to heed its councils. John Stuart translated the term as "wild men."

[14] See Swanton, *op. cit.*, 442, for a list of estimates. Many others were made in the eighteenth century.

[15] Major Francis Ogilvie, "A List of the Towns & Number of Gun Men in the Creek Nation," 1764, Gage MSS, offers considerable data on the Creeks at that time.

[16] Commonly designated "poste des Alibamons."

[17] Estimates vary from 4,000 to 6,000.

the east, and the Gulf of Mexico on the south. The Choctaws had even less cohesion than the southern nations generally. In the main, there were three groups, the East Party, the West Party, and the Six Villages, the latter a small group of towns between the Pearl and the Pascagoula rivers. Before the Seven Years' War French influence was dominant among the Choctaws and especially in the region of the Six Villages. For many years the French at annual congresses had actually given the Choctaws ammunition, clothing, and other necessaries, and the Choctaws had therefore lost some of their pristine vigor. In 1736 the French had also erected Fort Tombigbee on the river of the same name,[18] but the English occasionally obtained a foothold in the East Party because of their superiority in trade. Less aggressive than most of the southern tribes, the Choctaws were erroneously held to be an inferior nation by some contemporary writers.[19]

Probably the most warlike of all the southern Indians were the tall and athletic Chickasaws. The main body of this tribe lived in seven towns in the valley of the upper Tombigbee. Their hunting range extended from the northern banks of the Yazoo to the Ohio. Although the Chickasaws were rather highly unified, they could muster no more than five hundred warriors.[20] They had made an alliance with the English even before the founding of Louisiana, and were faithful to that alliance so long as the British remained in the old Southwest. In large part the continuance of Anglo-Chickasaw friendship is explained by the incessant attacks made upon the Chickasaws from Louisiana. A long series of assaults by the French and their Indian allies upon the Chickasaws sadly depleted the manpower of the gallant little nation. One small group, despairing of successful resistance, moved away. It established a new home at Breed Camp[21] on the headwaters of the Coosa River. It numbered about eighty warriors in 1754. Even earlier another band of Chickasaws had taken root on the left bank of the Savannah near old Fort Moore, on lands furnished them by South Carolina.[22] However, the

[18] The site of the fort, in Sumpter County, Alabama, is now called Jones Bluff. It was built by Bienville as a base for an expedition against the Chickasaws.

[19] For accounts of the Choctaws and the Small Tribes see John R. Swanton, *Indian Tribes of the Lower Mississippi Valley and Adjacent Coast of the Gulf of Mexico* (Washington, 1911).

[20] See Adair, *op. cit.*, 402, note, for a list of estimates. Many others were made.

[21] The term "breed," which was colloquial for Chickasaw, was used because of the mixture of blood in the tribe.

[22] For a time after 1750 these Chickasaws lived on both sides of the Savannah.

main body replenished its supply of warriors by naturalizing Cherokees and Shawnees who married into the tribe,[23] until a pure-blooded Chickasaw (if there ever was such a thing) became a rarity.[24] This interbreeding, coupled with timely aid from the English, preserved Chickasaw independence.

In 1745 the Shawnees emigrated westward from the borders of Pennsylvania. The major part of the nation established new homes on the Scioto River. In 1747 about 140 warriors moved southward under the leadership of Peter Chartier, son of a Philadelphia candlemaker. Some of them amalgamated with the Upper Creeks of Mucolasses and Tuckabatchie, but Chartier and approximately 85 warriors formed two new towns on the headwaters of the Coosa River, midway between the Upper Creeks and the Cherokees. As allies of the French, Chartier and his followers, whom I shall call the Southern Shawnees, were to make effective use of this strategic position and were to constitute a thorn in the side of the English during the Seven Years' War.[25]

At the middle of the eighteenth century the European neighbors of the southern Indians were the English, the French, and the Spanish. At that time the great rivals were the English and the French, for the influence of the Spanish in Florida hardly extended beyond the walls of their forts after the failure of their last expedition against Georgia in 1742. After that year, in fact, the Spanish posts—St. Augustine, Pensacola, St. Mark,[26] and Picolata[27]—were loosely besieged by the Seminoles. Steadily reinforced by their brethren from the Creek towns, the Seminoles insistently pressed forward into Florida and drove the detested Spanish and their feeble Indian allies to the water's edge.

To judge from surface indications, the French were also much weaker than the English in the South. Louisiana at the mid-century was stagnant. It had only 6,000 whites in a total population of approximately 25,000; and its commerce, except for the trade in furs and deerskins, was meager. The French government was able to

[23] Kerlérec to ministry, Dec. 18, 1754, Archives Nationales, Colonies, C13A, 38. (Hereafter this body of documents is cited as ANC.)

[24] See Romans, *op. cit.,* 63.

[25] The most informative document on these Southern Shawnees is Atkin to Board of Trade, May 30, 1755, Loudoun MSS, Henry E. Huntington Library. But see also Kerlérec to ministry, Sept. 12, 1758, ANC, C13A, 40, and Reuben G. Thwaites, ed., *Collections of the State Historical Society of Wisconsin,* XVII (Madison, 1906), 331; XVIII (Madison, 1908), 19, 20, 41.

[26] Located on the Appalachie River near its mouth.

[27] Located on the St. John's River.

offer greater assistance to Louisiana than the Spanish to Florida. Theoretically, a body of 1,850 trained troops was steadily maintained in the *corps de Louisianne,* although in practice a much smaller number was usually fit for duty, and these scattered throughout a wide area.[28] On the other hand, it was estimated that the Carolinas and Georgia at that time contained 78,000 white inhabitants; and the Carolinas were growing steadily.[29] Besides, the southern English colonies could reasonably expect some assistance from Virginia, even though the major interests of the Old Dominion, so far as frontier affairs were concerned, lay in the Ohio valley. Their commerce, notably that of South Carolina, was flourishing. To be sure, after the disbanding of Oglethorpe's regiment in 1749 there were only three companies of English regulars in the South, stationed at various posts in South Carolina and Georgia,[30] but the Carolinas and Virginia were sufficiently wealthy and populous to raise considerable bodies of provincial troops. Moreover, in the event of war the southern English colonies could well calculate upon substantial aid from the mother country in both men and money, while Louisiana could not, if only because of English sea power. English sea power also largely nullified any faint hope that Louisiana—or Florida, for that matter—might be used as a base for a successful attack on those colonies from the Atlantic. Nor could the French hope to make an overland attack unless supported by the great majority of the southern Indians. Louisiana, however, was safe from assault by land unless the English secured the assistance of the Indians, but lay relatively open to attack by a combined English military and naval expedition. Since the English failed to execute plans for such an expedition, the last phase of the struggle for empire between the French and English in the South was largely dominated by the attempts of the great rivals to secure the aid of the Indian nations for land operations.

Assuredly, if skill in Indian diplomacy had been the decisive factor in the conflict for dominion in the South and if French superiority in that field had been as overwhelming as some writers have believed it was, Louisiana would have been relieved of all fear

[28] For a description of the French forces in 1754 see ANC, C13A, 38: 213.

[29] In 1752 the white populations of Georgia and South Carolina were estimated at 3,000 and 25,000 respectively; those of North Carolina and Virginia were calculated at 50,000 and 125,000 in 1755. "An account of the number of white inhabitants in His Majesty's colonies in North America . . . ," CO, 5/7.

[30] The three companies were raised in accordance with an order in council of 1744. When Oglethorpe's regiment was dropped from the service in 1749 veterans from it were placed in the three companies.

of invasion by land, the westward advance of English settlers would have been sharply checked, and the infant colony of Georgia would perhaps have been ruined. In fact, the southern Indians were as shrewd politicians as their white neighbors, and their policies, though affected by diplomatic suasion, were dictated in large part by principles of self-interest. To them the strategy of balance of power had not the slightest mystery. Neither the French nor the English could obtain Indian alliances without giving, or at least promising, substantial advantages. Possibly the French *were* somewhat more adept in dealing with the southern tribes than were their English rivals. Their officials sedulously hid any contempt they may have felt toward the Indian, and carefully masked their Gallic gaiety so as not to offend the levity-despising savages, but many English leaders, though by no means all, likewise mastered the arts of Indian negotiation. It is not at all difficult to find instances of ineptitude on the part of the English. Nevertheless, it is significant that the French indulged themselves in an unending feud with the Chickasaws and that they allowed a second feud with the Cherokees to continue until the French and Indian War was well under way. There were no fundamentally sound reasons why they should have waged war against these tribes. Nor can it be said that the French had a major advantage because their soldiers and merchants intermarried among the Indians. English traders and soldiers in the South also took to themselves Indian consorts. Bernard Romans [31] even claims that there was greater intermingling between the English and the Choctaws after 1763 than between the French and the Choctaws before that year.

Possibly the only substantial advantage held by the French in diplomacy was unified control. While French policy was entirely in the hands of the governor of Louisiana, several English provinces, and after 1757 also an imperial superintendent of Indian affairs, negotiated with the southern tribes. This division of authority among the English not only caused confusion in purpose, but also permitted their rascally Indian traders to conduct themselves much as they pleased and even to undermine official policies. On the other hand, the English were quite consistently able to offer more in the way of gifts. During the period 1732–55 South Carolina alone spent over £26,000 on Indian affairs, a considerable portion of which went for presents,[32] and the imperial government spent upon the southern Indians in one way or another between £1,000 and £8,000 annually

[31] *Op. cit.,* 82.

[32] Lyttelton to Board of Trade, Nov. 30, 1757, CO, 5/376.

from 1732 to 1748.[33] To be sure, the government of Louis XV, when possible, sent every year a considerable supply of gifts to the Choctaws and to the Upper Creeks living in the neighborhood of Fort Toulouse; and many thousand livres were spent each year upon Indian delegations visiting New Orleans.[34] Moreover, the generosity of the English was partly counterbalanced by the efficiency of the French in distribution, for the French usually offered their presents at or near the homes of the Indians and wisely included the influential old men among the beneficiaries. The English after 1735 ordinarily required the Indians to visit Charleston and Savannah for presents, and thus deprived the old men of largesse.[35]

The major reason why many southern Indians preferred the French to the English undoubtedly lay in the fact that the French did not seriously encroach upon the lands of their savage neighbors. The English steadily advanced toward and into the lands of the Creeks, Cherokees, and Catawbas; and it required no great penetration on the part of the savages to discern in the westward march of the pioneers a grave threat to their own existence. Charges assiduously circulated by the French to the effect that the English would not be sated until they had taken for themselves all the territory east of the Mississippi therefore often obtained credence.

Although the English were at a disadvantage in Indian relations because of shortcomings in diplomacy and because of their expansive tendencies, they could exercise through their mastery of the southern Indian trade an influence which in the last analysis outweighed all others. In times of peace the English were consistently able to offer the Indians goods of higher quality at lower rates for the deerskins[36] and furs which the Indians sold to them. As a mat-

[33] Memorial by James Crokatt to Holderness, Nov. 14, 1751, CO, 5/385. In 1747 the London government decided to send out £3,000 worth of presents annually to South Carolina and Georgia. One supply was sent, but the distribution was characterized by inefficiency and corruption. At the end of King George's War the home government therefore decided not to continue this gift, and refused to alter its decision in spite of heavy pressure on the part of South Carolina and the Georgia trustees.

[34] See ANC, C13A, 38: 223.

[35] Nor did the English traders make presents to the old men, since they had no deerskins. See Atkin to Board of Trade, May 30, 1755, Loudoun MSS.

[36] Deerskins often served the same purposes as leather. They could be washed, dyed, and mended, and in South Carolina were sometimes used in the making of breeches. See an interesting advertisement by Mary Robinson in the *South-Carolina Gazette,* Aug. 17, 1738. Professor Verner W. Crane suggests that certain pieces of headgear worn in England in the eighteenth century and known as "South Carolina hats" may have been made from deerskin.

ter of fact, the French did not deal with the Cherokees, Catawbas, and Chickasaws; and they were able to trade with the Small Tribes, the Choctaws, and occasionally with the Creeks in the vicinity of Fort Toulouse, only through royal assistance. Annually supplies of goods were furnished by the crown at cost prices in France. In return, those engaged in the trade were forced to sell their skins and furs to the crown at fixed rates or pay an equivalent in cash. Nevertheless, royal bounty did not enable the French to compete with the English on even terms; and deficiencies in quantity, quality, and diversity continued.[37] Moreover, after 1749 the trade was monopolized by the military officers at the posts, who sought to make exorbitant profits. In times of war the French were, of course, at a special disadvantage. Consequently, even the Choctaws from time to time besought English traders to come among them. The Spanish offered virtually no competition in trade before 1763; after that time French traders from Spanish Louisiana vied with the English for the trade with the Choctaws and the Small Tribes on the Mississippi.

The English trade had ramifications from Germany to the Mississippi, and even beyond that river. The trade goods, consisting of guns, ammunition, clothing, rum, tobacco, paint, tomahawks, and trinkets of various sorts, were shipped from England by commercial houses to merchants at Charleston, Savannah, and other seaports; these in turn sold the goods to storekeepers at Augusta and other interior towns; and the Augusta storekeepers and their fellows sold them to traders who carried them by means of packhorse trains into the Indian country. Commonly these journeys were timed for the early spring, in order to reach the Indians as soon as they returned from their hunting, which took place in the fall and winter. When the traders had completed their dealings with the Indians, they paid their accounts with their storekeepers in deerskins, furs, and the other less important articles that they had received from the Indians. The frontier merchants similarly met their obligations to the business houses of the seaports. In part, these houses met their London bills with the same articles.[38] The best skins found their way to Eng-

[37] Goods sent out to Canada by the French were superior to those shipped to Louisiana.

[38] There is a valuable discussion of the trade in a letter by Governor James Wright of Georgia to the Board of Trade, Nov. 10, 1764, CO, 323/20. At that time Wright estimated that the goods used annually in the trade conducted by inhabitants of Georgia were worth £12,000 in England. Freight charges to Savannah and insurance required £1,500, and the Savannah merchants demanded 15 per cent of the prime cost as their gross profit. The Augusta storekeepers therefore had to pay about £15,360 for the goods. They raised prices 20 per cent on

land and to Germany; the inferior ones were used in the colonies.[39] The community of interest between those linked together in this chain, which was almost entirely based on credit, is obvious; because of economic factors the traders did not lack friends at Charleston, Savannah, and London.

The trade with the southern Indians was lucrative. Exports of deerskins from Charleston between 1731 and 1765 never fell below 150,000 pounds per annum. The French and Indian War caused little, if any, diminution in the number of deerskins exported from Charleston,[40] but exports from Georgia during the same period dwindled to the negligible figure of 5,791 pounds.[41] From 1765 to 1773, however, Georgia exports remained consistently above 200,000 pounds per annum, and totaled over 300,000 pounds in 1768. From 1765 to 1768 Mobile exported 150 hogsheads of skins annually. Exports of beaver skins, though large from the North, were of little importance in the South, 5,412 pounds being the largest annual total from Georgia after 1755.[42] Since prices of deerskins at Charleston

their investment, and the traders therefore paid about £18,360 for the same articles. The expenses of the trader incurred in transportation and handling were usually about 30 per cent of the cost of the goods to him. It therefore cost the Georgia traders some £23,961 to bring their wares to the Indian. The traders charged the Indian a little less than 18 per cent upon their gross investment, and would therefore bring in skins and furs worth about £28,000 to them. It may well be that the profits were underestimated by Wright, since his information came from those engaged in the trade and since at that time the London government was considering taxation of the trade in order to finance the imperial Indian departments. It should also be pointed out that the traders obtained their goods at the seaports in the earlier part of the eighteenth century, and that some probably continued to do so. Moreover, the traders were often employees of Augusta and Charleston merchants rather than independent operators.

Shipowners carried deerskins at low rates since it was unsafe to load ships entirely with rice because of its weight. George Louis Beer, *British Colonial Policy, 1754–1765* (New York, 1907), 222.

[39] Crane, *op. cit.*, 111. [40] *Ibid.*, Appendix A, Tables III and IV.

[41] The falling off in exports of deerskins from Georgia during the war no doubt partly resulted from an increased use of Charleston, rather than Savannah, as a shipping point to Europe. It is significant that in 1761 Georgia laid a tax upon skins sent from that province to South Carolina.

[42] These figures are taken from "An Aggregate and Valuation of Exports of Produce from the Province of Georgia, with the Number of Vessels employed therein, annually distinguished, from the Year 1754, to 1773, Compiled by William Brown, Comptroller and Searcher of his Majesty's Customs in the Port of Savannah," Romans, *op. cit.*, chart opposite p. 104, and from Montfort Browne to Hillsborough, Aug. 25, 1768, CO, 5/585. Romans, *op. cit.*, 66, states that both the Chickasaws and the Choctaws refused to hunt beaver, although these animals were abundant in their hunting grounds. In their opinion beaver was proper quarry for squaws and white men only.

ranged from twenty shillings (South Carolina currency) down to thirteen shillings the pound during the last four decades of British rule,[43] it is clear that the Indian trade was of considerable economic importance. The colonies in the South chiefly benefiting from it were South Carolina and Georgia, although West Florida had a substantial share in it after 1763. Attempts by Virginia to secure the Cherokee trade had little success, and North Carolina never displayed much interest. East Florida settlements were too far distant from most of the tribes to obtain any significant portion of the trade.

The English trade, though economically important, was, as has been suggested, of even greater political consequence, for it proved to be both a formidable weapon in the hands of the English and a threat to their safety. The Indians could be pleased by giving them prosperity through trade, and at times they could also be coerced by cutting off the trade. But an ill-conducted trade might easily cause an Indian war, and regulation was extremely difficult. In general, the traders were unscrupulous and abandoned wretches who trafficked heavily in rum, cheated their clients abominably, and abused them in every imaginable way.[44] Their activities, carried on in the wilderness, could hardly be supervised efficiently even under the best conditions. Competition was vicious, especially when traders from two or more colonies did business in the same town, as was commonly true in the South. When the misdeeds of the traders became unbearable, the Indians might rise and slaughter indiscriminately both the traders and the settlers on the frontiers. Attempts to secure an orderly trade as well as a profitable one were therefore made by all the southern colonies. Three methods of attack were possible: strict regulation of private traders, operation of a public system, or a combination of the two. All three were tried, but the influence of the traders, their merchants, and their friends was usually strong enough to keep the trade in private hands, although public management or the use of a public company as a "yardstick" was better calculated to preserve order. In emergencies the colonies were apt to resort to the public system or the yardstick arrangement, whereby

[43] Statement based on prices quoted for deerskins occasionally from 1732 to 1775 in the *South-Carolina Gazette*. South Carolina currency was worth approximately one seventh of sterling. David D. Wallace, *The Life of Henry Laurens*... (New York and London, 1915), 53.

[44] A host of references regarding the evil character of the traders could be cited. Good examples are David Taitt to Stuart, March 6, 1772, Newton D. Mereness, ed., *Travels in the American Colonies* (New York, 1916), 524–25; Adair, *op. cit.*, 443–44.

the traders through the competition of a public company were compelled to some extent to modify their habits. The backbone of a managed private system was always the requirement that the trader obtain a license and be bonded to obey regulations set up by colonial executives. Infractions of these rules might be punished by revocation of the license and forfeiture of the bond. Such regulations were often laid down in great detail. Very commonly they required observance of a price schedule, the use of proper weights and measures, and the restriction of the trader's activities to a certain Indian town or subtribe. They usually forbade the employment of Indians and Negroes as assistants, and the purchase of "green" skins.[45] Of course, even the most adequate system of trade regulation was of little avail when it was confined to one colony and traders from several provinces were competing.

[45] That is, skins not yet dressed in the Indian fashion. The dressing was done by the squaws in the towns. It is obvious that it was advantageous to the trader that they should continue to do so. Moreover, such a restriction tended to prevent the traders from going out to the hunting grounds, where they could not be watched and where they would be tempted to hunt for themselves.

CHAPTER II

THE INDIAN POLICY OF JAMES GLEN: MANEUVERS BEFORE 1754

IT CANNOT be said that English management of Indian affairs in the South during the decade before the outbreak of the French and Indian War was uniformly or even generally adequate. Intercolonial rivalry of long standing between South Carolina, Virginia, and Georgia over the Indian trade and control of Indian relations caused much confusion. Early in the century South Carolina had largely gained the Cherokee trade. In part this success is explained by the failure of Virginia traders to find a satisfactory road to the Cherokee country until about 1740, in part by an assertion by South Carolina of jurisdiction over the Cherokee country and by the passage of ordinances in South Carolina requiring all licenses for the Cherokee trade to be issued in Charleston. This strategy was relatively successful in spite of the fact that the imperial government frowned upon it. Yet the hopes of Virginia were not completely destroyed, and Virginia was to make sporadic attempts to regain a share in the Cherokee trade until 1766.[1] Ill feeling between officials of the two provinces was plainly evident during and after 1751, when considerable numbers of Lower Cherokees moved over the hills, partly because of a scarcity of game in their own hunting grounds and a conflict with the Creeks, but also in order to open with Virginians a trade denied them by South Carolina.[2]

Interestingly enough, the legal methods used by South Carolina to prevent Virginian participation in the Cherokee trade were em-

[1] W. Neil Franklin, "Virginia and the Cherokee Indian Trade, 1673–1752," *The East Tennessee Historical Society's Publications,* No. 4 (1932), 17–21.

[2] See Council Journals of South Carolina, Historical Commission of South Carolina (hereafter cited as CJSC), xviii, 296–99; Lewis Burwell to Glen, Oct. 26, 1751, Indian Books of South Carolina, Historical Commission of South Carolina (hereafter cited as IBSC), ii, 186–87; minute of Va. council, Nov. 11, 1752, CO, 5/1429. A rumor of 1745 that Virginia traders were trying to persuade the Catawbas to remove to the northward greatly disturbed the South Carolina assembly. CJSC, xiv, 42–43.

ployed with some effect against South Carolina by her youthful southern neighbor. By her charter Georgia extended to the Savannah River and, as a result, the Creeks and a portion of the Cherokees fell within her domain. In 1735 Georgia by statute required all persons trading within her bounds to secure licenses at Savannah. A bitter conflict between South Carolina and her impudent young sister colony followed. The act did not prove to be decisive; both provinces continued to share in the commerce with the Creeks and the Cherokees, but the trade with the former, especially with the Lower Creeks, tended to fall more and more into the hands of Georgians, while that with the latter remained largely in the hands of South Carolinians. Since this rivalry made it possible for traders to evade restriction by either province, and since private trading remained in vogue in both South Carolina and Georgia until 1762 —in Georgia under acts of 1735 and 1758 and in South Carolina under acts of 1739 and 1752—the Indian commerce was often in a chaotic state. A reasonably competent observer claimed that both colonies despairingly abandoned efforts to restore order, and that the South Carolina Indian Commissioner, whose duty it was to revoke the licenses and to sue the bonds of erring traders, failed to take action against a single person for many years before 1754.[3] Nor was the rivalry between the two colonies confined to trade, for there was also an interrelated conflict over the management of Indian politics. The relatively wealthy and powerful South Carolina held that the establishment of Georgia should not affect her own traditional dominance in southern Indian policy; presumptuous Georgia would allow South Carolina exclusive control only of the Catawbas. Georgia claimed the Creek nation as her own major sphere of interest and also a share in conducting relations with the Cherokees and Chickasaws.[4] This rivalry inevitably created confusion in the Indian country, not only because it brought on direct conflicts but also because it helped to render proper regulation of the trade impossible.

The growth of the English southern colonies before 1754 created less ill will among the Indians than might have been expected, for the tide of expansion rose rather gradually. As early as 1745 Virginia was granting lands beyond the Allegheny divide. A number of Virginian settlements were formed in the valley of the Kanawha River during the next ten years without causing more than minor irritation on the part of the Overhill Cherokees, who occasionally

[3] Atkin to Board of Trade, May 30, 1755, Loudoun MSS.

[4] See Henry Parker to Glen, April 16, 1751, IBSC, ii, 9–11.

hunted toward the Ohio. The flood of population from Pennsylvania, Maryland, and Virginia southwest into the uplands of the more southerly provinces began in the 1740's, but neither it nor its confluent streams from the seacoast stirred up great Indian unrest until the following decade. North Carolina settlements did not reach the Cherokee country until after 1763, although the lands of the Catawbas aroused the covetousness of whites in both Carolinas in the 1750's. North Carolina governors made no effort to protect the rights of the Catawbas and proceeded to grant their lands, even though it was highly doubtful that those lands lay within the confines of North Carolina. Resulting dissatisfaction among the Catawbas was somewhat lessened, however, by action on the part of James Glen, governor of South Carolina, who held the reins of office in Charleston from 1743 to 1756. Glen asserted that their territory lay within his government and refused to authorize surveys within a radius of thirty miles of the Catawba towns.[5] Nor were relations between South Carolina and the Cherokees very much affected by land questions before the French and Indian War. In part this fact is explained by the existence of a provincial statute passed in 1739 that outlawed the purchase of Indian lands by private persons,[6] in part by efforts of Glen to prevent a clash. When settlers moved into the region of Long Canes Creek in upper South Carolina, Glen purchased the Cherokee claims to the left bank of that stream. Serious repercussions among the Cherokees were thereby averted, although this measure was not completely successful, since the three South Carolina commissioners who secured the cession in 1747 dealt only with the Lower townsmen and paid the purchase price exclusively to them, a procedure not relished by the Overhills.[7] An advance by the pioneers west of Long Canes Creek during the first years of the French and Indian War was to cause considerable Cherokee unrest.[8]

Before 1754, however, the gravest of the British-Indian disputes over land in the South arose from the growth of Georgia. The

[5] Charles Pinckney to John Pownall, July 5, 1754, and enclosed representation to Board of Trade, CO, 5/375.

[6] Thomas Cooper and David J. McCord, eds., *Statutes at Large of South Carolina* (Columbia, S. C., 1836–41), III, 525–26.

[7] Old Hop to Glen, April 29, 1752, IBSC, iii, 14–15; "Historical Relation of Facts Delivered by Ludovick Grant, Indian Trader, to His Excellency the Governor of South Carolina," Jan. 12, 1756, *South Carolina Historical and Genealogical Magazine* (hereafter cited as *SCHGM*), X (1909), 62–63.

[8] James Beamer to Glen, Feb. 11, 1756, IBSC, v, 105–6. On the formation of settlements in upper South Carolina between 1740 and 1760 see David D. Wallace, *The History of South Carolina* (New York, 1934), II, 42–46.

Creeks had not unwillingly ceded to Oglethorpe all lands between the Savannah and the Altamaha as far as the tide flowed, except for a small strip near Savannah town. Nor had they made any objection to the establishment of Augusta in 1735, because that village was an ideal Indian trade center, but they were alarmed by English occupation of lands above tide level; and they were particularly displeased because of a settlement made without legal authority by forty families from Virginia and North Carolina on the Ogeechee River shortly before 1754.[9] Moreover, British-Creek relations were seriously disturbed until 1759 by the claims of the Indian "princess" Mary Musgrove to the islands of St. Catherine's, Sapelo, and Ossabaw, and the strip near Savannah reserved by the Creeks in their agreements with Oglethorpe. This "princess," best known as Mary Bosomworth, because of her marriage to the Reverend Thomas Bosomworth, secured a claim to part of these lands from the Creek chief Tomichichi as early as 1737. Later she obtained formal deeds from the Creeks. Georgia at the time had no legislation barring such transactions, and the proprietary and royal governments found it impossible to ignore her claim. Their repeated refusals to acknowledge its validity were highly displeasing to Creeks who, at the urging of the Bosomworths, continued to insist that the deed be recognized.

If intercolonial rivalries, the nefarious activities of the traders, and the expansionist habits of the English tended to alienate the southern Indians, it is nevertheless true that the trade was so substantially useful to the Indians that it tipped the balance in favor of the English at the beginning of James Glen's administration. Anglophile Creeks had even requested South Carolina to erect a fort in their nation to counterbalance the influence of Fort Toulouse; and the Cherokees had asked that the English build a post to protect them from attacks by Ohio valley tribes in the French interest. In October, 1743, Lieutenant Governor William Bull of South Carolina had made an agreement with a delegation of Upper Creeks whereby an English fort was to be built in their country with their assistance. Bull actually collected some supplies for the purpose, and commissioned one Captain Wood to supervise construction. But the commons house refused to grant the necessary funds on the ground that such a fort was not needed.[10] In 1738 even the Choctaws, disgusted because of the unsatisfactory trade given them

[9] Regarding the early history of this squatter settlement see Reynolds to Lyttelton, Sept. 8, 1756, IBSC, v, 211–12.

[10] CJSC, x, 430, 441–42, 447–48, 456–57; George Hunter to Board of Trade, Oct. 31, 1743, CO, 5/370.

by the French, had renewed overtures for the establishment of a commerce with the English. In 1744 they again solicited such a commerce, inevitably a forerunner of more friendly political relations.

From the beginning to the end of Anglo-French conflict in America English management of Indian affairs on the southern frontier, except during Oglethorpe's sojourn in America, was largely in the hands of South Carolinians. From 1743 to 1756 it was Governor James Glen of South Carolina who stubbornly occupied the center of the stage. This energetic Scotsman delighted in Indian politics, and was tremendously pleased when praised for his proficiency in that field; nor did he lack admirers, in spite of the fact that provincial enemies and the Board of Trade unfailingly discounted his achievements. It is true that the genius for Indian affairs which the not-too-modest governor arrogated to himself was not so great as he would have had the world believe. Nevertheless, he had some understanding as well as much zeal; his policies and his actions dominate more than one chapter in the history of English relations with the southern Indians.

Glen was well aware that the southern English colonies were reasonably safe from direct French or Spanish aggression. Nevertheless, he feared—and with some reason—that the French might be able to inspire and arm an Indian confederacy that would be sufficiently powerful to drive the English back to the Atlantic seacoast. He realized that the French could hardly succeed in such a design so long as English policy toward the southern Indians was judicious and English presents were liberal. But, though prudence and money could ensure the continued existence of the southern colonies, something more was needed to protect English back settlements from invasion by hostile warriors in alliance with France. Moreover, the back settlements were exposed to attack because of intertribal strife. Before 1742 the Cherokees, Creeks, and Catawbas were at war both with the Six Nations and with trans-Ohio tribes in the French interest, and gangs of scalp seekers ranged back and forth behind the English settlements. Nor were these feuds much alleviated by a Cherokee-Iroquois peace negotiated in that year by Lieutenant Governor George Clarke of New York. That peace, in fact, permitted the Six Nations to use the Cherokee country as a base for raids upon the Catawbas and Creeks, and thereby caused much ill will between the Cherokees and their neighbors and contributed materially to the continuance of a Cherokee-Creek conflict that had broken out in 1740. When war parties, especially those of the northern tribes, could not satisfy their lust for plunder and hirsute spoils at the expense of red enemies, they not infrequently fulfilled their desires by ravaging white settlements. More than once during Glen's administration northern warriors, particularly Shawnees, penetrated to the Congarees; as late as 1753 they slew an inhabitant of Monk's Corner, only a few miles from Charleston itself. Inevitably, importunate appeals for protection came to Glen from the back country.[11]

There were several alternatives open to Glen in the formation of an Indian policy. A moderate man might well have satisfied his official conscience by maintaining existing friendships with the southern Indians and by raising blockhouses and enlisting rangers to protect the South Carolina frontier. A man of vision and subtlety, observing the rising tide of westward emigration, might also have tried to erase the Indian obstacle from its path by permitting or even fomenting intertribal conflicts, at the same time maintaining sufficient influence among the Indians to prevent the formation of a hostile confederacy, but Glen was neither cautious nor very subtle. He believed in protecting the frontier and was friendly to immediate westward extension of the English settlements, provided such extension did not create serious Indian enmity. The primary objectives of his policy, however, were to establish English ascendancy in the southern nations and to maintain the strength of those nations by mediating their conflicts. He hoped to create a solid Indian bulwark against aggression by the French and also to secure a great body of Indian allies who might serve as auxiliaries in a successful attack on Louisiana. Glen also believed that English ascendancy in the Indian nations would lead to an expansion of the skin trade and would open the way eventually for new settlements. His policy was an impressively simple and logical piece of large-scale planning.

Glen's Indian policy did not lack critics, especially in the South Carolina assembly. The governor wished to erect forts in each of the great southern nations as centers of English influence and trade. Some critics claimed that, even though useful, such posts would be unduly expensive. At least one foresaw the danger that the garrisons might be cut off if the neighboring Indians declared war upon the English.[12] The most bitter criticism, however, was

[11] Stephen Crell to Glen, April 6, 1751, proclamation by Glen, April 7, 1753, IBSC, ii, 8–9, iii, 181–82; CJSC, pt. 1, xxii, 33–34; Glen to Board of Trade, June 25, 1753, CO, 5/374.

[12] Atkin to Board of Trade, May 30, 1755, Loudoun MSS.

caused by Glen's attempts to maintain the strength of Indian nations supposedly in the English interest through mediating intertribal wars. Persons versed in Indian customs and psychology objected vigorously. They pointed out that the chief business of the male savage was war, and that repute among the Indians was based in large part upon the exhibition of military prowess. Obviously, if the braves of the various nations were upon amicable terms, they would inevitably turn their arms against their European neighbors; and, as these critics could justly argue, there was great probability that they would assail the very persons who had benevolently helped to settle their earlier quarrels.[13]

Although the sanguine Glen continued during and after King George's War to dream of subjugating Louisiana, he made but little real progress. On receipt of the news of the outbreak of hostilities between England and France in 1744 he immediately began to lay plans for the capture of Fort Toulouse.[14] In the following year John Fenwick, a member of the South Carolina council well versed in Indian politics, begged the Board of Trade to send a British-Indian expedition under Glen's leadership against New Orleans.[15] The Creeks effectively put an end to the former project, however, by refusing to permit English troops to pass through their territory;[16] and the imperial government failed to support Fenwick's proposal. Glen contended that Louisiana (and Florida also) would fall easy prey to an attack by such forces as could be raised in the southern colonies, supported by a naval contingent,[17] but it was to no avail.

In spite of the fact that Glen was unable to bring about military and naval operations on a grand scale against the French colony, his manipulations in Indian diplomacy before 1754 sorely disturbed the governors of Louisiana, the Marquis de Vaudreuil and the Chevalier Louis de Kerlérec, who succeeded Vaudreuil in 1753. Year by year, with Glen's encouragement, James Adair, John Campbell, John Petticrew, Jerome Courtonne, and other English traders visited the Chickasaws, bringing them badly needed arms and supplies in exchange for deerskins. The traders encouraged

[13] See William Bull to Amherst, June 17, 1761, CO, 5/61.

[14] [Glen] to Newcastle, July 14, 1744, CO, 5/388.

[15] Representation by Fenwick to Board of Trade [1745], CO, 5/371; *Journal of the Commissioners for Trade and Plantations, from January 1741–2 to December 1749* . . . (London, 1931), 162, 164.

[16] Glen to Board of Trade, Sept. 29, 1746, CO, 5/371.

[17] See Glen to Board of Trade, Feb. 3, 1748, CO, 5/372.

the "breeds" to continue their defense against Franco-Choctaw aggression, and they often carried substantial presents of guns and ammunition from the province of South Carolina. Gallophile Choctaws frequently attacked these traders en route. Some were killed, and others were captured and sent to France; but the majority safely reached their destination under the protection of Chickasaw parties that met them at Breed Camp and escorted them along the Chickasaw trading path. The traders also taught the Chickasaws the use of entrenchments, and thereby enabled them to ward off a major French attack in 1752. Thus the "breeds" were enabled to defend themselves and to interrupt occasionally communications between New Orleans and the Illinois country. Galling as the activities of the traders were to French officials, they were hardly dangerous to Louisiana until Glen attempted to win over the Choctaws by the use of similar tactics. The overtures made by the Choctaws for a trade in 1744 were not lost upon Glen, who saw in them an opportunity to obtain a powerful Indian ally at the very backdoor of New Orleans. Declarations to Glen by French prisoners that New Orleans was almost defenseless and that it had been necessary to mount guns to overawe dissatisfied Choctaws visiting the town roused the governor to action.

Sometime in 1744 or 1745,[18] when the famous Indian trader James Adair was in Charleston, Glen sought him out, and the two Scotsmen settled upon a plan of action calculated to win over the Choctaws. Adair and his partner set out for the Chickasaw country in 1745; the partner was slain by Choctaws on the trading path, but he himself arrived safely. In the Chickasaw nation he found John Campbell, a trader acquainted with the Choctaw tongue who willingly joined in the enterprise. In accordance with the Glen-Adair plan, "Jemmey" and Campbell invited a group of Choctaws to the Chickasaw towns to see for themselves the quantity and quality of goods carried by the English traders and to witness the low prices at which they were sold. As Glen and Adair had foreseen, the Choctaws immediately requested a similar trade for themselves, whereupon the two traders declared that Glen had forbidden it, unless the Choctaws displayed friendship for the English by attacking the French. Glen and Adair hoped, of course, that the Choctaws could be so embroiled with their allies that they would be forced into the English camp. While the Choctaws correctly read the English strategy and many of them stood by their French friends,

[18] Adair says 1744; Glen, 1745.

others, especially in the East Party, were carried away by their covetousness. Red Shoes, the most notable Choctaw chief of the time, was completely won over; and in 1746 Choctaw parties inflicted casualties upon the French near Mobile. In the same year a delegation of chiefs led by Little King, younger brother of Red Shoes, set out for Charleston, arriving in April, 1747. At Charleston this delegation entered into an alliance with the English and offered to open a trading path between the Choctaw and the Chickasaw nations by destroying Fort Tombigbee. Meanwhile, however, Vaudreuil was making strenuous efforts to maintain French influence; and he was able to procure the assassination of Red Shoes by Gallophile Choctaws on June 8, 1747. Thereupon civil strife broke out between the French and the English parties in the nation.

In November, 1747, Glen attempted to further the so-called "Choctaw Revolution" by sending out a large supply of presents to the Choctaw tribe. The man upon whose shoulders fell the task of delivering these presents, as well as others to the Upper Creeks and Chickasaws, was John Vann, a partner in a firm recently formed to trade with the Choctaws. Included in his company were Charles McNaire, Matthew Roche, James Maxwell, Arthur Harvey, and possibly others. Unfortunately, though Vann might have been expected to execute his trust with precision and celerity, since success in his mission would aid his own firm, he did not actually disburse the Choctaw goods until August, 1748. Some question, moreover, exists as to whether all the presents were actually delivered. Vann's delinquency inevitably disheartened the Anglophile Choctaws, and also gave Vaudreuil time to win waverers and to incite the allies of the French to further efforts against their erring brethren. As a result, the English party steadily grew weaker; and the Little King was slain. A second supply of presents sent by Glen through the agency of John Highrider and John Petticrew arrived in the Choctaw nation in February, 1750, but it came too late.

Before the close of 1750 English interest among the Choctaws had dwindled almost to nought; and no serious attempt to revive it was made for some years. Glen himself was disgusted with the whole affair. His conduct of it was characterized as inefficient by the Board of Trade. Moreover, charges of bad faith laid against him by Adair and Charles McNaire greatly annoyed the governor. Each of these men claimed that he had inspired the Choctaw Revolution, that he had spent considerable sums of money to accomplish it upon a promise of reimbursement from Glen, and that

Glen had failed to keep his word. Curiously enough, Adair's claim gained no credence, whereas McNaire was able to secure a compensatory grant from the South Carolina assembly and a recommendation for another from the Board of Trade before his tale was shown to be almost completely unfounded.[19]

Although the Choctaws had largely returned to their French allegiance by the close of 1750, the two factions in the nation that arose from the Choctaw Revolution continued to exist until 1763. Vaudreuil was so thoroughly frightened by the Glen-Adair campaign that he hesitated before assisting in making peace between the rival groups in 1752, for fear that they might still combine against Louisiana.[20] A peace was negotiated, but was broken shortly afterward. Kerlérec thought it wise to permit this civil conflict

[19] Significant references in English official papers on the Choctaw Revolution are: CJSC, xv, 57–60; xvii, 16–17, 25; Commons House Journals of South Carolina, Historical Commission of South Carolina (hereafter cited as CHJSC), xxiii, 621–23; Glen to Board of Trade, Feb. 3, Oct. 10, 1748, July 15, 1750, CO, 5/372; Glen to Board of Trade, Dec. —, 1751, "The Examination of John Vann, taken before His Excellency in Council . . . ," n.d., Holderness to Board of Trade and enclosures, Feb. 7, 1752, CO, 5/373; Board of Trade to Glen, Dec. 20, 1748, Board of Trade to Holderness, March 19, 1752, CO, 5/402; Glen to Newcastle, Aug. 12, 1749, CO, 5/389; *Journal of the Commissioners for Trade and Plantations from January 1749–50 to December 1753* . . . (London, 1932), 277–78, 280–82, 292–93. See also James Adair, *History of the American Indians* (Williams ed.), 345–49, 354, and *South-Carolina Gazette*, Nov. 26, 1750. There is an interesting account of the revolution in Kerlérec to ministry, Sept. 12, 1758, ANC, C13A, 40.

Neither McNaire nor Adair was able to furnish documentary evidence that Glen had promised to reimburse him for monies he claimed to have spent in public service. It is clear that McNaire played no part in the Choctaw Revolution until it was well under way. A powerful faction in the South Carolina assembly hostile to Glen supported McNaire. James Crokatt, its agent in London, tried to convince the Board of Trade of the justice of McNaire's claim. A newly elected assembly exonerated Glen. Glen was not unwilling that McNaire should receive a public grant, but only because he believed traders should be encouraged to risk their funds in establishing a Choctaw trade. He freely acknowledged that Adair and Campbell had performed service useful to the public. He gave them small sums from his own pocket, and urged, without success, that the home government offer them additional compensation. Adair, however, was very bitter against Glen, and declared that the governor was a member of a "Sphinx Company," which was formed in 1747 to monopolize the Choctaw trade and which lost heavily. The description of the "Sphinx Company" given by Adair tallies with what is known of the firm ostensibly headed by McNaire. Either Glen was a partner in the company or he lent money to some of its members. Robert L. Meriwether, *The Expansion of South Carolina, 1729–1765* (Kingsport, Tenn., 1940), 196.

John Campbell was slain by Francophile Choctaws in the winter of 1750–51. Daniel Clark to Glen, March 26, 1751, IBSC, ii, 7.

[20] Vaudreuil to ministry, Jan. 28, 1752, ANC, C13A, 36.

to continue. The French ministry had taken no steps toward offering a better trade to the Choctaws, and Kerlérec also feared that the nation, if reunited, might attack New Orleans.[21] It was clear that the Choctaws could not be used effectively against the English in the Seven Years' War.

As Glen's diplomacy rendered the French extremely uneasy because of their Indian neighbors, so French policy created perplexing difficulties for the English among the tribes bordering upon the English colonies. French policy required that these tribes either seek the friendship of France or be consumed in internecine or intertribal conflicts. But the Creeks, Cherokees, and Catawbas did not fall entirely or even preponderantly under French influence either in King George's War or in the peace interval of 1748-54, nor were they destroyed. The French were able to maintain an energetic minority party of Upper Creeks (including Alabamas) in the neighborhood of Fort Toulouse, and they also managed to create a group of Gallophiles among the Lower Creeks. Malatchi of Coweta, son of the great chieftain Old Brims and the most notable leader of the Lower Creeks, was apparently permanently won over. In 1740, they instigated a Creek attack upon the Cherokees to punish them for aiding the Chickasaws. This action brought on a Creek-Cherokee war that continued intermittently until 1753. They were especially active among the Creeks from 1746 to 1750. In the latter year they scored a remarkable success when a French officer with a small command was received in friendly fashion at Coweta and the fleur-de-lis was run up above that town for the first time.[22] In 1751 Fort Toulouse was completely rebuilt, and a missionary was sent there to spread the Roman Catholic faith. But if, as Glen was informed, they entertained hopes of establishing new posts in the Upper Creek country and at Coweta,[23] they were disappointed. The fact that French prestige was highest in the Creek nation during the period of the Choctaw Revolution indicates that the Creeks turned from the English at that time to maintain a balance of power; certain it is that the effectiveness of the French propaganda was in-

[21] Kerlérec to ministry, Aug. 2, 1753, ANC, C13A, 37.

[22] George Galphin to William Pinckney, Nov. 3, 1750, and enclosed memorandum, IBSC, ii, 2–3. In 1750 Glen was so irritated by the attitude of Malatchi and the Lower Creeks that he desired the Georgia officials to join South Carolina in cutting off their trade in order to bring them to heel. Glen to Board of Trade, Oct. 2, 1750, CO, 5/372.

[23] Glen to Board of Trade, July 27, 1752, CO, 5/374.

creased by the rift between Georgia and the Creeks caused by the Bosomworth claim.[24] Nevertheless, Mary and Thomas Bosomworth, and the latter's brother Abraham, rendered considerable service in supporting the English cause as agents for South Carolina and Georgia.[25] Glen himself held several important conferences with the Creeks in order to bolster the English interest with harangues and presents; in 1753, after one of these meetings, he even thought he had won back Malatchi. It would appear, however, that the Creeks were less friendly in 1754 than they had been ten years before. Their fear of the rising English might was probably the chief cause. Such feeble efforts as were made by Spanish Florida to gain adherents among the Creeks during this period came to nought. Although the Creeks have been properly praised for their astute use of the principle of balance of power, they chose at this time to attack the Spanish rather than to encourage the continuance of Florida as a counterweight to the English and French colonies.[26]

Deeply concerned as he was in Creek and Choctaw affairs, Glen devoted even greater attention to the Catawbas and Cherokees, because the attitudes taken by these tribes were of more immediate importance to South Carolina. His endeavors to protect the Catawba lands in order to maintain the little nation as a friendly barrier have already been mentioned. To the same end Glen, when on a tour of the back country in 1746, smoothed over a rift that had developed during the previous winter between the Catawbas and other Indian groups incorporated into that tribe some years before. On the same tour he sedulously mediated a conflict that had broken out almost simultaneously between the Catawbas and the Savannah River Chickasaws. He was especially

[24] An amazing tumult caused by the Bosomworths at Savannah is described in Allen D. Candler, ed., *Colonial Records of the State of Georgia* (Atlanta, 1904–16), VI, 252–87. (Hereafter these documents, with fourteen volumes of Georgia colonial records in typescript form at the Georgia State Department of Archives and History, are cited as *GCR*.)

[25] See IBSC, iii, 19–20, 23–149, for data regarding a mission undertaken by Mary and Thomas Bosomworth for Glen in 1753. They frankly admitted that an innocent Creek was murdered at their instigation in order to achieve success. See also "A State of the particular Services of Abraham Bosomworth reduced Ensign in General Oglethorpe's late Regiment of Foot," March 12, 1751, CO, 5/389.

[26] John P. Corry, *Indian Affairs in Georgia, 1732–1756* (Philadelphia, 1936), Chapters VI–VII, contains a lengthier account of the rivalry between Georgia, Florida, and Louisiana in the Creek country from 1740 to 1754.

anxious to lend support to the Catawbas because he believed their troubles had been caused by French artifices.

The most dangerous activities of the French, in Glen's view, were among the Cherokees, whose country Glen not unreasonably considered the "key of Carolina." Two French agents accompanied by a score or so of representatives from Francophile tribes came to the Overhill towns early in 1746 to negotiate a peace. The Frenchmen brought a considerable supply of presents to gain this end and also, according to report, to obtain permission to erect a fort at Choté. Apparently they made some little progress. When Glen met a body of Cherokees at Saluda Old Town on his journey of 1746, they reaffirmed the chain of friendship; on the other hand, they were not pleased by a suggestion from Glen that the English build a fort at Choté. Soon afterward, however, two South Carolina agents, one appointed by the provincial assembly and the other by Glen, proceeded to the Cherokee country. English influence led to the death of one of the Frenchmen at Cherokee hands, and permission for the English to erect a fort was forthcoming early in 1747. The surviving French emissary was still in the Overhill country in 1751, but he was able to do little toward undermining English ascendancy.[27]

Anglo-Cherokee affairs, however, did not run a smooth course from 1747 to 1754. Early in 1748 relations were so strained with the Lower towns that Glen called the assembly into session to consider measures to meet a possible attack;[28] and in 1751 South Carolina and Georgia jointly cut off the trade in order to prevent an outbreak by the Lower Cherokees.[29] But these seeming crises were caused by misconduct on the part of the traders rather than by French intrigue, although the famous chief Attakullakulla, about whom disaffection supposedly centered in 1751, was reputedly in the French interest. Attakullakulla, frequently mentioned as the Little Carpenter, was a nephew of Old Hop, the Cherokee "emperor," and had been a member of the embassy of 1730. However, he had been captured, and carried off to Canada by Francophile Indians in 1741 or 1742. He spent about six years, technically as a captive, among these French Indians, returning to the Overhill country about 1748. Shortly afterward he made a protracted visit

[27] Glen to Board of Trade, Sept. 29, 1746, April 28, 1747, CO, 5/371; Glen to Board of Trade, Dec. —, 1751, CO, 5/373.

[28] CJSC, xv, 198–200.

[29] Glen to Henry Parker, Sept. 9, 1751, IBSC, ii, 140–41. In ii, 217–28, is the record of a conference between Glen and the Cherokees which ended the crisis.

to the French Indians, reappearing in the Overhill towns in the winter of 1750-51.[30]

Since the Creeks were not thoroughly under English influence and since the friendship of the Cherokees was not positively assured, it might have been wise for Glen to permit the conflict that had broken out between these tribes in 1740 to continue. Perhaps the fact that the war was fomented and encouraged by the French unduly swayed Glen's opinion. In any case, he made several attempts at mediation during his long administration, in spite of opposition expressed in the South Carolina assembly. A peace negotiated by him in 1745 was quickly broken, and a pacification arranged by him in 1749 was equally fruitless, even though it was fortified by a provision that Glen was to cut off the trade with that nation which violated the treaty. In 1753, however, the governor's efforts were crowned with complete success.[31] Glen also strove mightily to bring to an end the long-continued feud between the Catawbas and the Six Nations in order to prevent the destruction of the former. In 1751 Governor George Clinton of New York invited Glen to a conference at Albany, one object of which was to secure a general peace between Anglophile tribes, north and south. Glen, because of the Cherokee crisis of that year, was unable to attend; he sent William Bull[32] as his representative with a delegation of Catawbas headed by "King" Hagler. At Albany Bull and several New Yorkers secured the signatures to a treaty ending hostilities between the Catawbas and the Iroquois, but the approval of the latter was obtained only by dint of much persuasion and bribery.[33] The Iroquois again attacked the Catawbas in 1753, and the task of mediation had to be resumed.

Perhaps the most significant aspect of Glen's policy, in view of later developments, was his advocacy of the establishment of English posts at strategic locations in the southern Indian na-

[30] Affidavits by Robert Gaudey and Richard Smith, IBSC, ii, 77–79, 116–18. Attakullakulla was called Onaconou in 1730. See remarks made by him in *SCHGM,* X, 65–68.

[31] CJSC, xiv, 212, xviii, 122–27, xix, pt. 2, 55–56; CHJSC, xxvii, 465–67, 486; Glen to Board of Trade [1749], CO, 5/372; minutes of conference between Glen and Cherokees, July, 1753, Lachlan McIntosh to Glen, Nov. 2, 1753, IBSC, iii, 283–322, 343–44.

[32] Of Sheldon, son of the person of the same name mentioned above. Whenever the name is used hereafter it refers to the son.

[33] Glen to Clinton, May 24, 1751, Bull to Glen, July 25, 1751, Clinton to Glen, July 25, 1751, IBSC, ii, 94–97, 103–13, 125; Reverend John Ogilvie to Bull, June 29, 1752, Arent Stevens to Bull, July 30, 1752, *ibid.,* iii, 153–55.

tions for the purpose of of extending English power. Such grand-scale strategy was not new in South Carolina; in fact, Glen was following in the footsteps of other ambitious South Carolinian expansionists, notably the great Indian agent, Thomas Nairne, who had urged that posts be erected upon the Tennessee River as early as 1708, and John Barnwell, veteran of numerous Indian campaigns, who had called for the construction of forts on the Tennessee, on the Chattahoochee, and at other important spots. So effective were the arguments put forth by Barnwell and others who supported him that his ideas were incorporated into the Board of Trade plan of September, 1721, but the only immediate result of that plan, because the approval of the privy council was not forthcoming, was the founding of Fort King George on the Altamaha River in 1721. In 1725 Governor Nicholson of South Carolina had proposed to build a fort at the forks of the Altamaha, in the Lower Creek country, although he had failed to obtain funds from the assembly. The advisability of establishing a post in the Creek nation, in Cherokee territory, or in both, was also considered officially in South Carolina in 1727, 1728, 1729, and 1731, but no action was taken.[34] As mentioned above, Glen's predecessor in office had desired a stronghold in the Upper Creek country in 1743.

When Glen informed the South Carolina assembly in the spring of 1747 that the Overhill Cherokees had given permission for the establishment of a post in their territory, provincial opinion was in favor of erecting fortifications both in the Overhill country and in the Creek nation. Both houses agreed that the colony should supply the necessary funds. After a discussion that lasted from April to June it was decided to expend £10,000 (South Carolina currency) upon each post, but the money was not voted because of a conflict over prerogative.[35] In July, 1748, the assembly urged Glen to promise a delegation of Overhill Cherokees clamoring for a fort that their desire would be fulfilled—whch he did, circumspectly, without setting a date.[36] Nevertheless, the commons house failed to make any grant for that purpose until the French and Indian War was well under way.

In April, 1747, however, the South Carolina assembly provided between £200 and £300 to erect a post in the Lower Cherokee country to protect the backsettlers. When Glen described this

[34] V. W. Crane, *The Southern Frontier, 1670–1732* (Durham, N. C., 1929), 89–90, 94–95, 191–92, 220, 228–34, 276.

[35] CJSC, xvi, pt. 1, 9–18, 20–21, 25–27, 31, 34–36, 42–47.

[36] Glen to Board of Trade, July 26, 1748, CO, 5/372.

circumstance to the Board of Trade, he let it appear that the money had been provided for an *Overhill* fort, and urged the treasury at London offer £400 or £500 additional for the purpose.[37] The *Overhill* fort project was also approved by the home government, *in principle.* In June, 1748, in accordance with a report of the Board of Trade of the previous August, instructions were sent to Glen to enter into the necessary formal agreement with the Overhill Cherokees, and to submit a plan and an estimate.[38] Meanwhile Glen, enthusiastic over the seeming success of the Choctaw Revolution, submitted revised proposals calling for the establishment of no fewer than four posts, one in the Choctaw country, another among the Chickasaws, a third in the Overhill towns, and a fourth between the Lower Cherokees and the Catawbas![39] But the Board of Trade took no action regarding this new and grander scheme when it was considered in September, 1748, since the war with France was at an end. In July, 1750, Glen was able to report that he had secured title to a site for a fort in the Overhill country in return for a few presents, and submitted an estimate of £2,500 to £3,000.[40] This report was ignored, however, by the Duke of Bedford, to whom as secretary of state for the southern department it was referred by the board. Glen was thus placed in a very embarrassing position. A request by the South Carolina governor in 1752 for action in this matter (and also for the erection of a fort in the Creek country)[41] was ignored; and a similar request made in the following year by Charles Pinckney, acting as agent for Glen and his council, received the same treatment.

Although the home government failed to take any action regarding the Overhill fort project before 1754, a post was built in the Lower Cherokee country at the close of 1753. As we have seen, the commons house of South Carolina had approved of the establishment of a post somewhere in the Lower towns in 1747 and had even voted a small sum for the purpose. Since Glen had taken no action, because he considered the grant insufficient, the subject was reopened in the spring of 1748, at a time when unrest was rife among the Cherokees and incursions into the back settlements were more than ordinarily troublesome. A joint committee on Indian affairs once more brought up the project. The

[37] CHJSC, xxii, 479, 484; Glen to Board of Trade, April 28, 1747, CO, 5/371.

[38] Representation of Board of Trade to the king, Aug. 13, 1747, Board of Trade to Glen, Oct. 10, 1748, CO, 5/402; text of instruction in CO, 5/372.

[39] Glen to Board of Trade, Feb. 3, July 26, Oct. 10, 1748, CO, 5/372.

[40] Glen to Board of Trade, July 15, 1750, CO, 5/372.

[41] Glen to Board of Trade, July 27, 1752, CO, 5/374.

commons house failed to move, since relations with the Cherokees soon improved.[42] It was again resurrected during the Cherokee crisis of 1751. At that time Glen offered convincing reasons why such a post should be built: it would encourage the Indian trade; it would serve to persuade the Lower Cherokees to remain in their towns and even to bring back those who had gone over the hills to escape Creek attacks and to trade with Virginia; and it would protect the back settlements against Indian attacks, even against assaults by the Cherokees themselves. As part of a program to meet the crisis Glen and his council advocated sending an armed force to the Cherokee country to make a display of power, to erect a fort in the Lower Towns, and to choose sites for others in the Middle Settlements and in the Overhill country. But the commons house steadily refused its assent during a long session that continued until the end of August. In the following November Glen again urged on the assembly the necessity of a fort among the Lower Cherokees, suggesting the left bank of the Keowee River opposite the Cherokee town of Keowee as an appropriate location. The commons house hesitated for some months because doubt existed whether the proposed site lay within the boundaries of South Carolina. On March 13, 1752, however, it gave its approval, provided that all or as much as possible of the territory between Long Canes Creek and Keowee be purchased from the Cherokees. On the fourteenth of May an appropriation of £3,000 (South Carolina currency) was voted, and Glen was requested to use Indian presents previously furnished by the crown to buy the lands below Keowee.[43]

Why a new delay occurred is not perfectly clear, but the fort was not actually begun until eighteen months later. Probably Glen deferred action in the hope that he would be able to secure more funds, for he felt that the appropriation made by the assembly was no more than half the amount needed. But the Cherokee traders insistently called for action; and a delegation of Cherokees at Charleston in July, 1753, sharply accused Glen of breaking his promise to build a fort for their protection.[44] As a result,

[42] CJSC, xv, 198–200; CHJSC, xxiii, 352–53, 371–72.

[43] CHJSC, xxvi, 491–94, 538–39, 630–32, 643–44, 648–52, 657–58, xxvii, 52–55, 183–84, 250–51, 465–67, 486, 551–52; CJSC, xix, pt. 1, 56–57, 115–17, 121–23, 126–28.

[44] James Beamer to Glen, April 30, 1752, minutes of a conference between Glen and Cherokee traders, July 6, 1753, petition by Cherokee traders to Glen [July, 1753], IBSC, iii, 13, 309–13, 324–26.

Glen, with a company of Independent Regulars under Captain Raymond Demeré, left Charleston on October 14 for Ninety-Six to begin preparations. Difficulties developed in securing laborers and supplies; and when these were obtained, through the efforts of Captain James Francis of Ninety-Six, the workmen refused to go to Keowee unless accompanied by Glen. According to Glen, he consented because the operations might otherwise be long delayed, especially since some Cherokees who had strongly favored the erection of the post had recently died and others were being tempted to oppose it by certain Overhill traders.[45] About the end of October Glen, his troops, and the corps of laborers reached Keowee. There Glen conferred with leaders of a large body of Lower Cherokees, principally with the Raven of Toxaway. At first the Cherokees wished to give the land requisite for the fort. Glen, however, insisted on purchasing it, and along with it a strip of territory round about to serve for raising food for the garrison and a passageway the width of the fort from Long Canes to Keowee.[46] The fort was completed during November—according to one authority, in exactly twenty-two days. It was built of wood and was a square, each side of which was nearly two hundred feet in length. Glen left a small garrison under the command of Sergeant Thomas Harrison and was back in Charleston on December 11. In addition to £100 worth of presents used to purchase the land, nearly £1,000 was spent upon construction. Not long afterward the South Carolina assembly voted £2,000 (provincial currency) to reimburse Glen for the sums he had been obliged to forward in order to complete the task.[47]

If Glen had accomplished nothing more than the construction of Fort Prince George (for so this post was named), his administration would still have been notable in the colonial history of of the Carolinas.

[45] Glen to ——, Oct. 25, 1753, Glen to Board of Trade, Oct. 25, 1753, CO, 5/374.

[46] Glen declared in the letter cited in the following note that he purchased "many thousand acres of valuable soil" on this occasion; and in the spring of 1754 he informed some Cherokees at Charleston that by the treaty "they gave... all the land between the river [Keowee] and a place called the long Canes together with all the trees corn fields pastures grounds hills weeds and water...." But the treaty clearly shows Glen's purchase was not so extensive as these passages would indicate. On this point see also David D. Wallace, *Life of Henry Laurens* . . . (New York and London, 1915), Appendix IV. In passages quoted from manuscript sources I have deleted unnecessary capitals.

[47] Glen to Board of Trade, Aug. 26, 1754, CO, 5/375; Atkin to Board of Trade May 30, 1755, Loudoun MSS; *South-Carolina Gazette,* Dec. 17, 1753.

CHAPTER III

UNDECLARED WAR IN THE SOUTH

IN 1754, as the seemingly inevitable renewal of the Franco-British conflict in America approached, James Glen had reason to hope that his great plans for the expansion of English influence to the Mississippi might yet bear fruit. The home government was less indifferent to his proposals than formerly, for London officials also sensed the imminence of the struggle in America. By April, 1754, Lord Halifax, then president of the Board of Trade, had become thoroughly convinced that the French were attempting to encircle and to roll back to the sea the English colonies in America, and that forts should be erected in the Overhill Cherokee country, in Upper Creek territory, and at other strategic points to the northward to put a stop to French aggression.[1] When on June 1, 1754, Charles Pinckney renewed his solicitations, not merely for an Overhill fort, but also for one in the Middle settlements, he received a sympathetic hearing, especially since he produced evidence that the French had made proposals to the Cherokees for erecting a fort in the Overhill country which the Indians might well accept should the English not act quickly. Pinckney pointed out to the Board of Trade that French aggression among the Cherokees was a matter of grave concern to all the colonies, and to the mother country as well. Therefore, declared Pinckney, the posts should be erected at the expense of the imperial government, particularly since the cost would be beyond the means of South Carolina.[2] After considerable discussion the board decided to recommend substantial assistance for the construction of the two forts. In a formal report of June 20 it so urged Sir Thomas Robinson, secretary of state for the southern department;[3] and on July 5

[1] [Halifax,] "Proposals for building Forts & ca: upon the Ohio, & other Rivers in North America, April 30th: 1754," CO, 5/6.

[2] Representation by Pinckney to Board of Trade, June 1, 1754, William Pinckney to Charles Pinckney, April 9, 1754 (Extract), Glen to Charles Pinckney, July 28, 1753, CO, 5/374.

[3] Board of Trade to Robinson, June 20, 1754, CO, 5/386.

Robinson wrote to Lieutenant Governor Robert Dinwiddie of Virginia, giving him a credit of £10,000 for the defense of the American colonies. Part of this sum was to be employed to erect a fort in the Overhill country, the construction of which was to be arranged in consultation by Dinwiddie and Glen.[4] Why Robinson instructed the two governors to coöperate in a project that was Glen's, and Glen's alone, is a mystery, especially since Glen and Dinwiddie were on very bad terms. In a letter to Glen of the same date Robinson found it necessary to order him to cease obstructing efforts on the part of Dinwiddie to secure aid from the Catawbas and Cherokees, and to urge that South Carolina grant funds toward financing English operations in the Ohio valley.[5] Robinson's instructions created a confusion that was perhaps more comic than tragic, but serious enough withal. Meanwhile, on June 27 Charles Pinckney had again memorialized the board, on the basis of further informaton received from South Carolina. The French threat, he now contended, was actually more serious than he had first represented, and even more strenuous action should be taken. Not only an Overhill fort, but also posts in the Upper and Lower Creek towns were necessary; and another in the Catawba nation would be useful.[6] The board merely reserved these additional proposals for future consideration, since its attention was now directed elsewhere in America.

While Pinckney was arguing the case of South Carolina in London, Glen was developing a plan to extend English sway through the Cherokee country to the upper Mississippi and to drive a wedge between Canada and Louisiana. He forwarded it to England in August, 1754. The Cherokee country, he was still convinced, was the "key of Carolina"; the real danger of French aggression lay, not on the borders of New York and New England nor in the upper Ohio valley, where the English were numerous and powerful, but on the frontiers of the far southern colonies. The Tennessee River, in his opinion, constituted an excellent road into the heart of those colonies. Hence the need for the Overhill fort. But the Tennessee River could also serve as an avenue by which the English might reach and dominate the upper Mississippi. The Cherokees should be persuaded to acknowledge the sovereignty of the British crown and to offer a small tribute of deerskins in token thereof. A delegation of seven Cherokee chiefs

[4] Robinson to Dinwiddie, July 5, 1754, CO, 5/11.
[5] Robinson to Glen, July 5, 1754, CO, 5/211.
[6] This representation is in CO, 5/375.

should go to England to ratify the necessary instrument. In this delegation should be included Attakullakulla, Usteneka,[7] and a younger chief then rising to power, Ouconnostotah, otherwise known as the Great Warrior. The boldest part of the plan was a proposal to build one or two forts near the confluence of the Ohio with the Mississippi in order to secure a firm grip on the great river and to weaken Louis XV's American colonies by severing their connection. Glen would have been satisfied either with two small forts, one on the neck between the Tennessee and the Ohio rivers and another between the Ohio and the Wabash rivers, or with a single large fort on the south side of the Ohio below the mouths of the Wabash and Tennessee. He hoped the crown would meet the cost; otherwise, Pennsylvania and Virginia should contribute £3,000, South Carolina and New York £2,000, and Maryland and North Carolina £1,000 of the £12,000 fund that would be required. A regiment should be sent out as a garrison. The valley of the Tennessee once gained in this fashion could be colonized by the English.[8]

If the theater of military conflict in the North in the Seven Years' War had been confined to the frontiers of New England and New York, Glen might have succeeded in persuading his superiors to adopt his proposals, but the upper Ohio valley became a second theater of warfare, and the attention of the home government was therefore focused upon operations in that area as well as in the far North. Its response to Glen consisted of renewed demands that South Carolina lend all possible aid to Virginia. These instructions were highly displeasing to Glen, already deeply involved in his quarrel with Dinwiddie.

Although the lack of interest of the home government in Glen's scheme for driving a wedge between Canada and Louisiana was undoubtedly irritating to its author, certain significant developments in British Indian policy during the undeclared war in America would have proved far more displeasing to him had he continued to hold office after 1756.

As described above, remedial measures to promote unity in

[7] Usteneka was commonly known as "Judd's Friend," because he was reputed to have saved the life of a man named Judd. This name was often corrupted to "Judge's Friend." He is also often mentioned as "Mankiller," and as "Autacité," which has the same meaning in Cherokee. However, "Autacité" was merely a Cherokee title that was borne by many chiefs. To avoid confusion I have used the name "Usteneka" consistently.

[8] Glen to Robinson, Aug. 13, 1754, CO, 5/14.

the formation and execution of Indian policy had long been considered a more or less pressing necessity, especially in view of French endeavors to gain the affections of the Indians. Between 1746 and 1751 several persons of note familiar with the mismanagement of relations with the Iroquois by the Indian Commissioners of New York advocated the establishment of a special office for conducting such relations. These included Governor George Clinton of New York, Governor William Shirley of Massachusetts, Archibald Kennedy, and Benjamin Franklin. Whether their advocacy was the effective factor is not certain, but the home government was sufficiently impressed by the need for reviving English prestige among the Six Nations to urge in 1753 the consideration of the problem at the Albany Congress; and in April, 1754, Lord Halifax proposed the appointment of two royal superintendents to control political and commercial relations with the northern and southern tribes. Presumably Halifax's desire to employ such an official in the South was caused by his knowledge of the jealous rivalries existing between Virginia, South Carolina, and Georgia. At all events no evidence of a demand from that area for an independent royal agent has been discovered.

The plan advocated by Halifax was never adopted in its entirety, although some progress toward implementing it was made during the period 1754–56. In August, 1754, the Board of Trade, when urging the appointment of a commander in chief for the armies in America, suggested also that the military commander should direct Indian affairs in the capacity of "commissary-general." Late in October the board reverted to Halifax's proposal for a more or less independent civil official, so far as the Iroquois were concerned. On the twenty-ninth of that month, primarily in response to recommendations by the members of the Albany Congress and by the chiefs of the Six Nations, but also in accordance with opinions expressed by Thomas Pownall, George Clinton, and William Shirley, the board called for the appointment of William Johnson as royal agent to manage diplomatic relations with the Iroquois and their allies. Behind the scenes Johnson had been the real instigator of this report. He had hoped to obtain for himself a royal commission and freedom of action under the direction of London officials. However, General Edward Braddock was sent to America with instructions to offer Johnson a commission and to furnish him with funds, and also to select a superintendent for the southern tribes. Accordingly in April, 1755, Johnson was appointed, but Braddock failed to choose a southern agent. Not long after Braddock's death a bitter controversy arose between Johnson and William Shirley, Braddock's successor, regarding the nature of Johnson's office. Johnson's appeal for a royal commission was supported by Thomas Pownall and George Clinton, and, in February, 1756, resulted in complete success. Nevertheless, Johnson was forced to continue to draw upon the commander in chief for funds.

Johnson's success in establishing himself as a quasi-permanent Indian official with a substantial salary of £600 per annum was not lost upon one Edmund Atkin, a prominent South Carolinian who had come to England in 1750 upon private affairs and had since stayed on. Some time after the news of the Fort Necessity campaign reached England, Atkin, at the request of the Board of Trade, prepared a voluminous report on the state of Indian affairs in the South; and with the support of influential South Carolinians he sought for himself an appointment as agent for the southern Indians. Since the home government was already satisfied that such an office was needed, Atkin's desire was eventually gratified. On May 13, 1756, he was commissioned agent for the Indian nations on the borders of Virginia, the Carolinas, Georgia, and their allies.[9]

Meanwhile, the war was raging in America. When rumors of a projected Franco-Indian attack in force on the frontiers of Virginia and the Carolinas reached Dinwiddie in the late spring of 1753, the jealousy of Virginia had already been aroused by the activity of the French in the region between the forks of the Ohio and Lake Erie. From Virginia Dinwiddie immediately began to lay plans for a struggle in the Ohio valley. He called upon South Carolina for troops. He also requested assistance from Glen in securing bands of Catawbas, Cherokees, and Creeks to serve as auxiliaries on the upper Ohio, since Virginia was unable to enlist the tribes, except for the feeble Nottoways and Saponeys, on her own borders. Glen replied that he would send neither men nor money to the aid of Virginia, except under instructions from home. Should war actually break out, Glen was willing to coöperate in enlisting Indian auxiliaries, provided the conflicts between the Six Nations and the southern Indians were mediated. Glen had long been jealous—and especially so since 1751—of the attempts of Virginians to participate in the Cherokee trade. He was convinced

[9] On the origins and early development of the office of superintendent see John R. Alden, "The Albany Congress and the Creation of the Indian Superintendencies," *Miss. Vall. Hist. Rev.*, XXVII (1940), 193–210.

that Virginia was trying to seize the Indian trade of the whole continental interior. He feared that aggressive action on the part of the Old Dominion would lead to hostilities on the Upper Ohio. Glen correctly predicted that the reports of a Franco-Indian invasion would prove to be unfounded, and he urged Dinwiddie to take no important step in dealing with the French until after he had conferred with the governors of other interested colonies. A French war would be of grave concern to all the colonies.[10]

Dinwiddie paid little heed to Glen. Late in 1753 he planned a conference at Winchester for May of the following year to iron out differences between the Cherokees and Catawbas and their northern enemies. He asked the advice of South Carolina on the proper mode of issuing invitations to the two southern nations; but the South Carolina council, replying during Glen's absence in the Cherokee country, gave an unfriendly answer.[11] Dinwiddie then employed Abraham Smith, formerly a trader to the Cherokees from Virginia, to invite the two tribes to confer with the governor and to take up arms against the French. Smith made three visits to each nation in 1754. In March Dinwiddie boasted that they had promised him the services of 1,000 warriors whenever they were needed. However, for all his liberal promises of presents and a plentiful trade from Virginia, Smith was able to persuade only "King" Hagler and eighteen other Catawbas, with a few Cherokees, to confer with Dinwiddie at Winchester in May. A few more southern Indians met the Virginia governor at the same place not long afterward. Glen was urging the Catawbas to remain at home to defend their own towns and advising the Cherokees to send out war parties only against their enemies across the lower Ohio.[12]

Glen's hostility toward Dinwiddie's policy did not by any means abate in 1754. Rather, it was heightened as a result of new instructions from home inspired by Dinwiddie. These instructions compelled him to send a company of the Independent Regulars under his command to Virginia,[13] where it served during the campaigns of 1754 and 1755. In the summer of 1754 Glen called for

[10] Dinwiddie to Glen, May 23, 1753, Glen to Dinwiddie, June 21, 1753, CO, 5/13.

[11] In IBSC, iii, 244–48.

[12] See various papers in IBSC, iv, 31–32, 46–47, 60, 74–75, 81–82; also Glen to Dinwiddie, June 1, 1754, CO, 5/14.

[13] R. A. Brock, ed., *The Official Records of Robert Dinwiddie* ... (Richmond, 1883–84), I, 97.

the return of this company, and condemned Dinwiddie's attempts to secure help from the Cherokees and Catawbas. Again he refused to offer any assistance to Virginia in men or money at the mere request of the Virginia governor. He contended that Saint-Pierre's replies to Washington at Fort Le Boeuf had been cool and decent, that the attitude of the French was not aggressive, and that concerted action on the part of the English governors might compel the French to agree to a peaceable settlement, even after Washington's Fort Necessity campaign.[14] In the February preceding and also in May the South Carolina assembly, though commonly at odds with Glen, had approved his attitude toward Dinwiddie's policy. When he called it into session early in September to consider Dinwiddie's request for money, the assembly once more heartily endorsed his view of the situation and refused to grant funds to defend Virginia unless a conference of colonial representatives should judge it necessary.[15]

Before Braddock began his march to the Ohio Glen was informed by Sir Thomas Robinson that the course followed by Virginia had received the approval of the home government and that South Carolina was expected to aid her sister colony. The South Carolina assembly now responded by action that enabled Glen to forward £4,000 to Braddock in May, 1755, with a promise of an additional £2,000. Glen was also forced to abandon his attitude of complete opposition toward Virginia efforts to get help from the southern Indians. He now declared himself willing to permit some of the Cherokees and Catawbas to join the English forces on the Virginia frontier, but he continued to argue that the majority of both tribes should remain at home to defend their towns.[16] Moreover, protracted negotiations that he conducted during the spring and early summer of 1755 with the Cherokees, in an effort to complete some portion of his grand plan for control of the Cherokee country, made it quite certain that most of that tribe would not give heed to Dinwiddie's appeals. Without Glen's active assistance Dinwiddie could not enlist many southern warriors, for the Cherokees and Catawbas were loath to leave

[14] Glen to Robinson, Aug. 13, 1754, CO, 5/14; Dinwiddie to Glen, Aug. 15, 1754, IBSC, iv, 96–100.

[15] CHJSC, xxix, 462–77; CJSC, xxii, pt. 2, 52–54.

[16] Glen to Board of Trade, May 29, 1755, CO, 5/375; minute of S. C. council, June 3, 1755. (The minute of the South Carolina council referred to and many others cited herein without indication of specific location are to be found in photostatic copies in the Historical Commission of South Carolina.)

their towns open to attack by trans-Ohio tribes in their absence. Edward Guest, sent out as agent by Dinwiddie early in 1755, had a difficult task, especially since he was hindered by Richard Pearis, a Virginia trader who improperly claimed to be Dinwiddie's representative. Guest finally obtained a halfhearted promise of the services of a number of Overhill warriors, but a band of forty supposedly friendly Shawnees who were visiting the Overhills warned them that the path to Winchester was dangerous and easily persuaded them not to go. Ultimately, eighty Cherokees led by Usteneka actually accompanied Pearis [17] to Virginia, where they participated in an expedition against the Shawnees.[18]

Glen, and Glen only, could have enlisted a body of Cherokees and Catawbas who might have saved Braddock, but a month before Braddock's defeat Glen was still very busy procuring from the Cherokees a formal acknowledgment of English sovereignty. He had opened these negotiations in the summer of 1754 with a message urging them to send such an acknowledgment to the king and suggesting that a Cherokee delegation might go across the water in the spring of 1755 to complete a formal ratification. When this message reached the Overhill country a number of warriors immediately replied as Glen desired. Shortly thereafter these warriors repudiated their own action; and the "Emperor," Old Hop, because he had not initiated it, denied its validity. At Glen's behest, however, most of the South Carolina traders supported the proposal; and in September, 1754, Old Hop himself and other chiefs forwarded a second acknowledgment to Glen.[19] But Glen's design was not approved by his superiors. He then abandoned the idea of sending a Cherokee embassy to London; instead he invited Old Hop and other chiefs to Charleston to make a formal submission.

Old Hop excused himself from the long journey on the ground that he was a cripple. A delegation of Overhills headed by Attakullakulla and Ouconnostotah and another from the Lower towns were secured only after considerable effort by Glen's intermedi-

[17] Pearis was made a Virginia agent by Dinwiddie in September, 1755.

[18] Ludovick Grant to Glen, March 27, 1755, "talk" by the Warrior of Tennessee town to "King" Hagler, March 16, 1755, Ludovick Grant to Glen, April 29, 1755, IBSC, v, 41–47, 50–51, 53–59; H. R. McIlwaine, ed., *Journals of the House of Burgesses of Virginia, 1752–1755, 1756–1758* (Richmond, 1909), 379–81.

[19] Glen to Overhill chiefs [summer of 1754], Overhill chiefs to Glen, Sept. 21, 1754, IBSC, iv, 81–82, v, 6; "Historical Relation of Facts delivered by Ludovick Grant, Indian Trader, to His Excellency the Governor of South Carolina," Jan. 12, 1756, *SCHGM,* X (1909), 63–64.

aries, Richard Smith,[20] James Beamer,[21] and the latter's half-breed son. In May, 1755, these Cherokees reached Charleston, conferred amicably with Glen, and transmitted an offer from Old Hop to meet Glen halfway between Charleston and Choté. Glen's council and a committee from the commons house advised him to go. The governor accordingly proceeded upcountry without official escort, expecting to meet Old Hop and a few others. En route he learned that hundreds of Cherokees were coming down from the hills. To uphold English prestige he therefore collected about five hundred militia. In June a seven-day conference was held at Saluda Old Town. There the Cherokees, in exchange for £500 worth of presents and a promise of an Overhill fort, formally ceded their lands to the English. All in all, the affair cost something like £1,100, which Glen temporarily advanced from his own pocket. The Cherokees on this occasion undoubtedly knew what they were doing and were properly authorized to do it. In reality, however, the treaty which they signed meant little, since the English did not immediately follow up the agreement by occupying the Cherokee country. Glen later sturdily defended this purchase as intrinsically desirable; but he also declared, with strange logic, that it had prevented the defection of the Cherokees and Creeks after Braddock's defeat.[22] When Glen boasted of his achievement to Dinwiddie, the latter expressed a vigorous opinion, in which Governor Arthur Dobbs of North Carolina heartily concurred, that Glen's non-coöperation in general, and his Saluda conference in particular, were largely responsible for the lack of those Indian auxiliaries from the South who might have saved Braddock's army.[23]

As Glen and Dinwiddie could not agree on Cherokee and Catawba aid for Virginia in 1755, so they failed utterly to act in concert in building the Overhill fort. This might indeed have been expected. When he received Robinson's letter of July 5, 1754, Dinwiddie urged Glen to submit appropriate information and an estimate for the fort. In terms of Glen's great design it could

[20] Richard Smith had formerly traded to the Overhills from Virginia. He was a brother of Abraham Smith.

[21] A Cherokee trader from South Carolina.

[22] Ludovick Grant and Joseph Axson to Glen, March 23, 24, 1755, IBSC, v, 48–49, 49–50; minute of S. C. council, May 22, 1755; Glen to Board of Trade, May 29, 1755, April 14, 1756, CO, 5/375; memorial by Glen to Lords Commissioners of Treasury [1762], CO, 5/377.

[23] Minute of S. C. council, Oct. 11, 1755; Dobbs to Henry Fox, March 26, 1756, CO, 5/17.

not be a cheap and poorly constructed affair, and he proposed an estimate of £7,000. Dinwiddie was shocked. His sole interest in the fort lay in doing only what was absolutely imperative to get the help that he desired from the Cherokees. Quite logically he considered it preposterous to spend for that purpose the major portion of the £10,000 fund. He therefore sent Glen a modest £1,000, with a suggestion that the plans be modified and that any necessary further aid be secured from the South Carolina assembly. Although both Glen and his assembly considered £1,000 utterly inadequate, the governor soon lowered his estimate to two thirds of the original. Nevertheless, in the winter of 1754–55 the commons house refused to appropriate any money for the purpose. The fort, it was alleged, would lie outside the limits of South Carolina and would serve for the defense of the southern colonies generally. If Virginia with North Carolina and Georgia would share in the expense, South Carolina was willing to come in, but the commons preferred that the crown bear the whole burden.[24] Glen sought to obtain additional funds from Dinwiddie, even attempting to bring pressure through Braddock. In August, 1755, he went so far as to promise to send eight or nine hundred Cherokees to Winchester, if Dinwiddie would forward an additional £2,000 or £3,000. Dinwiddie had spent most of the £10,000 fund upon the Braddock campaign, and he refused to offer a sixpence.[25]

In the fall of 1755 Dinwiddie began even more strenuous efforts to gain the aid of the southern Indians, for Braddock's defeat had opened the Virginia frontier to hostile Indian incursions. Invitations to the Catawbas and Cherokees to meet commissioners from Virginia in February and March, respectively, were issued; and on December 23 Dinwiddie appointed Peter Randolph and William Byrd as Virginia's representatives. These gentlemen were assisted by two commissioners appointed by Governor Dobbs, whose opinion on Indian aid for Virginia coincided with that of Dinwiddie. One of the North Carolina commissioners was Hugh Waddell, a well-known figure on the North Carolina frontier. On February 20–21 Randolph and Byrd succeeded in negotiating a treaty with the Catawbas at their principal town whereby the Catawbas were to send forty men to the aid of Virginia within forty days. From March 13 to 17 they held conferences with Atta-

[24] Glen to Dinwiddie, Jan. —, 1755, CO, 5/375; CHJSC, xxx, 321–24, 341–44, 360–61, 372–73; CJSC, xxiv, pt. 1, 37–39.

[25] Minutes of S. C. council, June 3, Aug. 29, Oct. 11, 1755.

kullakulla, Ouconnostotah, and a large body of Cherokees upon Broad River, but they were unable to secure a promise of immediate assistance from the Cherokees. The Cherokees were not inclined to serve on the upper Ohio unless a fort were built in their country. Byrd and Randolph at length promised them that this fort would be built, with Virginia contributing its fair proportion. In return the Cherokees pledged themselves to send 500 warriors to Virginia within forty days of its completion. The Cherokees were also persuaded to promise that they would not permit the French to build a similar post in their country. A treaty signed on March 17 embodied the pledges. These dealings had the full approval of the North Carolina government, which shortly afterward undertook to erect a fort for the Catawbas.[26]

One party of Cherokees reached Winchester for service in April, 1756. Apparently this was the only immediate result of the labors of Randolph and Byrd, even though Glen reversed his former attitude in the winter of 1755–56 and urged the Catawbas to send parties to Virginia.[27] When Dinwiddie learned of the treaties negotiated by the commissioners, he was irritated, for he felt that the Overhill fort should have been completed by Glen early in 1755. But he regarded the situation on the Virginia frontier as desperate and believed that energetic measures were required. The burgesses agreed with him, even to the point of voting £1,200 toward the expense of the fort. To this sum Dinwiddie added £800, the residue of the royal grant of £10,000. He dispatched Major Andrew Lewis with sixty men to the Overhill country with instructions to construct the fort. At the same time he wrote to Glen to inform him of these steps and to request him to send out a party of South Carolinians to work with Lewis. His letter to Glen evidently miscarried.[28]

Meanwhile, Randolph and Byrd, disgusted by the poor results

[26] *Virginia Magazine of History and Biography,* XIII (1906), 225–64, gives the texts of the treaties and other informative documents concerning the mission of Randolph and Byrd. North Carolina began the erection of a fort for the Catawbas in 1757, but abandoned the task when the Catawbas demanded that the work be discontinued. Not long afterward the Catawbas again changed their minds and requested that the fort be completed, but North Carolina did not resume operations. See William L. Saunders, ed., *The Colonial Records of North Carolina* . . . (Raleigh, N. C., 1886–90), V, 783–84, 902. (Hereafter these volumes are cited as *NCCR*.)

[27] Glen to "King" Hagler, Feb. 12, 1756, IBSC, v, 106–7; also v, 122. Glen continued to insist that the Cherokees serve under his orders.

[28] *Dinwiddie Records,* II, 413.

of a mission that had cost £1,500, had gone on to Charleston in the hope of obtaining help from Glen. When they arrived, on March 24,[29] they discovered that Glen was making actual preparations for building the long-discussed fort. Indeed, a large Cherokee delegation at Charleston on December 5 had told Glen what their fellows later told Dinwiddie's commissioners: no fort, no aid to Virginia.[30] In January, 1756, Glen had once more placed the subject before the assembly. He urged the advance of sufficient funds added to the £1,000 furnished by the crown to do the job and assured the assembly that the crown would repay. On February 4 the assembly voted a loan of £1,000.[31] Shortly afterward Glen sent out John Pearson, a provincial deputy-surveyor, to choose a site on the Little Tennessee River. At first Glen planned to employ fifty Independent Regulars and fifty provincials for the task. He offered the command to Lieutenant Probart Howarth,[32] an experienced officer of the regulars, who had just returned to South Carolina from service under Washington and Braddock. Lieutenant Howarth did not want the appointment. When Randolph and Byrd urged Glen to oversee the work in person, the governor agreed, for he flattered himself upon his knowledge of the science of fortification. This he was the more ready to do when the assembly, at his urging, voted a second loan of £1,000 for the fort.[33]

Nor did Glen abandon his plans when the sums voted by the assembly were not forthcoming because of a disagreement between the two houses over a tax bill. A few public-minded citizens promptly lent £2,000 to the colony; and he set out from Charleston on May 19. He was accompanied by ninety Independent Regulars under Captain Raymond Demeré and by some 210 South Carolina provincials. With him went also William Gerard De Brahm, the well-known engineer, and Dr. Alexander Garden, a Charleston physician interested in botanical research. Glen and his entourage were far upcountry when William Henry Lyttelton, a lean young gentleman who had been appointed governor of

[29] Glen to Board of Trade, April 14, 1756, CO, 5/375; *South-Carolina Gazette*, April 1, 1756.

[30] Representation by Charles Pinckney to Board of Trade, Feb. 4, 1756, CO, 5/375.

[31] CHJSC, xxxi, pt. 1, 47–49, 65, 77.

[32] Howarth's given name, according to the *British Army Lists*, was Robert, but in the documents it is Probart.

[33] Glen to Attakullakulla, Feb. 17, 1756, IBSC, v, 113–14; CJSC, xxv, 147, 152–53; CHJSC, xxxi, pt. 1, 177, 180; Glen to Board of Trade, April 14, 1756, CO, 5/375.

South Carolina early in 1755, appeared at Charleston on June 1. On the very next day he decided to disband Glen's provincials and to make new arrangements. When Glen learned, in the middle of June, of his successor's arrival, he reluctantly returned from Ninety-Six to Charleston. Ironically, he had been superseded just at the moment when one of his most cherished projects was on the verge of completion.[34]

It will have been inferred that, in spite of continued antagonism between South Carolina and Virginia, the Cherokees remained on friendly terms with the English during the undeclared war in America. And so they did, although the disorderly behavior of the Cherokee traders tended to alienate them. The conduct of the traders had been such that in 1755 South Carolina and Georgia attempted a partial remedy by forbidding the use of rum in the trade,[35] without any helpful result. To be sure, the Overhills permitted a dozen Frenchmen, supposedly deserters and prisoners, to reside in their towns, and even protected them against the English, but the great body of the nation was faithful to its traditional ally.[36] They would not have been so loyal if the Chevalier Louis de Kerlérec had been as able as he was eager to offer them a trade.

If we may believe Kerlérec, he spent the fifth decade of his life, when he served as governor of Louisiana, striving endlessly to protect and enhance the power of his most Christian majesty Louis XV. Frequently and vehemently this experienced servant of the crown of France declared that he had exhausted health and private fortune in his master's service. He claimed that his indefatigable energy preserved Louisiana in spite of unending efforts on the part of the English to throw the southern Indian tribes against New Orleans, in spite also of the lack of support from France, and against the opposition of self-seeking Louisianians. And most of the officers in the military forces of Louisiana would *publicly* have sworn that Kerlérec did not exaggerate either his achievements or his disinterestedness. However, his enemies in Louisiana, particularly Gaston de Rochemore, commissaire-ordonnateur of

[34] CJSC, xxv, 273–74; Alexander Garden to Cadwallader Colden, April 20, Aug. 14, 1756, Jan. 10, 1757, *Collections of the New-York Historical Society for the Year 1921* (New York, 1922), 70–71, 90, 115; letters from Demeré to Lyttelton, June 15 and 24, 1756, and other papers, IBSC, v, 133–37, 143–44.

[35] Minute of S. C. council, July 21, 1755.

[36] John Elliott to Glen, Sept. 25, 1755, IBSC, v, 85–86.

the colony from 1758 to 1762, if merely dubious of the services of the governor to France, were certain that he amassed in Louisiana a tidy sum with which to face his old age, and that a goodly portion of that sum had been obtained by corrupt practices. Rochemore specifically charged that the military officers at the various posts, who retained throughout Kerlérec's administration a monopoly of the Indian trade, rewarded the governor for the privilege. Kerlérec, of course, made countercharges against Rochemore; he claimed that the commissaire-ordonnateur used his own office, the duties of which included the purchase and disbursement of supplies for the colony, to fill his purse. Indeed, Kerlérec defended his cause so successfully that in 1759 Rochemore's office was put under his own; three years later he was even able to send Rochemore to France in disgrace. With Rochemore's death shortly afterward Kerlérec seemed to have won his case *in toto,* but Rochemore's widow made a strenuous fight to clear her husband's name. Kerlérec suffered a brief imprisonment in the Bastille after his return to France at the close of the Seven Years' War. An investigation that was carried on for several years disclosed that M. Chiton, Kerlérec's secretary, had undoubtedly profited by connections with army officers engaged in the skin trade, that his employer had probably done likewise, and that Kerlérec's conduct had been far from satisfactory in other ways.[37]

Whatever may be said regarding the disinterestedness of Kerlérec, it must be admitted that he labored under great difficulties. The usual difficulties in obtaining Indian goods were multiplied by the outbreak of war, for a scheme formulated by Kerlérec to create a great reserve of supplies for such an emergency[38] had not been approved. Moreover, the French government was insistently demanding economy in Louisiana. In addition, he often lacked instructions from home, partly because the English intercepted correspondence at sea, partly because of the negligence of his superiors in France. Yet he was an exasperating opponent to the English. As he afterward declared, during the early years of the war he even hoped to organize an onslaught by the southern Indians (the Chickasaws, of course, excepted) upon the Carolinas

[37] This paragraph is based upon a mass of correspondence in Archives Nationales, Colonies. The major facts regarding Kerlérec and Rochemore are conveniently summarized in a Résumé de l'Extrait de l'Avis sur l'affaire de La Louisianne, ANC, C13A, 41.

[38] Kerlérec to ministry, Aug. 2, 1753, ANC, C13A, 37.

and Georgia. Thus he would not only have inflicted severe blows upon those provinces, but would also have relieved the English pressure upon Canada.[39]

Unfortunately for Kerlérec, Anglo-Cherokee relations from 1754 to 1756 were on a sufficiently sound footing, so that mere intrigue by the French could not greatly sway that tribe. Kerlérec was fully aware of this fact. He realized that it was necessary to establish a trade with the Cherokees to win their friendship. He was also convinced that it was necessary to erect a post upon the lower Ohio as a center of operations among them. But it was not until the late spring of 1757 that the post was built by M. Philippe Aubry, acting under orders from Major Macarty, French commander in the Illinois country. Fort Massac, as it came to be known, was located on the Ohio eleven miles below the mouth of the Tennessee. It was garrisoned by fifty men.[40] Nor was Kerlérec able to offer the Cherokees a trade. As early as 1754 a small faction among the Overhills made overtures to the French, partly in order to end attacks by Francophile tribes and partly to obtain a trade that would render them less dependent upon the English.[41] After 1755 this faction became even more friendly to the French. This was largely due to the efforts of the Chevalier Louis de Lantagnac, an officer who had previously spent some six years among the Cherokees (most of them as a trader from South Carolina), and who was now acting as agent of propaganda among them under the direction of the commander of Fort Toulouse.[42] Soon

[39] Kerlérec to ministry, Nov. 25, 1758, ANC, C13A, 40.

[40] *Wis. Hist. Colls.*, XVIII (1908), 210, note; John Charles Vian's deposition, Jan. 30, 1758, IBSC, vi, 128–29. The post was first named Fort de l'Ascension because it was completed on the anniversary of the Ascension. It was rechristened Fort Massac (or Massiac). To the English it was known as Fort Assumption.

[41] Kerlérec to ministry, Sept. 19, 1754, ANC, C13A, 38.

[42] According to Lantagnac, he was thirteen years of age in 1745 and an ensign stationed at Fort Toulouse. In November of that year he went hunting, became lost, was captured by a band of Chickasaws, and was carried off to Georgia. He was handed over to Glen by Georgia officials, was offered but declined a commission in the Independent Regulars, and idled away three years in Charleston. Then he was allowed to make a journey under parole with South Carolina traders to the Cherokee country. At length Glen personally lent him money to establish himself as a trader to the Cherokees; and he followed that occupation for five years. In 1755 he made his way to Savannah and thence to Fort Toulouse. Kerlérec accepted his story. Lantagnac mentions Vaudreuil as his *parent,* which indicates that Vaudreuil was his kinsman. Kerlérec to ministry, Oct. 1, 1755, Lantagnac to Kerlérec, n.d., ANC, C13A, 39. Lantagnac's story should be taken with a grain of salt. William Bull, who was certainly familiar with the

an odd group of scoundrels—Peter Chartier, a half-breed known as Savannah Tom, and French John, a Canadian and supposedly the slave of Old Hop—came to Lantagnac's assistance. They were supported by the Francophiles among the Upper Creeks and by the Southern Shawnees. Until the fall of 1756 the intrigues of this motley crew apparently had little effect. They might have been more successful, had Kerlérec and Vaudreuil been willing to conclude a formal alliance with the Cherokees, but both governors feared to promise the necessary trade. They believed that if that trade, once formally promised, were not forthcoming, the Cherokees would be thrown completely and finally into the arms of the English.

Kerlérec's greatest efforts in Indian diplomacy during the period 1754–56 were logically directed toward the establishment of French hegemony in the Creek nation. The Creeks as enemies would be far more dangerous to the safety of Louisiana than the Cherokees; and the chances of inciting the Creeks to assail the English were also much greater. Almost simultaneously with the outbreak of hostilities on the Monongahela M. de Massé, the French commandant at Fort Toulouse, offered presents to delegates from the Upper Creeks and invited them down to Mobile. There Kerlérec himself sought to turn them against the English, and not without reward. Shrewd propaganda to the effect that Fort Prince George was intended as a base for a joint Anglo-Cherokee attack on the Creeks and that the advance of English settlements on the Ogeechee demonstrated English designs upon all the Creek lands, impressed the Indians. Late in the year Kerlérec was able to make a greater effort, when two years' supplies of Indian goods for the Choctaws and Creeks arrived from France. He promptly invited both tribes to confer with him at Mobile. A special personal emissary was sent to urge Malatchi to attend, but he had fallen dangerously ill in the summer of 1754 and sent his regrets. At Mobile, between October and December, Kerlérec held a number of conclaves, first with the Creeks and later with the Choctaws, with satisfactory results. To the propaganda circulated among the Creeks earlier in the year he and his subordinates now added a most effective tale: that Malatchi had been given a slow poison by the English because of his opposition to them. The Creek delegates acknowledged a leaning toward

Independent Regulars, declares that Lantagnac accepted a commission in that body of troops when he first came to Charleston and that he served for a time. Bull to Board of Trade, Nov. 18, 1760, CO, 5/377.

the French, but pointed out, as they had done so often, that they could not exist without the English trade. Kerlérec attempted to remove that objection. After his return to New Orleans he sent several thousand livres worth of goods to Fort Toulouse for a temporary trade, in which, if English traders were not mistaken, prices were lower than their own. He also appealed to the ministry to enable him to offer a trade to the Creeks similar to that with the Choctaws, but in this he failed. However, Massé and the Chevalier Montaut de Monbéraut, his successor in 1755, assiduously and effectively fostered French influence among the Creeks throughout 1755 and the early months of 1756. Especially helpful to them during this period was a discovery made in the late summer of 1754 by Gun Merchant, chief of Oakfuskie town, that English trading prices to the Cherokees were lower than those to the Creeks. When Gun Merchant brought this news home in the spring of 1755 great dissatisfaction arose among the Upper Creeks.[43]

Neither Glen nor John Reynolds, first royal governor of Georgia who reached his post in October, 1754, was able to cope effectively with Kerlérec's intrigues among the Creeks. Both became seriously alarmed about the situation. Unfortunately, Reynolds, a former naval officer, was an arbitrary person hardly better fitted for his office, as one critic[44] declared, than an Indian chief. Moreover, the home government failed to supply him with presents for the Creeks until late in 1755, and Georgia was then too poverty-stricken to make up the deficiency. Because he had no cloth goods Reynolds felt compelled to present guns and ammunition, gifts of doubtful wisdom, to some Lower Creeks who appeared at Savannah in March, 1755. Not long afterward he was forced to send away visiting Cherokees and Savannah River Chickasaws without presents of any kind. Other groups of Creeks who desired to confer with Reynolds were urged to remain at home.[45]

Glen issued three separate invitations to the Creeks to visit him during the early months of 1755, but they would not come to Charleston. He and his council came to fear that the fate of the Chickasaws was sealed and that a Creek attack upon the English was imminent. Glen consequently convened the assembly at

[43] Kerlérec to ministry, Dec. 18, 19, 1754, Malatchi to Kerlérec, Dec. 18, 1754, ANC, C13A, 38; journal of [Lachlan McIntosh], IBSC, v, 60–75.

[44] General Huske. See Robert Phillimore, ed., *Memoirs and Correspondence of George, Lord Lyttelton, from 1734 to 1773* (London, 1845), II, 605.

[45] *GCR*, VII, 20–21, 46–47, 135, 172–73, 179, 182, 206, 211, 268.

the unseasonable time of September 15 to consider the situation.[46] To the assembly he described the state of affairs in the darkest colors. He declared that the French aimed at no less than the establishment of an overlordship over the Creeks, as the first step toward complete French sovereignty. In accordance with advice given him by the Creek traders Lachlan McGillivray and Lachlan McIntosh Glen requested the assembly to offset French activities by a law cutting Creek trade prices and providing for an ample supply of presents. He urged that steps be taken to forestall the French by securing Creek recognition of English overlordship. A joint committee on Indian affairs promptly recommended that Major Henry Hyrne, an officer with considerable experience in frontier affairs, be sent out as a special agent to offer presents to the Creeks and Chickasaws, and to invite a Creek delegation to a conference regarding trade prices. The commons immediately approved this report. Glen, however, declared that an agent was unnecessary and contended that the house had overstepped its powers by attempting to name him and to direct his work. Thereupon the commons house retorted that the supposed crisis must be largely imaginary. Indeed, a house committee after examining one Spencer, a partner of McGillivray, reported that McGillivray and McIntosh had greatly exaggerated the Creek requests for lower trade prices, and that they had done so in order to crowd out their poorer competitors. Before adjourning, the assembly did give the governor, the council, and a committee of the house power to make necessary changes in Creek trading rates.[47]

Lachlan McIntosh finally succeeded in persuading the Upper Creeks to send a delegation to discuss the trade question at Charleston; Malatchi, also invited, was dying.[48] The South Carolina trade committee made plans for a conference at the end of 1755 and urged Georgia to participate in it.[49] Meanwhile, however, Reynolds had received a supply of presents from England and had independently summoned the Upper Creeks to meet him at Augusta on December 1. Some sixty warriors headed by Gun Merchant, Wolf King, and Devil's Landlord eventually appeared at

[46] Minutes of S. C. council, Aug. 19, Sept. 1, 1755.

[47] Minute of S. C. council, Sept. 4, 1755; CJSC, xxiv, pt. 1, 102–5; CHJSC, xxx, 606–9, 623–25, 630–41.

[48] Malatchi died about the beginning of 1756. See Lachlan McGillivray to Glen and S. C. council, Feb. 17, 1756, IBSC, v, 117.

[49] Lachlan McIntosh to Glen, Oct. 8, 1755, David Douglass to Glen, Nov. 21, 1755, IBSC, v, 90, 95–96.

that place, but Reynolds was piqued when he learned that this delegation planned to spend only a few days at Augusta en route to Charleston. Entrusting negotiations to William Little, clerk of the assembly and holder of various other offices in Georgia, he departed for Savannah. Little distributed the presents, and was given no return but a demand that the Bosomworth claim be recognized. The demand was promptly refused.[50] The Creeks went on to Charleston, where they conferred with Glen and the special committee from January 10 to 25, 1756.

Glen was eager to please the Creeks. He hoped to persuade them to help the Chickasaws by exerting pressure upon the Choctaws and to obtain their permission to build a fort in one of their towns as a base for an attack on Fort Toulouse. But the Creek delegation complained about the Ogeechee settlements and trade prices. After much cajoling the Creeks promised to lend the desired support to the Chickasaws. They agreed to permit Glen to erect a storehouse for goods in their territory, though not a fort. In return Glen promised that trade prices would be lowered to the level of those of the Cherokees. These agreements were crystallized in a treaty signed on January 23, which was ratified for Georgia by Reynolds exactly one month later. But the South Carolina committee insisted on limiting the number of Creek traders as well as cutting prices. The commons house refused its consent, and action to meet the trade problem was therefore indefinitely postponed.[51] The treaty was not too well received in the Upper Creek towns, in spite of the fact that it was stoutly defended by its Indian signers. Relations with those towns were quiet, though not amiable, when Glen was succeeded by Lyttelton.

[50] Lachlan McIntosh to Glen, n.d., IBSC, v, 98; minute of S. C. council, Oct. 28, 1755; representation of Board of Trade, July 29, 1756, *GCR,* XXXIX, 198–222. See also second document in the next note.

[51] CJSC, xxv, 42–53, 55–60, 65–83, 90; Reynolds to Glen, Feb. 23, 1756, Glen to Board of Trade, April 14, 1756, CO, 5/375.

CHAPTER IV

ANGLO-CHEROKEE RELATIONS, 1756–57: LYTTELTON AND ATKIN

WILLIAM HENRY LYTTELTON, through family influence appointed governor of South Carolina on January 28, 1755, set out for his post on board H.M.S. *Blandford*. The man-of-war was captured by the French, and Lyttelton was carried to France. Released, he returned to England in September of the same year, for he had destroyed his instructions when the *Blandford* was about to be taken. In February, 1756, he was called before the Board of Trade for a special verbal instruction. Early in that month Charles Pinckney had informed the board that Glen and Dinwiddie had not yet built the Overhill fort; he had further insisted that South Carolina and Georgia were undone unless prompt action was taken. The board was impressed by Pinckney's arguments. Lyttelton was ordered to begin operations immediately after reaching America. If South Carolina failed to supply sufficient funds, further measures to deal with the financial problem would be taken by the home government.[1]

On the very day following his disembarkation at Charleston Lyttelton ordered the provincials raised by Glen to be disbanded, because he was persuaded that Glen's arrangements for building the fort were not well planned. But he also sent presents to Old Hop with an assurance that the project would not be abandoned. In accordance with the governor's orders, Demeré moved on to Fort Prince George with the regulars, and sent Sergeant William Gibbes to the Overhill towns with eighteen men under the escort of Attakullakulla to make preliminary preparations. On June 21 Lyttelton asked the South Carolina assembly for funds. Although he was forced to admit that Glen had erred in asking merely for a loan to build the fort and that the home government desired

[1] Representation by Pinckney to the board, Feb. 4, 1756, CO, 5/375; *Journal of the Commissioners for Trade and Plantations from January 1754 to December 1758* . . . (London, 1933), 210–13.

an outright grant, the assembly almost immediately voted to place £4,000 in his hands.[2]

For lack of a better engineer Lyttelton employed De Brahm to make plans for the fort and to supervise its construction.[3] On July 15 he appointed John Stuart and John Postell captains and instructed them to raise two provincial companies of sixty men each to serve under Demeré. Stuart was made the senior officer, probably because he had previously held a commission in the South Carolina militia.[4] Stuart and Postell recruited their men, chiefly in the northern parts of the province. Late in August all the provincials reached Keowee.[5] Meanwhile, Demeré had reconstructed Fort Prince George, since the works hastily erected by Glen were found unsatisfactory.[6] Leaving Ensign John Bogges with fifteen regulars at Fort Prince George, Demeré, with most of the regulars and provincials, departed for the Overhill country on September 24.[7] On October 4 he and his men reached a camp prepared for them by Gibbes near the Overhill town of Tomotley, then under the leadership of Attakullakulla.[8]

While Lyttelton's preparations were being completed, Major Lewis and his sixty Virginians had safely reached Chotě, on June 28. When Lewis informed an assemblage of Cherokees gathered to greet him that he was under orders to coöperate with the South Carolinians in building a fort, the Cherokees insisted upon two forts, one on the southern bank of the Little Tennessee to protect them against French-inspired attacks from the west, and another on the northern shore to shield them against Francophile

[2] Lyttelton to Board of Trade, June 19, July 19, 1756, CO, 5/375; Demeré to Lyttelton, July 28, 1756, IBSC, v, 170–72. Of course, part of the £5,000 thus made available for the fort had already been spent by Glen for materials, wages, etc.

[3] Lyttelton to Loudoun, Aug. 25, 1756, Public Record Office, War Office (hereafter cited as WO), 34/35, pt. 1.

[4] CJSC, xxv, 310–11, xxvi, pt. 1, 81; Stuart's commission, July 15, 1756, in Record Book of Probate Court, 1754–1758, Judge W. E. Vincent, Charleston Co., 563, Charleston County (S. C.) Courthouse; Demeré to Lyttelton, Sept. 1, 1756, IBSC, v, 203–4. Demeré states that Lyttelton considered Stuart's seniority as beginning at an earlier date, "as [Stuart] had served before as a captain." It seems probable that the service referred to was given as an officer in the Charleston militia, in which Stuart held the rank of captain in 1757.

[5] Demeré to Lyttelton, Aug. 29, 1756, IBSC, v, 194–96.

[6] Demeré to Lyttelton, July 6, 1756, IBSC, v, 149; also v, 200.

[7] Sergeant Thomas Harrison, commandant at the fort since its erection, was given leave of absence by Demeré. Bogges held the post until the spring of 1757. He was succeeded by Lieutenant Shaw, who commanded until the fall of 1757.

[8] Demeré to Lyttelton, Sept. 12, Oct. 13, 1756, IBSC, v, 224–27, 241–47.

tribes from the Ohio. Since Lewis believed that otherwise he would get no help for Virginia, he agreed; in return the Cherokees promised to send 400 men to Virginia as soon as the works on the northern bank were completed. Later the Cherokees would pledge only 100 men. On a site one mile above Choté Lewis erected a log fort 105 feet in length, which was finished by the end of July.[9] Finally, however, Lewis was accompanied to Virginia by only seven Overhill warriors and three women, even though Lyttelton, anxious to aid in the common cause, sent up a large quantity of presents for the Cherokees.

In part Lewis's failure to secure many allies is explained by the fact that, in accordance with his instructions, he left no garrison at the Virginia fort; in part it was caused by the intrigues of Southern Shawnees, Upper Creeks, and Frenchmen residing in the Overhill towns. Lewis came to believe that the Cherokees sought to have the two English forts erected merely to secure presents and to have English soldiers in their country as virtual hostages. He was also satisfied that Attakullakulla was thoroughly in the French interest, and that the little chief hoped to persuade the French to build a fort at Tellico town to counterbalance the English posts. As a result of Lewis's reports Dinwiddie became convinced that the Cherokees were waiting to see which side would win the war and that they would join the apparent victor. Early in October the burgesses voted £2,000 to maintain a garrison of fifty men in the Virginia fort. In November Dinwiddie renewed his appeals to the Overhills for help, promising that a garrison would be sent. Nevertheless, Dinwiddie was so distrustful of the Cherokees that he was resolved to postpone dispatching a garrison until he was certain of their friendship.[10] Only a few small parties of Cherokees and Catawbas came to the assistance of Virginia in 1756, and these rendered no service of value.[11]

The erection of the South Carolinian fort, a much more imposing structure than that built by the Virginians, was accomplished not without difficulties, caused largely, if we may believe Demeré, by the incompetence and peculiar temperament of De

[9] Lewis to Demeré, July 7, 1756, Demeré to Lyttelton, July 28, 30, 1756, IBSC, v, 157–58, 170–72, 173.

[10] Reports by Demeré and Lewis to Lyttelton, Sept. 12 and 14, 1756, IBSC, v, 224–31; *NCCR*, V, 612–14; *Dinwiddie Records*, II, 538–40, 543–44, 548–49, 553–54; *South-Carolina Gazette*, Nov. 4, 1756.

[11] *Dinwiddie Records*, II, 560–61; John C. Fitzpatrick, ed., *The Writings of George Washington* ... (Washington, 1931—), I, 508, 524–26.

Brahm.[12] Demeré and the engineer quarreled hotly over the site. Demeré was well pleased with that chosen by Pearson, but De Brahm finally insisted upon another spot. Weary of conflict, Demeré consented and permitted De Brahm to carry on operations as he would. Demeré reported that the works thrown up under De Brahm's direction were both costly and defective. A month after construction had begun De Brahm was on bad terms with most of the officers and was constantly threatening to leave for Charleston.[13] In December he caused a crisis when he announced that the fort would be finished in three days and informed Captain Postell's provincials that they were free to return to South Carolina after that time. In order to prevent Postell's men from leaving, Demeré and Stuart were forced to read to the soldiers the articles of war and Stuart's commission and instructions, thus making it clear that their departure would constitute desertion.[14] Finally, although the fort was still unfinished, De Brahm slipped away for Charleston on the night of December 25, thereby earning for himself the Cherokee sobriquet of "warrior who ran away in the night." Even after his departure the difficulties he had caused continued, for he had formed a friendship with Postell, and it was some little time before Postell was reconciled to his fellow officers.[15] However, the troops were able to move into the fort at the close of 1756. At the same time, in accordance with the wish of Lyttelton, it was named "Loudoun" [16] in honor of the commander in chief from 1756 to 1758. But work on the fort continued under Demeré's direction until April, 1757.[17] One problem, which Demeré was unable to solve, that of bringing the heavy guns over the hills, was settled by John Elliott, a Cherokee trader, who managed to transport them to the fort on horseback.[18]

Demeré also found it difficult to handle the Cherokees. It soon developed, however, that Stuart and, to a lesser extent, Lieuten-

[12] Demeré's judgment of De Brahm seems sound.

[13] Demeré to Lyttelton, Oct. 13, Nov. 7, 18, 1756, IBSC, v, 241–47, 268–71, 280–83.

[14] IBSC, v, 307–10.

[15] Demeré to Lyttelton, Dec. 27, 1756, Jan. 2, May 18, 1757, IBSC, v, 324–27, 341–44, vi, 42–45.

[16] Demeré to Lyttelton, Dec. 8, 1756, IBSC, v, 295–97. In his reports to Lyttelton Demeré used the term for the first time on January 2, 1757. The fort was located a short distance above the confluence of the Little Tennessee and Tellico rivers, in what is now Monroe County, Tennessee.

[17] Demeré to Lyttelton, March 28, April 11, 1757, IBSC, vi, 6–9, 30–32.

[18] Demeré to Lyttelton, Nov. 28, 1756, IBSC, v, 291–94.

ant Robert Wall of Postell's company, were especially gifted for Indian diplomacy. Through them Demeré found it possible to meet various problems. In fact, Demeré was so pleased with Stuart that he urged his appointment as commandant of the fort in the event that the regulars were withdrawn upon its completion; suggested Stuart as the person most suited to carry on at the fort a trade desired by the Cherokees; and hinted that the management of relations with the whole tribe should be placed in Stuart's hands.[19]

It was fortunate indeed that Stuart and Wall were so gifted, since French intrigues among the Cherokees seemed likely to bear fruit. A gang of Southern Shawnees inspired by Lantagnac and Chartier labored effectively in the Overhill towns of Tellico and Chatuga in the early fall of 1756. As a result, the Mankiller of Tellico and some twenty-four fellow townsmen conferred with French officers and with delegations of Southern Shawnees and Upper Creeks at Fort Toulouse on October 18. The Shawnees and Overhills urged a joint attack upon the English, the Upper Creeks to strike the first blow. The Upper Creeks brought these negotiations to an end by sagaciously refusing to be used as tools. Shortly afterward the Mankiller and most of his following set out for home, but four or five Tellico men proceeded to Mobile with Lantagnac, and thence to New Orleans.[20] At New Orleans in November the warriors represented themselves as emissaries of the Cherokee nation, and signed a preliminary treaty of alliance with Kerlérec. Because Kerlérec was still reluctant to enter upon any engagements with the Cherokees involving a definite promise of a trade the preliminary agreement stipulated that France would regard the Cherokees as allies *if* they attacked the English and *if* the agreement were satisfactory to the governor of Canada

[19] Demeré to Lyttelton, Oct. 26, 1756, Jan. 2, 1757, IBSC, v, 257–60, 341–44. Demeré wrote to Lyttelton in the former letter: "I am extreamly pleased that your Excellency approves of my having a friendly communication with Capt. Stewart I should be much to blaim was I not to cultivate the same; I take him to be a very worthy gentleman fit & capable for any kind of service I only wish myself as capable as he is for the management of Indian negotiations . . . Captain Stuart and Lieut. Wall are extreamly beloved by the Indians . . . ." It is not unlikely that Stuart did carry on a trade at the fort. Lyttelton later declared that some of the officers indulged in trading operations and that he reluctantly permitted them to do so because they received no payment for their trouble and expenses in negotiating with the Cherokees. Lyttelton to Board of Trade, Aug. 7, 1758, CO, 5/376.

[20] Samuel Pepper to Lyttelton, Nov. 18, 1756, IBSC, v, 284–88, also vi, 86; *South-Carolina Gazette,* Nov. 18, 25, 1756.

and to Francophile Indians at war with the Cherokees. In the event that all these stipulations were fulfilled Kerlérec would provide a good trade to the Cherokees. By the treaty Kerlérec hoped immediately to strengthen French influence among the Cherokees. At the same time he could refuse a permanent alliance; or he could ratify one, were he enabled to open a trade. But Vaudreuil failed to offer his approval, and for several years Kerlérec's efforts to obtain the trade goods necessary to consummate the alliance were without result.[21]

Demeré and Stuart were early informed of the departure of the Tellico delegation for Fort Toulouse, and they were inclined to believe that it had not gone without the approval of Old Hop and Attakullakulla. They suspected Attakullakulla of playing a double game and tried for some time without success to discover his real sentiments.[22] However, the Mankiller of Tellico, after his return home in December, appeared at the fort and asked audience with Demeré. Demeré and Stuart plied him with liquor and coaxed him into such good humor that he remained overnight at the fort. Between cups the troublesome chief confessed that his mission had been dictated by Old Hop and the Little Carpenter, and displayed beads that he had worn as token that he was Old Hop's ambassador.[23] On December 23 Attakullakulla, who had become attached to Stuart, supped with him at the fort. Stuart accused the little chief of perfidy. Attakullakulla denied that he had instigated the action of the Tellico warriors and pledged eternal friendship to the English. He kept his pledge. To prove his friendship he insisted upon going immediately to Charleston with Stuart to confer with Lyttelton. Demeré consented, and he told Lyttelton that the Overhills were so fond of Stuart that they would be "prodigiously affronted" if he did not return. Stuart was instructed to inform the governor of the state of affairs in the Overhill country.[24]

On December 27 Stuart, Attakullakulla, Usteneka, Willinawa,[25]

[21] Lyttelton to Board of Trade, April 22, 1757, CO, 5/375; Kerlérec to ministry, Dec. 13, 1756, and enclosed English translation of preliminary treaty, WO, 34/38, pt. 1; Kerlérec to ministry, Jan. 30, 1757, covering a French copy of the treaty, ANC, C13A, 40; Berryer to Kerlérec, Nov. 18, 1758, ANC, B, 107.

[22] Demeré to Lyttelton, Oct. 29, Nov. 7, Dec. 8, 1756, IBSC, v, 265–66, 268–71, 295–97.

[23] Note by Demeré, Dec. 10, 1756, Demeré to Lyttelton, Dec. 11, 1756, IBSC, v, 298–303.

[24] Demeré to Lyttelton, Dec. 17, 1756, IBSC, v, 303–6.

[25] Brother of Attakullakulla.

and a band of Overhills that grew to the number of sixty-seven set out for Charleston. The winter was a remarkably severe one, and the group suffered greatly from inclement weather, but reached their destination safely late in January. Conferences between the Indians and Lyttelton continued from January 31 to February 17. Attakullakulla asked several times to be sent to England to offer his homage again to George II, a request that Lyttelton felt obliged to refuse. He also descanted on the abuses committed by the Cherokee traders. Lyttelton pleased him by rescinding John Elliott's license, and was able to send off the Cherokees in excellent humor. The Little Carpenter even promised to attack the French.

Through Demeré Lyttelton had earlier promised payment for scalps of Frenchmen and Francophile Indians. He now secured the passage of an act by the provincial assembly on February 4 which provided a bounty for such scalps, established a double reward when they were taken in towns friendly to the English, set prices on the heads of Lantagnac and French John, and offered payment to Indians for information. It is safe to assume this action was taken upon the advice of Stuart, and that Lyttelton's success in dealing with the Overhill delegation was partly due to Stuart. Certain it is that the governor anxiously sought his opinion on the works at Fort Loudoun.[26]

Stuart was delayed in returning to Fort Loudoun by attacks of gout that forced him to lie idle at Fort Prince George and again at Hiwassie. The Cherokees therefore preceded him, and he did not reach the fort until about the beginning of June.[27] During his absence Demeré had had his troubles. Almost immediately after Stuart's departure for Charleston, the Mankiller and his following made a fruitless trip to Hiwassie—the Tellico people believed the French would erect a post at that place, which lay on the path then used between Forts Prince George and Loudoun. Shortly afterward,

[26] Demeré to Lyttelton, Dec. 27, 1756, IBSC, v, 324–27; CJSC, xxvi, pt. 1, 7, 14–62; CHJSC, xxxi, pt. 2, 35; Lyttelton to Board of Trade, April 22, 1757, CO, 5/375; *South-Carolina Gazette,* Feb. 3, 24, 1757. Stuart was credited with knowledge of the science of fortification, possibly because he had previously had some part in the inspection and maintenance of the works at Charleston, more likely because of experience he had acquired in service under Admiral Anson.

[27] John Chevillette to Lyttelton, April 5, 1757, Demeré to Lyttelton, April 11, May 18, June 10, 1757, IBSC, vi, 25–27, 30–32, 42–45, 49–50. Stuart submitted bills of £35, 10 and £354, 17, 6 (South Carolina currency) to the provincial government for expenses incurred in connection with the Cherokee delegation. His charges were considered exorbitant. He was given only £45. CHJSC, xxxi, pt. 2, 109.

however, the Mankiller appeared at Fort Loudoun and remained there overnight, assuring Demeré of his loyalty. On January 11 Lieutenant Wall managed to persuade the chief to announce publicly his friendship for the English.[28] Nevertheless, Demeré soon learned that the Mankiller was as untrustworthy as he had been before. In March three of the Tellico men who had visited New Orleans returned, and the French flag was run up over their town. When he discovered that the fleur-de-lis was a symbol, not of sovereignty, but of peace between the French and the Cherokees, Demeré decided to take no action.[29] However, except for Tellico town, the Overhills remained friendly. In the spring of 1757 both Ouconnostotah and Attakullakulla led parties toward the lower Ohio in forays against Francophile Indians,[30] while other Overhills came to the assistance of Washington in defending Virginia.

Early in June Demeré learned that eight Southern Shawnee warriors had appeared at Tellico and had proposed to join the Tellico people in a raid on the Virginia frontier. After consulting Captain Stuart and Lieutenant Howarth (who had brought up thirty additional regulars in the preceding winter), Demeré urged Old Hop to sanction an Anglo-Cherokee attack on the Shawnees. Impressed by the rewards offered for the scalps of hostile Indians in the Cherokee towns, Old Hop consented. But when the time for action came only two Overhills, one of them a son of Old Hop, joined the detachment under Lieutenant James Adamson that made the attack. It was successful and resulted in the slaying of four Shawnees.[31] Toward the close of the following month French John and Savannah Tom boldly appeared at Tellico with invitations to the Cherokees to visit Fort Toulouse or Mobile, and Demeré was unable to persuade the Cherokees to attack them. After Savannah Tom had brutally murdered the insane wife of a soldier as she wandered into Tellico in an attempt to reach Fort Loudoun, Demeré sent a detachment to deal with the two scoundrels, but they had fled.[32]

It was with reluctance that Captain Raymond Demeré had

[28] Demeré to Lyttelton, Jan. 2, 6, 13, 1757, and following documents, IBSC, v, 341–44, 348–51, 354–65.

[29] Demeré to Lyttelton, March 26, April 2, 1757, IBSC, vi, 6–9, 21–25.

[30] *South-Carolina Gazette,* June 9, 1757.

[31] Demeré to Lyttelton, June 10, 1757, Adamson to Lyttelton, June 13, 1757, IBSC, vi, 49–50, 55–56.

[32] Demeré to Lyttelton, July 30, 1757, Aug. 10, 1757, IBSC, vi, 61–68, 68–74. French John was drowned in the Mississippi in 1759.

entered upon service in the Overhill country, and he had several times asked to be relieved. On August 14 he was able to deliver his command to his younger brother Paul, who also held the rank of captain in the Independent Regulars. On August 19 Captain Raymond Demeré, Stuart, and Postell left for Charleston.[33] As Captain George Mercer of the Virginia provincials then stationed in Charleston pointed out, the younger Demeré was not the proper sort of person to deal with the Indians.[34] The deficiencies of the new commander in that respect, however, were not disclosed for some time.

William Henry Lyttelton was eager to make a name for himself in the New World. If a forceful and pleasing personality had been the sole requisite, he would assuredly have succeeded. Like his predecessor, Glen, Lyttelton believed that the greatest glory he could attain as governor of South Carolina would be to play a major rôle in a successful assault on Louisiana. Unfortunately for Lyttelton's ambition, the English did not try to seize Louisiana during the Seven Years' War. When Sir Jeffrey Amherst and Admiral Boscawen came to America for the campaign of 1758, they carried orders from William Pitt to make an attempt, if possible, on New Orleans and Mobile in the following winter; and Lyttelton was instructed by Pitt to render effective assistance. Amherst and Boscawen hoped to land a considerable force from a fleet operating on the Gulf coast. Lyttelton was eager to lead a supporting expedition of 2,000 provincials and Independent Regulars to Mobile via Fort Toulouse. Preliminary plans were made, but Amherst learned in March, 1759, that weather conditions in the Gulf of Mexico would hardly permit a fleet to operate there in winter. He therefore temporarily abandoned the whole project, for his troops were needed in the North during the remainder of the year.[35] The same military necessity prevented Amherst from moving in succeeding years. Although Lyttelton and other southern governors continued to hope that the French menace from New Orleans would be removed, the war ended be-

[33] Demeré to Lyttelton, Aug. 26, 1757, IBSC, vi, 78–81.

[34] Stanislaus M. Hamilton, ed., *Letters to Washington and Accompanying Papers* (Boston, New York, 1898–1902), II, 227.

[35] Pitt to Lyttelton, Jan. 27, 1758, CO, 5/213; Lyttelton to [Boscawen], Aug. 22, 1758 (Secret), Lyttelton to Pitt, Nov. 4, 1758, CO, 5/18; Lyttelton to Amherst, Nov. 30, 1758, Amherst to Lyttelton, Jan. 12, 1759, Lyttelton to Amherst, Feb. 7, 1759 (Extract), Amherst to Lyttelton, March 21, 1759, CO, 5/54.

fore an attempt could be made.[36] Lyttelton was compelled to seek out other fields of endeavor.

Lyttelton was rather successful, however, in his attempts to persuade South Carolina to do its share toward the winning of the war, for he remained a popular figure almost to the end of his term of office. Especially remarkable during his administration was the willingness of the assembly to raise funds for fortifications and Indian affairs. Soon after his arrival the assembly voted, in addition to the sum given for Fort Loudoun, £22,000 (provincial currency) for fortifications and contingent expenses.[37] Lyttelton was therefore able to have Forts Prince George and Moore repaired in 1756.[38] In March, 1757, the asembly voted £10,000 (provincial currency) to erect a fort at Port Royal, considerable sums for other seacoast defenses, and additional outlays to maintain 200 provincial troops in service.[39].

It is true that South Carolina's record in regard to raising troops during most of Lyttelton's administration was not a remarkable one. The province was wealthy rather than populous; her Negroes were potential enemies; and the province was actually the English bulwark on the south. South Carolina therefore could not and did not send a single provincial soldier to the aid of her sister colonies during the Seven Years' War. Moreover, her inhabitants showed disinclination even to serve in levies raised for the defense of the colony. In the summer of 1757, when a considerable number of provincials from other colonies and a substantial body of regulars were sent to South Carolina to ward off a threatened invasion by the French and Creeks,[40] the assembly disbanded the 200 provincials then in service and voted £20,000 (South Carolina currency) to raise 700 men. Since less pay was offered than previously, very few men enlisted.[41] Although Lyttelton strove desperately to fill the seven companies voted, by offering bounties and by forcibly enrolling vagrants, he was able to muster only 500 provincials at the end of 1758.[42] Pitt's request

[36] The British government expected that the army which captured Havana in 1762 would proceed against New Orleans, but that force suffered too heavy losses at Havana. Amherst to Lord Albemarle, Sept. 6, 1762, CO, 5/62.

[37] Lyttelton to Board of Trade, July 19, 1756, CO, 5/375.

[38] "Returns of the Cannon. Stores. Ammunition &C. in the several Forts remote from Charles Town with their State and Condition . . . ." CO, 5/376.

[39] Lyttelton to Board of Trade, May 24, 1757, CO, 5/375.

[40] See Chapter VI.

[41] Henry Bouquet to Loudoun, Aug. 25, 1757, CO, 5/48.

[42] Lyttelton to Pitt, Aug. 7, 1758, CO, 5/18; Lyttelton to Board of Trade, Dec. 2, 1758, CO, 5/376.

that South Carolina maintain 700 men during 1759 was considered by the assembly in July of that year. Lyttelton supported it by a warning of a possible Cherokee war. In order to obtain favorable consideration he even offered to give up a special grant of £3,500 (provincial currency) that he had received annually from the province. The commons house voted to maintain only three companies of foot (which were mainly occupied in garrison duty) and two of rangers—and that not beyond January 1, 1760.[43] That more were not secured was hardly the fault of Lyttelton.

Lyttelton was anxious to coöperate with officials of other colonies and with British military officers in America. In contrast to his predecessor he heartily supported the efforts of Dinwiddie to procure Cherokee and Catawba auxiliaries and instructed South Carolina officers and traders to help Dinwiddie's emissaries. This policy began to bear fruit early in 1757. In addition to Cherokee parties which went out against the French in the Lower Ohio valley numerous groups proceeded to Virginia. On April 6 Dinwiddie estimated that 300 friendly Indians, of whom somewhat fewer than one half were Cherokees, had been sent out scouting and scalping. In mid-May the number had mounted to 400, including Saponeys, Nottoways, Tuscaroras, Catawbas, and Cherokees.[44] On March 18 one Cherokee party of twenty-five men returned with the scalps of five hostile Indians, and in June a captured French ensign named Belêtre and four more scalps were brought in by Cherokee scouts. In the action that resulted in the capture of Belêtre the Swallow Warrior, a Cherokee chief of some prominence, was slain.[45] Before the end of May most of the other tribesmen returned home, but many of the Cherokees remained in service. Some 200 additional Cherokees appeared in Virginia between June and September.[46]

The presence of the Cherokees in Virginia caused an infinite amount of difficulty, however. One band ravished a girl, and also slew a friendly Chickasaw in order to obtain the Virginia bounty offered for scalps. In April Washington, who as commander of the Virginia regiment was greatly occupied with these savage al-

[43] Message by Lyttelton to the commons house, July 9, 1759, addresses by the house to Lyttelton, July 9, 13, 1759, CO, 5/56.

[44] *Letters to Washington,* II, 54–55, 58; *Dinwiddie Records,* II, 605–6, 620.

[45] *Letters to Washington,* II, 79–81, 89–90; *South-Carolina Gazette,* May 12, 1757.

[46] *Dinwiddie Records,* II, 629, 640, 656; *Letters to Washington,* II, 189–90, 206–7.

lies, wrote: "The Indians are all around teazing and perplexing me for one thing or another so that I scarce know what I write." Regarding one Cherokee party he said a month later: "They are the most insolent, most avaricious, and most dissatisfied wretches I have ever had to deal with."[47] Washington must have heaved a great sigh of relief when he learned that Edmund Atkin, long expected, had arrived at Williamsburg about the first of May, and that Atkin would assume at least temporarily the management of the southern Indians in the pay of Virginia. Washington was going to be disappointed if he thought his troubles with his savage allies were ended.

Edmund Atkin was born at Exeter, England, on February 27, 1707. He was one of the numerous children of a certain John Atkin of that place.[48] He migrated to South Carolina in early youth,[49] and established himself in Charleston as a merchant in partnership with another John Atkin, possibly an older brother, sometime before 1732.[50] John and Edmund Atkin prospered, as did many merchants of pre-Revolutionary South Carolina. They eventually owned much land, especially in the northern part of the province. Edmund Atkin acquired sufficient reputation to be appointed a member of the South Carolina council on May 25, 1738.[51] He held various other minor offices in Charleston in the early 1740's, and received considerable publicity in 1745 for capturing Tom Bell, a confidence man whose exploits had rendered him notorious throughout the colonies.[52] Atkin was well educated and was possessed of genuine courage; he was also pompous and slow-moving. Late in life, on May 1, 1760, he married at Charles-

[47] Samuel Hazard, ed., *Pennsylvania Archives,* First Series (Philadelphia, 1852–54), III, 175–76; *Writings of Washington,* II, 25, 35–37.

[48] Atkin's will, May 22, 1760, Record of Wills, Charleston County, Vol. IX, 1760–1767 (A), Charleston Co. (S. C.) Courthouse; W. U. Reynell-Upham and H. Tapley-Soper, eds., *The Registers of Baptisms, Marriages, & Burials of the City of Exeter* (Exeter, 1910–33), II, 45. Atkin's given name is spelled both "Edmund" and "Edmond." He was apparently christened "Edmund," but he used "Edmond" in his correspondence and in his will. Possibly he adopted the latter form because he had many friends of French descent. He was intimate with the Manigault family of South Carolina. His surname is often incorrectly given in documents as "Atkins," less commonly as "Atkyns" and "Atcyns."

[49] *NYCD,* VII, 211.

[50] There is an advertisement in the *South-Carolina Gazette,* Feb. 19, 1732, signed by Edmund Atkin.

[51] *Journal of the Commissioners for Trade and Plantations from January 1734–5 to December 1741* ... (London, 1930), 284.

[52] Bell was jailed in Charleston, but soon escaped.

ton Lady Anne Mackenzie, daughter of George, third Earl of Cromartie, an impoverished Highland noble who had fought for Bonnie Prince Charlie.[53]

In October, 1750, Atkin sailed for England,[54] where he remained almost six years. In May, 1754, the Board of Trade inquired why he was not at his post as councilor at that critical time. Although Atkin replied that he planned to leave for Charleston in October,[55] he failed to do so. Sometime before the close of 1754 the board requested Atkin, who as a member of the South Carolina council was well acquainted with Indian affairs in the South, to present information on the subject. A lengthy paper which he placed in the hands of Halifax on May 30, 1755, was not without merit, for it contained shrewd analyses of French and British Indian policies in that area. He pointed out that the distribution of Indian presents by the English southern colonies had been inefficiently handled for many years, and that the trade had been virtually unregulated since 1735. To remedy the situation an imperial superintendent should be appointed for the southern Indians. He should disburse all presents, make all treaties, and take the major rôle in trade regulation. Johnson should have similar powers over the Six Nations and their allies. Parliamentary legislation would be necessary to establish this system and to provide the funds necessary to operate it. Atkin was inclined to favor obtaining the requisite funds in large part through enforcement of the Molasses Act of 1733. These proposals were undoubtedly not displeasing to London officials. Atkin's paper also contained a grandiose conception of the dignities and emoluments to be given the superintendents. He even asked that each agent should have the command of a regiment of regulars and a company of rangers.[56]

Atkin desired the southern superintendency for himself. He was supported by influential persons from South Carolina, and later by Lord Loudoun, but Halifax, Henry Fox, Newcastle, and

[53] Lady Anne, after Atkin's death, married Dr. John Murray, a physician of Charleston. She died at that place in January, 1768. See D. E. Huger Smith and Alexander S. Salley, Jr., eds., *Register of St. Philip's Parish, Charles Town, or Charleston, S. C., 1754–1810* (Charleston, S. C. 1927), 158; Lord Dover, ed., *Letters of Horace Walpole ... to Sir Thomas Mann ...* (New York, 1833), I, 417–18, 424, 428; *South-Carolina and American General Gazette,* Jan. 22, 1768.

[54] *South-Carolina Gazette,* Oct. 8, 29, 1750.

[55] Board of Trade to Atkin, May 29, 1754, CO, 5/402; Atkin to John Pownall, June 8, 1754, CO, 5/374.

[56] Atkin to Board of Trade, May 30, 1755, Loudoun MSS.

other English officials hesitated before offering him the appointment. When it was finally given, he was empowered merely to make treaties with the southern Indians. Moreover, because Halifax and Fox retained doubts of his zeal and abilities, Fox privately instructed Loudoun to replace Atkin if he thought such action justified. While Johnson's commission under the sign manual constituted him "sole" superintendent in the North, that word was omitted from Atkin's. Attempts by Atkin to secure funds for his expenses from the imperial government failed, as did his efforts to procure instructions from the Board of Trade to the southern governors urging that the southern colonies give the superintendent a measure of control over the trade. The board merely ordered the governors to coöperate with Atkin, and referred him to Loudoun for funds and instructions. Atkin therefore followed Loudoun to New York, at which place he arrived on October 6, 1756.[57]

Early in November Atkin carried on consultations with Loudoun and Sir William Johnson at Albany. He accompanied the latter to Johnson Hall, where the two superintendents held a conference with a delegation of Iroquois. Both agents were eager to bring about a peace between the Iroquois on the one hand and the Cherokees and Catawbas on the other, so that these tribes could devote all their energies against the French Indians; and they secured the approval of the Iroquois delegation to the opening of pourparlers. Negotiations initiated as a result of this conference led to the sending of Cherokee emissaries to the Six Nations in 1757 and to the signature of a treaty of peace between the Iroquois and the Cherokees and Catawbas in 1758.[58] Atkin was not so fortunate in his dealings with Loudoun, for Loudoun was reluctant to equip the superintendent for his work. Atkin followed the commander in chief from Albany to New York, from New

[57] "Observations touching the intended Appointment for Mr. Atkin," n.d., "Proposal made by Mr. Atkin," n.d., Atkin to Loudoun, May 14, 1756, "Instructions humbly proposed to be given to the Agent & Superintendant of Indian Affairs in the Southern District," n.d., Atkin to Loudoun, Oct. 6, 1756, Loudoun MSS; *Journal of the Commissioners for Trade and Plantations from January 1754 to December 1758* . . . , 242–43. See also John R. Alden, "The Albany Congress and the Creation of the Indian Superintendencies," *Miss. Vall. Hist. Rev.*, XXVII (1940), 210.

[58] *NYCD*, VII, 208–15; James Sullivan, Alexander C. Flick, Almon W. Lauber, and others, eds., *The Papers of Sir William Johnson* (Albany, 1921–), II, 858–64, 875–76, 878, 886; E. B. O'Callaghan, ed., *The Documentary History of the State of New York* (Albany, 1850, quarto ed.), II, 445–46; IBSC, vi, 116–18.

York to Boston, from Boston back to New York, and then from New York to Philadelphia before Loudoun paid his salary for the first half of 1757 and furnished him with a supply of Indian presents. Loudoun was very eager to get help from the southern Indians in operations against Fort Duquesne, and he wished Atkin to assume control of the Indian trade in the South. But, when the superintendent asked him for £2,000 in expense money and for permission to draw upon him for further necessary sums, Loudoun referred him to the southern governments for financial support. Consequently, the superintendent's hope for an Indian department independent of those governments was largely destroyed, for it was not to be expected that they would be consistently generous to him, financially or otherwise. The appointment of Atkin was no doubt a mistake; that mistake was hardly rectified by maintaining him in office without sufficient support. Finally, in the spring of 1757, Atkin traveled southward from Philadelphia to Williamsburg.[59]

Dinwiddie was anxious to secure the services of Atkin, not only to relieve Washington and to deal more effectively with the southern Indians, but also to end confusion resulting from clashes between the Indian agents of Maryland, Pennsylvania, and Virginia. At Williamsburg Dinwiddie tried vainly to obtain Atkin's services and the use of his Indian presents without cost to Virginia. He finally offered to pay Atkin £100 to £150 in expense money, and to furnish him with presents, if he would undertake to act on behalf of Virginia;[60] and Atkin agreed. After holding a conference with "King" Hagler and a gang of Catawbas at Jamestown in order to end a minor conflict that had arisen between Dinwiddie and the Catawbas,[61] Atkin joined Washington on June 3.

Atkin began operations at Fort Loudoun (Virginia)[62] with the loyal support of Washington. By assuming a haughty demeanor he succeeded—not without difficulty—in abating the insolence of certain Cherokee auxiliaries.[63] In July, however, his arbitrary methods created a dangerous incident. He believed that a party

[59] *NYCD,* VII, 208–10; Atkin to Loudoun, Nov. 26, 1756, March 26, 1757, Loudoun MSS; Atkin to John Pownall, March 1, 1757, CO, 323/13.

[60] *Dinwiddie Records,* II, 617; minute of Va. council, May 7, 1757, CO, 5/1429. Dinwiddie hoped that Loudoun would recompense Virginia.

[61] Minutes of the conference, May 18–19, 1757, Loudoun MSS.

[62] Located at Winchester. It has been confused with the Tennessee fort in John C. Fitzpatrick, ed., *Writings of Washington,* II, 345, note 33.

[63] *Pa. Archives,* First Series, II, 177–79; *Writings of Washington,* II, 52–53.

of ten Indians which appeared at Winchester at that time were French spies. In spite of protests from Washington he imprisoned the whole group. It turned out that two or more of those jailed were friendly Cherokees. They were identified as such by other Cherokees, who promptly sent messengers to inform their compatriots in the field and at home that they were being attacked at Winchester. The situation was saved by Washington, who satisfactorily explained Atkin's mistake. Fortunately, it was found possible to have the messenger sent southward by the Cherokees overtaken before he could deliver his tidings.[64] Atkin likewise had difficulties with the many persons entrusted with the management of Indian affairs by Pennsylvania and Maryland. These included George Croghan, deputy of Johnson acting for the former province, and Richard Pearis, who had secured an appointment as agent for Maryland in the nick of time to escape discharge by Virginia. The southern warriors were receiving presents from three provinces, and felt responsible to none. Atkin, supported by Dinwiddie, took the sensible view that efficiency required the distribution of presents by one authority only. He felt that he should be that authority, even though the Cherokees and Catawbas were serving in northern provinces. He forced Croghan and other agents to agree that presents from Pennsylvania and Maryland, as well as those from Virginia, should go through his hands, but the Pennsylvania and Maryland agents soon broke their pledges.[65]

During his stay in Virginia Atkin also managed to involve himself in a quarrel with several officers in Washington's regiment.[66] Yet his sojourn was not without accomplishment. When he departed from Williamsburg in the fall he left behind an organization to deal with Virginia's Indian problems. At the request of Washington and Dinwiddie he appointed the well-known Christopher Gist as his deputy and placed him in charge of such southern Indians as should come to Virginia after his own departure. Under authorization from Dinwiddie he also set up a system whereby parties of Cherokees and Catawbas coming to Virginia would be

[64] *Writings of Washington,* II, 97–98, 114–15; *Letters to Washington,* II, 156–57, 165, 167.

[65] *Pa. Archives,* First Series, II, 129–31, 179–81, 183–87, 197–201, 268–73; *Writings of Washington,* II, 188–89; *Dinwiddie Records,* II, 639, 645, 671. Cf. A. T. Volwiler, *George Croghan and the Westward Movement, 1741–1782* (Cleveland, 1926), 129.

[66] *Letters to Washington,* II, 102–7.

supervised by John Watts,[67] Richard Smith, and Thomas Rutherford, "conductors" and guides.[68]

Both Dinwiddie and Washington considered that the southern Indians had rendered substantial services to Virginia in 1757, although the former thought those services expensive.[69] Moreover, Dinwiddie believed that Atkin, although "very slow in all his Affairs," had performed useful labors.[70] Expense accounts submitted by Atkin amounting to £809 Dinwiddie thought "monstrous" high but he eventually gave Atkin £459 in fulfillment of those accounts. Dinwiddie also undertook to maintain the Indian officials appointed by Atkin in service until October, 1758.[71] Late in the fall Atkin resumed his journey southward by land.

[67] A Cherokee trader used as an interpreter by both Atkin and Stuart. He was the father of a half-breed of the same name who later became prominent in the councils of the Cherokee nation. He died in 1770.

[68] *Writings of Washington,* II, 40–41, 58–59; *Letters to Washington,* II, 86, 214–15; minutes of Va. council, May 24, Oct. 14, 1757, CO, 5/1429.

[69] *Writings of Washington,* II, 156–58; Dinwiddie to Pitt, Sept. 12, 1757, CO, 5/18.

[70] *Dinwiddie Records,* II, 673, 689–90.

[71] *Dinwiddie Records,* II, 707; minutes of Va. council, Oct. 18, 20, 1757, CO, 5/1429. Gist was actually kept in service and paid by Virginia until 1759.

CHAPTER V

THE LOSS OF THE CHEROKEE ALLIANCE

AS EARLY AS 1757 the continued requests of the English for military help from the Cherokees were placing so dangerous a strain on Anglo-Cherokee friendship that the English should have taken all possible precautions to preserve that friendship. The Cherokees excused themselves for not offering greater assistance during the campaign of that year because of the failure of the Old Dominion to man her Overhill fort and because of unsatisfactory trade conditions. Before the close of 1756 Dinwiddie had laid plans for placing a garrison in the fort, and had chosen Captain John McNeil of Washington's regiment as commander. He feared, however, that a garrison might be destroyed as the result of French intrigues. Although he promised Old Hop that troops would be sent by the spring of 1758, he failed to take action. In January, 1758, after Dinwiddie had left his post, the Virginia council planned to use £3,000 either to pay a detachment of regulars to be furnished by Loudoun or to send sixty provincials.[1] But no garrison was ever supplied, no doubt largely because Virginia secured all the Cherokee help she desired in the spring of 1758. Lewis's fort rotted away.

Nor did Virginia effectively meet the Cherokee demand for a satisfactory trade; in fact, Virginia bungled this problem completely. Immediately after reaching Williamsburg Atkin requested Dinwiddie to obtain for him power to license and to regulate the activities of Virginia traders. Dinwiddie, with technical accuracy, argued that the superintendent had not been authorized to meddle in the trade; and he refused even to consult with Atkin regarding the problem. Dinwiddie was convinced that low rates would serve as a more powerful argument than any other to maintain the good will of the Cherokees, and that public trading companies selling goods at cost should be created in all the colonies bordering upon the Indian country. It appears that he made no attempt to persuade the governors of the colonies to the southward of the merits of his reason-

[1] Minutes of Va. council, Jan. 28, 1757, Jan. 24, 1758, CO, 5/1429; *Letters to Washington,* II, 61; *Dinwiddie Records,* II, 657.

ing. Nevertheless, in June, 1757, he secured the enactment by the burgesses of a law establishing a board of trustees to carry on a public trade. By the terms of the act the trade was to include the Indians on the frontiers of Virginia; actually only the Cherokees were affected. A capital fund of £5,000 was provided to meet contingent expenses and probable deficits arising from the venture. A large supply of wares was ordered from England, and Dinwiddie promised Old Hop that the trustees would begin operations in the spring of 1758.

Atkin's long experience in Indian affairs enabled him to point out grave defects in the Virginia act. The Cherokees desired, not so much low prices, as plentiful supplies of goods and decent treatment from their traders. Moreover, he feared that the cheap rates offered by the Virginia company would drive all private traders out of business and that the burgesses, because of financial losses, would eventually repeal the act. If and when the burgesses abandoned the scheme, an almost impossible state of affairs would exist; private persons would not be able to reënter business because they could not offer the low rates established by the public company, upon which the Cherokees were certain to insist. In January, 1758, Atkin communicated his objections to the Virginia council. He urged modification of the act so as to maintain prices at a reasonably profitable level and to force employees of the Virginia company to secure licenses from the superintendent. There is no evidence that Virginia officials heeded Atkin's advice,[2] nor was the company ever active. The first and only shipment of goods was sent out in the fall of 1759, and it was stopped en route because of the outbreak of the Cherokee War.[3]

If Virginia had entrusted the licensing power to Atkin, it is not impossible that the other southern colonies would have taken similar action. Such a development, if permanent, would have constituted a long step toward more satisfactory trade regulation. Late in 1757 the assembly of North Carolina gave Atkin authority to license all traders operating within the borders of that colony; [4] and

[2] *Dinwiddie Records,* II, 487, 640, 657, 692–93; Atkin to Nathaniel Walthoe, Jan. 26, 1758, and enclosures, Loudoun MSS.

[3] Richard Smith to Lyttelton, Feb. 10, 1760, IBSC, vi, 219. In regard to the Virginia public trading company of this period see also W. Neil Franklin, "Virginia and the Cherokee Indian Trade, 1753–1775," *The East Tennessee Historical Society's Publications,* No. 5 (1933), 25–27.

[4] *NCCR,* V, 912–13, 917; Walter Clark, ed., *The State Records of North Carolina* ... (Goldsboro, N. C., 1895–1905, 16 vols., numbered XI–XXVI to follow *NCCR*), XXV, 356–58.

in 1759 Henry Ellis agreed, provided South Carolina did likewise, to permit the superintendent to suspend or vacate licenses issued by Georgia.[5] In August, 1758, Lyttelton was inclined to believe that two royal agents residing in the southern Indian nations should have such power,[6] but he was not disposed to place it in Atkin. He might have accepted Ellis's proposal if Virginia had followed the example of North Carolina, for Lyttelton tended to coöperate in dealing with the Indian problem.

By the spring of 1757 Lyttelton was well aware that the South Carolina trade system was completely ineffective.[7] The South Carolina assembly, which also realized the need for reform, resolved in April of that year to place the Indian trade of the province in the hands of a few reputable persons who would sell goods at prices and under rules dictated by the assembly. A committee was appointed to search out persons who would be willing to do business under such circumstances. If such persons could not be found, the assembly would consider the establishment of a public trade. At the time Lyttelton, though inclined to favor a regulated private monopoly, was not disposed to give his approval without special permission from the Board of Trade.[8] Apparently difficulty was met in finding individuals desirous of operating under such an arrangement, for in the following year Lyttelton seriously considered setting up a public trading organization. However, the traders carried plentiful supplies of goods to the Creeks and Cherokees in 1758; and Lyttelton feared that a South Carolina monopoly, by entering into competition with the Virginia company, might cause a serious intercolonial dispute. He came to believe that the trade problem could finally be resolved only by creating a monopoly managed by royal officials under authorization from Parliament. For the moment he thought it best not to undertake changes.[9] Since private trading from Georgia was also allowed to continue, no action of great consequence leading to improvement in the trade was taken for some years in the South.

Lord Loudoun was eager to secure 500 southern Indians to support General John Forbes in an attack on Fort Duquesne in the

[5] *GCR,* VIII, 5–8.

[6] Lyttelton to Board of Trade, Aug. 7, 1758, CO, 5/376.

[7] See reports by Captain Raymond Demeré to Lyttelton, Feb. 5, March 26, April 2, 1757, IBSC, v, 375–77, vi, 6–9, 21–25.

[8] CHJSC, xxxi, pt. 2, 95–96, 103–4; Lyttelton to Board of Trade, May 24, 1757, CO, 5/375.

[9] Lyttelton to Board of Trade, Aug. 7, 1758, CO, 5/376.

campaign of 1758. He had instructed Atkin to obtain these auxiliaries, and had furnished him a supply of presents, but Loudoun feared that Atkin would be dilatory. He therefore used the power lodged in him by Henry Fox to appoint a second agent in the South. In February, 1758, he commissioned William Byrd, with whom he was on very friendly terms, to assist Atkin, or, if Atkin failed in his duty, to assume charge of negotiations. Loudoun also urged Lyttelton to coöperate to the fullest extent; and he authorized Atkin and Lyttelton to draw upon the military establishment for expenses should the South Carolina assembly refuse to furnish sufficient funds. Byrd traveled by sea and reached Charleston on March 11. Lyttelton persuaded his assembly to place over £5,700 (provincial currency) at his disposal for Indian presents and expenses. He also sent Probart Howarth to invite the Cherokees to send delegates to meet Byrd at Keowee. So far all had gone well. Nor did the arrival on March 23 of Atkin, long delayed in North Carolina by illness, cause any difficulty. Although Loudoun had feared that Atkin would refuse to work with Byrd, Atkin accepted him without protest as a coworker, and abandoned the whole mission to him, pleading his recent sickness and an impending journey to the Creek nation as reasons for his own inaction. Byrd proceeded promptly to Keowee.[10]

Howarth traveled through the entire Cherokee nation, and both Howarth and Byrd spent some time at Keowee, yet Byrd was accompanied to Virginia by only fifty-seven Cherokees. Captain Paul Demeré, Ensign Lachlan McIntosh (who had assumed the command at Fort Prince George in the fall of 1757), John Watts, and Richard Smith had already sent forth more Cherokee warriors than Loudoun had requested. Every one of the Lower towns except Estatoe had furnished a contingent. Before the end of March large numbers of Overhills, including braves from every town except Tellico and Chatuga, had also gone to war. By May 1, 652 Cherokees had joined Forbes's army. Moreover, some 200 others had gone out on scalping expeditions to the lower Ohio. Even so, Byrd and Howarth might have obtained more help than they did, if the trader James

[10] Loudoun to Lyttelton, Feb. 13, 1758 (Private), WO, 34/36, pt. 1; Byrd to Loudoun, March 21, 1758, Atkin to Loudoun, March 25, 1758, CO, 5/50; CJSC, xxvi, pt. 2, 136–38. Loudoun also ordered Abraham Bosomworth, who had acquired a captaincy in the regulars, to assist Byrd in the Cherokee country. Loudoun to Bosomworth, Feb. 15, 1758, WO, 34/38, pt. 1. But this order seems to have been rescinded. Later in the year, however, Bosomworth assisted in managing the Cherokees who joined Forbes.

May had not urged the Middle Cherokees to remain at home.[11] Oddly enough, Attakullakulla refused to take the field in the spring of 1758. A conference between the little chief and Byrd led to no result. After a parley with Lyttelton at Charleston in April Attakullakulla promised to join the army, but insisted that he must first visit Choté, which place he reached in June. Even then he refused to go out to war, since a Cherokee magician warned that disaster would occur if he started out at the appointed time. Captain Paul Demeré made himself unpopular by insisting forcefully that Attakullakulla fulfill his pledge. Finally, the Little Carpenter promised to set out for Virginia in the fall.[12]

The Cherokees had been useful but troublesome allies in Virginia in the campaign of 1757. They were much less useful and much more troublesome in the following campaign. Several gangs operating toward Fort Duquesne performed minor services and threw fright into the Indian allies of the French on the upper Ohio. But Forbes failed to move, and the Cherokees came to despise the English for their inaction. James Glen, who had remained in South Carolina after quitting office and had gone north in the spring of 1758, vainly attempted to aid Forbes in holding the Cherokees in camp until the army began its advance.[13] On July 10 only 200 warriors remained; early in September there were only 80. But the disaffection of the Cherokees had displayed itself even more ominously early in May, when homeward-bound war parties indulged themselves in stealing horses from settlers near Bedford, Virginia. Several affrays and a pitched battle between the Cherokees and the outraged frontiersmen followed, in which there were a number of casualties on both sides.[14] The specter of a Cherokee war imme-

[11] Reports to Lyttelton by McIntosh of March 4 and 20, 1758, by Paul Demeré of April 2, 1758, and other papers, IBSC, vi, 129–30, 137–39, 141–45; CJSC, xxvi, pt. 2, 177–83; minute of Va. council, May 25, 1758, CO, 5/1429. In Philadelphia Byrd received much more credit for enlisting Cherokees than he deserved. See Forbes to Pitt, July 10, 1758, CO, 5/50; Stanley M. Pargellis, ed., *Military Affairs in North America, 1748–1765*... (New York, London, 1936), 431.

[12] CJSC, xxvi, pt. 2, 148–66; Lachlan McIntosh to Lyttelton, June 5, 1758, Attakullakulla to Lyttelton, June 5, 1758, IBSC, vi, 151–52, 152–53; Lyttelton to Board of Trade, Aug. 7, 1758, George Turner to Lyttelton, July 21, 1758, CO, 5/376.

[13] Glen was related to Forbes. He returned to South Carolina, and departed for Great Britain in June, 1761.

[14] *Writings of Washington*, II, 169, 181, 188–89, 201–2, 253–54, 361, 375; *Letters to Washington*, II, 304–16; Forbes to Pitt, June 17, July 10, Sept. 6, Oct. 20, 1758, CO, 5/50. The initial break between the Cherokees and the English probably took place in March, 1758. At that time Lachlan McIntosh

diately arose before the eyes of Lyttelton and Francis Fauquier, who assumed office as lieutenant governor of Virginia on June 5. The Cherokees, however, confessed to Paul Demeré and to McIntosh that they had been the aggressors. Early in August the Lower townsmen were even inclined to comply with a request from Forbes for more warriors. Then news came that the Virginians about Bedford had inflicted several casualties upon another returning party of Cherokees. The Cherokees seemed determined to seek revenge. Lyttelton took a firm stand; they could have peace with presents in compensation for their slain or they could have war. A delegation of Cherokees that came to Charleston early in the fall to discuss the situation chose the presents.[15] Thereafter for some months the Cherokees were fairly quiet.

That the whole Cherokee nation did not fly to arms against their allies in the winter of 1758–59 was certainly not to be explained by any wisdom on the part of General John Forbes. It was at least partly because of the influence of Attakullakulla that the Overhills remained friendly in the fall of 1758. At that time Attakullakulla himself with several followers joined Forbes's army. Little Carpenter afterward declared that he had been sent north by Old Hop to assure peace between his countrymen and Virginia. Whether or not he was persuaded against his will to join Forbes, he and nine followers left the army two days before the capture of Fort Duquesne. The Cherokee chief later explained that he considered the services of himself and his men no longer necessary, since he had previously learned from certain Shawnees that the French had deserted the fort. Forbes failed to remember that Attakullakulla had not enlisted in the English forces, and did not bother to request him to explain his action. Instead, he had the Cherokees pursued, disarmed, and conducted ignominiously to Winchester. At Winchester Attakullakulla conferred with Christopher Gist and demanded an audience with Fauquier, who received him at Williamsburg in January, 1759. Fauquier discovered that the Little Carpenter was "conscious and cast down on acct of his bad behaviour." What-

---

reported that two whites had been slain by a party of Cherokees going to war. Possibly these were murdered in revenge for the killing of four Cherokees near the upper settlements of South Carolina a little earlier, since the Lower Cherokees believed that frontiersmen had perpetrated this deed. McIntosh to Lyttelton, March 21, 1758, IBSC, vi, 139.

[15] Lyttelton to Board of Trade, Oct. 2, 1758, and enclosures, CO, 5/376; CJSC, xxviii, 33–40. James Beamer estimated that the Cherokees lost thirty warriors at the hands of the Virginians in 1758. His figure is probably too large. The conduct of the Virginians was by no means unimpeachable. Minute of Va. council, Oct. 24, 1758, CO, 5/1429.

ever the chief thought of his own conduct, he left Williamsburg on good terms with Fauquier. Early in April he reached Charleston and again pledged his friendship to the English, although Lyttelton at first gave him the cold shoulder.[16] One finds it difficult to believe that the treatment he received from Forbes and Lyttelton at this juncture accounts for the loyalty to the English that Attakullakulla displayed on many occasions in later years.

Although the Cherokee nation had accepted Lyttelton's presents in compensation for the warriors who fell in Bedford County, Indian custom demanded that they be avenged in blood. In the early months of 1759 there was much talk among the young Overhill braves of attacking the English; and war belts were exchanged between the Overhills on the one side and the French and their Indian allies on the other. Paul Demeré believed that Old Hop himself participated in the exchanging of belts. Demeré was also disturbed by rumors that the French were building forts on the Tennessee and Coosa rivers preparatory to an assault on Fort Loudoun. Demeré had cause for his apprehensions. In March The Mortar, the most talented Upper Creek chieftain of his generation and a confirmed Francophile,[17] reached the Overhill towns with French propaganda and inflammatory advice; and he was accompanied by several Cherokees from the Overhill country to Fort Toulouse. His visit had an even more sinister result. During his stay he held a secret conference with Moytoy, chief of Settico town, who shortly thereafter departed from home with twenty-five followers. In April these warriors slew thirteen to fifteen settlers on the Yadkin and Catawba rivers. They successfully eluded a party of Catawbas who pursued them, and returned to Settico early in May. Demeré demanded satisfaction, that is, the death of one Settico tribesman for every white person slain on this expedition. At this critical moment Attakullakulla returned home from Charleston. He had promised

[16] Lyttelton to Board of Trade, Oct. 2, 1758, Feb. 21, May 8, 1759, CO, 5/376; CJSC, xxviii, 77–89; minutes of Va. council, Jan. 19, 20, 23, 1759, CO, 5/1429; H. R. McIlwaine, ed., *Journal of the House of Burgesses of Virginia, 1758–1761* (Richmond, 1908), 266–67.

[17] The Mortar, known as Yahatastonake and Otis (Otassu) Mico by the Creeks and as Le Loup by the French, was a member of a prominent family among the Upper Creeks. In 1757 he was apparently living at Oakfuskie town. In the latter years of the Seven Years' War he wandered about from place to place with a band of followers. His band camped at various times on the upper Coosa, on the Tennessee, and at Hiwassie town. He returned to the Upper Creek country in 1763. The main facts regarding this remarkable savage will appear in later chapters.

Lyttelton that he would be responsible for the good behavior of the Cherokees, and he tried to persuade his fellows to comply with Demeré's demand. His efforts were in vain,[18] and he went off in disgust on a supposed raid against the French.

A wave of anti-English feeling was also rising in the Lower towns. Tugulkee, young son of the Creek leader Malatchi, held numerous secret conferences with the Cherokees in the neighborhood of Keowee during July and the first days of August. He proposed a joint Creek-Cherokee attack on the English traders for August 24 and a subsequent assault on the frontiers. A delegation of Cherokees accompanied Tugulkee when he set out for the Creek nation on August 3, but the Lower townsmen refused to take up arms unless the Creeks struck the first blow, a decision which ended the conspiracy. However, Richard Smith, who was sent by Lyttelton to negotiate with the Lower Cherokees, discovered that they were no more ready to give satisfaction for the murders committed by their nation than were the Overhills. Moreover, they complained to Lyttelton—apparently without complete justification—that they were not obtaining sufficient trade, and that white settlers were making extensive encroachments upon their lands above Long Canes; and they requested a conference with Lyttelton at Charleston to deal with these matters. Lyttelton replied that they could send an embassy to Charleston, for the delegates would serve as hostages while reinforcements and supplies were sent to the Cherokee country. After learning of the Settico raid he realized that a crisis was at hand, and he was making plans to meet it. He had already cut off the trade with Settico town; he had ordered the officers at the posts to prevent arms and ammunition from reaching the Cherokees and, if necessary, even to impound the traders' supplies; he had instructed Captain John Stuart, who was then in command of Fort Lyttelton,[19] to reinforce Demeré with seventy provincials; and he had made arrangements to throw provisions into Forts Loudoun and Prince George.[20]

[18] Little Carpenter failed because Ouconnostotah exerted himself to save the culprits. Ouconnostotah was pro-English, but was related to some of the Settico men.

[19] Erected at Port Royal in 1757–58 under Stuart's direction.

[20] Lyttelton to Board of Trade, April 14, Sept. 1, 1759, CO, 5/376; Demeré to Lyttelton, May 2, 12, 15, 1759, IBSC, vi, 177–79, 184–85, 190–91; minutes of Va. council, Sept. 3, Dec. 12, 1759, CO, 5/1429; *South-Carolina Gazette,* May 12, Aug. 18, 25, Sept. 8, 1759. Lyttelton displayed no interest in a proposal by the Cherokees that their quarrel be mediated by Henry Ellis. *GCR,* XXVIII, pt. 1, 313–14.

At the beginning of September the fickle Cherokees seemed somewhat more friendly than before. Attakullakulla, Old Hop, and Kanagataucko,[21] a chieftain who was rapidly gaining influence, labored for peace in the Overhill country. At that time the Tellico men actually furnished guards to escort a party convoying flour to Fort Loudoun. Moreover, Round O, chief of the town of Stickoee and recognized leader of several Middle Cherokee towns which were not on the best of terms with their neighbors, informed the Lower townsmen that he would assist the English in the event of war. As a result, the Lower Cherokees sent a friendly "talk" to Lieutenant Richard Coytmore, a young officer of the Independent Regulars who had become commandant at Fort Prince George by the spring of 1759.[22]

This seeming improvement in Anglo-Cherokee relations was only temporary. Soon the Lower Cherokees were again displaying a hostile attitude, no doubt partly because they detested Coytmore, who, with two other officers of his command, had ravished Cherokee women.[23] Coytmore, expecting an outbreak, prevented trading goods destined for the Overhill towns from leaving Fort Prince George. On hearing early in September of Coytmore's action the Tellico and Settico men slew a trader;[24] and a numerous body of Overhills appeared at Fort Loudoun to demand ammunition. Partly no doubt because his own supplies were low, Demeré refused, thereby adding fuel to the flame. This was soon to be fanned by French propaganda to the effect that the stoppage of ammunition was a prelude to an English attack. Nevertheless, Demeré believed on September 13 that most of the Overhills were friendly; and he was able to persuade Ouconnostotah and Usteneka to go on to Fort Prince George to escort Stuart's command and a supply of provisions over the hills. He assured the chiefs that Stuart would give them ammunition.

Ouconnostotah and Usteneka, with eighteen other warriors and three traders, reached Fort Prince George on September 26. Stuart and his command, reduced to fifty-two men by desertion, had arrived at Keowee only four days previously. When Ouconnostotah

[21] Or Standing Turkey. His Indian name is variously spelled—Conogotocko, Conogotoco, Kanagataukco.

[22] *South-Carolina Gazette,* Sept. 22, 1759.

[23] James Adair, *History of the American Indians* (Williams ed.), 260–61; CJSC, xxviii, 137.

[24] There was a rumor, apparently unfounded, that one or two members of the Fort Loudoun garrison were slain at this time.

and his associates, as well as a Lower Cherokee delegation, demanded ammunition from Coytmore and Stuart, the two officers refused. They believed that a refusal would lead to immediate hostilities, but that in any event the Cherokees would soon take up arms. Possibly they overestimated the war spirit among the Cherokees, for the two parties, numbering in all thirty-eight men, thirteen women, and five children, merely joined and marched toward Charleston to place their demand before Lyttelton himself. En route Usteneka left his comrades for the purpose, it was rumored, of surreptitiously organizing an attack on Stuart's force, in the event that Stuart endeavored to reach Fort Loudoun. If Usteneka entertained the thought, he did not attempt to execute it. Correctly forecasting that the Cherokees would not attack while Ouconnostotah and his followers were in the settlements of South Carolina, Stuart hurriedly sent flour and cattle to Fort Loudoun. A few days later Stuart and his men set out. They reached Fort Loudoun safely on October 27. On December 5 the garrison at that post mustered 200 men; it was believed in Charleston that supplies for six months were available at the fort.[25]

Meanwhile the refusal of the Cherokees to offer satisfaction for the Settico raid and the antagonistic attitude assumed by a large part of the nation had impelled Lyttelton to adopt strong measures. He called the South Carolina assembly into session on October 4. On the following day he asked for a grant to finance military operations, should they prove necessary, against the Cherokees. On October 10, according to Lyttelton, the council was unanimous for declaring war against the Cherokees. The commons house recognized the gravity of the crisis, but was opposed to a declaration. However, that body agreed on October 12 to pay 1,500 militiamen to be drafted by Lyttelton, with the understanding that Lyttelton would lead a strong force to demand, or, if need be, to take satisfaction in the Cherokee country. The house made available for immediate use some £5,000 (provincial currency), but declared that it would not pay the militia beyond January 1, 1760. In spite of a very energetic protest from the governor the lower house would do no more. He therefore adjourned the assembly on October 13. Meanwhile Lyttelton had written to Fauquier, urging that Virginia undertake to maintain the garrison at Fort Loudoun, since South Carolina would be unable to do so; to Dobbs, asking that North

[25] Coytmore to Lyttelton, Sept. 26, 1759, WO, 34/35, pt. 2; Lyttelton to Board of Trade, Oct. 16, 1759, and enclosures, CO, 5/376; *South-Carolina Gazette,* Oct. 6, 17 (Extraordinary), 20, Nov. 17 (Supplement), Dec. 29, 1759.

Carolina send a contingent of militia to join him; and to Atkin, who was then on a mission in the Creek country,[26] requesting him to incite the Creeks and Chickasaws to dispatch parties against the Cherokees.[27] Lyttelton also sought assistance from the Catawbas.

If Lyttelton's council had been unanimous for a declaration of war on October 10, it was not so a week later, when the Cherokees led by Ouconnostotah reached Charleston. Four members of the council, including William Bull, then favored a more cautious, though possibly a less honorable, policy. They advocated making a final demand for satisfaction. To ensure so far as possible its success, they recommended a complete stoppage of the trade and the detention of several leaders of the Cherokees then in town as hostages. The council was unanimous, however, in advising Lyttelton not to treat with the Cherokee delegation, since the Overhills in it were not authorized to negotiate and since the nation would probably not execute a treaty signed by the delegation. In conferences between the Cherokees and Lyttelton that lasted from October 18 to 21, Ouconnostotah, who acted as spokesman for his fellows, merely asked for peace on the basis of mutual forgiveness of offenses. In accordance with the advice of the council, the governor refused to deal with Ouconnostotah, but he continued to believe it necessary to frighten or force the Cherokees into submission. On October 22 he informed the Cherokees that he was about to march to Fort Prince George with the militia, and that they must accompany him, since otherwise they might be attacked by angered settlers as they proceeded upcountry. At the same time Lyttelton completely cut off the Cherokee trade from South Carolina.[28]

[26] See the following chapter.

[27] Lyttelton to Board of Trade, Oct. 16, 1759, CO, 5/376; CJSC, xxviii, 127; Lyttelton to Amherst, Oct. 16, 1759, and enclosed resolutions of commons house, CO, 5/57; *South-Carolina Gazette,* Oct. 6, 1759.

[28] CJSC, xxvii, 131–39; Lyttelton to Board of Trade, Oct. 23, 1759, extract of letter from speaker of the commons house of South Carolina to James Wright, Dec. 1, 1759, CO, 5/376. From the Lyttelton letter cited it would appear that the whole council approved his decision. But such was apparently not the case. The journal of the council and the extract of the speaker's letter show the division of the council as described in the text. It is significant that a special injunction forbidding the governor of South Carolina to embark upon an Indian war without the consent of his council was inserted in the instructions of Thomas Boone (in CO, 5/404), when Boone was appointed governor on May 4, 1761. Bull caustically wrote later: "What are called spirited measures against ... [Indians], tho' they cast a glazing light, yet if they should fail in the execution, serve rather to show what we cannot, than what we can do, and therefore in my opinion, are justifiable only when recourse is had to them as the dernier resort." Bull to Board of Trade, Aug. 31, 1760, CO, 5/377.

Sound policy dictated that Lyttelton should not have undertaken to reduce the Cherokees to submission by the display or the actual use of force, unless he could rely upon the services of a formidable and well-supplied body of troops. At the time only three companies of foot and two of rangers were in the service of the province. To be sure, there may have been a certain amount of enthusiasm in the province for Lyttelton's expedition. The *South-Carolina Gazette*[29] printed the chorus of a song:

> Our Governor doth now command
> Then come, my Sons, with Sword in Hand;
> With him let's fight; with him let's stray,
> Over the Hills and far away.

Nevertheless, Lyttelton was able to raise in all only 1,400 men to serve with the 150 Independent Regulars available for the expedition. He hoped that North Carolina would send 500 men to join him as he approached Fort Prince George. It was not certain, however, that the combined forces of the Carolinas, even though supported by contingents of Catawbas and Savannah River Chickasaws, would be sufficient to overawe the Cherokees. It was even more doubtful that Lyttelton would be able to force a passage over the mountains to relieve Fort Loudoun. Moreover, although this fort was more accessible from Virginia than from South Carolina, Lyttelton could not be certain that the Old Dominion would successfully undertake to relieve its garrison. Lyttelton might well have appealed for assistance to Sir Jeffrey Amherst, the military commander in America after 1758. Too confident that he would not fail, Lyttelton informed Amherst of the critical Cherokee situation, but omitted to call for help. This was a most unfortunate lapse on his part, for Amherst heartily approved of the strong course adopted by the governor. The general was more than willing to send a body of regulars to South Carolina, since the campaign of 1759 was now over in the North. In fact, Amherst, expecting an appeal from Lyttelton, prepared two regiments for embarkation at New York.[30] Merely because Lyttelton did not ask for them these troops remained at New York.

Lyttelton's march toward Keowee was not a pleasure junket. In the last week of October the majority of his forces converged upon the Congarees. At Amelia a detachment headed by Lyttelton him-

[29] Nov. 3, 1759.

[30] Lyttelton to Amherst, Oct. 16, 1759, WO, 34/35, pt. 1; Lyttelton to Amherst, Oct. 23, 1759, WO, 34/35, pt. 2; Amherst to Lyttelton, Dec. 21, 1759, Amherst to Captain John Stott, Dec. 23, 1759, CO, 5/57.

self encountered some forty Cherokees led by the friendly Round O en route to Charleston. These were also taken under protection and forced to accompany the South Carolina troops. But four members of Round O's party fled the army at the Congarees and hurried off to rouse the Cherokee nation, and Lyttelton felt obliged to place the other Cherokees under guard. The weather was inclement, and the South Carolinians were severely stricken by measles. Lyttelton hoped to meet a strong Catawba contingent as he moved upcountry, but only six Catawbas appeared for service, for the nation was suffering terribly from smallpox.[31] Twenty-eight Savannah Chickasaws joined Lyttelton at Saluda. However, a rumor that the South Carolinians were to be attacked as they crossed a stream twelve miles below Keowee proved false. Lyttelton reached Fort Prince George safely on December 9 with 1,300 men; a further contingent of 200 men arrived at the fort on the evening of the same day. Shortly afterward the governor released all but twenty-eight of the Cherokees held by him.[32]

Lyttelton felt uncomfortable at Fort Prince George. He had at his disposal only about 1,700 men, including the garrison; and the term of service of the militia expired on January 1. News from North Carolina was disheartening. Colonel Hugh Waddell had been entrusted by Dobbs with the task of leading 500 militiamen to Lyttelton's aid. The North Carolina assembly provided the necessary funds, and Waddell was given powers enabling him to call the militia into service. Then Waddell's command, except for eighty men, deserted on the pretext that no provincial legislation existed compelling service outside the colony. The legal defect was remedied, but Waddell did not move, for he could not gather his forces and reach Keowee in time to assist Lyttelton.[33] Moreover, smallpox had spread from the Catawbas to Keowee town, and Lyttelton feared that the pestilence would strike his troops, even though he cut off communication between the fort and the town. Lyttelton's ardor cooled. Under the circumstances he was no doubt glad to be able to negotiate with the Cherokees. On his march upcountry he had received a message from Attakullakulla asking for a conference

[31] It was reported in the *South-Carolina Gazette,* Dec. 15, 1759, that almost one half of the Catawbas perished. The same paper ascribed the heavy toll to a practice followed by the Catawbas of throwing themselves into a river when attacked by the scourge.

[32] Lyttelton to Board of Trade, Oct. 23, Dec. 10, 1759, CO, 5/376; *South-Carolina Gazette,* Nov. 3, 17, 24 (Supplement), Dec. 8, 1759.

[33] *NCCR,* VI, 136–37, 152, 220–21.

at Fort Prince George. With credentials from Old Hop authorizing him to treat on behalf of the whole nation, the Little Carpenter reached the fort a few days after Lyttelton.

Awkward as Lyttelton's position was, he sternly demanded as one of the terms of a settlement that twenty-four Cherokees who had participated in forays resulting in the murder of twenty-four whites after November 24, 1758,[34] should be surrendered to him for punishment. He released four more of the Cherokees held at the fort, and declared that he would hold the remaining twenty-four until the guilty warriors were given up. Attakullakulla informed the governor that he lacked sufficient authority to compel his nation to abandon all the culprits to their fate. He surrendered two murderers, and urged Lyttelton to release in exchange Ouconnostotah and a second chief, Tistoe of Keowee. He indicated that their help was needed to persuade the nation to give up the twenty-two men still at large. Lyttelton consented—unwisely, since Ouconnostotah's former friendship for the English had turned, because of his unjustified imprisonment, into a deadly hatred. In any case, it was not possible to seize the guilty Cherokees immediately, for they sought safety by flight as soon as they learned of their peril. In order to obtain a settlement Lyttelton was compelled still further to modify his demands. On December 26 the governor, Attakullakulla, Ouconnostotah, and certain other Cherokees signed a treaty which provided that the Cherokee murderers should be given up one by one as they were apprehended, and that one of the twenty-two hostages held in the fort should be freed in exchange for each offender delivered. The treaty also stipulated that the trade was to be reopened, and that the Cherokees were to expel all Frenchmen and Francophile Indians from their territory.[35]

Although a day or two after signature of the treaty, one more luckless Cherokee was abandoned to Lyttelton's mercies, the governor was not at all sure that the remainder would be delivered at the fort. But he was helpless. His troops were mutinous. On December 28 smallpox broke out among them. Realizing that his forces could not be maintained at the fort, Lyttelton issued orders for a

[34] It is not clear how Lyttelton arrived at a total of twenty-four whites slain. Incidents mentioned in the text would not account for more than seventeen. No doubt other incidents not reported in documents occurred.

[35] Text of treaty, in CJSC, xxviii, 155–56; Lyttelton to Amherst, Dec. 27, 1759, WO, 34/35, pt. 2; Lyttelton letters of Dec. 29, 1759, cited in following note; Alexander Hewatt, *An Historical Account of the Rise and Progress of the Colonies of South Carolina and Georgia* (London, 1779), II, 218–25.

return to the low country. He left behind twenty men to reinforce the garrison of Fort Prince George, provisions he claimed to be sufficient for six months, many Indian presents, and orders to send supplies to Fort Loudoun. The three Cherokee murderers were put in chains and carried off to Charleston. The governor reached the provincial capital on January 8, 1761. The Cherokees were thrown into prison, and Lyttelton was accorded a reception befitting a conquering hero.[36]

[36] Lyttelton to Board of Trade, Dec. 29, 1759, Jan. 21, 1760, CO, 5/376; Lyttelton to Pitt, Dec. 29, 1759, CO, 5/19; Lyttelton to Amherst, March 31, 1760, WO, 34/35, pt. 2; Hewatt, *op. cit.*, 226. Lyttelton requested the home government for orders regarding the disposition of the Cherokee murderers already in or to be placed in his hands. He proposed pardoning some and selling the remainder as slaves in the West Indies.

CHAPTER VI

ANGLO-FRENCH RIVALRY IN THE CREEK COUNTRY, 1756–59

LYTTELTON'S interest in Indian affairs was by no means confined to the Cherokees and Catawbas. Almost immediately after taking office he invited the Creeks to visit him in Charleston. The "talks" that he received in reply, though friendly in tone, failed to indicate that the Creeks would accept the invitation. Instead, most of the Upper Creeks let it be known that they were dissatisfied with the treaty concluded by Gun Merchant the previous winter; they desired neither lowering of their trading rates nor a fort in their country. They asked that the English squatters on the Ogeechee be forced to remove, since their presence near the Creek towns led to brawls. Nor were the Lower Creeks eager for changes in trading prices.[1] Anxious to discover the truth regarding the situation in the Creek country, Lyttelton decided early in September, 1756, to send an agent to find out the real sentiments of those Indians, to probe into French activities, and to persuade the Creeks to send a delegation to Charleston. He should also secure information of the disposition of the Choctaws. For this special mission Lyttelton chose Samuel Pepper, who had gained considerable knowledge of the Creeks as commander of Fort Moore in the 1740's.

Before Pepper could leave Charleston bad tidings reached Lyttelton from Augusta. Early in September Edward Brown and seven other settlers on the Ogeechee had pursued and attacked a party of Creeks who had stolen Brown's horses. Two Creeks were slain and a third was wounded. Immediately the Ogeechee people abandoned their homes and thronged into Augusta and Fort Moore, seeking protection against an expected Creek attack. Lyttelton promptly sent reinforcements to Lieutenant White Outerbridge, the commander at Fort Moore, and a message to the Creeks offering large quantities of goods to console the relatives of the slain In-

[1] Upper Creek headmen to Lyttelton, Aug. 9, 1756, Lower Creek headmen to Lyttelton, Aug. 12, 1756, IBSC, v, 175–76, 176–77.

dians.[2] Pepper departed from Charleston on September 23. Meanwhile Reynolds, although without funds to pay them, undertook to raise seventy rangers to assist in protecting Georgia,[3] and sent Thomas Ross to the Creeks to smooth over the affair. Toward the end of September Ross, accompanied by John Petticrew, Jr., who carried Lyttelton's message, left Augusta for the Creek country. Since the slain Indians proved to be Upper Creeks and since the Lower townsmen displayed no concern,[4] Ross pushed on to the Upper Creek villages. There he learned that a considerable faction was disposed to demand the lives of two white men in revenge for their slain. Handsome Fellow, an Upper Creek chieftain,[5] and a delegation traveled to Savannah in October to place this demand before Reynolds. Ross set out with Handsome Fellow, but became fearful for his own life and fled from his companions, turning up naked and terror-stricken at Coweta town.[6] At Savannah Handsome Fellow was received by Reynolds and the Georgia council. Reynolds countered his demand with presents and with a statement—apparently an error—that two white men had died as the result of wounds received in the affray between Brown's party and the Upper Creeks; and the chief left Savannah satisfied.[7]

Early reports from Reynolds regarding the Ogeechee fight, with representations from Charles Pinckney alleging that South Carolina was exposed to French attack, had led the Board of Trade to fear that the southern English colonies were in grave danger.[8] Accordingly, Lieutenant Colonel Archibald Montgomery was dispatched from Great Britain to Charleston in 1757 with 1,000 Royal Highlanders. Fears for the safety of the southern colonies were also felt at a conference at Philadelphia in March, 1757, attended by Loudoun, Dinwiddie, and governors William Denny and Horatio Sharpe of Pennsylvania and Maryland. This conference decided

[2] *GCR,* VII, 390–91, 395, 396–97; Lyttelton to Board of Trade, Oct. 17, 1756, CO, 5/375; Lyttelton to Creeks, Sept. 16, 1756, IBSC, v, 207. Brown and his friends fled and were apprehended, but were not punished.

[3] *GCR,* VII, 400, XVI, 84.

[4] Outerbridge to Lyttelton, Sept. 25, 1756, and enclosed "talks" from Lower Creeks, IBSC, v, 214–16.

[5] Also known as Oboylaco.

[6] Daniel Pepper to Lyttelton, Nov. 30, 1756, IBSC, v, 333–35. See also v, 236–40.

[7] *GCR,* VII, 419–25. Reports of the affray show that one white man was slightly wounded, but there is no indication beyond rumor that any white man died. *Ibid.,* VII, 390–91, 395, 396–97.

[8] Representation by Pinckney, Dec. 2, 1756, CO, 5/375; Report of Board of Trade, Dec. 24, 1756, CO, 5/7.

that 500 regulars from Loudoun's army and 800 provincials from Virginia, Pennsylvania, and North Carolina should be sent to Charleston. Lieutenant Colonel Henry Bouquet, acting as commander of the troops in service in South Carolina and Georgia by direction of Loudoun, reached that place on June 15 with 500 Royal Americans and 200 Virginians. It was expected that 500 additional provincials would arrive shortly afterward, but it does not appear that they did. However, Montgomery and his Highlanders reached land on September 1.[9] Fortunately, the rumored attacks by the French and Creeks failed to materialize; and all the troops sent to South Carolina were withdrawn to the north in the spring of 1758.[10]

In urging that troops be sent to the southern colonies the Board of Trade had discounted reports from Lyttelton that the Creek situation was serious though not alarming. Lyttelton had read the signs more accurately than Reynolds. Samuel Pepper and his presents were well received by both the Upper and the Lower Creeks. In November, 1756, Gun Merchant and Wolf King, chief of the Upper Creek town of Mucolasses, boldly asserted that the warriors slain upon the Ogeechee had received their just deserts. Pepper was then inclined to believe that the Upper Creeks would visit Lyttelton in the following spring.[11] Shortly afterward Wolf King even offered to permit the English to build a fort at Mucolasses, which was located only seven miles from Fort Toulouse. Pepper judiciously advised Lyttelton not to accept this offer until such time as the Upper Creeks generally gave their approval. Indeed, Pepper discovered that English prestige was being undermined by the misconduct of traders from both South Carolina and Georgia, including storekeepers who served as magistrates at Augusta; and that The Mortar's power was growing. Moreover, Pepper was unable to execute projects he had formed to destroy Lantagnac and Peter Chartier.[12]

[9] *Letters to Washington,* II, 51–53; Lyttelton to Board of Trade, June 19, 1757, CO, 5/375; Lyttelton to Pitt, Sept. 3, 1757, CO, 5/18. Bouquet stationed one company of Virginians at Savannah. He considered dispatching another company of Virginians to the fort built by Lewis, but refrained. He came to the conclusion that the fort was of no value and indefensible.

[10] Lieutenant Colonel Adam Stephen was able to inform Washington that the only wounds sustained by two companies of Washington's regiment stationed in the South were those inflicted by love. Those wounds were probably not very serious, since the Virginia officers considered the Charleston belles less attractive than those of the Old Dominion. *Letters to Washington,* II, 180–81.

[11] Pepper to Lyttelton, Nov. 18, 1756, IBSC, v, 284–88.

[12] Pepper to Lyttelton, Dec. 21, 1756, March 30, April 7, 1757, IBSC, v, 336–39, vi, 11–19, 27–30.

Nor could Pepper persuade the Upper Creeks to compel the Choctaws to abandon their attacks upon the Chickasaws, an object that Lyttelton had very much at heart. The Chickasaws had been so heavily beset by their Francophile enemies that they had been unable to hunt effectively since 1753. In the spring of 1756 they had even summoned their brethren at Breed Camp and on the Savannah to return home for a last-ditch defense. But at the same time they had sworn to remain faithful to their English alliance "while sun shines and water runs." Their loyalty was not unappreciated in South Carolina and Georgia. In 1755 and 1757 Jerome Courtonne, a Chickasaw trader, brought to the nation presents of much-needed arms and other supplies; and a band of Chickasaws led by their redoubtable chief Paya Mattaha [13] was graciously received at Charleston in 1757 and loaded with presents.[14]

Pepper managed through the aid of Gun Merchant to meet Chickasaw and Choctaw delegations at Oakfuskie town and to persuade them to make peace. He realized that this peace would not be kept. In the spring of 1757 he believed that the position of the Chickasaws was desperate, and he proposed that they should be encouraged to remove to the banks of the Ogeechee, where they would serve as a bulwark for Georgia.[15] But the "breeds" continued the struggle, the ardor of the Choctaws waned when the French were unable to supply them with goods, and a temporary Chickasaw-Choctaw peace was made at the end of 1758. Soon afterward the Chickasaws signally avenged the wrongs inflicted upon the English by the Southern Shawnees. Early in 1759 these Indians marched from the headwaters of the Coosa to the neighborhood of Fort Massac to establish new homes. John Brown, a half-breed partner of Jerome Courtonne, organized a body of 140 Chickasaws, who sought vainly for them in February. But two months later Brown and 200

[13] Paya Mattaha was the leading warrior in a nation of warriors. Consistently friendly to the English, he became one of John Stuart's most valuable chessmen in the game of Indian diplomacy. Romans, *A Concise Natural History of East and West Florida,* 64, states that Paya Mattaha killed his man more than forty times. His influence extended even to the Choctaws after 1763.

[14] Chickasaws to Glen and council, April 5, 1756, IBSC, v, 123–24; Jerome Courtonne's journal, July 18, 1755—April 23, 1756, v, 124–32; vi, 132–33; CJSC, xxvi, pt. 2, 13–21; Ellis to Board of Trade, and enclosures, Oct. 22, 1757, *GCR,* XXVIII, pt. 1, 97–101; *South-Carolina Gazette,* July 7, 1757. Peter Timothy, long-time publisher of the *South-Carolina Gazette,* even declared, in an issue of Nov. 18, 1756, that only the Chickasaw alliance prevented a Franco-Indian attack on the southern English colonies.

[15] Pepper to Lyttelton, April 7, May 25, June 28, 1757, IBSC, vi, 27–30, 45–47, 57–59.

Chickasaws headed by Paya Mattaha discovered the Shawnees and inflicted severe punishment upon them, punishment which would have been even heavier had not the Chickasaws run out of ammunition.[16]

Although Pepper had failed to achieve all of his objectives, his mission on the whole was distinctly successful, since he did much to uphold English influence among the Creeks. For some time in the spring of 1757 he boldly maintained headquarters at Mucolasses. An English flag floating over that town during his residence indicated his triumphs. One of his aides, William Bonar, even managed to penetrate into Fort Toulouse in the guise of a packhorseman. Bonar brought back detailed information regarding its fortifications and its garrison. Shortly afterward, when Bonar was seized by the French and hurried off toward Mobile, Pepper scored again, for Wolf King and a party of Upper Creeks were persuaded to rescue the captive.[17] Pepper was also able to apprehend Lieutenant Robert Wall and John Brown, a Cherokee trader, as they fled toward Fort Toulouse, presumably to furnish the French with valuable information regarding the Cherokee country.[18] In addition, Pepper opened negotiations with the Choctaws, inviting them to visit Lyttelton in Charleston. A final conference held by the Carolina agent with the Upper Creeks at Oakfuskie was amicably con-

[16] Jerome Courtonne to Lyttelton, May 13, 1759, and "talk" from Chickasaws to Lyttelton, IBSC, vi, 185–89; *South-Carolina Gazette,* May 5, 26, 1759.

[17] Pepper to Lyttelton, May 7, 25, 27, 1757, IBSC, vi, 35–40, 45–47, 48. Pepper urged that Bonar be rewarded with a commission in the South Carolina provincials. His recommendation was evidently heeded, since a Lieutenant William Bonar was in command of Fort Johnston in December, 1759. CJSC, xxviii, 149. Bonar drew several useful maps of the Creek towns.

[18] Wall and Brown were both of Virginian birth, the latter being the father of the John Brown mentioned earlier in this chapter. Wall was accused of desertion, and both Wall and Brown were charged with robbing the trader Elliott near Keowee, with counterfeiting, and with treason. Although Wall denied the charges, there is little doubt that he was a rascal. Brown offered to turn state's evidence, but he managed to make his escape en route back to Charleston, while Wall succeeded in persuading Tugulkee to intercede for him. Tugulkee urged Lyttelton in such strong terms not to permit Wall to be put to death that the governor felt obliged to accede to his demand, since Tugulkee was then expected to assume the position of leadership formerly held by his father. As it happened, Lyttelton was eventually forced to release Wall for lack of evidence. Early in 1759 Wall was again seized upon suspicion of treason, but no doubt regained his freedom. Pepper letters of May 25 and 27, 1757, cited in preceding note; Robert Wall to John Hatton, June 1, 1757, and other papers, IBSC, vi, 45–48, 56–59, 84; CJSC, xxvi, pt. 2, 6–9; *South-Carolina Gazette,* May 26, June 27, 1757, Jan. 5, 1759.

ducted, although once again certain warriors manifested a desire for revenge for the Ogeechee slayings. The Upper townsmen promised to visit Lyttelton in the near future. A last conference with the Lower Creeks was without untoward incident, and Pepper was able to return to Charleston in the summer of 1757 with the satisfaction of a task well done.[19]

At Charleston in July, 1757, Lyttelton exchanged greetings with a body of Upper Creeks headed by Handsome Fellow.[20] Early in the following year the governor held a friendly parley with Wolf King and seventy followers, although he was obliged to refuse a request by the chief for lower trade prices.[21] Neither of these delegations, however, represented all the Upper Creeks. Lyttelton actually had much less contact with the Creeks after the conclusion of Pepper's mission than did Henry Ellis, who succeeded Reynolds as governor of Georgia on February 16, 1757, although Lyttelton demanded that Ellis recognize his leadership in Indian relations. On the whole, it was well that Ellis played the primary rôle, for he proved to be a competent and judicious diplomat.[22]

In May, 1757, Ellis received a large supply of Indian presents from the home government. He was consequently able during the next year to carry on extensive negotiations with the Creeks. Although Pepper had been unable to persuade them to send an embassy to Charleston, they now responded to invitations from the governor of Georgia. Large groups of Upper and Lower Creeks reached Savannah at the end of October, 1757. On November 3 they signed a treaty pledging themselves to maintain neutrality in the conflict between England and France and ceding to the British crown the lands claimed by the Bosomworths. Tugulkee, at the instigation of the Bosomworths, promptly denounced the treaty, but in the following June the Creeks again formally acknowledged Brit-

[19] Pepper to Lyttelton, June 28, 1757, IBSC, vi, 57–59. The South Carolina commons house, irritated because it had not been consulted regarding Pepper's appointment, threatened not to pay his accounts unless it received all the documents regarding his mission. Lyttelton refused, and the house eventually receded from this position.

[20] CJSC, xxvi, pt. 2, 22 ff.

[21] CJSC, xxvi, pt. 2, 100–20; Lyttelton to Board of Trade, Feb. 18, 1758 (incorrectly dated 1759 in transcript in Historical Commission of South Carolina), CO, 5/376.

[22] No discussion of the problems confronting Lyttelton, Ellis, and other English officials as the result of the formation of the New Hanover settlement is included in the text, because Indian relations were only very slightly involved.

ish ownership. Tugulkee and other warriors of Coweta town were affronted and displayed their resentment by going off to Mobile to plot with the French. The Bosomworths, however, were willing to accept a compromise. Ellis informed the London government that a settlement was necessary in order to end their intrigues.[23] Ellis's suggestion was approved; and in 1759 the Bosomworths accepted in exchange for their claims a royal grant of St. Catherine's Island and 2,000 guineas, provided the islands of Ossabaw and Sapelo should bring that sum at sale.[24] Thereafter the wiles of the Bosomworths were devoted to strengthening English influence; and the settlement, without offending the Creeks, furnished much land for the population of Georgia.

Ellis also succeeded in securing the passage of an act by the Georgia assembly in February, 1758, to outlaw private land purchases from Indians within the boundaries of the colony and to establish a system of trade regulation to replace that enacted by the proprietary government. Those making such a purchase were to be fined £1,000. The licensing of traders was placed in the hands of the acting governor. Persons operating without licenses were to be fined £100 for each offense, and were to suffer loss of all their goods. This act remained upon the statute books until the Revolution. Ellis demanded £200 bonds from the Georgia traders for its observance.[25] Both the governor and the assembly seemed eager to apprehend offenders,[26] but the act was easily evaded by the traders, who left the province before the courts could hear their cases. Nor did amendments passed in 1759, 1764, and 1765 insure the punishment of apprehended traders.[27]

The Creeks as a whole remained quiet and strictly neutral from 1757 to 1759. In spite of donations of English presents and the efforts of Ellis to remove causes of dispute, they might have given active assistance to the French, had it not been that Kerlérec during that period was able to offer very little in the way of presents

[23] Text of treaty with Creeks, Nov. 3, 1757, in CO, 5/18; Ellis to Board of Trade, Nov. 25, Dec. 7, 1757, June 28, July 20, 1758, *GCR,* XXVIII, pt. 1, 114–17, 119–21, 220–22, 227; Lyttelton to Board of Trade, April 14, 1759, CO, 5/376.

[24] Ellis to Board of Trade, July 26, 1759, June 27, 1760, *GCR,* XXVIII, pt. 1, 306–10, 390–94. The Bosomworths characteristically refused to pay Isaac Levy, a New York merchant who had bought from them a share in their claim. Levy received a small compensation from the imperial treasury in 1769.

[25] *GCR,* XVIII, 247–49; Ellis to Board of Trade, Feb. 18, 1758, *ibid.,* XXVIII, pt. 1, 171–74.

[26] *GCR,* XIII, 294–96, XVI, 281–94; CJSC, xxviii, 21.

[27] *GCR,* XIX, 247–49, 360–61, 594–95, 703–5.

and even less in trade. From the beginning of the war until August, 1758, not a single ship carrying Indian goods reached New Orleans from France. Kerlérec managed to purchase some supplies from merchants at New Orleans, from the Spanish at Vera Cruz, and especially from English colonial merchants who were not above trading with the enemy, though not in sufficient quantities; the king's magazines at New Orleans were often empty or virtually so.[28] Both the Creeks and the Choctaws were irritated because the annual presents were not forthcoming; and the latter bluntly informed Kerlérec in May, 1757, that they could and would open a trade with the English if he did not satisfy them.[29] It was not until the spring of 1759 that Kerlérec was able to distribute any considerable amount of presents to the Choctaws, a year's supply which he gave out at Mobile. He then felt that he was perhaps too late to save the Choctaw alliance. His fear was well grounded.[30]

The disaffection shown by the Choctaws toward the French could not be hidden from the English. Indeed, Kerlérec declared before the close of 1756 that English traders, using the tactics formerly employed by Glen and Adair, were offering the Choctaws a trade in exchange for an Anglo-Choctaw alliance.[31] Both Lyttelton and Ellis were deeply interested in reports that fifty Choctaws brought deerskins into the Upper Creek towns to deal with English traders in 1757.[32] Lyttelton came to believe, no doubt largely on the basis

[28] Kerlérec to ministry, Dec. 12, 1756, ANC, C13A, 39; Kerlérec to ministry, Jan. 28, March 13, Aug. 28 (two letters), 1757, Nov. 25, 1758, ANC, C13A, 40; Kerlérec to ministry, Dec. 21, 1760, ANC, C13A, 42. In the last document cited Kerlérec lays heavy stress upon the usefulness of the goods brought in by English merchants. On the activities of these merchants see also Bull to Pitt, Feb. 18, 1761, CO, 5/20. Benedict Thoms, a soldier who fell into the hands of the French after the capture of Fort Loudoun by the Cherokees in 1760, tells an interesting story. At New Orleans he was placed on board an English sloop which loaded a cargo of deerskins, logwood, and other items, and landed it at Boston harbor. Ironically enough, English goods had helped to bring about the fall of Fort Loudoun. See Thoms's affidavit, May 2, 1761, and his "Account," May 4, 1761, in CO, 5/20.

[29] Kerlérec to ministry, May 13, 1757, ANC, C13A, 39.

[30] Kerlérec to ministry, May 6, 1759, ANC, C13A, 41.

[31] Kerlérec to ministry, Dec. 12, 1756, ANC, C13A, 39.

[32] Lieutenant White Outerbridge to Lyttelton, Dec. 2, 1757, IBSC, vi, 98; Ellis to Board of Trade, Nov. 25, 1757, *GCR,* XXVIII, pt. 1, 114–17. The Choctaws did not actually deal with English traders. They were persuaded by the French at Fort Toulouse to exchange their skins with the Alabamas for old goods. The Alabamas in turn secured new goods for the skins from the English. Upper Creek traders to Outerbridge, Dec. 26, 1757 (incorrectly dated 1758), IBSC, vi, 101-2.

of information furnished by Samuel Pepper, that it was possible to secure a Choctaw alliance. A Choctaw chief residing among the Upper Creeks who visited Charleston at the beginning of 1758 with Wolf King was given a letter to his brethren by the governor. In June, 1758, James Wright, London agent for South Carolina, urged that the imperial government furnish Lyttelton £3,500 worth of Indian presents to consummate such an alliance; and apparently Wright's request was granted about the beginning of 1759,[33] although evidence is lacking to show that the goods were actually delivered at Charleston and used as intended. The real threat to French hegemony in the Choctaw country arose, oddly enough, not from the activities of Lyttelton and Ellis, but from those of Edmund Atkin.

When Edmund Atkin left England in 1756 he planned to arrange personally the signing of new treaties with the great southern tribes friendly to the English. Even before he reached Charleston, he determined, for reasons unknown, to negotiate with the Creeks first, and with the Cherokees later. This decision was seemingly not displeasing to Lyttelton, who in May, 1758, urged the South Carolina assembly to grant the superintendent financial assistance.[34] Lyttelton seems to have been on friendly terms with Atkin.[35] Probably they discussed the possibility of winning over the Choctaws. Whether the assembly did supply Atkin with funds is not certain. Atkin attended several sessions of the council during the summer of 1758, and on May 30 secured recognition by seniority as president of that body.[36] About the end of September he left for Savannah. Ellis had vainly asked for instructions from home regarding the attitude he should take toward Atkin. When Atkin early in October informed Ellis of his intention to travel into the Creek country, the governor declared there was no need for such a journey, since the Creeks were quiet; he suggested that Atkin should strive to improve relations between the Cherokees and Virginia, but Atkin was determined to proceed. Thereupon Ellis gave him a commission as justice of the peace, furnished a small body of Georgia rangers to escort

[33] Memorial by James Abercromby to Pitt, Jan. 20, 1759, Samuel Martin to John Pownall, Feb. 20, 1759, CO, 5/1329; Board of Trade to Lords of Treasury, March 1, 1759, CO, 5/1367.

[34] CJSC, xxvi, pt. 2, 187–88.

[35] Lord George Lyttelton, sponsor of the governor, apparently was on amicable terms with Atkin in England. Atkin later declared that Lyttelton was the only southern governor who supported him. Atkin to Pitt, March 27, 1760, CO, 5/64.

[36] CJSC, xxvi, pt. 2, 204–5.

him upcountry, and supplied some Indian presents.[37] Atkin rode on to Augusta, whence he notified the Creeks of his coming. He did not move further until the spring of 1759, although Anglophile Creeks repeatedly urged him not to delay.[38] Possibly he hesitated because he lacked authority over the English traders; during his sojourn on the Georgia frontier he requested Lyttelton and Ellis to furnish him with declarations that upon his recommendation they would suspend or vacate trading licenses. Ellis was strongly against granting such a power to the superintendent, but agreed to offer it, if Lyttelton concurred. Lyttelton merely gave Atkin an appointment as agent for South Carolina without salary and issued a proclamation ordering all traders not to impede his work.[39]

Atkin collected an armed guard, and made an impressive entrance into the Creek nation. At Cussita town, where he remained for some time, he found nineteen Choctaw warriors awaiting him to petition for a trade. To this he agreed, provided the Choctaws forbore hostilities against the Chickasaws and sent a delegation to meet with him in the Upper Creek country to conclude a treaty of friendship. Gun Merchant, two other Creek chiefs, and an English trader were also commissioned to bear the same message to the Choctaw nation. The French were unable to persuade the Choctaws to ignore Atkin's invitation. More than 300 members of that tribe waited upon Atkin at the Upper Creek town of Wauleyhatchie. According to the superintendent, they represented the whole nation. On July 10 a treaty was signed. In return for a trade the Choctaws agreed to make peace with the Chickasaws and to consider the French enemies. The Choctaws promptly entered into a formal pacification with the Chickasaws. Two English traders, William Hewitt and one Thompson, with equal promptness carried a consignment of goods past Fort Toulouse into the Choctaw nation. They did a splendid bit of business, and returned safely under escort of several hundred Choctaws to the Upper Creek towns. From 1759 to 1763 English traders visited the Choctaws, but they failed to develop a great traffic before the close of the Seven Years' War. Since they could not avoid traveling through the Upper Creek vil-

[37] *GCR,* VII, 826–27; Ellis to Board of Trade, Oct. 25, 1758, *ibid.,* XXVIII, pt. 1, 231–33.

[38] *GCR,* VIII, 163; James Adair, *History of the American Indians* (Williams ed.), 268.

[39] *GCR,* VIII, 5–8; CJSC, xxviii, 75–77. Lyttelton took action on Feb. 7, 1760, to revoke the licenses of Spencer and Elsinore, Creek traders accused of misconduct by Atkin.

lages, they were dependent upon the good will of the Creeks. Strained relations between the Creeks and the English after 1760 prevented most traders from going to the Choctaws.[40]

Atkin was less successful in his negotiations with the Creeks. He gave numerous "talks" in the Upper towns, and his "talks" were not always fully understood by his audiences. Moreover, the superintendent unwisely refused to confer with The Mortar and Gun Merchant when he learned that they were spending much time at Fort Toulouse. On September 28, while Atkin was addressing a gathering at Tuckabatchie, a near tragedy occurred. Aggrieved by Atkin's haughty attitude, Tobacco-Eater, an Alabama tribesman, attempted to assassinate the superintendent. He struck Atkin upon the head and again upon the arm with a tomahawk, but a friendly Creek named Molton, with the trader John McGillivray and one Waggonfield, Atkin's secretary, prevented him from completing his design. According to Atkin, this incident won him much sympathy among the Creeks, and they very generally swore firm friendship to the English. He claimed that two of their chiefs secretly promised to assist in an attack on Mobile, if the English would send an expedition by sea. Adair, however, declared that Atkin alienated the affections of the Creeks and that his conduct at this time was the real cause of outbreaks by the Upper Creeks in the following year.[41]

Accompanied by several Creeks, Atkin left Oakfuskie town about the end of November, and reached Fort Moore on December 23. Before leaving Oakfuskie the superintendent had sent messages to the Cherokees urging them to render submission to Lyttelton. He now made preparations for traveling into the Cherokee country, and persuaded his armed escort to go to Lyttelton's assistance. He abandoned the project when he learned of Lyttelton's agreement with the Cherokees. For three months he remained in the neighborhood of Fort Moore.[42]

Henry Ellis was not satisfied that Atkin had maintained English prestige among the Creeks. In October, 1759, he invited the chiefs of the Lower Creeks to visit him. They complained of Atkin's con-

[40] At its very beginning the Alabamas were hostile to the Anglo-Choctaw traffic. By threatening to cut off the trade of the Alabamas Atkin forced them to promise they would not attempt to hinder the commerce with the Choctaws.

[41] The activities of Atkin among the Creeks are described in Atkin to Pitt, March 27, 1760, and enclosures, CO, 5/64, and Adair, *op. cit.* (Williams ed.), 268–70, 314. See also John Reid's deposition, Oct. 5, 1759, *London Chronicle,* VII, 17; *South-Carolina Gazette,* June 30, July 21, Aug. 4, Sept. 1, 22, Oct. 20, Nov. 17 (Supplement 2), 1759.

[42] *South-Carolina Gazette,* Dec. 15, 29, 1759, Jan. 5, 26, 1760.

duct, although they expressed friendly sentiments toward the English.[43] On January 6, 1760, Ellis informed the Board of Trade that Atkin was unfitted for his office. But Ellis was not impartial, for he wished to have the southern Indian superintendency abolished. He declared that Atkin could not have handled the Cherokee crisis of 1759 so effectively as Lyttelton.[44] Lyttelton himself had not been quite so successful as Ellis appeared to believe.

[43] *GCR,* VIII, 163–70.

[44] *GCR,* XXVIII, pt. 1, 329–31. There was a rumor current in 1760 that Atkin would be dismissed. William Knox, afterward undersecretary of state for the colonies but then provost marshal of Georgia, tried to persuade Ellis and Lyttelton to recommend him for Atkin's position, should the rumor prove to be true. He received no encouragement from Lyttelton. William Knox to [John Ellis], May 20, 1760, Lyttelton to Knox, Jan. 2, 1761, Knox MSS, William L. Clements Library.

CHAPTER VII

THE CHEROKEE WAR

THE applause heaped upon Governor Lyttelton because of the seeming effectiveness of his negotiations with the Cherokees at the close of 1759 was quite unmerited, for he had neither appeased the Indians nor impressed them with English power. Hostilities were soon begun by the Cherokees. Immediately after Lyttelton's departure from Fort Prince George they brought in one more murderer to the fort and secured the release of another hostage. However, Lieutenant Coytmore was informed on January 13, 1760, that John Kelly, a trader, had been killed at Hiwassie town, and that the Middle and Valley townsmen were coming down to the fort to free, by peaceful means or otherwise, their brethren still held there. On the sixteenth Coytmore received a message from Saluy, young chief of the Lower town of Estatoe, that he would visit the fort in three days to exchange three or four murderers for hostages. Before Saluy appeared, several traders fled for their lives to the fort; some of their fellows, they reported, had been attacked by the Cherokees. Coytmore was therefore on the alert when Saluy approached on January 19, with twenty-five warriors. Every member of Saluy's party carried a weapon concealed under a blanket or a matchcoat held over his head, ostensibly to ward off a driving rain; and over a hundred Cherokees were observed by Coytmore's men in partial concealment on a hill a short distance away. Saluy, of course, hoped to be admitted to the fort as a friend, and then to stage an attack upon the garrison from within and without. Coytmore penetrated the scheme and ordered his men to prepare for battle. Saluy was invited to enter with three or four warriors and the murderers, and the chief accepted the invitation. When the gate swung open, all twenty-five warriors began to press in. Coytmore hurriedly ordered it closed after the chief and twelve companions had gained the interior of the fort. Their arms were ill hidden, but they dared make no hostile gestures. Realizing that Coytmore was prepared for action, Saluy deceitfully affirmed his friendship. He indicated that the murderers were still without, and he was given permission to escort

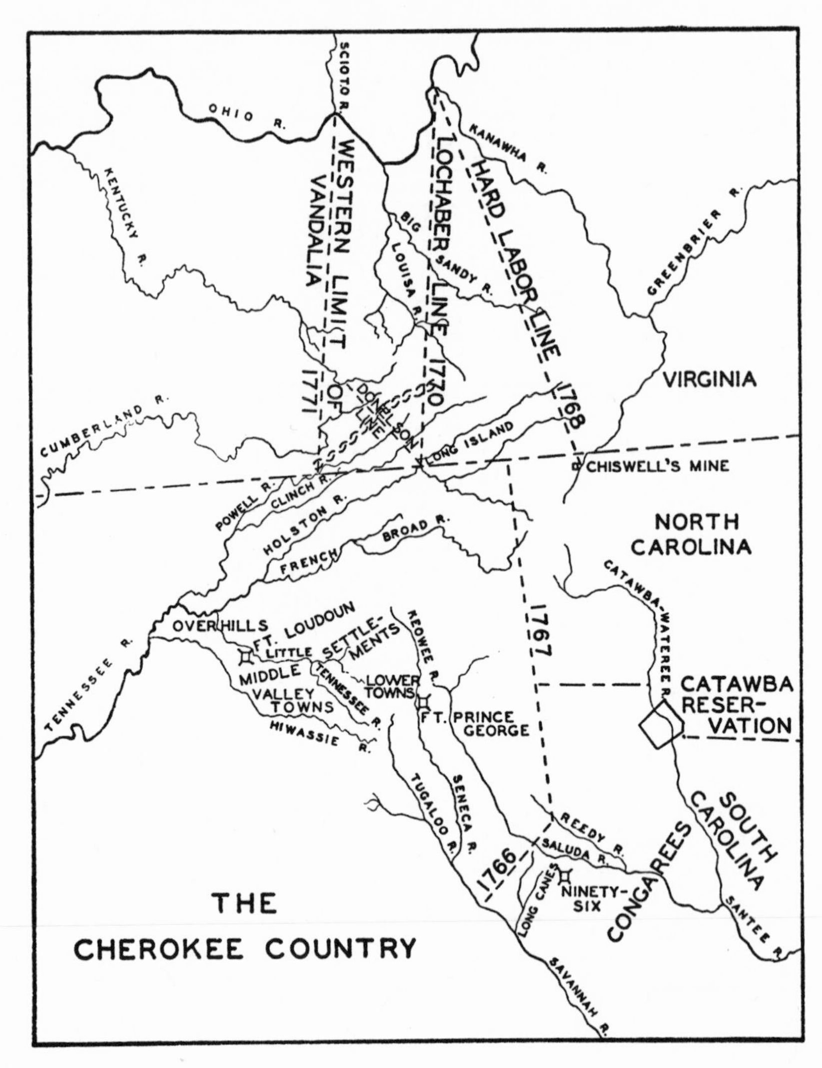

Map 2

them into the post. He returned with frivolous excuses. Saluy's band then left the fort amid protestations of friendship. Two of the hostages managed to mingle with them and thus to make their escape.

After this ominous episode Saluy's people returned home and

slew several traders, including John Elliott. Late in January with other Lower Cherokees they descended upon the frontiers of South Carolina and Georgia. The settlers between the Saluda and the Savannah rivers fled before them to the low country. Many took refuge in Augusta; others found safety in a log fort erected by Lyttelton at Ninety-Six and in stockades that had been built by the settlers themselves. Even so, the Cherokees took a frightful toll. Some forty or fifty persons, including men, women, and children, fell prey to their muskets and hatchets. Beyond the Congarees the whole South Carolina upcountry was a scene of desolation and distress.[1]

Meanwhile Fort Prince George was invested by the Cherokees, although for several weeks there was no firing upon the fort. On February 14 Ouconnostotah and Attakullakulla, who had returned to the Overhill country after the conclusion of the treaty of December 26, reappeared at the fort to demand the release of the Overhills still held within its walls. Coytmore, of course, refused. Early on the morning of February 16 Ouconnostotah, carrying a bridle, appeared on the far shore of the Keowee River. When asked why he carried the bridle, the chief replied that he intended to catch a horse to ride to Charleston to place his demand before Lyttelton; and he asked an interview with Coytmore. Coytmore, a junior officer, and a trader named Ambrose Davis went down to the river to speak with him. Ouconnostotah asked for a guide and a horse. When Coytmore consented, the warrior brandished his bridle and fled, whereupon twenty-five or thirty Cherokees who had concealed themselves under the bank of the river opened fire. Coytmore was mortally wounded and his companions were injured. Davis was shot in the buttocks, but contrived to carry the commandant into the fort. Davis then seized a rifle and shot one of the ambuscaders, and the Cherokees opened a general fire upon the fort. According to Ensign Alexander Miln, who assumed the command, the garrison wanted to kill the remaining hostages in revenge for the attack on Coytmore and to prevent them from aiding their brethren. When Miln instead ordered them placed in irons, the hostages resisted, drawing their knives and tomahawks. In the mêlee that resulted one soldier was killed and another wounded. The exasperated garrison then slaughtered every Indian within the fort. Miln

[1] Coytmore to Lyttelton, Jan. 23, 1760, and Coytmore's journal enclosed, CO, 5/57; John Pearson to Lyttelton, Feb. 8, 1760, IBSC, vi, 218; Lyttelton to Board of Trade, Feb. 22, 1760, CO, 5/376; *South-Carolina Gazette,* Jan. 19, Feb. 16, 23, 1760.

claimed that the Cherokees within and without the post had planned a simultaneous attack. The Indians outside withdrew when they observed the fate of their comrades. Not long afterward Coytmore died.[2]

Whatever justification there may have been for the slaying of the hostages, the deed greatly embittered the Lower and Middle townsmen. For a time they continued their assaults on the frontiers, with less success than before. On February 27 two attacks made upon the garrison of Fort Dobbs on the North Carolina frontier were repulsed with some loss to the aggressors.[3] On March 3 and 4 a body of 200 or more braves assailed the stockade at Ninety-Six, but it was defended by militiamen under Captain James Francis, and the Cherokees were beaten off. They vanished on March 6, leaving behind six dead warriors, whose bodies were thrown to the dogs by the garrison and whose scalps were used to decorate the stockade. A few of the defenders suffered wounds.[4] Thereafter the frontiers were quieter, although Cherokee raiding parties were not inactive.[5] Fort Prince George remained virtually in a state of siege, while the garrison of Fort Loudoun was placed in a desperate position.

On January 26 Captain Paul Demeré reported from Fort Loudoun that he had provisions for four months; that all was quiet in the Overhill country; that Settico town alone displayed a hostile disposition; and that Attakullakulla, highly displeased by the outbreaks of the Middle and Lower townsmen, had reaffirmed his loyalty to the English.[6] But Attakullakulla's influence was temporarily on the wane, partly because of his very loyalty. When Old Hop died, about the beginning of 1760, Kanagataucko was chosen "emperor" through the influence of Usteneka and Ouconnostotah, al-

[2] Miln to Lyttelton, Feb. 24, 1760, and Miln's journal enclosed, IBSC, vi, 219–21. Four hostages, according to Miln, had died between February 8 and 14. If so, fourteen were slain by the garrison in the affair of February 16. Too great reliance should not be placed upon Miln's account. He strenuously attempted to exculpate himself and the garrison from blame. He even claimed that the hostages had a bottle of poison and that they planned to inject it into the fort's water supply. It seems unlikely that four warriors died of natural causes within one week and that the hostages were actually a serious threat to the garrison.

[3] *NCCR,* VI, 229–30.

[4] James Francis to Lyttelton, March 6, 1760, IBSC, vi, 227–28; *South-Carolina Gazette,* March 15, 1760.

[5] For a more extensive account of the depredations of the Cherokees see Robert L. Meriwether, *The Expansion of South Carolina, 1729–1765* (Kingsport, Tenn., 1940), 222–27.

[6] Lyttelton to Board of Trade, Feb. 22, 1760, CO, 5/376.

though the Little Carpenter greatly desired the honor. Actually Ouconnostotah became the Overhill leader, while Usteneka held second rank. Under their guidance the war party became steadily stronger. Firing upon the fort began on March 20 and continued for four days. Attakullakulla, unable to restrain his brethren, temporarily retired to the woods. Not long afterward Demeré was forced to cut the ration of corn to one pint per day to each man. Through their Indian wives the garrison obtained some food from the Overhills in exchange for paint, ribbons, and other knickknacks. But it became more and more difficult to procure supplies through the squaws, and eventually goods to trade for provisions were exhausted. In fact, the Overhills were themselves short of corn. Although the Indians quieted down after their failure to carry the fort, the garrison continued to feel uneasy, especially since two messengers sent by Demeré to Virginia for aid were unsuccessful in their mission. One was killed by a Piankashaw party; the other was captured by the same party, escaped, and was brought into Fort Loudoun by Ouconnostotah. On May 16 William Bull believed that the garrison could not hold out two months.[7]

Lyttelton was informed of the first Cherokee outbreaks on the last day of January. On February 2 the governor and his council recognized that war existed, and determined to ask the commons house, which was scheduled to meet two days later, to vote funds to raise a large force. Also, messengers were sent by land and by sea to beg Amherst to furnish 1,500 to 2,000 regulars to assist in crushing the Cherokees.[8] And on the same day another express was sent

[7] Bull to Board of Trade, May 16, 1760, CO, 5/377; minute of Va. council, Nov. 7, 1761, Council Journals of Virginia, 1722–1773, Virginia State Library; *South-Carolina Gazette,* May 3, 1760. The most logical candidates for selection as "emperor" were Old Hop's sons, his nephew Attakullakulla, and the latter's brother, Willinawa. Nevertheless, Old Hop himself in the fall of 1756 was anxious that the Great Warrior and his brother, known as Kittagusta, or "Prince" of Chotê, should inherit his power. "Talk" by Old Hop to Stuart and Lieutenant Wall, Oct. 25, 1756, IBSC, v, 264–65. Kanagataucko was also apparently a nephew of Old Hop. He may have been deposed before 1765. See Andrew Lewis to Fauquier, June 3, 1765, CO, 5/43. In any case, Kanagataucko soon lost his influence. In 1770, at the instigation of Ouconnostotah, the Cherokees deposed an "emperor" (not named) because he was irresponsible and not sufficiently friendly to the English. At the same time, through Ouconnostotah's influence, Attakullakulla was given the imperial dignity. Stuart to Gage, April 24, 1770, Gage MSS; William Bartram, *Travels through North and South Carolina, Georgia, East and West Florida, the Cherokee Country, the Extensive Territories of the Muscogulges or Creek Confederacy, and the Country of the Chactaws* (London, 1792), 362–63.

[8] CJSC, xxviii, 157–58; Lyttelton to Amherst, Feb. 2, 1760, CO, 5/57.

to Fauquier, to urge him to send reinforcements and provisions to Fort Loudoun "as speedily as can be," since the nature of the terrain prevented an easy approach from South Carolina to the Cherokee country. On February 5 Lyttelton ordered reinforcements to Forts Moore and Augusta. On the following day the assembly convened. The censure meted out to the commons by Lyttelton the preceding October still rankled. Nevertheless, the house voted to raise a regiment of 1,000 men and to offer rewards to white men, Indians, and Negroes for Cherokee scalps. Lyttelton promptly laid plans to send 500 militiamen to the relief of Fort Prince George. Unfortunately, before February 22 Lyttelton received letters from home with news that he had been promoted to the governorship of Jamaica on November 14, 1759, and orders to proceed to England for instructions. William Bull, appointed lieutenant governor on the same day, was to serve in his stead until a new governor should be appointed.[9] Since Lyttelton did not leave the province until April 5, but relaxed his grip upon public affairs, and since Bull considered it improper to seize the reins so long as Lyttelton remained at Charleston, for many weeks little was done by the South Carolina government to deal with a desperate situation.[10]

Amherst believed that Lyttelton's policy in the Cherokee crisis was sound; and that it would have succeeded, had the Cherokee hostages been kept at Charleston, where the Cherokees could not have hoped to rescue them. He responded immediately to Lyttelton's call for aid, although he wished it had come sooner. He collected 1,200 men from the 1st and 77th regiments, and placed them under Archibald Montgomery.[11] Montgomery was ordered to proceed immediately to Charleston by sea. Amherst was loath to spare these men from the coming campaign against Canada; Montgomery was therefore instructed to lead a punitive expedition against the Cherokees, and thereafter to return north with all possible speed. He was specially instructed neither to garrison the South Carolina forts nor to act defensively, unless a grave emergency existed. He was even ordered to keep the transports in port at Charleston to insure a speedy return to New York, and, if necessary, to sail northward

[9] Lyttelton to Board of Trade, Feb. 22, 1760, CO, 5/376; Board of Trade to Lyttelton, Nov. 14, 1759, CO, 5/403.

[10] See James Grant to Amherst, April 17, 1760, CO, 5/58.

[11] Bouquet was not considered for this command because Lyttelton informed Amherst that he had engaged in land speculation with Frederick Haldimand and others in South Carolina during his service there in 1757–58, and that he was therefore *persona non grata*.

without the convoy of a warship. Montgomery's force was promptly organized at Perth Amboy, but Amherst was able to secure transports only by threatening an embargo on shipping from New York harbor, and it was not until March 20 that Montgomery set sail.[12] On April 1 his force reached Charleston. It was disembarked at Samuel Brailsford's plantation seven miles above the town, and marched directly to Monk's Corner.

Montgomery was unable immediately to move upcountry because Lyttelton and Bull had made no arrangements for transporting his impedimenta. According to Lieutenant Colonel James Grant, second in comand of the troops sent by Amherst, Montgomery, to obtain action, had to threaten to leave the colony immediately. In any case, the assembly met on April 15 at Bull's call and shortly afterward empowered Bull to impress the necessary wagons. On April 23 Montgomery was able to leave Monk's Corner. Traveling by night to avoid the heat of the day, he reached the Congarees on May 2. On the morning of May 24 he arrived at Ninety-Six, and on the 28th he marched toward the Lower Cherokee towns. Lyttelton and Bull had failed to raise more than a small fraction of the regiment voted by the assembly, and Montgomery was accompanied by only 335 provincial rangers. Bull, however, did make arrangements to send forty Savannah River Chickasaws and forty Catawbas to serve as scouts. Montgomery was ill satisfied with the assistance given him by South Carolina. From Ninety-Six he reported that not a single person of prominence in the province had joined the army, although there was much talk in the colony of meting out terrible punishment to the Cherokees. Montgomery did not criticize Bull. The lieutenant governor had done all within his power. Nor did Bull wish the Cherokees to be extirpated or driven permanently into the arms of the French; he desired that they should be chastised enough to teach them the value of English friendship.[13] Atkin's conduct at this critical moment was also respectable. He reached Charleston from Augusta on March 24, participated after April 5 as a member of the council in preparations for the campaign, set out for the army on May 16, and joined it on May 23.[14]

[12] Amherst to Lyttelton, Feb. 26, 1760, Amherst to Montgomery, March 6, 1760, Amherst to Pitt, March 8, 1760, CO, 5/57.

[13] Grant to Amherst, April 17, 1760, Montgomery to Amherst, May 24, 1760, CO, 5/58; Bull to Board of Trade, May 6, 8, 29, 1760, CO, 5/377; *South-Carolina Gazette,* April 7, 1760.

[14] *South-Carolina Gazette,* March 29, May 17, June 7, 1760.

Besides assisting Montgomery to launch his expedition, Bull attempted in various ways to strengthen the English position. At his request the assembly on April 19 raised the reward for Cherokee scalps to £35 (South Carolina currency), and agreed to pay James Adair and three other whites to lead parties of Creeks and Chickasaws against the Cherokees.[15] Because of his urging the assembly also voted £1,000 sterling for presents to bolster the English interest among the Creeks, Chickasaws, and Catawbas.[16] Bull was especially anxious to relieve the garrison of Fort Loudoun to prevent occupation of the fort by the French. Moreover, as a slave owner, he feared that the Overhill country, like the mountains of Jamaica, might become a refuge for fugitive Negroes. He therefore twice urged Fauquier to send a relieving expedition into the Overhill towns while the Cherokees were gathering on the eastern slopes of the mountains to oppose Montgomery. He also sent one Henry Lucas to the Overhill country with a supply of ribbons and paint in the hope that these trifles could be traded for provisions for the garrison.[17]

Although Bull commissioned men to lead parties of Creeks against the Cherokees, there was small prospect of securing the assistance of the Creek nation. In fact, a crisis in Creek affairs arose before Montgomery reached the Cherokee country. From Augusta Atkin had sent messages to the Creeks at the beginning of the Cherokee War urging that they either remain neutral or offer assistance to the English. He received friendly replies from both the Upper and the Lower towns.[18] But Bull and Ellis, with good reason, feared that the Creeks might ally themselves with the Cherokees. Ellis was deeply concerned for the safety of Georgia. At the outbreak of the Cherokee War there were fewer than 100 Independent Regulars in Georgia, stationed at Frederica and Augusta. Ellis could also rely upon forty-odd rangers raised by Reynolds, for in June, 1759, this body of horsemen had been definitely placed in the pay of the British military establishment in America. And, under authorization from Amherst, Ellis was then in the process of increasing the rangers to 150 men.[19] However, Georgia could muster no more

[15] CHJSC, xxxiii, pt. 1, 126–28; minute of S. C. council, April 22, 1760.

[16] CHJSC, xxxiii, pt. 1, 154–58.

[17] Bull to Board of Trade, May 6, 8, 1760, CO, 5/377.

[18] *South-Carolina Gazette,* April 7, 1760.

[19] Amherst to Ellis, June 1, 1759, CO, 5/55; Ellis to Amherst, July 20, 1759, Amherst to Ellis, Oct. 25, 1759, Ellis to Amherst, Jan. 12, 1760, CO, 5/57. The Independent Regulars in Georgia had originally been placed under the command of the governor of South Carolina because Georgia lacked a royal gover-

than 1,300 militia. When the Georgia backsettlers began to pour into Savannah and its environs Ellis therefore also called upon Amherst to send a large force of regulars to the South.[20]

Ellis seems to have done everything within his power to defend his province. He immediately sent rangers to patrol the frontiers, and secured the transfer of most of the regulars at Frederica to Augusta. Like Bull, he tried to embroil the Creeks with the Cherokees, offering £5 for every Cherokee scalp the Creeks brought in. In person and through agents such as the Bosomworths and the wealthy trader George Galphin he distributed £1,000 worth of goods to persuade the Creeks to go on the warpath against the Cherokees. While the Lower Creeks did bring in five Cherokee scalps, Ellis was not able to foment a Creek-Cherokee war. He did manage to maintain good relations between Georgia and the Lower Creeks. Neither he nor Bull was able to assure the friendship of the Upper Creeks, although on the other hand the Cherokee embassies that sought aid from them were also unsuccessful.[21] On May 8 Bull was inclined to think that the Upper Creeks would preserve neutrality, but shortly afterward he received advices from Augusta that the English interest among the Creeks was in a tottering state. Pro-English and pro-French factions were so bitter against each other that they were almost at blows; the Francophiles were threatening to slay an Englishman for every Cherokee slain by the Anglophiles. On May 14 he believed that a crisis in Anglo-Creek relations was near at hand.[22] It was even nearer than he thought. On that very day the long-continued intrigues of Kerlérec and his aides among the Creeks began to bear fruit, much to Kerlérec's satisfaction. The Oakfuskie townsmen arose and slew their traders, and their example was followed by several towns among the Upper Creeks. Handsome Fellow was the apparent leader, but The Mortar had planned the attack. Eleven whites were killed, although Wolf King, Gun Merchant, and Devil's Landlord saved some traders. Others fled to Pensacola, where they were relieved from distress by merchants from Rhode Island and New York who were

---

nor. This arrangement, much to the disgust of Ellis, was allowed to continue after Georgia became a royal province. The rangers subsisted precariously before 1759 upon funds granted by Loudoun and bills drawn by Ellis in the hope that he would be reimbursed.

[20] Ellis to Amherst, Feb. 13, 1760, CO, 5/58.

[21] Ellis to Board of Trade, Feb. 15, April 16, 1760, *GCR,* XXVIII, pt. 1, 333–35, 369–70; Bull to Board of Trade, May 8, 1760, CO, 5/377; *South-Carolina Gazette,* March 15, 22, 29, May 10, 1760.

[22] Bull to Pitt, May 14, 1760, CO, 5/377.

trading with a very gay Frenchman from Mobile. Still others reached the Lower Creek towns, which refused to join in the slaughter and sent the fugitives off to Savannah in safety. With the news of this attack the frontiers of Georgia were completely abandoned, except by some merchants in and about Augusta who lived in rude stockades.

Both Bull and Ellis feared that the murder of the Upper Creek traders would be followed by a general Creek outbreak. Bull ordered Fort Moore abandoned and its garrison removed to Fort Augusta, encouraged the merchants in the neighborhood of Augusta to remain and protect their goods, and held himself in readiness to march to their assistance with all available militia. He also called upon Amherst for orders to Montgomery to remain in South Carolina. But the cautious policy pursued by the two governors prevented the Creeks from joining the Cherokees.

Although the South Carolina assembly gave Bull authority to cut off the trade in order to bring the Creeks to heel, Bull did not take any action, since many of the surviving traders did not immediately return to their stations. Nor did Georgia formally cut off the trade. Instead, Bull and Ellis wisely made liberal presents to those Creeks innocent of the outbreak, and informed the nation as a whole that it would not be held responsible for the acts of a few malcontents. No categorical demand for the punishment of the murderers was made. As a result, friendly delegations of Upper and Lower Creeks visited Charleston in July, and others made their appearance at Savannah; and the Francophile party failed to gain ground among the Creeks. Gradually the tension in Anglo-Creek relations lessened during the summer of 1760.[23]

With the wisdom of experience Bull doubted that the Cherokees would offer open battle to Montgomery, although he hoped that Montgomery would be able to destroy the towns and food supplies of the "volatile" enemy. When Montgomery left Ninety-Six he expected to be opposed by the Cherokees at Twelve-Mile River below Keowee, but he crossed that stream without trouble. He struck hard at the Lower settlements. On June 2 a British detachment attacked and burnt Estatoe, slaying sixty or eighty Cherokees and capturing forty, including women and children. Some of the In-

[23] Bull to Board of Trade, May 29, June 17, July 20, Aug. 15, 1760, CO, 5/377; Bull to Pitt, Feb. 18, 1761, CO, 5/20; Ellis to Board of Trade, Sept. 5, 1760, *GCR,* XXVIII, pt. 1, 461–64; Kerlérec to ministry, June 12, 1760, ANC, C13A, minutes of S. C. council, June 2, 4, 5, 22, July 23, 24, 1760; *South-Carolina Gazette,* May 31, June 14, 21 (Supplement), July 19, 1760.

dians lost their lives in their huts, which were set ablaze by the soldiers. Other Lower Cherokee towns between Estatoe and Keowee were also burned. Montgomery's men arrived at Fort Prince George on June 4 in a state of exhaustion, after marching sixty miles without sleep. They had lost only three or four men, but a few others were wounded.

While bivouacked at Fort Prince George Montgomery came to the conclusion that he would be unable to penetrate the Overhill country, and that he could not even send provisions to Fort Loudoun. He therefore decided to invite the Overhills to make peace, particularly since the Lower townsmen, who were after all the worst offenders, had been dealt crushing blows. Instruments were ready at hand, for Miln had unscrupulously seized and held captive several friendly Cherokees, including two chiefs, Tistoe of Keowee and Old Warrior of Estatoe. On June 5 Montgomery sent Tistoe to inform the Middle and Overhill tribes that Montgomery could destroy them, but would prefer to make peace, and to demand that Fort Loudoun be supplied with corn and that Attakullakulla and Stuart be sent down to Fort Prince George to begin negotiations. Old Warrior was commissioned to bring in representatives of the Lower settlements. Montgomery demanded prompt action from the Cherokees. In these measures he was joined by Atkin, who also sent "talks" to the Middle and Overhill towns. Montgomery's bid for peace almost succeeded. Both the Middle and the Overhill Cherokees had been angered by the slaughter of the hostages and by the seizure of the warriors mentioned above at Fort Prince George. They were reluctant to send delegates because of a fear that they would be imprisoned or slain. But the Middle townsmen were short of ammunition, while the Overhills lacked corn. The Overhills actually made preparations to send a great delegation, but were deterred at the last moment by a message sent to them by one Welsh, a rascally trader, who assured them the delegates would be slain by the English.[24]

[24] Montgomery to Amherst, June 4, 1760, Bull to Amherst, June 21, 1760, CO, 5/59; Grant to Amherst, Jan. 17, 1761, CO, 5/61; minutes of S. C. council, June 10, 30, 1760; A. Hewatt, *An Historical Account of the Rise and Progress of the Colonies of South Carolina and Georgia* (London, 1779), II, 231; *South-Carolina Gazette,* June 10 (Extraordinary), June 21 (Supplement), Aug. 23, 1760. The June 10 issue of the gazette cited contains most of a letter written by Lieutenant Colonel Grant to Bull on June 4 from Fort Prince George. Bull suppressed portions of the letter which indicated that Montgomery would not attempt to relieve Fort Loudoun and which described the nefarious activities of Miln and other officers at Fort Prince George.

When his overtures for peace did not receive a favorable answer, Montgomery determined to strike a blow at the Middle Cherokees. Baggage and tents were left at Fort Prince George so that the little army could move rapidly. Montgomery left the fort on June 24 and marched some fifty miles without meeting opposition, although the terrain was well calculated for defense. On June 27, however, when he was six miles from the Middle Cherokee town of Etchoe he was confronted with a numerous body of Cherokees, composed mainly of Lower and Middle townsmen, although a few Overhills were present. According to Montgomery, it included a few Creeks and Choctaws. After sharp fighting he drove off the savages. Soon afterward the rear guard under Captain Peter Gordon foiled an attempt to capture the horses and cattle belonging to the expedition. Montgomery claimed that the Cherokees lost fifty warriors in these combats. On June 28 the army reached Etchoe and destroyed the huts of the Indians. There it was fired upon from the hills, but a sallying party drove off the attackers. Montgomery remained two days at Etchoe to rest his men, and then turned back toward Fort Prince George. He was convinced that it was impossible to advance farther, for the country before him was exceedingly difficult, and he was burdened with wounded soldiers. Attakullakulla believed Montgomery could have reached Fort Loudoun, and resistance would have melted away before him. Peter Timothy, publisher of the *South-Carolina Gazette,* expressed the same opinion. Possibly Attakullakulla and Timothy were right; a George Rogers Clark might have marched on to Fort Loudoun. Whatever the answer to this difficult question, Montgomery retreated from Etchoe in the night of June 30. On July 2 attacks were made on the flanks of the army, but these were beaten off, with a loss of perhaps a dozen warriors to the Cherokees. The Indians then disappeared, and Montgomery proceeded safely to Fort Prince George. Altogether his force had lost twenty men killed and seventy wounded.[25]

Montgomery believed that he had now executed his orders and had done all that was possible, although the Cherokees had certainly not been brought to terms. At Fort Prince George he left a large supply of flour (unfortunately damaged by the sweat of the horses

[25] Montgomery to Amherst, June 23, 1760, Montgomery to Amherst, July 2, 1760 (Extract), and enclosed "Return of Killed and Wounded of the Detachment . . . under Montgomery," CO, 5/59; Bull to Board of Trade, July 20, 1760, CO, 5/377; letter from Fort Loudoun, May 29, 1760, *Virginia Gazette,* July 11, 1760, copy in volume of papers on Cherokee Indians, 1760–1774, Division of Manuscripts, L. C.; *South-Carolina Gazette,* Sept. 6, 1760.

that had carried it), and then marched toward Charleston to embark for New York. According to Bull, "consternation" reigned in South Carolina when the news spread that the regulars were leaving. The assembly urged him to bring pressure upon Montgomery to stay in the province. Bull begged him to remain at least until Amherst had had an opportunity to reply to the appeal that had been sent upon receiving news of the slaughter of the Upper Creek traders. He felt that the garrison of Fort Loudoun was probably lost, that Fort Prince George might be successfully attacked, and that the Creeks might well join the Cherokees. However, he admitted to Montgomery that the South Carolina settlements could be defended until Amherst could send a second force to carry on offensive operations.[26] At first Montgomery declined even to consider Bull's request, since his orders positively forbade him to engage in defensive operations and since he felt certain that, so long as the regulars remained in the province, South Carolina would not raise forces sufficient for offensive operations. He pointed out that the provincial rangers, enlisted to serve only until July 1, had already disbanded, and that the few foot soldiers who had been raised by the province were neither paid, nor properly clothed, nor anxious to serve. Bull wrote bitterly to the Board of Trade: "I conceived this country to be in a worse situation on many accounts by these troops under these circumstances leaving us, than if they had never been sent here." Nor did letters from Amherst, arriving when Montgomery was only eighty miles from Charleston, please Bull, for the general insisted that Montgomery's force return north immediately. Finally, Bull was able to persuade Montgomery to send Major Frederick Hamilton back to the Congarees with four companies of regulars, on the plea that this detachment could support the frontier forts and would encourage provincial recruiting.[27]

When on July 30 Bull informed the South Carolina assembly that Montgomery was leaving only a detachment and that he proposed to follow defensive tactics in the hope that lack of trade would bring the Cherokees to heel, the commons house dissented energetically. It promptly voted to increase the reward for Cherokee scalps to £100 (provincial currency), and to raise a regiment of foot and seven companies of horse to take the offensive. Indeed, a motion to equip 500 Negroes to serve against the savages was lost only

[26] Bull to Montgomery, July 12, 1760, CO, 5/376.

[27] Bull to Board of Trade, July 20, 1760, CO, 5/377; Bull to Amherst, Aug. 15, 1760, Montgomery to Amherst, Sept. 11, 1760, CO, 5/59.

by the casting vote of the speaker.[28] But Bull continued to hope that the Cherokees would sue for peace, and determined in any case not to attack until the following winter, when assistance might be secured from neighboring provinces. To assure the safety of the province meantime he sent fifty men with light artillery to the post at Ninety-Six, supplied settlers in the stockades with ammunition, and sent out rangers to patrol the frontier. His policy seemed justified when he learned on August 15 that at a great meeting the Middle and Lower Cherokees had expressed a desire for peace on the basis of a mutual exchange of prisoners and withdrawal by the English from Forts Loudoun and Prince George.[29] Three days later Charles McLamore, a renegade mulatto, arrived at Bull's home on the Ashley River with dispatches from Captain Paul Demeré announcing that Fort Loudoun had capitulated to the Overhills on August 8.

Easier access to Fort Loudoun could be had from Virginia—by way of the Holston and Tennessee rivers—than from any other English colony. Long before the fort was finished Captain Raymond Demeré had expressed an opinion that, if it were ever attacked by the Cherokees, relief must come from Virginia.[30] Virginia had contributed largely toward creating the situation that led to the Cherokee War by its insistent demands for the services of warriors and by its failure to prevent clashes between those warriors and its own inhabitants. Yet the Old Dominion was not to play a very handsome part in that war. Late in October, 1759, Fauquier sent 300 men to defend the southwestern frontiers of Virginia. In November the burgesses voted to maintain these men in service, but forbade their leaving the province.[31] When Lyttelton's appeal of February 2 was placed before the burgesses, that body again voted to maintain 300 men in that area, for defensive purposes only.[32] At the end of the first week of May, 1760, Fauquier and his council read another appeal—from Bull, sent on April 28—to rescue the Fort Loudoun men. Fauquier again convened the assembly on May 19.

[28] CHJSC, xxxiii, pt. 1, 365–66, 368–73.

[29] Bull to Board of Trade, Aug. 15, 1760, CO, 5/377; Bull to Amherst, Aug. 15, 1760, CO, 5/59.

[30] Demeré to Lyttelton, Oct. 29, 1756, IBSC, v, 265–66.

[31] Fauquier to Board of Trade, Dec. 17, 1759, CO, 5/1329. Fauquier states that he did not receive Lyttelton's request of October, 1759, that Virginia undertake to relieve Fort Loudoun.

[32] Minute of Va. council, Feb. 21, 1760, CO, 5/1429; Fauquier to Amherst, Feb. 23, April 5, 1760, CO, 5/58. It should be noted that Virginia was supporting over 400 men at Fort Pitt at this time.

The burgesses then responded by voting to raise 700 men, who were to join the force of 300 then on the frontier in carrying one year's supply of provisions into Fort Loudoun or in performing whatever service Bull might propose.[33] Not until the end of June were the 700 men enlisted.[34] It was already too late to strike while the Cherokees were heavily engaged by Montgomery.

Fauquier and Bull had hoped that North Carolina would raise a body of militia to join the force sent by Virginia. Dobbs called his assembly into session on April 22, asking for 500 men to be employed against the Cherokees. The assembly seemed to be willing to send 300 men to join the Virginians, but did not pass until May 27 a supply bill of £12,000 (provincial currency) intended to finance these troops. Dobbs claimed that the delay of the assembly in acting and certain provisions in the bill regarding methods of enlistment were intended to make it impossible to use the troops, and that the assembly passed it merely to secure the issuance of £12,000 in paper currency. Whether or not Dobbs was justified in this stand, he vetoed the bill. North Carolina therefore did not even attempt to assist Virginia.[35]

William Byrd, who accepted the command of the relieving expedition and then attempted to resign it, made all sorts of difficulties about beginning his work. En route to the army early in July he declared he had insufficient arms and supplies. He then thought he ought to build small posts twenty-five miles apart all the way to the Holston River, and a strong fort on Long Island in that stream. Such a fort would ensure a successful expedition against the Cherokees in the spring of 1761! Should he execute this plan? What should he do if the Cherokees asked him for peace? If the Fort Loudoun people were still holding out when he reached the Holston River and he believed the garrison could be brought off by a strong rescue party, should he attempt it? Fauquier peremptorily ordered him to leave peace negotiations to Bull, to build no more than one small fort at the Long Island and possibly another at Samuel Stalnaker's plantation some distance above the island; to proceed, supplies or no supplies; and to get in touch with Demeré, rescue his force, support it, or cover its retreat as the situation demanded.[36] Byrd received no news regarding Fort Loudoun

[33] Minute of Va. council, May 8, 1760, CO, 5/1429; Fauquier to Board of Trade, June 2, 1760, CO, 5/1330.

[34] Fauquier to Board of Trade, June 30, 1760, CO, 5/1330.

[35] *NCCR*, VI, 437–38; minute of Va. council, June 25, 1760, CO, 5/1435.

[36] Minutes of Va. council, May 24, July 8, 23, 1760, CO, 5/1435.

until August 27, when four traders who had undergone the siege and had escaped from that post on August 1 reached his encampment. Byrd had then progressed no farther than Sayer's Mill [37] on the Kanawha River. They informed him that the garrison had abandoned all hope at the time of their flight; Byrd thereupon sent out Major Andrew Lewis with 300 men to the Holston River to search for any persons who might have escaped from the fort and fled toward Virginia. On September 8 Attakullakulla appeared at Lewis's camp a little above Long Island; he told Lewis that Captain Stuart, his body-servant, an interpreter named William Shorey, Attakullakulla's wife and brother, and three or four other Cherokees were only five miles away. The little group had fled from the Overhill country, and had discovered Lewis's trail; and the chief had tracked Lewis to his camp. Attakullakulla then returned to his waiting companions, and brought them to Lewis.[38] Stuart had had an amazing experience.

During May Ouconnostotah and the Overhills had kept constant watch about the walls of Fort Loudoun. Since he was certain that the garrison could not cut its way to freedom, Ouconnostotah was not inclined to attack. But The Mortar appeared in the Overhill country at the very moment when his Upper Creek friends were slaughtering the English traders. He advocated using at Fort Loudoun the strategy that Saluy had employed unsuccessfully at Fort Prince George. Attakullakulla ruined this scheme by informing Demeré. Ouconnostotah then employed a different stratagem. On June 2, in an attempt to entice the garrison from the fort, he let it be known that the Overhills were sending out their warriors against Indian enemies. Again Attakullakulla warned Demeré. Lieutenant Maurice Anderson and a trader were so unwise as to leave the protection of the walls, and were slain before a sortying party could rescue them, but the garrison was saved. Nevertheless, Demeré's position became steadily more desperate. Henry Lucas reached the fort safely before the end of May with his paint and ribbons, and Demeré was able to buy from the Overhills with these trifles sufficient supplies to maintain the garrison for fourteen days. But the Overhills themselves were still suffering from a shortage of corn, and it became more and more difficult to procure it.

After the first week of June Fort Loudoun heard no more from the outside world except what information the Overhills chose to

[37] Or Sawyer's. Located on a creek known by the same name.

[38] Minute of Va. council, Sept. 16, 1760, CO, 5/1435; Lewis to Byrd [Sept. 9, 1760], CO, 5/377; *South-Carolina Gazette,* Oct. 11, 1760.

give; and very little news regarding Demeré and his men reached the settlements. At the beginning of July the garrison was daily expecting to be relieved by Montgomery. It was then subsisting in part upon the flesh of horses.[39] But Montgomery did not come. After July 7 no bread was to be had at the fort. Scanty supplies of hogs and beans reached the vanishing point. Fresh horseflesh sickened the men, and soon the Cherokees cut off even that source of food. By stripping themselves of personal adornments and even clothing the garrison and the few traders and women enclosed within the walls managed to buy a little corn from the Overhills. Ouconnostotah guarded the fort ever more closely. Two half-breeds who left it on July 27 and arrived at Charleston a month later reported that the garrison was miserable beyond all description, and that it felt "abandoned and forsaken by God and Man." On August 4 and 5 considerable numbers of soldiers deserted the fort, attempting to make their way to the settlements or throwing themselves upon the mercy of the Overhills. The remainder of the garrison threatened to do likewise; and on August 6 the officers held a council of war to consider the situation. It was decided to sue again for terms of peace, since food was lacking for more than three days. On the following day Stuart and Lieutenant James Adamson conferred with Ouconnostotah and the Cherokee chiefs at Choté. Stuart was able to negotiate a capitulation according to which the garrison was to march freely with its arms to Virginia or South Carolina. Those who were sick were to be cared for in the Cherokee towns, and the cannon and other supplies at the fort were to be abandoned to the barbarians. Fourteen one-pounders, 80 small arms, 1,000 pounds of powder, and 2,000 pounds of ball accordingly fell to the triumphant Cherokees. Peace and trade were to be restored.[40]

[39] Bull to Amherst, May 29, 1760, CO, 5/58; Bull to Board of Trade, June 17, 1760, CO, 5/377; Bull to Board of Trade, June 30, 1760, CO, 5/376; *South-Carolina Gazette,* May 31, June 21 (Supplement), July 5, Aug. 13 (Extraordinary), 1760.

[40] *Journals of the House of Burgesses of Virginia, 1758–1761,* 286–87; Bull to Amherst, Oct. 19, 1760, CO, 5/60; *South-Carolina Gazette,* Aug. 13 (Extraordinary), 16, 23, 1760. When Amherst learned, without details, that Fort Loudoun had capitulated, he remarked that it was the first instance of royal troops surrendering to Indians. He made the stupidly arrogant comment, "I must own I am ashamed . . . they must be blameable for so doing." Amherst to Bull, Oct. 14, 1760, CO, 5/59. Was Braddock the least wise of the British military commanders in dealing with Indians? The lesson of Fort Loudoun, that unsupported posts in the Indian country were at the mercy of the savages, was completely lost upon Amherst, as Pontiac's uprising was to prove in terrible fashion.

On August 9 Demeré and his people, undoubtedly with deep misgivings, set out for Fort Prince George. One account states that some of the Overhills were restrained from attacking them as they emerged from the fort only by the intervention of Ouconnostotah.[41] During the day the great chief and a large body of Cherokees escorted them, then gradually withdrew. Not a single warrior was in evidence when the whites camped in the evening on Cane Creek, some fifteen miles from the fort and about two miles from Tellico town. Usteneka visited the English after dark, but did not remain. After reveille on the following morning an advance guard discovered many Indians hidden in ambush within sixty yards of the camp, and gave an alarm. Stuart hurriedly called the men to arms. Some of the soldiers attempted to flee, while others opened fire. There is some evidence that the Cherokees, who were reported to number about 700 warriors, originally intended merely to make prisoners of the English. In any case, they responded to the soldiers' fire with a rain of bullets and arrows. Demeré was wounded in the first volley, scalped, and barbarously slain. Adamson, the junior officers, and between twenty and thirty men also lost their lives, but many soldiers threw down their arms and urged their comrades to do likewise; and after the death of Demeré Usteneka stopped the slaughter with the cry that the Cherokees should be satisfied. The survivors were stripped, marched off to the various Overhill towns, and subjected to unspeakable cruelties en route. Eighty more of Demeré's men suffered death before the lust of the Cherokees for blood was sated. Stuart, more fortunate than his fellow officers, was seized by Onatoy, a brother of Round O; and he managed to persuade his captor to take him to Tomotley and thence to Fort Loudoun in search of Attakullakulla. At the fort a few hours after the massacre they found the little chief, who rejoiced in the escape of his friend from the slaughter and undertook to protect him for the future.[42]

Immediately on receipt of the news of the attack on the Fort

[41] *South-Carolina Gazette,* Aug. 23, 1760.

[42] This paragraph is based largely on information secured from Stuart, given in a minute of the S. C. council, Oct. 22, 1760, and in an item in the *South-Carolina Gazette,* Oct. 4, 1760. Other accounts of the attack on Demeré's force are to be found in issues of the *Gazette* of Sept. 20, 27, and Oct. 4, 1760. Data in the issues of Sept. 20 and 27 seem to be quite unreliable. See also Bull to Board of Trade, Sept. 9, 1760, CO, 5/377; Bull to Amherst, Oct. 19, 1760, CO, 5/60; Hewatt, *op. cit.,* II, 238–39. There was a rumor current in 1760 that the Overhills slew as many persons as Lyttelton had imprisoned. Probably more than twenty-four persons were slain in the attack.

Loudoun people Ensign Miln sent a messenger to the Cherokees urging that Stuart and the survivors be released as part of a program leading to a general peace, but the triumphant Overhills would not listen. At the moment they were not in a mood to consider a pacification, partly because they could employ Stuart as a hostage and partly because they had learned that the English had hidden twelve bags of powder in Fort Loudoun in defiance of the treaty of capitulation. Rather, they were eager to capture Fort Prince George, not only to wreak vengeance upon Miln for his part in the slaying of the Cherokee hostages at that post, but also to obtain possession of large quantities of guns, ammunition, and woollens left there by Lyttelton. After a general council on August 27 they informed Stuart that they planned to depart for Keowee on September 6, and that he and a number of sailors from Beaufort in his company who were experienced in the operation of artillery must accompany them and must train the guns captured at Fort Loudoun upon Fort Prince George. The alternative was death. Fortunately Stuart was able to evade making a choice. Attakullakulla, by abandoning all his possessions, purchased Stuart from his captor and managed to take him away on August 30 or 31 upon a simulated hunting trip. On September 8 Stuart was safe in the camp of Andrew Lewis.[43]

Before September 6 some hope had been held in South Carolina that the war weariness of the Cherokees and the regard they had for Stuart might save the garrison of Fort Loudoun.[44] The news of the capitulation spurred Bull to open negotiations with the Cherokees for peace on the basis of a mutual exchange of prisoners; and he sent Charles McLamore back to the nation with his proposal. While Bull realized that such a peace would seem dishonorable according to European standards, he could well defend his policy on prudential grounds.[45] On the evening of September 6, however, information reached Charleston regarding the attack on the Fort Loudoun people and the projected Cherokee assault on Fort Prince George. Up to that time Bull had made no effort to raise the regiment voted by the assembly a month before. In the second week of September

[43] Bull to Amherst, Oct. 19, 1760, CO, 5/60; *South-Carolina Gazette,* Sept. 27, Oct. 4, 11, 1760. Hewatt, *op. cit.,* II, 239, states that Attakullakulla purchased Stuart from his captor when he first met Stuart after the massacre. Other accounts indicate the purchase was not made until after the Cherokee council of August 27.

[44] *South-Carolina Gazette,* Aug. 30, 1760.

[45] Minute of S. C. council, Aug. 22, 1760; Bull to Board of Trade, Aug. 31, 1760, CO, 5/377.

he issued commissions to officers to recruit and lead the regiment; and he laid plans for relieving Fort Prince George and attacking the Lower townsmen with the assistance of Hamilton's force.[46]

Bull's peace proposal was seriously considered by the Cherokees. They had hoped for aid from the Creeks and the French, but The Mortar came to Choté at the end of August with only fourteen warriors and without supplies. Moreover, they were somewhat daunted by Stuart's escape. A message from Byrd threatening their destruction unless they made peace also had an effect. The Overhills abandoned their intention of attacking Fort Prince George. On September 26 Ouconnostotah and Usteneka, with some 2,000 Cherokees, raised the English flag at Nucassee town and sent out a peace "talk" to Bull. They offered to exchange prisoners at Ninety-Six. Bull made arrangements to send thirty-three Cherokees taken by Montgomery and held at Charleston to Ninety-Six, but these negotiations fell through. At a formal meeting on October 14 the Cherokees decided to make no commitments to Bull until they had gone to Choté to consider overtures from Byrd, who had also made proposals to them. In any case it would not have been easy for Bull to arrange a peace, since the Cherokees were then disposed to demand that the stores at Fort Prince George be abandoned to them and that the post be razed.[47]

On Sunday, September 19, Andrew Lewis and his men, with Stuart, Attakullakulla, and their party, joined Byrd at his camp on the Kanawha. While Byrd had no authority to negotiate with the Cherokees, he concluded, after many conferences with the chief, that Attakullakulla might be used as an instrument to bring the war to a successful close. He decided to dispatch Attakullakulla to the Overhill country as his ambassador. The Little Carpenter was to demand from the Cherokees that they send fully empowered delegates to Byrd by October 20; that they free at that time all English prisoners; that they give up certain warriors to Byrd for execution; that they drive all Frenchmen from their towns; and that they acknowledge Attakullakulla as their "emperor." If these stipulations were met, Byrd would undertake to free the Cherokees held by the English and to reopen the trade. He hoped that fear of his army would compel the Indians to accept his terms. He also hoped that Little Carpenter might be able to embroil the Creeks and Cherokees, so that the latter would be forced to make peace. If the chief

[46] Bull to Board of Trade, Sept. 9, 1760, CO, 5/377.

[47] Minute of S. C. council, Oct. 22, 1760; Bull to Amherst, Oct. 19, 1760, CO, 5/60; *South-Carolina Gazette,* Oct. 11, 25, 1760.

failed in this mission, he was to bring in to Byrd all his friends and whatever British prisoners he could carry off. Although documents connect with this plan only the name of Byrd, it seems certain that much of it originated with Stuart, and that his influence with Attakullakulla as well as the little chief's ambition led the latter to undertake the task. Attakullakulla set out on September 21, while Stuart remained at Byrd's camp to await the result of his mission. Bull and his council approved the scheme, although Bull feared that the war party among the Cherokees would be greatly strengthened if it failed and Byrd did not attack. He pointed out that Byrd's force was to be disbanded on December 1, and that his threats were pure bluff.[48]

Attakullakulla reached Choté in October and placed Byrd's proposals before a large body of Cherokees that assembled to meet him, but the little chief was unable to achieve complete success in his mission. In part his failure was caused by the inactivity of Byrd on the Kanawha, for the Cherokees had come to realize that they had nothing to fear from him; in part it was apparently caused by the activities of Lantagnac, who arrived shortly after Attakullakulla at Choté with nine or ten Frenchmen and a supply of presents from Fort Massac. Lantagnac earnestly pledged himself to return in three weeks with French soldiers and Creek warriors to aid in seizing Fort Prince George, and he left his French companions at Choté as proof of his good faith. This performance encouraged some Cherokees, notably Saluy, to carry on the war. Attakullakulla did secure promises from the Cherokees to suspend hostilities until March, provided Byrd did not advance, and to negotiate further in the spring. These promises were not of much value, but Attakullakulla managed to carry off ten English prisoners, and brought them safely to the Virginian encampment on the Kanawha on November 1.

On the Kanawha Little Carpenter bade farewell to Stuart, who proceeded on November 5 to Williamsburg, no doubt to inform Fauquier regarding the Cherokee situation. On Christmas Day Stuart reached Charleston, in good health, so the *South-Carolina Gazette* reported, in view of the hardships he had undergone.[49] Stuart's services, his sufferings, and his romantic escape had made him an object of public admiration and sympathy. On January 21, 1761, Bull urged the assembly to compensate him for losses in personal

[48] Minute of Va. council, Oct. 6, 1760, CO, 5/1435; Bull to Amherst, Oct. 19, 1760, CO, 5/60; *South-Carolina Gazette,* Oct. 11, 1760.

[49] Minute of Va. council, Nov. 12, 1760, Co, 5/1435; Bull to Amherst, Nov. 18, 1760, CO, 5/60; *South-Carolina Gazette,* Nov. 29, Dec. 6, 30, 1760.

property and for extraordinary expenses incurred in the public service, and to reward him for his devotion to duty. The commons house, which had hitherto looked askance at bills submitted by Stuart for unusual expenses, responded handsomely. It immediately resolved that the thanks of the house should be given to Stuart for his labors among the Cherokees, in particular for "his conduct & perseverance (amidst a variety of calamities) in the defence of Fort Loudoun"; that he be presented a gratuity of £1,500 (provincial currency) in compensation and as a mark of approbation by the commons; and that he be recommended "in the warmest manner by this house to the lieutenant governor, as a person highly deserving the favour of his honour, & promotion in the service of this province."[50]

[50] CHJSC, xxxiii, pt. 2, 29, 31, 34.

CHAPTER VIII

THE CHEROKEE WAR *(Continued)*

DURING a session of the South Carolina assembly held in October, 1760, the commons house harshly censured Bull's efforts to make peace with the Cherokees after the capitulation of Fort Loudoun, accused Bull of indolence in the conduct of the war, and demanded that it be pushed with unrelenting vigor. At the same time the house requested him to call upon Amherst for aid and to inform the general that the province had expended no less than £75,000 during the previous year and was in financial straits.

There was little foundation for the charges laid against Bull by the house. While it was engaged in throwing verbal brickbats at the lieutenant governor, 268 rangers commanded by Major William Thomson proceeded to Fort Prince George under Bull's orders to supply that post with provisions. This task was successfully completed at the middle of October without molestation from the Cherokees. Meanwhile, also under directions from Bull, provincial officers were striving to enlist troops, not only in South Carolina, but in North Carolina. At that time Bull hoped that Amherst would be able to send a detachment in time to join the provincials in laying waste the Cherokee towns during the following winter. If the Indians still refused to make peace, he proposed to organize a second raid in the spring to destroy their crops.[1] A month later Bull placed a different plan before Amherst: provincials from Virginia and North Carolina, supported if possible by regulars from Fort Pitt, should attack the Overhills in the spring, while the South Carolina men, assisted by another force of regulars, should smash through the Lower and Middle Cherokee towns to Choté. Fauquier and Dobbs supported this plan, but Amherst refused to send any troops to Virginia. Fauquier expected to place 1,000 men in the field; and

[1] CHJSC, xxxiii, pt. 2, 8–9, 11–12; Bull to Amherst, Oct. 19, 1760, CO, 5/60. For another criticism of Bull see Alexander Garden to Cadwallader Colden, *Collections of the New-York Historical Society for the Year 1921*, 362–63; but see also Ellis to Board of Trade, Sept. 6, 1760, *GCR*, XXVIII, pt. 1, 461–64, for a defense of Bull's policy.

Amherst believed that the Virginians, with or without help from North Carolina, would be strong enough to attack the Overhills.[2]

Immediately after learning of the fall of Fort Loudoun Amherst had actually made arrangements to dispatch another body of regulars to South Carolina. He detailed 1,200 men for this service, and a number of Mohawks and Stockbridge Indians under the leadership of Captain Quintin Kennedy were also collected for the expedition. Upon the recommendation of Montgomery, who was unable to serve and who gave Lieutenant Colonel Grant most of the credit for such successes as had been scored by the regulars in the first expedition, Amherst conferred the command upon Grant. As Montgomery had been, Grant was placed under orders to engage in offensive operations only; and he was instructed, if South Carolina failed to make adequate preparations for attacking the Cherokees, to return promptly to New York. He was not to meddle in peace negotiations with the Cherokees; they should be conducted by Bull and the South Carolina assembly. He was to assume the command of all troops serving offensively against the Indians. Grant set sail from New York on December 30. Although the little fleet carrying his men was scattered by a storm, all the ships reached Charleston Bar on January 6, 1761. However, Grant decided not to move upcountry until March, because grass to feed horses and cattle was lacking until that time.[3]

Bull was certainly not inactive during the winter of 1760–61. To occupy the Cherokees while preparations for Grant's march were under way Bull laid plans to send 600 foot and 400 rangers from their training camp at the Congarees to make a demonstration of force by marching to Fort Prince George. He dropped this project at a hint from Amherst. Late in November Bull did send out under Major Thomson a force of 450 rangers which traveled to and from Fort Prince George without molestation. Thomson placed a large supply of flour, a wagonload of salt, and 70 steers in the fort. In January Bull ordered a third relieving force, consisting of 550 rangers, to the fort with provisions. Again the rangers were not attacked, but they encamped carelessly six miles below the fort on their return journey and 125 horses belonging to them were stolen by lightfooted Cherokees. Since the Overhills threatened, if they were attacked,

[2] Bull to Amherst, Nov. 18, 1760, CO, 5/60; Fauquier to Amherst, Dec. 15, 1760, Amherst to Fauquier, Jan. 21, 1761, CO, 5/61.

[3] Amherst to Bull, Nov. 27, 1760, Amherst to Grant, Dec. 15, 1760, commission from Amherst to Grant, Dec. 15, 1760, Amherst to Grant, Dec. 21, 1760, CO, 5/60; Grant to Amherst, Jan. 7, 1761, CO, 5/61.

to kill all their captives, Bull secured a grant from the assembly of £6,000 (provincial currency) to buy goods with which to ransom the English prisoners. With Grant's approval he reappointed Lachlan McIntosh as commandant of Fort Prince George, to replace the odious Miln. At the fort McIntosh made excellent use of a large supply of goods furnished by Bull.[4]

The most perplexing problems confronting Bull in the winter of 1760–61 were those connected with raising provincial troops to serve under Grant. Grant reported that peace was "a most unfashionable topick" in Charleston, but that the South Carolinians seemed disinclined to take any active part in the war. According to Grant, some Charleston citizens desired war because of the money spent by the regulars in the provincial capital, while others wanted it because they were unduly concerned regarding their frontier plantations. He even went so far as to declare that the war then existed chiefly in the imaginations of Miln and his subordinates at Fort Prince George, whose representations of danger alarmed the province; that the Cherokees were more sinned against than sinning; and that they sincerely desired peace, but knew not how to obtain it.[5] While the bias of the regular army officer is evident in Grant's attitude, his strictures had some justification. On December 17 the provincial rangers mustered over 500 men, but Bull had been unable to enlist more than 400 men in the provincial regiment, and some of these were probably raised in North Carolina. Bull therefore sent out officers with cash to enlist as many as possible of 300 provincials recently disbanded by Dobbs because of inability to meet their pay. These officers had considerable success. Nevertheless, Colonel Henry Middleton, who commanded the South Carolina troops, could muster no more than 600 rangers and 600 foot when Grant advanced from Ninety-Six on May 18.[6]

[4] Bull to Board of Trade, Dec. 17, 1760, April 30, 1761, CO, 5/377; Bull to Amherst, Dec. 27, 1760, CO, 5/60; Bull to Amherst, Jan. 24, 1761, CO, 5/61. McIntosh is mentioned in correspondence as being a lieutenant when he first served at Fort Prince George. He was actually an ensign until Jan. 11, 1761. Then, upon Grant's recommendation, he was promoted to a lieutenancy by Amherst. Amherst to Grant, Jan. 14, 1761, CO, 5/60; *British Army Lists.*

[5] Grant to Amherst, Jan. 7, 1761, CO, 5/61.

[6] Bull to Board of Trade, Dec. 17, 1760, Jan. 29, 1761, CO, 5/377. At least 100 men—perhaps many more—of Middleton's infantry were enlisted in North Carolina. Bull was not satisfied that the South Carolinians had responded properly to the call to service, but he defended the province on the ground that it contained only 6,000 able-bodied white men and 57,000 potential "intestine" black enemies.

Since Grant's expedition was delayed for several months, North Carolina and Virginia had ample time to raise troops to attack the Overhills while Grant was advancing through the Lower and Middle towns. Nevertheless, it was not until April 23 that the North Carolina assembly voted funds to support 500 provincials for the purpose.[7] By *August 10* the men had been enlisted and were bivouacked at Fort Dobbs. Even then they lacked arms and waited for William Byrd to give the order to advance.[8] Byrd had again been appointed to command the expedition against the Cherokees from the north!

Virginia was not quite so dilatory as North Carolina. Fauquier made no real effort early in the year to enlist men, chiefly because he feared that the burgesses would refuse to pay them.[9] In March the burgesses voted to send 1,000 men against the Cherokees. The house, however, refused to allow the Virginians to advance without the support of a body of regulars. The excuse for this stand was that the Virginians might be overwhelmed, if the Cherokees concentrated their forces against them. But Amherst reiterated the opinion he had given when the campaign of 1761 was first planned—that the Virginians would be sufficiently strong to move against the Overhills without the aid of regulars and without assistance from North Carolina.[10] Although Byrd then asked the burgesses to permit him to enlist 700 more men, that body merely ordered him to march.[11] On July 19 Byrd was stationed at Samuel Stalnaker's plantation. He had only 600 men, and his supplies were inadequate. A week later he had decided to remain at Stalnaker's.[12]

While the military preparations of the English were on foot, opposition to the continuance of the war grew stronger among the Cherokees. During the latter months of 1760 and the early part of 1761 extensive negotiations were carried on between the Cherokees and Miln; and Bull received peace "talks" from some of the Lower and Middle towns. To be sure, the Overhills were apparently less

[7] Dobbs to Amherst, April 24, 1761, CO, 5/61.

[8] Bull to Amherst, Aug. 17, 1761, CO, 5/61.

[9] Fauquier to [Byrd], Feb. 16, 1761, *Journals of the House of Burgesses of Virginia, 1758–1761*, 270–71.

[10] Fauquier to Amherst, March 13, 1761, Amherst to John Robinson, March 25, 1761, CO, 5/60. Apparently the burgesses were not greatly worried regarding the safety of Byrd's men in 1760.

[11] Fauquier to Amherst, April 17, 1761, and enclosed address of the burgesses, CO, 5/61.

[12] Byrd to Bull, July 26, 1761, CHJSC, xxxiv, 242–43; Bull to Amherst, Aug. 17, 1761, CO, 5/61.

inclined to treat than were their brethren. Lantagnac failed to keep his promise to bring immediate aid to the Cherokees from Fort Toulouse, but a Settico chief and others who had accompanied Lantagnac to the French fort returned in December with supplies. About the same time Ouconnostotah brought in ammunition and goods from Fort Massac. Bull was consequently worried by a contemporaneous rumor—which proved to be without substantial foundation—that the French were building a post halfway between Fort Massac and Fort Loudoun.[13]

The Lower Cherokees displayed less and less interest in the war. The continued shortage of food and other supplies bore heavily upon them; they were pleased by the removal of Miln; and they liked Lachlan McIntosh. Finally, the bold Saluy himself laid down the tomahawk. This favorable turn of events was in part the result of good work by McIntosh. Coöperating with Attakullakulla he was able also to ransom prisoner after prisoner; by April 25 no fewer than 113 persons, over 70 of whom had served at Fort Loudoun, had been delivered at the fort.[14] However, some 100 persons were still held captive. Attakullakulla even attempted to negotiate a general peace through McIntosh, but Bull and his council refused to deal with Little Carpenter because they believed that the nation as a whole did not support him.[15]

Fortunately for the English, during this period the pro-French faction among the Creeks failed to gain in strength; rather, as time wore on and the French did not offer the trade so often promised, their influence tended to wane. Bull and James Wright, who succeeded Ellis on November 3, 1760, continued to make liberal presents to them. Numerous Creeks, notably the faithful Wolf King, visited Savannah and Charleston. Some difficulties developed in the Creek trade when it was gradually reopened in the latter part of 1760. Early in 1761 at least twenty-seven individuals or firms of South Carolina, many of them new entrants into the field, were engaged in it. Bull feared that the quantity of goods reaching the Creek country was too large, and that a portion might find its way to

[13] Bull to Amherst, Dec. 17, 1760, CO, 5/60; *South-Carolina Gazette*, Jan. 31, March 14, 1761.

[14] Dr. Thomas Walker and John Chiswell, acting as agents for Virginia, also ransomed a number of prisoners.

[15] Minutes of S. C. council, March 25, 26, May 6, 1761, Public Records of South Carolina, Historical Commission of South Carolina, iii, 334–35, 344; Bull to Amherst, April 15, 1761, "Talk" from Saluy to McIntosh, April 1, 1761, CO, 5/61; *South-Carolina Gazette*, May 9, 1761.

the Cherokees. He therefore vacated nine licenses. This precaution was undoubtedly well taken, but the presence of Grant and his northern Indian allies in South Carolina assured Creek neutrality, for Bull astutely arranged matters so that Creeks visiting Charleston met Grant's Mohawks. As a result, the Creeks learned for themselves that the Mohawks were determined to assist the English and that Quebec had fallen. In February, 1760, Bull felt that a difficult corner in Anglo-Creek relations was definitely turned. The final blow to French hopes that the Creeks might intervene in the Cherokee War apparently came in the following month, when French officials admitted to a great conclave of Creeks at Fort Toulouse that they could not give a trade. According to report, even The Mortar then declared himself in favor of a policy of neutrality.[16]

At Ninety-Six Grant made his final dispositions for the campaign against the Cherokees. About 200 regulars who were unable to march were relieved from duty; and a considerable part of the provincials, both horse and foot, was stationed at the Congarees and at Ninety-Six to secure his line of communications. A striking force of 2,250 men, of whom more than one half were regulars,[17] followed Grant to Fort Prince George. On May 27 the army reached the fort, where it was joined by twenty Catawbas under "King" Hagler and as many Savannah River Chickasaws. These, added to the northern warriors under Captain Kennedy and eleven Chickasaws from the nation proper under Captain James Colbert, insured the army against surprise.

While on the march toward Keowee Grant received a message from Little Carpenter urging a peace settlement, but he refused to treat unless all the Fort Loudoun captives were freed and all the Cherokees laid down their arms. At Fort Prince George Little Carpenter again tried to secure peace. He urged Grant to delay his operations until he had had an opportunity to ask the Cherokees to submit to Grant's terms, but the commander politely refused.[18]

On June 7 Grant took the trail followed by Montgomery the previous year. Three days later considerable bodies of Cherokees

[16] Bull to Amherst, Jan. 24, 1761, CO, 5/61; Bull to Board of Trade, Feb. 17, 1761, CO, 5/377; minutes of S. C. council, Jan. 30, Feb. 6, 11, 26, 1761, Public Records of South Carolina, iii, 304, 314, 316–21, 324–26; Wright to Board of Trade, May 16, 1761, *GCR,* XXVIII, pt. 1, 551; *South-Carolina Gazette,* May 16, 1761.

[17] The troops left behind by Montgomery were included in Grant's army.

[18] Bull to Board of Trade, May 28, June 19, 1761, CO, 5/377; *South-Carolina Gazette,* June 13, 1761. While at Keowee Grant gave permission to Tistoe of Keowee and sixty or seventy friendly Cherokees to resettle near the fort.

attacked his army at a spot only two miles distant from that at which Montgomery had been assailed. In a sharp action nine members of the English force, including one Indian, were slain, and forty-seven were wounded; but the Cherokees were driven off with considerable losses. Grant immediately pushed on to Etchoe. Shortly afterward, leaving Middleton with 1,000 men to guard provisions at Etchoe, Grant advanced into the Middle settlements. No opposition worthy of the name appeared. Grant destroyed no fewer than fifteen Middle towns on the upper branches of the Little Tennessee River, and Indian refugees poured into the Overhill country. The army then rapidly made its way through the hills back to Fort Prince George. The men were in a state of utter exhaustion when they reached it on July 9. Grant's Indian allies, especially the Chickasaws under Captain Colbert, had rendered useful service in scouting and had not failed to bring in enemy scalps.[19]

Since Grant destroyed the crops as well as the huts of the Cherokees and made likely a severe food shortage in the Lower and Middle towns, he was inclined to believe that the Indians would have to sue for peace. Refraining from further action against the Cherokees, he remained at Fort Prince George in the hope that Ouconnostotah would join Attakullakulla in negotiating. This policy, which had the approval of Bull and Amherst, was justified. Lantagnac brought nine horseloads of ammunition from Fort Toulouse to the Overhill towns in May, but the Great Warrior was weary of the conflict. He let it be known that he was willing to accept a pacification,[20] and on July 6 Attakullakulla, with forty-three other Cherokees, appeared at Byrd's camp to sue for peace. Byrd referred him to Bull for terms, since Fauquier had agreed that South Carolina should deal for all the colonies concerned. On August 9 Tistoe of Keowee and Slavecatcher of Tomotley, commissioned to negotiate by Ouconnostotah himself and by Kanagataucko, reached Fort Prince George. Grant desired that the great chiefs of the nation, especially Ouconnostotah, should come in person. He therefore sent back these emissaries with John Watts, at that time a captain in the provincial rangers, to bring down more influential leaders. The Great Warrior hesitated, but finally refused, because he feared for

[19] Grant to Amherst, July 10, 1761, and Grant's journal of the campaign, June 7—July 9, 1761, CO, 5/61; Bull to Board of Trade, July 17, 1761, CO, 5/377; minutes of S. C. council, Aug. 5, Sept. 12, 1761, Public Records of South Carolina, iii, 380–83, 392–95.

[20] The Overhills apparently offered their brethren little assistance against Grant.

his life. However, Attakullakulla and eight other chiefs fully empowered to treat reached Fort Prince George on August 28.[21]

Foreseeing that the Cherokees would apply to Grant for peace terms, Bull had provided that officer with stipulations for a preliminary treaty. The first of these required the execution of one Cherokee leader from each of the four parts of the nation. Others provided for exchange of prisoners, reopening of the trade, permission for the English to build forts in the Cherokee country at will, and recognition of Attakullakulla as "emperor." In addition, the Cherokees were to bury the hatchet with the Catawbas and Chickasaws. Grant deleted the clause requiring recognition of Little Carpenter as "emperor," for he believed that Attakullakulla's authority could not be increased by a treaty stipulation. He laid the remaining provisions before the Cherokee emissaries on September 2. Attakullakulla indicated that they were not empowered to agree to the execution of four Cherokee leaders. Grant thought that the Indians had been sufficiently punished, and he was eager to obtain a settlement, especially since the South Carolina infantry was already disbanding for lack of pay. He therefore urged the Cherokee ambassadors to go on to Charleston to deal with Bull, at the same time making it clear that Bull would probably be willing to delete the offending clause. After some delay, caused by the intrigues of a trader whom Grant had thrown into irons, the Cherokees agreed.[22] On the following day they departed for Charleston in the company of Henry Laurens[23] and other officers.

On September 10 Bull and his council considered the situation in the light of the parley at Keowee and decided to convene the assembly so that the commons house could participate in the negotiations with Attakullakulla and his colleagues. Since there was a report that yellow fever existed in Charleston, the assembly was summoned to gather at Ashley Ferry. On Sunday, September 13, Laurens, Attakullakulla, and their party reached town; and on the

[21] Grant to Bull, Sept. 2, 1761, Byrd to Bull, July 26, 1761, CHJSC, xxxiv, 240–42, 242–43; Amherst to Grant, Aug. 1, 1761, Bull to Amherst, Aug. 17, 1761, CO, 5/61; Bull to Board of Trade, July 17, 1761, CO, 5/377; *South-Carolina Gazette,* June 20, Aug. 22, Sept. 5, 1761. Fauquier suggested that commissioners from Virginia and South Carolina join in dealing with the Cherokees. But Amherst and Bull argued that South Carolina should act for all the English, and Fauquier consented. Bull to Amherst, June 6, July 11, 1761, CO, 5/61.

[22] Bull to Grant, April 14, 1761, Grant to Bull, Sept. 2, 1761, CHJSC, xxxiv, 237–40, 240–42; Grant to Amherst, Sept. 3, 1761, CO, 5/61.

[23] Laurens had served as lieutenant colonel of the South Carolina regiment.

same day John Stuart, who had taken no part in Grant's expedition, escorted his Indian friend to Ashley Ferry,[24] where conferences began immediately. Two days later the assembly was formally opened.

Since Bull, like Grant, believed that the Cherokees had been effectively chastised, he did not insist that the Cherokee leaders suffer death; and he quickly came to an agreement with Attakullakulla on other points. But the commons house condemned Bull's policy of prudence, and proposed two further stipulations: that the Cherokees promise never to come below 26-Mile Creek,[25] except when authorized by proper authority, and that all white renegades who had lent aid to the Cherokees be given up. The latter recommendation of the house was inserted in the treaty. So was the former, by accident rather than by design. Bull states that it was mistakenly copied into the treaty when he was ill. The preliminary treaty was signed on September 22 by Little Carpenter.[26]

Attakullakulla returned to his nation to bring down a delegation of chiefs to ratify the final peace. When he reached Fort Prince George on his way to Choté, Grant suggested that it would be wise for the Cherokees also to send delegates to Virginia to notify that colony of the peace. The Indians decided to send out the two embassies. Ouconnostotah and Usteneka were still unwilling to risk their persons, but Attakullakulla, the "Prince" of Choté, seven other chiefs, and a number of warriors arrived at Fort Prince George in mid-November en route to Charleston. Attakullakulla was apparently escorted from Goose Creek to Charleston by John Stuart

[24] Minutes of S. C. council, Sept. 10, Nov. 13, 1761, Public Records of South Carolina, iii, 390–91, 411–13; item from Charleston in *Virginia Gazette*, Oct. 2, 1761, in volume entitled, Cherokee Indians, 1760–1774, Division of Manuscripts, Library of Congress.

[25] A stream running across the trading path below Keowee, supposedly twenty-six miles from Keowee.

[26] Address by commons house to Bull, Sept. 18, 1761, CHJSC, xxxiv, 254–56; minute of S. C. council, Sept. 22, 1761, Public Records of South Carolina, iii, 398–403; Bull to Board of Trade, Sept. 23, 1761, CO, 5/377. In criticizing the terms of the preliminary peace the commons house showed animosity toward Grant. Yet Grant had rendered the province very useful service, especially when viewed in the light of the inadequate military support given him by the province. Shortly afterward a heated controversy arose as to the relative merits of the regulars and the provincials which was enlivened by a bloodless duel between Grant and Middleton. Since Grant and many of his officers and men were Scots, an anti-Scottish feeling developed in South Carolina. Incidentally, Grant reported to Amherst that the South Carolina men, both horse and foot, behaved well.

and Henry Laurens.[27] In December he held numerous "talks" with Colonel Othniel Beale, who acted for Bull during his illness. The definitive treaty, signed on December 17, differed from the preliminary document in two important details. Attakullakulla complained that the backsettlers would occupy the east bank of 26-Mile River if the Cherokees were not permitted to hunt below that stream, and that the Lower townsmen would consequently be sorely crowded by the whites. Bull readily offered to let 40-Mile River serve as a limit, and Attakullakulla agreed. A second change was necessary because Bull would not promise to reopen the trade except at Keowee.[28] Five days later Thomas Boone, a former resident of South Carolina who had been appointed governor on May 4, 1761, reached Charleston. He and the council smoothed over a minor difficulty that arose from the dissatisfaction of the Cherokees with the presents given them; and the Indians left Charleston in excellent spirits. They brought home to their nation peace with honor, but they lost some of their horses to thieving backsettlers.[29] The war was finally ended.

While all these negotiations were going on, Byrd resigned his command to Lieutenant Colonel Adam Stephen and hurried off to explain to Amherst his failure to attack the Overhills; and Fauquier traveled to New York for the same purpose. Probably the general was not difficult to satisfy, since he had privately doubted that the Virginians would do more than make a feint.[30] Early in October Stephen was finally joined by Hugh Waddell with over 300 North Carolinians and a few Tuscaroras.[31] Although Stephen and Waddell did not advance beyond Long Island their presence at no great distance from the Overhill towns possibly encouraged the Overhills to make peace. On November 17 Kanagataucko reached Stephen's camp with the news of the preliminary treaty,[32] but Stephen and his men remained on the Holston until peace was assured and spring

[27] "Talk" from Attakullakulla to Bull and Grant, Nov. 16, 1761, CHJSC, xxxiv, 260–62; Bull to Board of Trade, Dec. 5, 1761, CO, 5/377; *South-Carolina Gazette,* Nov. 28, 1761.

[28] Minutes of S. C. council, Dec. 12, 16, 17, 1761, Public Records of South Carolina, iii, 420–22, 422–26, 427–34.

[29] Minutes of S. C. council, Dec. 26, 28, 1761, Public Records of South Carolina, iii, 441–42, 443–44; *South-Carolina Gazette,* Feb. 2, 1762.

[30] Minute of Va. council, Sept. 11, 1761, CO, 5/1435; Amherst to Bull, July 2, 1761, CO, 5/61.

[31] Minutes of Va. council, Oct. 17, 19, 1761, CO, 5/1435.

[32] Minute of Va. council, Dec. 10, 1761, CO, 5/1435; minute of Va. council, Nov. 7, 1761, in MS volume of council journals of Virginia, 1722–1773, Virginia State Library.

was on the way. One of the Virginia officers, Lieutenant Henry Timberlake, took the opportunity to visit the Overhill towns. Timberlake and Thomas Sumter turned up at Williamsburg in April with Usteneka and seventy other Cherokees. Long jealous of the prestige held by Attakullakulla because of his visit to London in 1729–30, Usteneka begged to be sent to England. Fauquier agreed, and Usteneka, two other Cherokee warriors, Timberlake, Sumter, and an interpreter set out. Unfortunately, the interpreter died on the voyage, and there was no one in London who could converse with the Cherokees. In spite of linguistic difficulties they were dined by Henry Ellis, painted by Sir Joshua Reynolds, and received at court. Usteneka was a thorough Anglophile when he disembarked at Charleston at the beginning of November, 1762.[33]

Kerlérec was apparently almost the last person in America to learn that the Cherokee War was over. In the late spring of 1762 he was planning to use part of a substantial supply of Indian goods that arrived from France in April to encourage the Cherokees to redouble their efforts against the English; and he commissioned Lantagnac to invite the Cherokee chiefs to visit him.[34] Justification for the error made by Kerlérec is not difficult to find; some time in the early months of 1762 Ouconnostotah visited New Orleans. But the Great Warrior was not disposed to renew hostilities when he returned to Choté late in June.[35]

The name of Edmund Atkin is not mentioned in connection with Anglo-Cherokee relations after May, 1760. When Montgomery marched westward from Fort Prince George, Atkin did not accompany him, but remained with the wounded at the fort.[36] In July, 1760, as the result of earlier arrangements made with Dobbs and Lyttelton, he traveled to Pine Tree Hill on the Catawba River to negotiate with the Catawbas regarding the problem caused by the encroachments of North Carolinians upon their lands. There he

[33] London officials did not know whether or not Usteneka was pleased by the treatment he received at London until reports were sent from Charleston. For accounts of Usteneka's visit to England see Samuel C. Williams, ed., *Lieut. Henry Timberlake's Memoirs* (Johnson City, Tenn., 1927), and Anne K. Gregorie, *Thomas Sumter* (Columbia, S. C., 1931), 6–23.

[34] Kerlérec to ministry, June 24, July 26, 1762, ANC, C13A, 43. At this time Kerlérec finally gave Lantagnac a lieutenancy.

[35] *South-Carolina Gazette,* July 31, 1762. The article on Ouconnostotah in the *Dictionary of American Biography* states that he may have accompanied Usteneka to England. There is no evidence to show that he did; and he could not have been at both Choté and London in June, 1762.

[36] *South-Carolina Gazette,* July 5, 1760.

secured the signature of a treaty in which they abandoned all their lands except for an area roughly fifteen miles square on the Catawba River and promised further assistance against the Cherokees. In return, Atkin pledged that a fort would be built for their protection. On August 5, with "King" Hagler and three of his followers, Atkin appeared at Charleston. On October 14 the South Carolina assembly implemented this treaty by voting £700 (provincial currency) to erect the fort,[37] but Dobbs refused for some time to recognize its validity. According to Governor Boone, Dobbs desired part of the lands reserved to the Catawbas for himself and used his official position to have surveys made to his satisfaction.[38] Whether these lands lay within North Carolina or South Carolina remained an open question until 1772, but in 1763 the reservation was finally recognized by all concerned. (See Map 2, p. 102.)

Atkin's dealings with the Catawbas in the summer of 1760 were his last official acts as superintendent. He sat upon the South Carolina council from August 11 to October 16, acting as president upon several occasions in the absence of Bull. Apparently his health had failed, for he resigned from the council on October 23 of the same year.[39] He died on October 8, 1761, at his Mars Bluff plantation near the Pedee River.[40]

Because of lack of information one hesitates to offer definite judgments regarding Edmund Atkin. However, certain very general conclusions may be drawn with safety. Atkin failed to establish a strong Indian department in the South. Although he made some attempts to secure control over trade, both commercial and political relations with the southern Indians during his period of office remained largely in the hands of the southern colonial governments, as they had been in the years before the French and Indian War. Atkin rendered some services of value in Virginia in 1757, and others during later years, but it is doubtful that he accomplished more than Henry Fox and Halifax had expected when they gave him his appointment. Atkin was probably not a man of marked ability. Condemnation of him may easily go beyond what he deserved, for he never received adequate support from the commander in chief. What he might have achieved if Loudoun and Amherst had supplied him with funds equal to those furnished to Johnson it is dif-

[37] CHJSC, xxxiii, pt. 2, 14–15; *South-Carolina Gazette,* Aug. 9, 1760.

[38] Boone to Board of Trade, Oct. 9, 1762, CO, 5/377.

[39] Minute of S. C. council, Nov. 1, 1760.

[40] Alexander S. Salley, Jr., ed., *Death Notices in the South-Carolina Gazette, 1732–1775* (Columbia, S. C., 1917), 29.

ficult to say. The actual services of Atkin to the crown were possibly worth his salary and the £1,500 in expense acounts[41] that were submitted for the whole period of his superintendency. The judgment of his contemporaries, except for Dinwiddie, was uniformly that Atkin was unfitted for his office.[42]

Except for the eccentric James Adair, no informed person living in the latter half of the eighteenth century contended that Atkin's successor did not deserve his post. At the close of the Cherokee War Attakullakulla informed Bull and his council that peace between the English and the Cherokees would be assured if his friend Stuart were sent to the nation as provincial Indian agent.[43] Better things, however, were in store for Stuart. Before assuming office as governor of South Carolina Thomas Boone had held a similar appointment in New Jersey. When he learned of Atkin's death, he called upon Amherst at New York, in November, 1761, and urged the general to recommend Stuart for the southern superintendency. Precisely why Boone undertook to push Stuart's fortunes is not certain, although it is very likely that the two men were personally acquainted, since Boone, a member of an old South Carolina family, had lived on Charleston Bay from 1752 to 1754, when Stuart was operating as a merchant in the same locale. In any case, Boone cogently argued that Stuart had saved the larger part of the garrison of Fort Loudoun, and convinced Amherst that his request was a disinterested one. Amherst's letter of recommendation to William Pitt, dated November 27,[44] reached London, after a very swift pas-

[41] For a brief discussion of Atkin's expense accounts see Helen Louise Shaw, *British Administration of the Southern Indians, 1756–1783* (Lancaster, Pa., 1931), 53–54.

[42] Lord Shelburne thought that Atkin was utterly unworthy of his position. "Shelburne's Observations upon a Plan for the future Management of Indian Affairs," Shelburne MSS, William L. Clements Library, lx. Dr. Alexander Garden, a Charleston physician personally acquainted with Atkin, wrote in 1758: "...how far the design and import of that appointment [of Atkin] will be answered by a man whose sole business is to cook good dinners for himself in Charlestown, time, and probably the defection of some one or other of these [Indian] nations, will shew." Garden to John Ellis, Aug. 11, 1758, Sir James Edward Smith, ed., *A Selection of the Correspondence of Linnaeus, and Other Naturalists...* (London, 1821), I, 427.

[43] A. Hewatt, *An Historical Account of the Rise and Progress of the Colonies of South Carolina and Georgia* (London, 1779), II, 276.

[44] Amherst to Pitt, Nov. 27, 1761, Gertrude S. Kimball, ed., *Correspondence of William Pitt, when Secretary of State, with Colonial Governors, and Military and Naval Commissioners in America* (New York, 1906), II, 487; Amherst to Stuart, March 18, 1763, Amherst MSS, William L. Clements Library; American Loyalist Transcripts, New York Public Library, liii, 449; *South-Carolina Gazette,*

sage, on December 26; and on January 12, 1762, the Earl of Egremont informed Amherst that Stuart had been appointed.[45] Stuart's commission was dated January 5, 1762,[46] and the news of his appointment reached him in May, 1762.[47] He did not actually receive the document until February, 1763. Before that time Stuart felt that he lacked authority to interfere in Indian affairs.[48]

March 19, 1753. It may or may not be significant that Lawrence Read, New York merchant who served as Superintendent Stuart's agent, was on very friendly terms with Boone. See *Collections of the New-York Historical Society for the Year 1899* (New York, 1900), 243–45. Read may have been a relative of Patrick Reid, Stuart's merchant partner at Charleston. The fact that the name is spelled differently does not preclude this possibility. It is perhaps of no great importance whether personal relationships in part motivated Boone's championship of Stuart. William Gerard De Brahm afterward claimed that he was responsible for Stuart's appointment. De Brahm to Earl of Dartmouth, Oct. 23, 1773, *Royal Historical Manuscripts Commission, Fourteenth Report,* Appendix, pt. 10, 173. Ordinarily, no reliance can be placed in De Brahm's statements. But it is possible that he urged Boone to support Stuart. It is also possible that he independently solicited the appointment for Stuart from the imperial government. Amherst's recommendation may have been supported by Anson, who was in the cabinet at the time.

[45] Egremont to Amherst, Jan. 12, 1762, CO, 5/214.

[46] There are two certified copies of the commission in the Gage MSS.

[47] Minute of S. C. council, May 31, 1762, Public Records of South Carolina, iii, 510–13.

[48] Stuart to Amherst, Feb. 25, 1763, Amherst MSS. One unsuccessful applicant for the southern superintendency was Major Robert Rogers, who secured a recommendation from the council of North Carolina and sought Amherst's favor, but failed to obtain it. At the time Rogers was in command of one of the companies of Independent Regulars in South Carolina. Dobbs to Egremont, Dec. —, 1761, *NCCR,* VI, 596; memorial by Rogers to Amherst, Oct. 24, 1761, WO, 34/47. Another unsuccessful aspirant was Lieutenant Colonel Adam Stephen. Fauquier recommended him to the Board of Trade, but informed the board that he did so at Stephen's request. Fauquier's letter of recommendation was written over a month after Stuart was appointed. Fauquier to Board of Trade, Feb. 24, 1762, CO, 5/1330.

PART II

IMPERIAL MANAGEMENT OF INDIAN RELATIONS UNDER JOHN STUART, 1763–75

CHAPTER IX

EVOLUTION OF THE OFFICE OF SUPERINTENDENT[1]

THE management of Indian affairs in the South between the close of the Seven Years' War and the clash of arms in 1775 was largely in the hands of John Stuart. Because as superintendent he was a part of the imperial system for governing the colonies and because his work was greatly affected by other units in that system, some further discussion of the powers and duties of the superintendents, their connections with officials at London, their relations with other officials in America, and their rank in the colonial hierarchy is essential. Since Stuart's labors were also conditioned by his own personality, an effort had been made in Chapter X to describe his background, his early career, his family, his social connections, and his character.

The imperial office of superintendent existed during a period of almost thirty years in that part of North America which became the United States, and disappeared only when the Thirteen Colonies gained their independence. Johnson continued as superintendent in the North until his death in 1774, and was followed by Guy Johnson, his nephew and son-in-law,[2] who held office until the close of the Revolution.[3] As we have seen, Edmund Atkin served in the southern district from 1756 to 1761. Stuart held the southern post until 1779. From 1779 to 1783 the southern district was divided into two parts, known as the eastern and western divisions. Thomas

[1] Substantiation for some points made in this chapter will be found in other chapters.

[2] Guy Johnson is incorrectly named as a son of Sir William in Clarence W. Alvord and Clarence E. Carter, eds., "The Critical Period, 1763–1765," *Collections of the Illinois State Historical Library,* X, British Series, I (Springfield, Ill., 1915), 467, note. Hereafter this volume and its companions in the British Series, "The New Régime, 1765–1767" (Springfield, Ill., 1916), and "Trade and Politics, 1767–1769" (Springfield, Ill., 1921), will be cited as *Ill. Hist. Colls.,* X, XI, and XVI.

[3] In 1783 Sir John Johnson, son of Sir William, was given a commission as superintendent and inspector general of Indian affairs, but the jurisdiction of his office was confined to Canada.

Browne managed the eastern division during the four years of its existence; and Alexander Cameron and John Graham controlled the western area from 1779 to 1781 and from 1782 to 1783 respectively.[4]

While the office existed, the superintendents, in theory if not always in practice, conducted the political relations of the English with the Indians. They were at least partly responsible for the protection of the Indians themselves against lawless land speculators and other evildoers. After 1763 the duties of the agents also included the formation and maintenance of the Indian boundary lines. Theoretically Edmund Atkin had substantial control of the meager Indian trade carried on from North Carolina after 1757; and Johnson and Sir Jeffrey Amherst as a temporary measure used the military officers at the western posts to supervise the trade in the St. Lawrence valley during the last years of the French and Indian War. But with these exceptions management of the trade remained in the hands of the colonial governments until 1765. From 1765 to 1768 Stuart and Johnson attempted to control the trade, until the home government finally ordered them to desist. Until his death Stuart made sporadic efforts to regain authority over it. In wartime the superintendents arranged for the enlistment of Indians as auxiliary troops. Johnson, Atkin, and Stuart raised Indian warriors to serve against the French and their allies before 1765; and all the superintendents tried to get Indian help against the Americans in the Revolution. As a matter of policy, the superintendents should have had complete charge of the distribution of the vast amounts of presents that were given the Indians to secure their good will, their approval to land cessions, and their aid in warfare, but the governors commonly purchased or received supplies of goods from England and gave them out independently.

The work of the agents was not confined to Indian affairs. Johnson commanded provincial troops in the Seven Years' War; and the superintendents organized and sent bands of Loyalists against the Americans during the Revolution. By the famous Proclamation of 1763 they and their subordinates were instructed to apprehend criminals who had taken refuge in the Indian reservation created by the proclamation and to return them to the colonies from which they fled. One most interesting activity of John Stuart was his su-

[4] Immediately after the death of Stuart, in March, 1779, Governor Peter Chester of West Florida appointed a board of commissioners to execute the duties of the southern superintendent until orders came from England. This board continued to act until the following September.

pervision of the manufacture of several maps important for the study of Indian boundary lines and the locations of Indian tribes and villages in the South.

If one were to accept as definitive certain writings of Professor Clarence E. Carter, long an earnest student of the pre-Revolutionary West, the following extensive discussion of the development of the office of superintendent would be more or less superfluous. Professor Carter has set forth an interesting contention to the effect that the office of commander in chief of the British armed forces in America tended during the pre-Revolutionary period to become a vice-royalty; that the military commanders were primarily responsible for the formation and execution of Indian policy; and that the superintendents were directly responsible to them. As he states it, "Another phase of supreme authority exercised by the military office was the administration of Indian affairs, which had been designated by the Crown in 1755 to the commander in chief in America; it continued to be so directed." He points out in support of this thesis that Johnson's first commission emanated from Braddock; [5] that Johnson by a royal commission given him in 1761 [6] was ordered "punctually to obey" the directions of the military commander; and that the salaries of the Indian officials were included in the budget of the military establishment. He also thinks that "It is not without significance that the areas included in the northern and southern superintendencies corresponded in general with the two military districts created in 1764, each under a brigadier general." Professor Carter continues:

> The superintendents believed that their functions were such as to give them a separate status; and though they were surely aware of the source of their powers they stoutly opposed the complete subordination of their departments. Sir William Johnson, for example, lodged a series of complaints, but he appears to have become reconciled to the relationship by the time General Gage became his superior. John Stuart, the southern superintendent, continued to chafe under the restriction for some time, however.

According to Professor Carter, it was therefore necessary for Lord Shelburne, in a letter of December 11, 1766, to remind Stuart, and

[5] Professor Carter fails to note that Braddock chose Johnson because the general's instructions required him to do so. Johnson's first commission was dictated by the Board of Trade and the secretaries of state. See John R. Alden, "The Albany Congress and the Creation of the Indian Superintendencies," *Miss. Vall. Hist. Rev.,* XXVII (1940), 201, 207–8.

[6] This commission was in the same terms as that given Johnson in 1756. It was apparently issued because of the accession of a new king, George III.

the superintendents in general, of their proper position. He quotes the following passage:

> As to what you propose of Instructions to be given to the Governors to correspond with the Superintendants, His Majesty thinks it will answer sufficiently that your regular and fixed correspondence be with the Commander-in-Chief of His Majesty's Forces, the System of Indian Affairs as managed by the Superintendants must ultimately be under his Direction. The different Governors can scarcely be supposed to coincide in opinion, nor is it possible for so many to act in Concert. You are therefore to take the Orders of the Commander-in-Chief on all interesting Occasions, who being settled in the Center of the Colonies will carry on the Correspondence with the Governors on all such Points ... and as he will be very particularly instructed by Administration, you are to look upon him as a proper Medium of material intelligence either to or from England or the Colonies.[7]

Professor Carter thinks that "Such instructions were sufficiently explicit to admit of no reservation, and seem definitely to have settled the relationship." [8] Nevertheless, this rather simple hypothesis in regard to a complicated relationship will be found on close examination to be quite unsatisfactory.

While it is certainly true that the military commanders in America were authorized to play an important rôle in Indian affairs and that some of these officers took considerable interest in such matters, it is equally certain that they never had supreme authority. After 1756 the military commanders no longer exercised the power to appoint the Indian superintendents; [9] they held commissions

[7] Shelburne to Stuart, Dec. 11, 1766, Gage MSS.

[8] Professor Carter's theory was set forth first in "The Significance of the Military Office in America, 1763–1775," *Am. Hist. Rev.*, XXVIII (1923), 475–88, again in the introduction to his edition of *The Correspondence of General Thomas Gage* (New Haven, 1931–33), and is most fully developed in an essay on "The Office of Commander in Chief: A Phase of Imperial Unity on the Eve of the Revolution," in Richard B. Morris, ed., *The Era of the American Revolution* (New York, 1939), 170–213. Certain arguments adduced by Professor Carter in his earlier writings to prove the complete subordination of the Indian agents to the military commanders have been eliminated or modified in his most recent discussion. Thus a statement that the commissions of the superintendents were originally given by the military commander and that they were renewed by the successive generals, an obvious error, has been deleted from his latest essay.

[9] The recommendation of the commander in chief was of prime importance in the selection of a superintendent when a vacancy occurred. Thus Gage's recommendation of Guy Johnson to succeed his uncle, made at Sir William's request, was instrumental in securing Guy Johnson's appointment. Strange to say, the nephew was not actually given a commission until three years later. He was at first merely authorized to exercise his uncle's authority. Evidently Lord Dartmouth hoped for a time to obtain the northern superintendency for one of his own sons. Gage to Dartmouth, July 18, 1774, *Gage Corr.*, I, 360; Dartmouth to Guy Johnson, Sept. 8, 1774, *NYCD*, VIII, 489; Peter Orlando Hutchin-

from the crown that required them "punctually to obey" instructions from the commander in chief. Obviously the superintendents were always required to render obedience to the commands of the ranking general in America in regard to political relations with the Indians, *provided those commands did not conflict with instructions received by the Indian agents from the Board of Trade and the secretaries of state.* This fact was recognized by all the superintendents. On several occasions Johnson tried, unsuccessfully, to persuade the home government to release him from this fixed obligation. While Stuart undoubtedly would have preferred to be freed from it, there is no evidence that he chafed under the restriction.[10] The Shelburne letter does not have the meaning attached to it by Professor Carter; it arose from a mere request made by Stuart that the southern governors be ordered to correspond with him, because these governors did not always reply to his letters.[11] Actually, Stuart frequently asked Gage—commander in chief from 1763 to 1775—for orders before 1766, much more commonly than he did after that time.[12] No other specific authority over Indian policy was given

son, ed., *The Diary and Letters of His Excellency Thomas Hutchinson* . . . (Boston, 1884–86), I, 232. Stuart was chosen largely though the influence of Amherst, and Cameron through that of Sir Henry Clinton. Germain to Clinton, June 25, 1779, Sir Henry Clinton MSS, William L. Clements Library. Guy Johnson was also given, until the home government could act, an *ad interim* appointment by Gage. Gage to Guy Johnson, July 17, 1774, Gage MSS. Cameron received a similar appointment from Clinton. Clinton to Germain, May 3, 1779, Sir Henry Clinton MSS.

[10] Professor Carter fails to cite evidence that Stuart protested against this obligation, nor do I find any. It is true that in 1764 Stuart suggested completely independent Indian departments as an ideal.

[11] Stuart to Sir Henry Conway, Aug. 8, 1766, CO, 5/67. The letter was received by Shelburne.

[12] Immediately on receipt of his commission Stuart wrote to Amherst: "His Majesty's service shall not suffer for want of my zeal and assiduity in executing such commands as Your Excellency may think proper to honour me with." Stuart to Amherst, Feb. 25, 1763, Amherst MSS. Stuart frequently asked Gage for instructions in 1764 and 1765. Concerning Shelburne's letter of Dec. 11, 1766, Stuart could therefore write to Gage: "The sense of administration expressed therein I shall strictly observe and be directed by. I always considered it as my duty to be ultimately directed by your Excelly in the management of Indian affairs within my department and shall with the greatest alacrity & satisfaction endeavor to execute your commands." Stuart to Gage, April 18, 1767, Gage MSS. This letter and Gage's reply might well have been noted by Professor Carter. Gage answered: "You express your reddiness to obey any orders I shall transmit you in a very obliging manner, for which I am much indebted to you. Tho' I apprehend that I shall seldom have occasion to trouble you further than to cooperate with you in every measure that shall appear to be conducive to the publick good." Gage to Stuart, May 16, 1767, *ibid.*

the military commanders by the British government in 1755 or thereafter.[13] So far as the Indian commerce was concerned, the military office was not authorized to interfere. During the Seven Years' War Johnson tried to obtain an order from Loudoun and Amherst giving him control of the trade, but both generals refused to comply, since they lacked power from London.[14] The authority of the colonial governments over the trade remained complete until 1766, except that such trading as was carried on between 1759 and 1765 in areas formerly occupied by the French and Spanish was necessarily under the control of the military until the pacification of those areas.

Professor Carter thinks it significant that the Indian departments coincided in general with the northern and southern military departments under the brigadier generals after 1764, but the coincidence was extremely superficial. The authority of the brigadier generals in the South was confined to the Floridas from 1764 to 1775, while Suart's department certainly was not limited to those two provinces; [15] and the brigadiers stationed in Canada did not exercise control over all that wide area covered by Johnson's department. Even if very substantial similarities existed after 1764, no conclusion could be drawn from the fact unless the similarities were purposive and the brigadier generals were given authority over the superintendents. Actually, the jurisdiction of the Indian agents was based, as we have seen, on Indian policy, and was limited to certain Indian tribes. Thus in 1755 Johnson was given control of relations with the Iroquois and their allies because they could be managed as a unit. When the tribes north and west of the Ohio River acknowledged English overlordship, they were also incorporated into his department, partly because the Six Nations had a claim to suzerainty over some of these tribes and partly because Johnson's aides could reach them more easily than Stuart's.[16] The authority of the southern agents was limited in similar fashion. Both Atkin and Stuart were appointed as superintendents for the Indian nations and their allies on the borders of the southern colonies; and when all the territory between the Ohio River and the Gulf of Mexico

[13] Braddock and his successors were empowered to *advise* the governors regarding distribution of Indian presents, but the governors usually did not bother to ask the generals for advice.

[14] See Amherst to Johnson, Feb. 22, 1761, WO, 34/38, pt. 1.

[15] The royal troops stationed in South Carolina and Georgia from 1763 to 1768 were under the command of an officer who reported directly to Gage.

[16] See Gage to Johnson, Feb. 25, 1765, Gage MSS.

became English in 1763, the few tribes in that area that had not previously had dealings with the southern agent came under his management as a matter of course. The well-known "Plan for the Future Management of Indian Affairs" of 1764 also contemplated the division of the Indians between the superintendents on the basis of tribes. The evolution of the northern and southern military districts surely followed a very different course, on principles peculiar to the organization and functions of the army. Their bounds did not closely coincide with those of the Indian districts during the Seven Years' War, and probably never did.[17]

The Indian agents were not subject to orders from the brigadiers until near the close of the Revolution. In 1766 Lieutenant Colonel William Tayler, acting brigadier in the Floridas after the death of General Bouquet, complained to Gage that he was not consulted on Indian affairs in West Florida; [18] and Gage ordered Stuart to concert with Haldimand, about to become brigadier in that area, on all Indian problems involving peace and war.[19] Stuart immediately protested, pointing out that Indian affairs, to a greater or a lesser extent, always involved peace and war. He could not consider himself to be "charged with or responsible for the trust which seems to be reposed in me by His Majesty" if his every action in East and West Florida had to meet Haldimand's approval.[20] Gage, who had intended merely to secure coöperation between the military and the Indian officials, then indicated to Stuart that his wish was nothing more than that Haldimand should be kept informed of the state of Indian affairs, so that the latter could make military arrangements accordingly.[21] Stuart was perfectly satisfied. It is true that after the division of the southern department in 1779 Stuart's successors were compelled to obey commands of ranking military officers in the South.[22]

Nor is Professor Carter's point that the expenses of the Indian

[17] This conclusion is based in part upon statements by Mr. Dale V. Morford, who has made an extensive study of the military departments. It is obvious that there were no such departments when Johnson was given his first commission.

[18] Tayler to Gage, Sept. 25, 1766, Gage MSS. Tayler had previously been in command at St. Augustine. After Haldimand's arrival he went to England.

[19] Gage to Stuart, Dec. 10, 1766, Gage MSS.

[20] Stuart to Gage, Jan. 7, 1767, Gage MSS.

[21] Gage to Stuart, Feb. 27, 1766, Gage MSS.

[22] Germain to Sir Henry Clinton, June 25, 1779, Sir Henry Clinton MSS. Gage was peeved when minor military officers meddled unnecessarily in Indian affairs. When one of them obtained a land cession from the Creeks, he refused to pay the bills incurred and declared the cession void. Gage to Stuart, Dec. 31, 1764, Gage MSS.

services were included in the budget of the military establishment unsusceptible of criticism. When the superintendencies were set up it seems to have been the intention of government that the outlays of the agents should be regulated from England, and that their bills should be drawn upon the military commander only for convenience. However, until 1768 the military commander did exercise the power, subject to directions from home,[23] to stipulate the amounts to be spent for the Indian departments. But the superintendents, although they continued to draw their bills upon the commander in chief until 1776, operated after 1768 upon budgets established by the home government, amended when necessary by the secretary of state for the colonies. From 1776 to 1779, when Stuart was operating from Pensacola, he drew bills directly upon the treasury, because it was extremely difficult to communicate with the head of the army from that place. During this period Stuart also was permitted to expend as much as his department seemed to require, the treasury of course retaining the right to refuse his bills if it appeared that they were unjustified.[24] Stuart's successors were placed upon budgets, £1,955 being allotted to each division. Outlays for general purposes beyond these allotments were to receive special sanction from the colonial secretary; and expenses arising from military operations were to be met by ranking military officers.[25]

From the origins of the office to the close of the Seven Years' War the superintendents considered themselves to be directly, though not primarily, responsible to London; both Johnson and Atkin wrote to officials at the imperial capital during the war. On August 5, 1763, Johnson and Stuart were formally instructed to report to the Board of Trade;[26] and from 1763 to 1768 they corresponded with and received orders from the board and the secretary of state for the southern department. After the colonial secretary was added to the cabinet in 1768, they reported to and received orders from him.[27] Although the superintendents were also compelled to corre-

[23] After the defeat of France in the Seven Years' War the Earl of Egremont instructed Amherst that not more than £1,000 should be spent to conciliate northern tribes offended by the withdrawal of the French. Amherst insisted that Johnson act according to this instruction. Amherst to Johnson, Sept. 9, 1763, Amherst MSS.

[24] Germain to Stuart, Sept. 5, 1776, CO, 5/77.

[25] Germain to Cameron, June 25, 1779, CO, 5/80.

[26] Board of Trade to Stuart, Aug. 5, 1763, Gage MSS.

[27] Since the colonial secretary sat with the board after 1768 there was no reason for the agents to continue correspondence with the board.

spond with the chief military officer in America and to render obedience to his commands, instructions from England determined their actions after 1763, when home officials chose to act. Since George Grenville was neither the first nor the only English statesman who read the dispatches from America, Indian policy was generally supervised from London, at times with the greatest of care. When instructions from London were lacking, those offered by the commander in chief sometimes filled the gap. There were some very important phases of Indian affairs, principally those connected with the formation and surveying of Indian boundaries in the South, in which the military commander never exercised any authority. In the large majority of cases orders to the agents, whether from England or from the commander in chief, were based on the recommendations of the agents themselves, because Indian problems were so intricate and required so much intimate knowledge. As a rule, the agents scrupulously obeyed instructions from home.[28] Stuart's conduct in this respect was especially noteworthy, for he was apt to translate the most tentative suggestions of the secretaries of state into action. When the plans of the superintendents were set aside, as they were on a few important occasions, such action was usually taken because they necessitated expenditures beyond what were considered wise and necessary.

It should be noted that relations between the superintendents and the military commander were probably as much determined by the nature of the Indian problem, by geography, and by the personalities of the men involved as by official mandate. Only one of the military commanders, Gage, could reasonably claim knowledge of Indian affairs, while the superintendents were quite naturally very well informed upon their specialty. Johnson, Stuart, George Croghan, and Alexander Cameron, Stuart's most capable aide, were without doubt masters in the art of Indian diplomacy. Because Indian management required thorough acquaintance with Indian psychology, customs, and policy, military commanders and home officials were wise to allow the superintendents a relatively free hand. Geographical factors also tended to give the agents liberty of action, for the critical scenes in Indian affairs were usually enacted hundreds, and even thousands, of miles from military headquarters. Communications, slow at the best, were also uncertain, whether by land or by sea. Atkin and Stuart could send reports to the military

[28] Johnson's purchase of eastern and central Kentucky from the Iroquois at Fort Stanwix in 1768 was a notable exception.

commander by sea from Charleston without too much trouble, but when Stuart was at Pensacola or Mobile, means of sending messages to and from New York were few and precarious, for traveling directly by land was almost impossible, and but few ships sailed from the Gulf of Mexico to northern ports. Even though Stuart frequently sent duplicates of his dispatches so as to guard against loss, some of his correspondence arrived too late to be of use, and a part of it failed to reach its destination. Ordinarily Stuart could correspond from West Florida with London almost as easily as with New York, and after the Revolution began he could do so with greater facility.

In what light did the military commanders and the superintendents view their relation, and how did they conduct themselves toward each other? The Johnson-Shirley imbroglio, already mentioned, was not symptomatic of the usual relations between the commander in chief and the Indian agents. Loudoun at one time rather querulously asserted his supervisory authority over Johnson, although he declared upon the same occasion that he had no intention of interfering with his work and apologized for having formed some of the Stockbridge Indians into a body of auxiliaries without Johnson's consent.[29] In general, Loudoun realized his ignorance of Indian matters, and his influence upon Johnson was rather small, in spite of the fact that a war was in progress. He rendered Johnson some service by supporting him against pretensions of the northern governors.[30] Of course, Loudoun's dealings with Atkin were upon a different basis.

In announcing his appointment as commander in chief in December, 1758, Amherst merely stated that he was instructed to correspond with and to aid the superintendents in obtaining Indian help against the French.[31] Although Amherst differed with Johnson on matters of policy, and insisted that the latter's method of treating the savages as children and securing their good will by conciliation and liberal presents was unwise and unproductive of results commensurate with the cost, he caused little difficulty about honoring Johnson's warrants during the critical years of the war. After the French had been subdued, he recommended economy so persistently that Johnson limited his expenditures to the most moderate figures. Amherst also initiated a practice of having the disbursements of subordinate officers in the Indian service certified by the military

[29] Loudoun to Johnson, Dec. 25, 1757, *Johnson Papers*, II, 764–67.

[30] Stanley M. Pargellis, *Lord Loudoun in North America* (New Haven, 1933), 254–56.

[31] Amherst to Johnson and Atkin, Dec. 13, 1758, *Johnson Papers*, III, 12–13.

when such disbursements took place at the posts, as was usually the case in the northern department. The result was that the expenses of the northern district were greatly lowered. Croghan prophesied in 1762 that this policy of economy would result in an Indian outbreak.[32] When his prediction came true in the following year, Amherst was blamed for the uprising, and Johnson's credit was exalted at his expense.[33] However, Amherst did assist Johnson in an attempt to regulate the fur trade in the St. Lawrence valley after the fall of Niagara in 1759. Also, like Loudoun, he insisted that the colonial governors should not meddle in the conduct of political relations with the northern Indians.[34] Amherst had little to do with Atkin.

Relations between Gage on the one hand and Johnson and Stuart on the other are largely explained by Gage's respect for their abilities. Gage had had ample opportunity to estimate Johnson's quality in the Seven Years' War; not long after he assumed office he became aware of the equal talents of Stuart. In fact, official intercourse between Gage and Stuart was characterized by a very friendly and coöperative spirit, although the two men never met personally. Gage exercised more positive influence over Indian affairs than any other military commander, but it may be said that he usually followed, rather than led, Johnson and Stuart. It was his generous support that made it possible for them to establish a measure of direct imperial control over the Indian trade between 1765 and 1768. Until the close of 1766 neither Johnson nor Stuart received any sanction whatever from home to interfere in the management of the trade, but Gage helped them to enforce their regulatory systems in 1765 and 1766. His action was the more remarkable because he had been forbidden to incur any new expenses without a specific grant from Parliament, except in emergencies, in the event of which he might spend money with the hope that the treasury would agree with him as to the necessity of the disbursement and would honor his bills. Since management of the trade inevitably required additional expenditures, it is evident that Gage sanctioned large outlays at the urging of Stuart and Johnson when the policy of the home government was one of retrenchment.

Moreover, Gage was generous in honoring the heavy bills pre-

[32] Croghan to Johnson, March 31, 1762, *Johnson Papers,* III, 662–63.

[33] Johnson and Croghan rejoiced over Amherst's discomfiture. See Croghan to Johnson, Feb. 24, 1764, *Johnson Papers,* IV, 339–41.

[34] On relations between Johnson and Amherst see *Johnson Papers,* III, 184–86, 343–47, 353, 514–16, 597–98, 604–5, 662–63, 964–66.

sented by Johnson and Stuart as a result of their attempt to control the trade; he made no great effort to lessen their expenditures until the war office rebuked him because the accounts of the Indian departments were too large. Finally, Gage did protest to Johnson, especially regarding the expenses of Edward Cole, Indian commissary at Fort Chartres in the Illinois country from 1766 to 1768. Cole had been reckless, if nothing worse, in his expenditures; Gage nevertheless felt compelled even in Cole's case to honor the accounts presented to him.[35] Gage actually refused to honor accounts presented by Major Robert Rogers, who was for a time both military commandant and Indian commissary at Michilimackinac. However, both Gage and Johnson distrusted Rogers, and they had agreed that his bills should not be paid.[36] Although Gage continued Amherst's policy of forcing the lesser Indian officials to secure certification of their expenditures by military officers when that procedure was possible,[37] he was pleased when he was relieved of the duty of doling out funds to the Indian departments, for the accounts of the Indian services had been one continuous headache for him. As Lord Shelburne once declared, the labors of the superintendents were such that they needed the power to draw whatever sums they thought expedient.[38] Gage, too, felt that it was outside his power to judge of the necessity of their expenses.[39] Immediately after receiving the Shelburne letter of December 11, 1766, he expressed a hope that the Board of Trade would assume complete control of the superintendents' financial transactions.[40]

Gage also displayed a benevolent and helpful attitude toward the superintendents by ordering his subordinates to assist the officers of the Indian establishments whenever possible. In those vast areas of America that were beyond the bounds of civil authority, the army men could and sometimes did help the Indian officials. Particularly pleasing to the Indian agents were Gage's attempts to strengthen their influence.[41]

[35] *Johnson Papers,* VI, 176–77, 187, 198–200; *Gage Corr.,* II, 461.

[36] For the opinion of Gage and Johnson on Rogers see *Doc. Hist. N. Y.* (quarto ed.), II, 513.

[37] It seems unlikely that military officers were consistently available in the South.

[38] Shelburne to Board of Trade, Oct. 5, 1767, *Ill. Hist. Colls.,* XVI (1921), 77.

[39] See Gage to Barrington, Dec. 10, 1766, *Gage Corr.,* II, 392–95.

[40] Gage to Shelburne, April 4, 1767, *Gage Corr.,* I, 129–31; Gage to Barrington, April 24, 1767, *ibid.,* II, 413–14.

[41] Gage considered the practice of furnishing the governors of East and West Florida with funds for Indian presents a very bad one, not only because presents

Some further conception of the relations between the superintendents, Gage, and the home government may be gathered from the manner in which appointments to and removals from lesser offices in the Indian departments were made. For the sake of efficiency they should have been completely within the jurisdiction of the superintendents, but the latter not infrequently found it prudent to heed the recommendations of higher officials.

Customarily Johnson selected all his subordinates, except the secretary of his department, who was named by the Board of Trade upon his recommendation. However, two of his aides were chosen by agreement between the secretary of state for the southern department, the commander in chief in America, and Johnson himself. Sir Henry Conway requested Gage to appoint Robert Rogers as both military commandant and Indian commissary at Michilimackinac. Gage replied that he could not give Rogers a commission for the latter position unless Johnson were willing and Rogers were placed under Johnson's orders. Johnson responded to the pressure from London, and Rogers duly received his commissions, taking directions concerning Indian affairs from Johnson and military instructions from Gage.[42] The troubles that arose from Rogers's appointment are well known. Major Joseph Gorham's case was very similar. The Duke of Richmond requested Gage to offer Gorham a commission as superintendent of Indian affairs in Nova Scotia without salary; Gage consulted Johnson's wishes and, with Johnson's approval, Gorham was made deputy superintendent in Nova Scotia under Johnson's direction.[43] In these unusual cases Gage had insisted that Johnson should have as much freedom of choice as possible. In one appointment Johnson had no voice whatever. In 1773 Lord Dartmouth gave one Captain John Campbell a commission as "Commandant of the Indians and Superintendant and Inspector of Indian affairs in the Province of Quebec in North

from these governors duplicated Stuart's, but also because the governors were thereby enabled to hold useless meetings with the Indians that damaged Stuart's plans. Thus Governor Grant of East Florida held a congress with the Lower Creeks in 1767 merely because he had presents to distribute. At Stuart's request Gage recommended to Shelburne, without avail, that the superintendents have complete control of the disbursement of Indian presents. Stuart to Gage, July 21, 1767, Gage MSS; Gage to Shelburne, Aug. 20, 1767, *Gage Corr.*, I, 144–45.

[42] Gage to Conway, Jan. 16, 1766, *Gage Corr.*, I, 79; Gage to Johnson, Feb. 3, 1766, Gage MSS; Johnson to Rogers, June 3, 1766, *Johnson Papers,* V, 238–39.

[43] Richmond to Gage, June 30, 1766, *Gage Corr.*, II, 42; Gage to Richmond, Sept. 11. 1766, *ibid.*, I, 107; Gage to Johnson, Feb. 17, 1767, Gage MSS.

America." Johnson was not consulted by Dartmouth, but Campbell was placed under his command.[44]

Stuart appointed all the members of his department without exception, although he was not unwilling to listen to suggestions from the military commander or a secretary of state. Thus he appointed the Chevalier Montaut de Monberaut as deputy superintendent in West Florida in 1765 upon the recommendation of Gage; and he chose Lieutenant John Thomas as his deputy for the Small Tribes on the eastern bank of the Mississippi in 1770, when Lord Hillsborough hinted that Thomas might possibly be useful, if Stuart wished to employ him. Both these men were discharged by Stuart upon unimpeachable grounds, and Stuart incurred no criticism as a result. Eventually he reinstated Thomas because Lord Dartmouth expressed an opinion that Thomas's misconduct arose largely from mistaken zeal, but Dartmouth insisted that Thomas should mend his ways. Declarations by Hillsborough and by William Knox that appointments to and dismissals from office in the Indian departments were prerogatives of the superintendents[45] indicate the usual procedure in such matters.

The coming of the Revolution necessitated changes in the duties of the superintendents. The northern department rather quickly became a machine to furnish auxiliary forces of Indians to the British army. Stuart retained his interest in the problems of trade and Indian boundaries to the end of his life, although most of his energies were devoted to the maintenance of British influence among the southern tribes and the raising of Loyalist troops. Because communication between Pensacola and the military commander was almost impossible and because the South was not the scene of major land operations during the early years of the conflict, Stuart was virtually independent during his last years. When inferior men assumed Stuart's duties after his death and the South became the main theater of war, the southern Indian agents were relegated to the status of leaders of irregular forces immediately under the direction of the ranking military officers in the South.

Relations between the superintendents and the colonial governors were ordinarily somewhat more awkward than those between the agents and the military commanders. The governors and colonial assemblies were usually unwilling to give up control over

[44] *Royal Historical Manuscripts Commission, Eleventh Report,* pt. 5, 397; Dartmouth to Campbell, Aug. 31, 1773, CO, 5/241.

[45] Hillsborough to Lord Campbell, Jan. 11, 1772, *Doc. Hist. N.Y.* (quarto ed.), II, 573; William Knox to David Taitt, Oct. 25, 1779, CO, 5/80.

Indian affairs, whether in connection with trade or political negotiations. Thus the proprietary governors of Pennsylvania between 1755 and 1760 insisted on treating with the Indians on the borders of that colony; and Johnson, though supported by the military commanders, could not prevent them from doing so. As time wore on, Johnson was bothered less and less by the interference of the northern governors in Indian diplomacy; but his attempt to manage the trade on an imperial basis met such strong opposition from Lieutenant Governor Guy Carleton of Quebec that Johnson was forced to modify his trade restrictions. On the whole, relations between Johnson and the governors of New York were friendly enough. Those of Atkin with the southern governors, which are described above, were not characterized by a coöperative spirit.

Stuart probably suffered more from attempts by the governors to manage Indian affairs than any other Indian official. Before the Revolution no fewer than six colonies bordered upon his district, and it was impossible to secure from them recognition of his sole authority over political relations with the Indians. Governors William Bull, James Wright, Francis Fauquier, George Johnstone of West Florida, and James Grant of East Florida, and others interfered in such matters and made Stuart's path a thorny one. Specially annoying to Stuart was the fact that the governors could and sometimes did give out Indian presents without reference to the superintendent, thereby duplicating his presents and lessening his influence. West Florida was actually furnished £1,000 annually for such gifts, while East Florida was given £1,000 for Indian expenses and contingencies.[46] In 1765 Stuart urged that all presents go through his hands in order to secure economy and efficiency and that he be granted £5,000 annually for goods,[47] but to no avail. Also very distasteful to Stuart was the employment by the governors of traders as emissaries to the Indians, a practice that he condemned over and over again.[48] His criticisms were completely justified when the same traders used the prestige they had thus acquired to wean the Indians from British allegiance in the Revolution.[49] Nor were the governors coöperative when Stuart tried to enlist their aid in

[46] Both Johnstone and Grant brought out large supplies of presents when they assumed their posts. The annual grants for Indian expenses were omitted for brief periods in the budgets of both colonies.

[47] Stuart to John Pownall, Aug. 24, 1765, CO, 5/66.

[48] For example, see Stuart to Fauquier, Nov. 24, 1766, CO, 5/67.

[49] Notably George Galphin and Edward Wilkinson, American agents for Indian affairs.

his endeavors to bring the Indian trade into some semblance of order by an exercise of imperial authority. Stuart's lot was especially hard in that his difficulties with the governors continued even during the Revolution. When the superintendents became integral parts of the British war machine they finally escaped from interference by the governors.

Peculiarly embarrassing to the superintendents was the fact that they had no official rank in the imperial system. When the home government arranged for precedence among the civil and military officials during the Seven Years' War the Indian superintendents, as neither fish nor fowl, were ignored. It was therefore possible for governors and military officials to claim precedence over them at Indian conferences, to the confusion of the superintendents, since prestige was all-important in Indian diplomacy. Fortunately, only governors actually claimed precedence at such gatherings in the South; and able men like Stuart and Johnson were able to overcome the handicap.

Stuart was specially annoyed because of his anomalous position. He was inducted into the councils of East and West Florida in the fall of 1764,[50] but these appointments gave him no standing in other southern colonies or in his dealings with Gage's subordinates. After 1767, although Stuart was willing to accept instructions from Gage, he wished to be protected by official mandate against any attempt by the southern brigadiers to assert authority over him; and he desired to be freed from presumptuous demands made upon him by minor officers such as Lieutenant Ralph Phillips, commander of the troops in South Carolina and Georgia in 1767, who attempted to dictate where Stuart should hold a private interview with an Indian chief.[51] Finally, in 1769, he appealed to Lord Hillsborough to settle the rank of the superintendents in the colonial hierarchy, at the same time disclaiming any wish for lofty precedence.[52] Hillsborough, however, did not wish to stir up a hornet's nest. He declined Stuart's request, offering as consolation to recommend that Stuart be made a member of all the councils in his district, if Stuart so de-

[50] Minute of council of W. Fla., Nov. 24, 1764, CO, 5/625; list of councillors of East Florida, in Grant to Board of Trade, Nov. 22, 1764, CO, 5/540.

[51] Stuart to Hillsborough, July 30, 1769, Lieutenant Ralph Phillips to Stuart, June 5, 1767, Stuart to Phillips, June 5, 1767, CO, 5/70. Phillips, promoted to a captaincy soon after this incident, belonged to the Royal Americans, and was sent from Fort Pitt to Charleston in 1763. After 1765 he commanded the regulars stationed in South Carolina and Georgia. He was transferred to Ticonderoga in 1768.

[52] Stuart to Hillsborough, Jan. 3, 1769, CO, 5/70.

sired.[53] Stuart responded that seats in these councils would be of great value in that they would permit him to consult with and advise the governors in person about their Indian problems; he asked that the several commissions be dated from the time when he became superintendent.[54] Hillsborough thereupon urged the Board of Trade to arrange that the Indian agents be made ex officio members of the councils in their districts.[55] The proper warrants, made out early in 1770, were drawn up in such a way as to exclude Stuart from acting as governor in case of a vacancy.[56]

This palliative did not end Stuart's attempts to secure precedence, for he valued dignities. In 1777, believing that Guy Johnson had been given a commission as colonel in the army, he requested that he be given a similar commission, especially in view of the fact that he was Guy Johnson's senior in service by thirteen years.[57] Johnson, however, had been made only a colonel of the Indians in his district. Lord George Germain proffered a similar title to Stuart, warning him that it gave him no control over officers in the regular army and that it was intended only to exalt Stuart's prestige among the savages in his department.[58] Accepting this appointment, Stuart promised to refrain from meddling with the regular army,[59] a promise which he seems to have kept.

In conclusion, it may be said that the Indian departments were perhaps as haphazardly established and maintained as any other part of the loosely organized eighteenth-century British colonial system.

[53] Hillsborough to Stuart, March 24, 1769, CO, 5/70. The "Plan of 1764," of which Hillsborough was a sponsor, would have given the superintendents seats in all the councils in their districts.

[54] Stuart to Hillsborough, July 30, 1769, CO, 5/70.

[55] Hillsborough to Stuart, Dec. 9, 1769, CO, 5/70.

[56] Hillsborough to Stuart, Feb. 17, 1770, CO, 5/71; W. L. Grant and James Munro, eds., *Acts of the Privy Council of England, Colonial Series* (London, 1908–12), V, 228–29. Stuart was also forbidden to act judicially in cases involving civil property. He occasionally attended council meetings in all the far southern colonies after 1770.

[57] Stuart to Germain, April 14, 1777, CO, 5/78.

[58] Germain to Stuart, Oct. 11, Nov. 5, 1777, CO, 5/78. The commission was dated Oct. 21, 1777.

[59] Stuart to Germain, March 5, 1778, CO, 5/79.

CHAPTER X

JOHN STUART[1]

ABOUT the year 1670 Alexander Steuart,[2] descendant of the royal house of Scotland, established himself as a merchant in Inverness, then as now the principal town in the Scottish Highlands. He was the great-grandson of Walter, eighth baron of Kincardine in Strathspey; and the Kincardine barons could trace their ancestry in direct male line to Robert II through his illegitimate son, Alexander Stewart, Wolf of Badenoch. Alexander Steuart was also related by blood to the chiefs of the clans of Grant, McIntosh, MacGregor, Cameron, and McLean, but he belonged to a younger branch of the Kincardine family and the fortunes of the family were temporarily on the downgrade. In fact, the barony was sold to the Gordons about the time he removed to Inverness. The Kincardine Steuarts were nevertheless to leave their mark on British and American history. Most famous of them in the first half of the eighteenth century was John Roy ("Red-haired John") Stuart, who would have inherited the barony, had it not been lost, and who was therefore in a sense the head of the family. He was a poet of some note, although he is even better known for his participation in the rising of 1745 as the boon companion of Bonnie Prince Charlie.

On September 2, 1676, Alexander Steuart, who had prospered moderately as a merchant, was presented with a son, baptized John,[3]

[1] Most of the facts regarding Stuart's personal history have hitherto been shrouded in almost complete mystery. Such biographical notices as have appeared, including that in the *Dictionary of American Biography*, are quite inadequate and unreliable.

[2] Whether to use the form "Stewart," "Steuart," or "Stuart" is often difficult to decide. My choice, so far as possible, is based on correct contemporary usage.

[3] The birthdate of John Steuart is given in a letter written by him to John Stuart, Sept. 8, 1749, in William Mackay, ed., "The Letter-Book of Bailie John Steuart of Inverness, 1715–1752," *Scottish History Society*, Second Series, IX (1915), 458. (Throughout this chapter this work will be cited by the author's name alone.) On the ancestry of the Bailie and his relationship to the Kincardine family and John Roy Stuart see Mackay, Introduction, ix; note by the Bailie, Dec. 23, 1743, *ibid.*, 442; Charles Fraser-Mackintosh, ed., *Letters of Two Centuries,*

who by 1700 had also become a merchant, operating both with his father and independently.[4] Bailie John Steuart, as this son is commonly known because he once served as a magistrate of Inverness, carried on extensive commercial activities, dealing in oatmeal, iron, fish, coal, beef, pork, furs, wine, and a host of other commodities. Ships that he owned in full or in part, perhaps a dozen, plied the North Sea, the Baltic, the Atlantic, and the Mediterranean. Nor was he averse to a profitable bit of smuggling, no great sin in his day.[5] He was also interested in the development of a lead mine in Glenelg, and served as an agent for James, first Earl of Bute from about 1707 to 1712,[6] and for the Earl of Moray from some time prior to 1715 to 1734. Of a sanguine, speculative nature, he prospered for many years, but after 1734 he sustained reverses. He lived chiefly upon the bounty of his children and his sons-in-law during his old age. The Bailie's home on Church Street in Inverness was commodious, and his family was for many years supported in comfort and even luxury. A member of the Episcopalian Church of Scotland, he was a pillar of that organization in Inverness. The Bailie was a shrewd business man, though apparently honest and kindly. Especially notable was his fondness for his children. He bore considerable repute among his fellow citizens, served on the town council from 1713 to 1716, and was a magistrate from 1713 to 1715. He died on April 20, 1759.[7]

As magistrate of Inverness Bailie Steuart signed a statement to the effect that he and his colleagues were arming the burghers to act against the Old Pretender,[8] but he was actually an ardent, though a cautious, Jacobite. He displayed an active sympathy for those who suffered because they followed the Old Pretender; and in 1718 he wrote, "all things goe fair befor the win[d] for the government, and the unfortunate still Learn patiance." [9] He engaged in

Chiefly Connected with Inverness and the Highlands from 1616 to 1815 (Inverness, 1890) 231–33. There is a brief sketch, not too accurate, of John Roy Stuart in the *Dictionary of National Biography*. Alexander Steuart was born in 1644 or 1645, and died on April 27, 1720. His wife (name unknown) died in August, 1728. Mackay, 114, 288, 458.

[4] Mackay, Introduction, lx.

[5] The Bailie characterized an accusation of smuggling made against him as a "malicius, willanus falshood." But several letters in Mackay show clearly that he did indulge in smuggling.

[6] Bailie Steuart to George Gordon, June 1, 1723, Mackay, 212–13.

[7] Mackay, Introduction, lvii, note 2.

[8] *Scottish History Society,* Third Series, XXV (1925), 73–74.

[9] Bailie Steuart to Norman McLeod, Aug. 23, 1718, Mackay, 88, also Introduction, xlvii.

extensive business affairs with Hanoverian officials; on the other hand, he was very friendly with several renowned Jacobites, including his cousin, John Roy Steuart, and Simon Fraser, Lord Lovat, with whom he was connected by marriage.[10] The Bailie was accused of taking part in the rising of 1745, but the charge was probably false so far as active soldiering was concerned, although his heart was unquestionably with Bonnie Prince Charlie.[11]

The Bailie's family was a large one. By his first wife, Marion, daughter of Robert Rose of Merkinch, he had two daughters, Marion and Margaret. His first wife died not long after they were married. He later espoused Christian, daughter of Norman MacLeod of Drynoch,[12] by whom he had one daughter and at least ten sons.[13] Christian Steuart survived the Bailie by some years.[14] John, appar-

[10] *Scottish History Society,* First Series, LVII (1901), 45.

[11] He was denounced as a very active volunteer in Prince Charlie's army. *Scottish History Society,* First Series, VIII (1890), 128–29. But he was sixty-nine years of age in 1745, and could hardly have undertaken arduous soldiering. In 1751 he attempted to secure a pension from the court of France as a Jacobite, but failed because he had not taken the field. Bailie Steuart to James [Stuart], Jan. 17, 1752, Mackay, 475–76. Both he and his son Francis bitterly attacked the victors for their cruelty to the vanquished. *Scottish History Society,* First Series, XXI (1895), 188–89, 204–6, 211–12.

[12] Mackay, Introduction, x, gives the name of the Bailie's second wife as Anne, as does Alexander Mackenzie, *History of the Macleods, with Genealogies of the Principal Families of the Name* (Inverness, 1889), 217. John Burke, *A Genealogic and Heraldic History of the Landed Gentry*... (London, 1838), III, 26, gives her name as Christiana. Burke is no doubt correct, although Christian is a more accurate spelling. In Bailie Steuart to Norman MacLeod, Nov. 25, 1728, Mackay, 299, Anne MacLeod is rather definitely fixed as the Bailie's second wife's sister. In his will Allan Stuart, a child of this second marriage, refers to "the best of mothers, Christian Stuart." *Collections of the New-York Historical Society for the Year 1897* (New York, 1898), 246; *Collections of the New-York Historical Society for the Year 1908* (New York, 1909), 258.

[13] Robert, apparently the oldest son, went to sea, and died on a return voyage from Italy in 1721. Alexander was serving as an apprentice to William Cumming, an Edinburgh merchant, in 1720. He married Cumming's daughter, and was later a wine merchant at Leith. Norman died in 1745. Apparently he was born in 1722. Bailie Steuart to [Norman MacLeod], Oct. 28, 1722, Mackay, 192. James was born in or about 1724. Bailie Steuart to David Munroe, July 12, 1740, *ibid.,* 422–23. He went to India and prospered in the service of the East India Company. Little can be learned regarding William, a younger son. Data on other children of the second marriage will appear in the text. Margaret and Marion, the daughters of the first union, married respectively John Reid and Alexander Wedderburn, Scottish merchant captains.

[14] Allan Stuart's will, dated Sept. 25, 1762, referred to in a previous note, contained a bequest of £50 to his mother.

rently the third child of this second union, and the subject of this sketch, was born on September 25, 1718.[15]

John Stuart,[16] like all the Bailie's children, attended the excellent grammar school of Inverness. Nothing more can be learned regarding his boyhood. In 1735 he was sufficiently mature to mismanage some minor business transaction. In the same year, according to his father, "Johnie" suffered a very severe illness, but the "boy" recovered completely.[17] Late in 1735 or early in 1736 the Bailie sent him to London for further study. Excellent reports concerning his character came back to Inverness from Scottish merchants in London who watched over him; and the Bailie rejoiced. "He is a good humoured honest lad, and does not want a good capacity," wrote the fond father. By October, 1736, Stuart had found employment in London,[18] but he did not remain long in the capital. Less than a year later he was employed in some commercial capacity at San Lucar de Barrameda,[19] the old Andalusian port at the mouth of the Guadalquivir, from which Columbus sailed on his third voyage to America and Magellan on his journey around the world. After two or three years' residence at San Lucar, where

[15] Writing to his first cousin, John Steuart, Writer to the Signet and Commissary of Inverness, on Sept. 27, 1718, the Bailie declared that his wife had borne a son (unnamed) two days before, and that his cousin and one "Mr. Buttler" had been named as godfathers. Commissary Steuart later promised to assist in paying for John's final schooling in London. Bailie Steuart to Commissary Steuart, Sept. 27, 1718, Bailie Steuart to Patrick MacKattie, Oct. 23, 1736, Mackay, 93, 398–99. It therefore seems altogether likely that John was the boy born on Sept. 25, 1718, and that he was named, in part at least, after Commissary Steuart. That this conclusion is correct is borne out by the facts that the Bailie's sons Norman and William were named after Norman MacLeod and William Steuart, M.P., their respective godfathers, and that William Steuart, M.P., was expected to do something for his namesake. Additional corroboration is found in a process of elimination which makes it clear that none of the other known male children of the Bailie could have been born at this time. Still further proof is found in the facts that John is described as a "boy" in 1735 and that he finished school in 1736, as mentioned in the text. The date given in the *Dictionary of American Biography* and elsewhere for Stuart's birth, 1700?, is of course inaccurate.

[16] Although the Bailie consistently spelled his name "Steuart," John just as consistently used the form "Stuart," although he is often referred to as "Steuart" or "Stewart."

[17] Bailie Steuart to the Laird of McKinnen, younger, Sept. 6, 1735, Mackay, 392.

[18] Bailie Steuart to Patrick MacKattie, Sept. 11, 1736, Bailie Steuart to John McLean, Sept. 18, 1736, Bailie Steuart to Patrick MacKattie, Oct. 23, 1736, Mackay, 397, 397–98, 398–99.

[19] Notes by Bailie Steuart, Oct. 1 and Nov. 12, 1737, Mackay, 409, 412.

he learned Spanish, he returned to London and engaged in business there.[20]

Possibly the War of Jenkins' Ear forced Stuart to leave Spain. If so, the war also gave him new employment. In 1740 the British government decided to send George Anson on a marauding expedition against the Spanish possessions in the New World and the Philippines. Certain high officials insisted that Anson would be unable to obtain provisions for his fleet, and that two persons, one of whom was named Hubert Tassell,[21] should be sent upon the expedition with goods worth £15,000 to purchase supplies en route. Anson objected vigorously, because he felt that these so-called agents-victualler would be unnecessary and because he believed that they desired to accompany him only for profit, but he protested without avail. The government even lent £10,000 to Tassell and his colleague to finance them.[22] The agents-victualler needed a clerk with a knowledge of Spanish, and therein lay opportunity for Stuart. They employed him at a salary of £100 per annum, and permitted him to carry some goods of his own upon a private venture. He became a member of the Royal Navy, for he was enrolled as an able-bodied seaman.

We have extensive acounts of the disasters and glories that came to those who participated in the Anson expedition, although little regarding individual exploits and relationships has come down, and hardly a scrap regarding John Stuart. Anson set sail on September 18, 1740, with six fighting craft and two provision ships, carrying 1,939 men. Storm, scurvy, and travail took a heavy toll, but the *Centurion,* Anson's flagship, successfully circumnavigated the globe, by way of Cape Horn, the China coast, and the Cape of Good Hope. There were only 135 men on board the flagship when she reached Spithead on June 15, 1744. However, in her hold there was treasure worth £500,000, the largest part of which had been obtained through the capture of the Manila Galleon, *Nuestra Señora de Cavadonga,* in June, 1743. Among the fortunate survivors was Stuart. He undoubtedly made an excellent record, for he won the praise of Anson, and he was promoted to captain's clerk on the *Centurion,* succeeding the Honorable John Fortescue, on June 1, 1743. One authority believes that Stuart may have been

[20] Fragment of letter by Bailie Steuart, 1739 or 1740, Mackay, 422.

[21] Or Tassel. Tassell's colleague was apparently one Hutchinson.

[22] G. C. Laird Clowes, ed., *A Voyage Round the World . . . By George Anson . . . Compiled From Papers and other Materials of . . . Anson, and published By Richard Walter . . .* (London, Boston, 1928), 7–9.

made a midshipman at the same time. In any case, Stuart received a substantial sum as his share of the prize money, which, taken with his salary, must have lifted him to comparative affluence.[23]

The knowledge that "Johnie" had returned safely to England gave the Bailie and his wife "unexpressable joy for which we bless and adore the mercy of God to us in preserving and restoring our Child in health and prosperity after passing throw so many Dangers, and so great a schen (scene) of Mortality and Distress." [24] The unfortunate Bailie began to draw upon his son for funds even before the *Centurion* reached harbor. After his return Stuart lived at Portsmouth and London for a year. A proposal from Sir James Stuart of Burray, a Jacobite relative, that he settle upon the island of Orkney seems not to have interested him.[25] Nor did he take any part in the '45, although his sympathies, like those of his father, may have been with the Young Pretender. Instead, he shipped for another voyage as purser on a man-of-war in the fall of 1745.[26] Whether or not he actually sailed is unknown, for nothing certain can be said regarding his career from 1745 to 1748.

Stuart sailed for South Carolina in the spring of 1748. On June 8 of that year an advertisement appeared in the *South-Carolina Gazette* announcing that the firm of Stuart and Reid had imported a large supply of goods in the *Lark*, Captain Douglas, recently arrived from London, and that they offered for sale all sorts of cloth goods, cutlery, haberdashery, stationery, iron wares, Indian trading goods, wines, and other commodities at their store on Charleston Bay near

[23] Contemporary accounts of the Anson expedition are to be found in the volume cited in the preceding note; John Philips, *An Authentic Journal of the late Expedition Under the Command of Commodore Anson*... (London, 1744); Pascoe Thomas, *A True and Impartial Journal of a Voyage to the South Seas and Round the Globe*... (London, 1745). A secondary account by a naval expert is to be found in Henry Boyle Somerville, *Commodore Anson's Voyage into the South Seas and around the World* (London, Toronto, 1934). On Stuart's participation in the voyage see Somerville, *op. cit.*, 275, 277; Bailie Steuart to Alexander Gordon, Jan. 13, 1744, Bailie Steuart to George Udnie, March 23, 1744, Mackay, 442–43, 445. Stuart's share in the prize money was estimated by an acquaintance of his father's to be £10,000 to £12,000. *Royal Historical Manuscripts Commission, Report on the Laing Manuscripts Preserved in the University of Edinburgh* (1914–25), II, 289. This estimate is probably considerably above the actual sum.

[24] Bailie Steuart to George Udny, July 6, 1744, Mackay, 449–50.

[25] Note by Bailie Steuart, July 27, 1745, Mackay, 453.

[26] Bailie Steuart to Stuart, Sept. 13, 1745, Mackay, 454–55. The Bailie wrote: "May Godd bless and derect us and all our dear freinds." One suspects that the "freinds" were Prince Charlie and his followers.

the "Vendue House."[27] Reid was Patrick Reid, obviously a Scot, who had been established in South Carolina for some years and who had previously been in partnership with one James Ogilvie at Charleston.[28] He sailed for England on November 3, 1746,[29] and apparently returned on October 1, 1747.[30] Probably the partnership was formed during his stay in Great Britain.

Many reasons might be brought forth for Stuart's determination to emigrate to South Carolina. Numerous family friends and acquaintances were already in South Carolina and Georgia, and he had probably been well informed regarding those colonies for some years. George Urquhart of Cromartie, Stuart's uncle by marriage, was captain of the *Hope,* which carried seventy passengers and servants from the Highlands to South Carolina in 1737 for William Backshell, later clerk of the South Carolina council. In fact, Bailie Steuart performed some business services in connection with this voyage for Backshell and attempted to secure employment in that province through him for his own son Alexander.[31] It may be significant that the Udneys, Scottish merchants at London who served as agents for both the Bailie and his son, traded to South Carolina and were for a time the agents of Stuart and Reid.

The new partnership encountered financial difficulties almost immediately. By August, 1749, Stuart was once more in England, in order to improve the credit of the firm and to secure goods. At that time he was married.[32] His wife was called Sarah; but neither the maiden name of Sarah Stuart nor the date of the marriage is known.[33] On June 9, 1750, at London the first child of this mar-

[27] Tradition, reflected in the brief sketch of Stuart in the *Dictionary of American Biography,* has represented Stuart as coming to America with Oglethorpe, or with the Highlanders who settled at New Inverness, but there can be no question that the date of his arrival in America was 1748. In a letter to John Pownall, Oct. 17, 1765, CO, 323/21, and in a petition to the Board of Trade, Sept. 23, 1766, CO, 5/67, Stuart clearly indicates 1748 as the year of his emigration. In 1774, when applying for the superintendency vacated by the death of Sir William Johnson, Stuart declared that he had been "in this country" 26 years. Stuart to Dartmouth, Sept. 12, 1774, CO, 5/75.

[28] CJSC, xiii, 36–38.

[29] *South-Carolina Gazette,* Nov. 3, 1746.

[30] *SCHGM,* XXVIII, 153.

[31] Notes and letters by Bailie Steuart, Mackay, 404–7.

[32] Bailie Steuart to Stuart, Sept. 8, 1749, Bailie Steuart to James Steuart, Nov. 8, 1751, Mackay, 458, 472.

[33] According to tradition in South Carolina, Stuart married Sarah Fenwick, daughter of Colonel John Fenwick, but conclusive evidence is lacking. The writer is inclined to believe that the tradition is erroneous. There is a legal document executed on April 28, 1750, by Elizabeth, Countess of Deloraine, older

riage, christened Sarah Christiana, was born.[34] Shortly afterward the little family went to Yorkshire and thence to Newton Hall, East Lothian, to visit Stuart's parents and his sister Anne, who had married Richard Hay-Newton of that place.[35] Accompanied by his wife and daughter, Stuart sailed for America in the fall of 1750, and after a long and arduous passage arrived in South Carolina in April, 1751.[36]

The affairs of Stuart and Reid failed to improve greatly after the former's return to Charleston. They established a branch at Beaufort under the management of Francis Stuart, John's younger

sister of Sarah Fenwick, which is witnessed by one "S. Fenwick." See Miscellaneous Records, Vol. 86B, 1758–1763, Charleston County, S. C., 987–88, Charleston County (S. C.) Courthouse. If the initial stands for Sarah—and it is likely that it does, since no other Fenwick of the time seems to have had a Christian name beginning with the letter *s*—the tradition is surely inaccurate. Doubt as to the tradition is also aroused by a letter from Stuart to William Henry Drayton of July 18, 1775, in the Gage MSS. Not long before this letter was written Stuart's daughter Christiana had married Edward Fenwick, son of Edward Fenwick, younger brother of Colonel John. Declares Stuart: "Yet long before I left Charles Town I knew that such a report [that Stuart was attempting to incite the Indians to attack the Americans] prevailed; and had been given to understand that you had established a belief of it in a family with which my daughter is since become connected." It is hardly likely, though it is not impossible, that Stuart would have mentioned the Edward Fenwick family in this fashion if he himself had long been connected with it through marriage to Sarah Fenwick. If tradition is correct, Christiana Stuart and Edward Fenwick the younger were first cousins, but the relationship would have been no bar to marriage.

[34] W. Bruce Bannerman and Major W. Bruce Bannerman, eds., *The Registers of St. Stephen's, Walbrook and of St. Benet Sherehog, London, Pt. I* (London, 1919), 135.

[35] Anne Stuart married Hay-Newton some time before July, 1742. They had several children, one of whom became an officer in the 64th Regiment and served in America. The Hay-Newtons were very kind to the Bailie and his wife, who apparently spent their last years at Newton Hall. Hay-Newton died on June 29, 1776. Mackay, 452, note. Anne died in the following year. Burke, *Landed Gentry* (1838), III, 26. Notes by the Bailie, in Mackay, 467–69, mention the approaching reunion at Newton Hall. A blank in the Bailie's papers follows, which indicates that it was actually held.

[36] Bailie Steuart to James Stuart, Jan. 17, 1752, Mackay, 478–79. Although Stuart was in financial difficulties in 1751, he offered his father a pension of £20 per annum. He proposed that his father settle at Boulogne (home of many exiled Jacobites), where living expenses were very reasonable. The Bailie would have had the rent of his home in addition to the pension. He visited Boulogne, but decided to maintain his home at Inverness, for he thought life in a strange country would prove to be unsatisfactory, especially since his son's precarious financial condition would make remittances uncertain. Bailie Steuart to James Steuart, Nov. 8, 1751, *ibid.*, 472. Stuart seems to have given his father considerable sums between 1744 and 1751. He also helped, or tried to help, his brothers Francis, James, and Patrick to a start in the world.

brother, who emigrated to South Carolina late in 1748.[37] This branch did £1,500 worth of business in its first year, and Frank was given a one-third interest in the profits made at Beaufort.[38] Stuart and Reid also combined with one John Wilkins in setting up a store at Pon Pon.[39] The Udneys, however, failed to offer sufficient credit, and Reid went to London in 1752 in an attempt to form a connection with another firm.[40] Probably Reid's mission was not too successful, for Stuart's financial condition remained precarious. Reid's death in May, 1754,[41] was the final blow to Stuart's career as a merchant. He advertised until January, 1755, that he was continuing the business in Charleston formerly carried on by the partnership.[42] In November, 1754, however, Charles Pinckney was offering for rent a "brick house, with very good offices, and very convenient back stores, situate on the said [Charleston] Bay, and late in the possession of Messrs. Stuart & Reid, but now in the tenure of Mr. John Stuart."[43] On April 1, 1755, writs against all of Stuart's property were issued, and it became evident that his goods, Negroes, lands, and other possessions were insufficient to satisfy his obligations. By the end of August judgments for thousands of pounds had been handed down against him. Whether or not all the claims against him were eventually paid is not shown by the records of the Court of Common Pleas at Charleston, but one presented by George Saxby for £2,000 and another by George Inglis, James Lennox, David Deas, and Robert Wells for £10,000 (provincial currency) were satisfied in 1768.[44]

[37] Francis, or Frank, was born about 1728. He was described at the time of his emigration as "modest, sober, sensible." Obviously, he went to America at John's invitation. See Robert Chambers, ed., *Jacobite Memoirs of the Rebellion of 1745* ... (Edinburgh, London, 1834), 232–41, 246, note.

[38] Bailie Steuart to James Stuart, Jan. 17, 1752, Mackay, 478–79.

[39] Advertisement by Stuart, Reid & Wilkins, *South-Carolina Gazette,* Oct. 23, 1752, and later issues; record of the case of John Stuart, Patrick Reid, and John Wilkins v. Jacob Turner, 1754, Court of Common Pleas, Charleston County (S. C.) Courthouse.

[40] Bailie Steuart to John Stuart, Sept. 28, 1752, Mackay, 485–87.

[41] Reid's will, made May 11, 1754, and probated May 24, 1754, is to be found in a record book of the Probate Court, 1752–1756, Judge W. E. Vincent, Charleston County, 246–48, Charleston County (S. C.) Courthouse. Reid had married Elizabeth Cossens, a widow, on April 16, 1753. He left a minor son, William. He was a brother of James Reid, ancestor of many South Carolinians.

[42] *South-Carolina Gazette,* Aug. 8, 1754, and later issues, also Jan. 16 and 23, 1755.

[43] *South-Carolina Gazette,* Nov. 14, 1754, March 27, 1755.

[44] Court Book of Common Pleas, 1754–1763, 31, 34, 36–37, 39, Charleston

Although Stuart had failed as a merchant, he had established for himself a place in Charleston life. Immediately after his arrival in America he became a member of the St. Andrew's Society of Charleston,[45] of which he was secretary from 1752 to 1755[46] (perhaps longer), and president from 1772 until the Revolution.[47] He also became a member of the Charleston Library Society before 1752, serving as steward for that organization for that year.[48] By 1754 he was affiliated with the Charleston "Grand Lodge of the Free and Accepted Masons." For several years he served as steward, assisting in making arrangements for a festival that the Masons celebrated every December 27 by attending church in the morning and by spending the remainder of the day at the inn of John Gordon, who was reputed to keep the best public house in America.[49] We may conclude that Stuart was a man of convivial tastes, especially since he suffered so greatly from gout after 1756 that he was at times completely incapacitated.[50] Stuart also held several local offices. In March, 1752, he was elected one of five firemasters for the parish of St. Philip's;[51] and he was a tax assessor for the parish for the year 1753.[52] In November, 1754, he was chosen as a member of the commons house of assembly from the parish of St. Helena, serving

---

County (S. C.) Courthouse; records of cases in Court of Common Pleas, George Inglis, James Lenox, David Deas, and Robert Wells v. Stuart, filed May 23, 1755, George Saxby v. Stuart, filed June 26, 1755, Isabella Graeme v. Stuart, Joseph Fuller v. Stuart, Benjamin Smith v. Stuart, all filed Aug. 30, 1755, Charleston County (S. C.) Courthouse.

[45] *St. Andrew's Society, of the City of Charleston, South Carolina* ... (Charleston, S. C., 1892), 32; J. H. Easterby, *History of the St. Andrew's Society of Charleston, South Carolina, 1729–1929* (Charleston, S. C., 1929), 45. Other members of the society were Stuart's brother Francis; his brother Allan, elected in 1757, when he came to Charleston with Lieutenant Colonel Archibald Montgomery; Charles Stuart, son of John Roy Stuart and deputy superintendent in the South; Captain Raymond Demeré; Alexander Cameron; James Grant; Patrick Reid; and others whose names appear herein. Stuart's son John became a member in 1780.

[46] *South-Carolina Gazette,* Nov. 6, 1752, Nov. 26, 1753, Nov. 27, 1755.

[47] *South-Carolina Gazette,* Dec. 3, 1772, Dec. 5, 1774.

[48] *South-Carolina Gazette,* Jan. 10, 1752. The MS journal of the society, preserved by the society, indicates that Stuart must have disposed of his share before 1759.

[49] *South-Carolina Gazette,* Dec. 5, 11, 1754, Jan. 9, 1755, Dec. 28, 1758.

[50] In 1771 Stuart asked for leave to go to England to obtain treatment for his gout. But the Earl of Hillsborough gave him permission to go only to the northern colonies. Stuart apparently did not visit the northern colonies; and there is no evidence that he ever returned to Great Britain after 1751.

[51] *South-Carolina Gazette,* April 6, 1752.

[52] *South-Carolina Gazette,* March 5, 1754.

in the house until early in 1756.[53] Stuart was unable to secure a remunerative civil post until his appointment as Indian agent, although not for lack of effort. On January 5, 1755, he petitioned for the position of commissary general of South Carolina, just vacated by the death of his colleague in the commons house from St. Helena, John Dart. Since the commissary general, among other duties, served as a disbursing agent for the province, the position could be a lucrative one. Stuart and other applicants, including Daniel Pepper, were passed over in favor of William Pinckney.[54] In July, 1761, he asked William Pitt for an appointment as clerk of the South Carolina assembly, an office made vacant by the death of Childermas Croft in the preceding May, but he was again unsuccessful.[55]

But the twelve years before the Revolution were prosperous ones for Stuart, as they were for many South Carolinians. His initial salary of £600 as superintendent was substantial; and his stipend was increased in 1768 to £1,000, which was larger than that received by some of the southern governors. Moreover, perquisites of his office were probably worth another £500.[56] His landholdings increased rapidly during this period, for he acquired 10,200 acres in South Carolina and Georgia, most of which, however, was unimproved land. He also had a grant of 5,000 acres in East Florida.[57] Two plantations on Lady's Island, opposite Beaufort, which he pur-

[53] *South-Carolina Gazette,* Nov. 7, 1754; minutes of S. C. council, April 12, Nov. 25, 1755; CJSC, xxv, 63, 132. There was another John Stuart residing in St. Helena Parish in 1737–38, but he does not seem to have been prominent. Although Stuart's home was in Charleston, it would appear that he was the person elected.

[54] CJSC, xxiv, pt. 1, 4, 8, 12–13, 36–37.

[55] Bull to Board of Trade, May 28, 1761, CO, 5/377; memorial by Stuart to William Pitt, July 26, 1761, Chatham MSS, 73, British Museum. In this memorial Stuart describes his career from 1756 to 1760. It is therefore valuable, but some of the dates given by him are incorrect. Thus he states that he was made captain in the provincials in 1757.

[56] John Graham, whose office covered only one half of the southern Indian department, estimated that the perquisites attached to it were worth £500 in 1782.

[57] In 1765 Stuart petitioned the Board of Trade for a grant of lands in either East or West Florida, asking that he be given two separate parcels under the usual terms in regard to quitrents. Stuart to John Pownall, Oct. 17, 1765, CO, 323/21. In 1766 he requested a grant of 10,000 acres in East Florida. Petition by Stuart to Board of Trade, Sept. 23, 1766, CO, 5/67. He was given 5,000 acres in East Florida. *Acts of the Privy Council, Colonial Series,* V, 814. Stuart's will, dated Feb. 16, 1776, indicates that he also had claims in West Florida before that time.

chased many years before the Revolution were the only ones that produced a profit. Improved steadily in the course of passing years and devoted to indigo culture, they came to yield, according to Stuart's heirs, a revenue of £1,000 per annum. As the Revolution came, he owned over 200 slaves, and was possessed of considerable plantation equipment. After 1772 he lived in a handsome three-storied cypress mansion at the corner of Tradd and Orange streets, which he built at a cost of £2,350 and equipped with new furniture from England worth several hundred pounds more.[58] His property was probably worth £12,000 to £14,000 in 1775.[59]

John and Sarah Stuart had at least four children. Sarah Christiana married James Graham, a merchant, on July 9, 1767,[60] and died in London on September 24, 1774.[61] Graham had been engaged in business at Savannah before 1767, but removed at that time to London, where he served as Stuart's agent for a decade. He was a brother of John Graham, lieutenant governor of Georgia and Indian superintendent in the western division of the southern district after 1782.[62] Christiana, a second daughter, born in 1752, encountered a romantic but tragic fate. She fell in love with Edward

[58] The house is still very well preserved, and is now occupied by Mr. John Mead Howells, who graciously conducted the writer through it on a tour of inspection.

[59] This account of Stuart's property is based largely upon the claims presented by his heirs in 1787 before the commission appointed by the British government to investigate the losses suffered by the Loyalists. These may be found in Public Record Office, Audit Office 12/51, pp. 146–83. See also a memorial to the king by Mrs. Sarah Stuart, June 4, 1781, CO, 5/158. Stuart's heirs estimated his property to be worth at the very lowest calculation £15,000. Although it was sequestered by the South Carolina patriots at the beginning of the Revolution, his relatives succeeded in carrying off part of it in 1777 and 1780. His heirs asked the British government for £18,634 in compensation; and they were given £9,300. American Loyalist Transcripts, ii, 278–80. The major part of the property was definitely confiscated by the state of South Carolina in 1782, and was sold for over £6,328. But the state made no profit thereby, for one Petrie, and certain persons named Johnson and Simpson, produced records of mortgages which entitled them to the proceeds of the sale. "List of Confiscated Estates which are Insolvent to be given up for the Benefit of the Creditors," n.d., Historical Commission of South Carolina. This paper seems to conflict with claims by Stuart's heirs that his property was virtually unencumbered. I am indebted to Robert Barnwell for bringing it to my attention.

[60] A. S. Salley, Jr., ed., *Marriage Notices in The South-Carolina Gazette; and Country Journal (1765–1775) and in the Charlestown Gazette (1778–1780)* (Charleston, 1904), 8.

[61] *SCHGM*, XVII (1916), 89–90.

[62] On the Grahams see Wilbur H. Seibert, *The Loyalists in East Florida, 1774–1785* (1929), 11, 71, 336–37.

Fenwick, son of a prominent South Carolinian of the same name, and married him late in the spring of 1775, in spite of the opposition of the older Fenwick. The older Fenwick had espoused the cause of the colonies. He detested Stuart because of his loyalty to the crown and because of reports that he planned to use the Indians under his control against the Americans. The younger Fenwick was made of weak stuff ill calculated to carry him with honor through the storms of the Revolution. He seems to have had no great fondness either for the king or for the American patriots. It would appear that he desired to avoid politics for horse racing, a pastime in which he won many laurels. He was indiscreet enough to announce himself as a Loyalist in 1780; and when the state legislature banished him and forfeited his estates in 1782, he was so foolish as to give military information to General Nathanael Greene in order to regain his citizenship and his property. Consequently, he was detested by both the American patriots and the English; and for a time after the Revolution he was almost a man without a country. At the close of hostilities in the South he and his family removed to London, where Mrs. Fenwick died on November 6, 1785. At Greene's intercession the sentence of banishment placed against him was revoked in 1786, and he returned to South Carolina, dying there in 1800.[63] Both Sarah Christiana and Christiana were survived by children. A third daughter of John and Sarah Stuart died in early youth.[64] A son, named John Joseph, born at Charleston on November 23, 1757,[65] entered Westminster school in 1770.[66] In 1775, in order to please his father, he began the study of law at Lincoln's Inn, but he conceived a fondness for the army, which his father eventually gratified by securing him an ensigncy through the

[63] On Christiana and Edward Fenwick see [Fairfax Harrison and Others], *The John's Island Stud (South Carolina), 1750–1788* (Richmond, 1931), 36–47; Stuart to William Henry Drayton, July 18, 1775, Gage MSS.

[64] Stuart declared in a petition to the Board of Trade, Sept. 23, 1766, CO, 5/67, that he had three daughters and one son. But no reference to a third daughter after 1766 has been found.

[65] *SCHGM,* XXIII (1922), 185. The *Dictionary of National Biography* has a sketch of this son which states that he was born in Georgia in 1759 and that his name was John Alexander Stuart. But the information given here is apparently accurate, since it was taken from the parish register of St. Helena.

[66] E. A. Jones, *American Members of the Inns of Court* (London, 1904), 205. South Carolina newspaper items show that Mrs. Stuart, Christiana, and Master John sailed for Bristol in August, 1770. Christiana returned in 1773; Mrs. Stuart, in 1774.

favor of Lord George Germain.[67] John Joseph Stuart served at Guilford Court House, rose to the rank of lieutenant general in the British army, was knighted, and was made Count of Maida by Ferdinand, the Bourbon king of Naples, as a result of a victory won by him at Maida in Calabria over a Napoleonic army in 1806. He died in 1815 and was buried in Bristol Cathedral.[68]

According to Cherokee tradition, Stuart was also the father of a son by Susannah Emory, a three-quarters white granddaughter of the Cherokee trader Ludovick Grant. Cherokee legend indicates that the son was known as Oonodutu (or Oonotota) by the Cherokees and as Bushyhead by the whites; and that he was the ancestor of many persons bearing the name Bushyhead at the present day. Unfortunately, contemporary evidence proving or disproving this interesting tale is lacking,[69] but it does seem likely that Stuart had at least one consort in the Cherokee nation.[70]

Although Stuart was for many years a popular figure in Charleston, he had his enemies, among them the publisher Peter Timothy. Timothy belonged to the anti-Scottish party that developed considerable strength in South Carolina as a result of the Cherokee War; and he had a special grievance against Stuart in that Stuart unwisely gave his news on Indian affairs exclusively to Robert

[67] E. A. Jones, *American Members of the Inns of Court,* 205; Stuart to Germain, July 16, 1777, CO, 5/79; Stuart to William Knox, July 26, 1777, CO, 5/78. Jones states that Stuart's son served with Loyalist troops in the South early in the Revolution, but he was still in London when Stuart wrote the letters cited.

[68] See the sketch of Sir John Stuart in the *Dictionary of National Biography.* The frontispiece in Mackay is a reproduction of two miniature portraits of Sir John and of Christiana Fenwick.

[69] The tradition is reported in Emmet Starr, *History of the Cherokee Indians and Their Legends and Folk Lore* (Oklahoma City, 1921), 20, 305, 466–67. There are some discrepancies in the tradition. Starr states that Stuart married Susannah Emory. If so, it was by Cherokee ceremony only. Starr also declares that Stuart himself was known among the Cherokees by the names given his son, because Stuart had a great shock of blond hair. One would rather think that Stuart, in accordance with the style of his day, had his hair cut short and concealed with a wig. Documents of the eighteenth century do not show these names being applied to Stuart by the Cherokees. It is also curious that this son, who would have been seven-eighths white, appears nowhere in documents, and that he remained among the Cherokees.

[70] There is an interesting statement in a letter from Alexander Cameron to Stuart, Nov. 8, 1775, Sir Henry Clinton MSS. Cameron states that one Hugh Hamilton "is related to a good tribe being married to the Wolfs daughter Savingah, or your friend Bett—I can assure you sir that I owe her much this summer for there was nothing in agitation in this nation, but she found out & informed me."

Wells, a close friend and also a Scot, whose *South-Carolina and American General Gazette* competed rather successfully with Timothy's paper.[71] At various times during the ten years before the Revolution Timothy astutely hinted to his readers that his paper lacked Indian news only because Stuart was guilty of favoritism.[72] Occasionally he attacked Stuart more openly.[73] Another of Stuart's enemies was William Henry Drayton, whose hostility toward the superintendent probably originated in 1772, when Stuart balked an attempt by Drayton to secure a lease upon the Catawba reservation.

Stuart also became unpopular among the defenders of American rights generally, because, whatever had been his political beliefs in youth, he remained steadfast in his loyalty to the crown in the Revolutionary crisis. In 1774 he earned the enmity of the patriots by taking a prominent part in the ousting of Drayton from the South Carolina council. By September of that year he had found it necessary largely to withdraw from Charleston society, which he had previously enjoyed.[74] The outbreak of hostilities in the North placed him in a very delicate position, for the possibility that he might use his influence among the Indians to bring them down upon the frontiers of the southern colonies inevitably interested the "Liberty Boys." In May, 1775, a storm burst about his head. The patriotic party, in which both Drayton and Timothy were prominent, accused Stuart of plotting to arouse the Indians, and to incite a revolt of the slaves. Stuart was undoubtedly innocent of these charges, but his friends advised him to leave Charleston to avoid trouble. Although he was ill at the time, he went off to his plantations at Lady's Island and thence to Savannah. Warned by Governor Wright that Captains Barnwell and Joyner, agents of the patriot congress, had followed him and planned to seize him, Stuart managed to flee to an armed British ship lying in Savannah harbor. He was carried to St. Augustine, and continued to manage the affairs

[71] Wells was a man of considerable ability and was well educated. He amassed a fortune of £20,000 between his arrival in Charleston in 1752 or 1753 and the outbreak of the Revolution. He was empowered by Stuart to open the superintendent's mail when Stuart was absent from Charleston. Regarding Wells see William Charles Wells, *Two Essays: One upon Single Vision with Two Eyes; the Other on Dew* (London, 1818), Introduction, vii–viii, lv, and 348.

[72] For examples see issues of the *South-Carolina Gazette,* May 4, June 30, 1765, May 30, June 20, 1768, June 14, 1773. In an issue of May 30, 1774, Timothy very aptly described Wells's pro-Scottish attitude with the quotation, "Scratch me, Countryman!—and I'll scratch thee."

[73] See the *South-Carolina Gazette,* Aug. 15, 1768.

[74] Stuart to Frederick Haldimand, Sept. 13, 1774, British Museum, Add. MSS, 21, 672, pt. 6.

of the southern Indians from that place and later from Pensacola,[75] although his health failed and he became more and more dependent upon his subordinates. After a long illness he died of a "consumption" at Pensacola on Sunday, March 21, 1779, at three o'clock in the afternoon.[76]

Mrs. Stuart remained in South Carolina until September, 1777. With Mrs. Fenwick she was held for a time by the patriots in virtual captivity in the family residence as a hostage for good behavior on the part of her husband in regard to Indian affairs. She was allowed to go to Dorchester early in 1776, and she was released in the following summer, since it became apparent that no object was to be gained by her further detention.[77] She seems to have rejoined

[75] The charges made by the patriots, though long accepted by historians of South Carolina, have been rather thoroughly disproved by Philip M. Hamer in "John Stuart's Indian Policy during the Early Months of the American Revolution," *Miss. Vall. Hist. Rev.*, XVII (1940), 351–66. Stuart's papers show clearly that he did attempt to maintain his influence and that of the crown among the southern Indians, but that he was reluctant to send them against the frontiers and did so finally under pressure from his superiors. Even then he tried to use the Indians in conjunction with whites so that the latter would restrain the cruelty of the savages. In the Sir Henry Clinton MSS there is a very interesting paper entitled "Annecdote, March 76," which gives Stuart's explanation, related to Clinton in March, 1776, of the origin of the canard that he intended to arouse the Negroes. According to this document, Stuart received a private letter from Gage in February or March, 1775, in which the general said to the South Carolinians: "It is to be hoped for your own sakes that the delegates you send to Philadelphia will be moderate people, but you Carolinians are as hot as your climate—however it is well known that if a serious opposition takes place, you can do but little—You have too much to take care and think of, but should you proceed much greater lengths it may happen that your rice and indigo will be brought to market by Negroes instead of white people." Stuart showed this letter to William Bull, and to Bull only. Soon afterward the canard was bruited about, according to the patriots, on "the highest authority in the province." Stuart bitterly concluded that Bull had informed Drayton, his nephew, of this letter, thus giving the patriots an excuse for an attack upon Stuart. Probably Stuart's explanation is sound.

[76] Various dates have been given for the death of Stuart, but it cannot be doubted that the information in the text is correct, since it is based on statements by Alexander Cameron and Charles Stuart, deputies of the superintendent who frequently attended upon him at his last illness, in a letter to Germain, March 26, 1779, CO, 5/80. Governor Peter Chester of West Florida and General John Campbell, who were present at Pensacola at the time, also state that Stuart died on March 21, 1779. Chester to Germain, March 23, 1779, CO, 5/597, pt. 2; Campbell to Germain, March 22, 1779, CO, 5/597, pt. 1.

[77] William Moultrie, *Memoirs of the American Revolution*... (New York, 1802), I, 122–23; Cameron to Stuart, Aug. 31, 1776, CO, 5/78; Henry Laurens to John Laurens, Aug. 14, 1776, *Collections of the New-York Historical Society for the Year 1872* (New York, 1873), 226.

her husband in West Florida.[78] She returned to Charleston after the recapture of the city by the British, joining her son in an attempt to regain the family property. But Mrs. Stuart was in England in 1781, and spent the remainder of her life there. She was granted a special allowance by the British government for a time, and later the pension given to widows of officers holding the rank of colonel; and she also shared in substantial sums given to the Stuart family in compensation for Stuart's property, definitely forfeited by the government of South Carolina in 1782.[79] Mrs. Stuart died at her home in Weymouth Street, London, on July 21, 1798.[80]

Unfortunately, neither a portrait nor a description of Stuart's physical characteristics has yet been discovered.[81] That he had a very pleasing personality is shown not only by the affection conceived for him by Attakullakulla and other southern Indians, but also by the testimony of more fastidious judges. In 1772 Frederick Haldimand urged Stuart to pay a visit on General Gage at New York, and informed Gage that the general would be "charmé de le connaittre personellement." [82] Stuart's behavior was dignified even to the point of vanity. In spite of poor health he was industrious and traveled thousands of miles on the king's service. In the judgment of many competent and more or less disinterested contemporaries he was both faithful to his trust and competent in the execution of his duties. Thomas Pownall described him as "a very active, intelligent, and able man"; [83] the fiery George Johnstone, who seldom discovered good in his fellows, found Stuart to be "one of the most judicious and intelligent men I ever conversed with"; [84] and James Grant, although he quarreled with Stuart regarding the

[78] There is no direct evidence that Mrs. Stuart went to West Florida, but she was granted 1,000 acres of land in that province in 1777. Dunbar Rowland, ed., *Publications of the Mississippi Historical Society,* Centenary Series, I (Jackson, Miss., 1916), 416. Moultrie, *op. cit.,* I, 123, states that Edward Fenwick the younger was temporarily imprisoned because he was suspected of assisting Mrs. Stuart to flee South Carolina.

[79] Mrs. Stuart was given a pension as a colonel's widow because Stuart had held the title of "Colonel" of the southern Indians.

[80] *Gentleman's Magazine,* LXVIII (1798), 637.

[81] When Indian grapevine reports reached Fort Prince George that the two largest officers were slain at the very beginning of the attack on the Fort Loudoun garrison, it was concluded that Captain Paul Demeré and Lieutenant James Adamson were dead. Stuart cannot have been a tall man.

[82] Haldimand to Gage, April 12, 1772, Gage MSS.

[83] Thomas Pownall, *The Administration of the British Colonies* (London, Second Edition, 1765), Appendix, 38.

[84] Johnstone to John Pownall, Oct. 31, 1764, CO, 5/574.

powers of the superintendent, at the same time declared that he had great respect for Stuart as a man.[85] During eleven years of official association Gage found no reason to criticize Stuart's conduct. After Stuart's death Sir Henry Clinton, who was personally acquainted with the superintendent, wrote to Lord George Germain: "The loss of so faithful and useful a servant to His Majesty is at all times to be regretted, but at this critical juncture is most sincerely to be lamented." [86] That these testimonials were not empty statements of the sort frequently made by friends of embezzlers is indicated by a study of his career and a survey of his financial transactions.[87] He was undoubtedly an honorable man according to eighteenth-century standards, possibly also according to more exacting canons. It is clear that insinuations directed against Stuart's conduct by two historians of the twentieth century (which are dealt with elsewhere) are based on insufficient and distorted evidence. Notable was Stuart's loyalty to his aides. Alexander Cameron, as a member of a grand jury at Ninety-Six in November, 1774, signed presentments which denied the right of Parliament to tax or bind the colonists in any way whatsoever and called upon South Carolina to coöperate with her sister colonies in the defense of American rights. Stuart refused to take any action against Cameron until the facts of the situation could be learned. Since Cameron had been drunk and had acted contrary to his real sentiments, he was forgiven.[88]

No fewer than four other scions of the Stuart family of Inverness

[85] Grant to Stuart, Aug. 22, 1767, CO, 5/73.

[86] Clinton to Germain, May 3, 1779, Sir Henry Clinton MSS.

[87] Because Stuart's expenses during the Revolution were much larger than previously, Germain at one time suspected him of dishonesty, and the treasury refused to honor a large number of his last bills. But his executors were able to show that he was virtually penniless at the time of his death; and Germain later exonerated him. Germain's final conclusion was that Stuart's ill health during his last years permitted his deputies and aides to deceive him and to cheat the crown. Cameron ardently defended Stuart's reputation. Germain to Cameron, Aug. 5, 1779, CO, 5/80; Germain to Cameron, April 5, 1780, Cameron to Germain, May 1, 1780, Cameron to Germain, July 18, 1780, CO, 5/81. In Lieutenant Colonel William Tayler to Gage, March 4, 1767, Gage MSS, there is a curious remark that seems to hint that Stuart did some "honest grafting": "The superintendant's power and office cannot yet be thoroughly understood, it should not be quite uncontrolable, nor should his office ever admit of his being the principal merchant with the Indians . . . ." Tayler, as this passage shows, was very jealous of the authority of Stuart. The writer has seen no other evidence that Stuart was engaged in trade after 1763. James Adair, who was hostile to Stuart, would hardly have failed to mention participation by the superintendent in the trade.

[88] *South-Carolina Gazette,* Dec 12, 1774; Cameron to Stuart, Dec. 24, 1774, Stuart to Gage, Jan. 18, 1775, Gage MSS.

either visited or resided in America. Francis, already mentioned, established his home at Beaufort. He escaped the economic disaster that overtook his older brother,[89] and continued as a merchant until his death on September 22, 1766.[90] Francis held various local offices, serving as justice of the peace, tax collector of the parish of St. Helena, and member of the vestry. He married Anne, daughter of Lewis Reeve, at Beaufort on December 28, 1752,[91] and they had several children, descendants of whom are to be found in South Carolina at the present day.

Another son of the Bailie, Henry, often spoken of as Harry, was intimately associated with John Stuart in the conduct of Indian affairs during the early years of the Revolution. The Bailie was so hard-pressed financially when Harry reached the age for advanced schooling that he considered sending him with another younger son, William, to the Scots College at Douai; but the Bailie refrained, in spite of the fact that education at Douai would be free, since he could not bear to have his children enter the Roman Catholic faith. Henry came to America, apparently in 1753, and was assisted by his brother Francis in obtaining employment.[92] It seems likely that he played some little part in the Cherokee War.[93] He also became a merchant at Beaufort, establishing a partnership with William Shaw that endured until Shaw's death by drowning in 1769.[94] Immediately after the British occupation of West Florida Henry Stuart was at Pensacola,[95] although he did not remain long, presumably because business opportunities were lacking. He also held several local offices at Beaufort, including that of sheriff. Like John Stuart, he entertained Loyalist opinions, and he found it wise to leave for St. Augustine at the onset of the Revolution. For a time he served as special agent for the southern Indian department, and was then appointed by his brother deputy superintendent for

[89] Advertisements by Francis Stuart in the *South-Carolina Gazette*, Nov. 18, 1754, Oct. 9, 1755, and other issues, demonstrate that Francis was not only solvent when John went bankrupt, but that he sailed to Great Britain in 1755 and returned with a supply of goods.

[90] *South-Carolina and American General Gazette*, Sept. 26, 1766.

[91] *SCHGM*, XXIII (1922), 182.

[92] Bailie Steuart to James Stuart, Jan. 17, 1752, Bailie Steuart to Allan Stuart, Sept. 4, 1752, Mackay, 479, 482.

[93] Henry Stuart was a witness to the will of Lieutenant Coytmore, dated Feb. 16, 1760, Record of Wills, Charleston County, Vol. ix, 1760–1767 (A), Charleston County (S. C.) Courthouse.

[94] *South-Carolina and American General Gazette*, Aug. 7, 1769.

[95] Minutes of council of W. Fla., Nov. 25, 1764, Feb. 7, 1765, CO, 5/625.

the Small Tribes on the Mississippi. He fled to a British man-of-war when the Willing expedition came down the Mississippi. He died at Hampstead, near London, on May 21, 1783.[96]

Allan Stuart, who was somewhat older than Henry, studied medicine, served an apprenticeship at Inverness, and attended the University of Edinburgh,[97] but eventually became a lieutenant in the 77th Regiment and served in America in the Seven Years' War. He took part in the assault on Havana in 1762, and died shortly afterward as the result of wounds or disease.[98]

Patrick Stuart, a fourth brother, served for some time as mate on the ship of Captain Alexander Wedderburn, husband of his half-sister Marion. In 1750 John Stuart unsuccessfully attempted to secure another berth for him. Bailie Steuart then obtained a place for him as second mate with a Scottish captain named Tolmie, but Patrick emigrated to South Carolina in 1752 to seek his fortune.[99] Patrick apparently did not remain long in South Carolina. He soon joined the British navy. He was a lieutenant, serving on the *Centaur,* in 1773. In the fall of that year he came to Charleston from England, and he stayed in South Carolina until September, 1774. During 1773–74 John Stuart vainly tried to use his influence with General Gage and with the Earl of Dartmouth to secure promotion for him.[100] Patrick was given a land grant in West Florida in 1777, a fact which indicates that he may have been in that province during the Revolution.[101] In January, 1779, he was captured with H.M.S. *Weazle* by a French frigate in the West Indies. He was carried into Guadeloupe, and there was paroled.[102] No further mention of him has been found.

[96] *Gentleman's Magazine,* LIII (1783), 454.

[97] For various items regarding Allan Stuart consult Mackay, Index.

[98] *Johnson Papers,* III, 991; Allan Stuart's will cited above. Allan had married at London on Jan. 8, 1757, one Hester Boumeester (or Bonester). A. W. Hughes Clarke, ed., *The Register of St. Mary the Virgin, Aldermanbury, London,* Pt. III (London, 1935), 97.

[99] On Patrick's early career consult Mackay.

[100] *South-Carolina Gazette,* Dec. 6, 1773; *Royal Historical Manuscripts Commission,* Fourteenth Report, pt. 10, 165, 280; Stuart to Dartmouth, Sept. 3, 1774, CO, 5/75; Stuart to Gage, Dec. 25, 1773, July 4, 1774 (Private), Gage MSS.

[101] Dunbar Rowland, ed., *Publications of the Mississippi Historical Society,* Centennial Series, I (1916), 415.

[102] D. Bonner-Smith, ed., "The Barrington Papers," II, *Navy Records Society* (1941), 240, 254.

CHAPTER XI

THE CONGRESS OF AUGUSTA

THE year 1763, long recognized as a turning point in American history, brought material political changes in the South. During the peace negotiations at the close of the Seven Years' War France gave New Orleans and western Louisiana to Spain, although French officials continued to exercise temporary authority in those territories until Spain was able to take control in 1769. Moreover, France and Spain ceded eastern Louisiana and Florida respectively to Great Britain in the Peace of Paris of 1763. As a result, the French threat to the southern English colonies was virtually removed. The Spanish in Louisiana were more powerful after 1769 than were the Spanish in Florida before 1763, but did not constitute a major worry to British officials until the outbreak of the American War of Independence. Although the doings of the Bourbons caused much less concern in the South from 1763 to 1775 than previously, frontier problems in that area during those twelve years did not lose their importance. The westward expansion of the southern English colonies assumed greater proportion as a factor in relations with the southern Indians after 1763, and the Indian trade continued to be a matter of great concern. Furthermore, the British imperial government, through its attempt to control westward emigration by means of the Proclamation of 1763 and later restrictive measures, through its efforts to manage Indian diplomacy directly from London, and through its endeavors to assume the power to regulate the Indian trade, gave frontier problems in the South a new significance. The exercise of direct imperial authority over the southern wilderness inevitably led to quarrels between the government of the mother country and the American colonists. To what degree those quarrels contributed to the outbreak of the War of Independence cannot now be accurately estimated, but they did contribute, possibly only in minor degree. As Indian superintendent in the southern district, John Stuart was a major figure in all the frontier controversies in the South during the period 1763–75.

When Stuart assumed office early in 1763 there existed some

danger of a general uprising among the southern Indians comparable to the outbreak of Pontiac; and his first task was to prevent such a disaster. Unfortunately, the English victory in the Cherokee War had not dampened the martial ardor of the southern Indians; and Indian relations had remained in a disturbed state since 1761.

The Cherokees, although rather severely chastised, were not in the most friendly mood in 1763, especially since they held serious grievances against the English in regard to trade and lands. Governor Boone had prevented trade with the Cherokees from South Carolina until June, 1762, in order to compel them to free the last of their prisoners; and Georgia and Virginia traders who dealt with the Cherokees contrary to the public interest were not sufficiently numerous to relieve their wants.[1] Nor were the Cherokees satisfied when the trade was reopened from South Carolina. In order to prevent future conflicts Boone had taken up the idea that all the provinces concerned in the Cherokee commerce should establish public monopolies selling goods at cost. The South Carolina assembly, at his urging, passed an act in May, 1762, part of which established such a monopoly under five directors, Thomas Lamboll, Thomas Shubrick, Gabriel Manigault, John Savage, and Thomas Smith, Jr. They were given £6,000 (provincial currency) for operating expenses, and private trade was forbidden under pain of fines and imprisonment. The act provided, however, for the establishment of only one factory, and that at Keowee, since it was assumed that the Overhill country lay outside the bounds of South Carolina.[2] Consequently the Overhills traded when possible with Virginians and Georgians, but could not secure sufficient goods. On the other hand, Edward Wilkinson, who served under the trustees as factor at Keowee, had difficulty in disposing of the wares in his charge, although the directors spent no more than £18,000 (provincial currency) for goods during a period of two years. This state of affairs was not improved by Wilkinson's attempt to prevent private trade by arresting two Virginians engaged in it.[3] Since Boone's

[1] Boone to Amherst, June 25, 1762, CO, 5/62. In June, 1762, all the remaining prisoners, except two who were slain at Hiwassie town, were given up. In exchange the Cherokees captured by Montgomery were finally released.

[2] The act is printed in Cooper and McCord, eds., *Statutes at Large of South Carolina,* IV, 168–73. See also memorial by Charles Garth to Board of Trade, Nov. —, 1762, CO, 5/377.

[3] The Journal of the Directors of the Cherokee Trade, 1762–1765, Historical Commission of South Carolina, which contains the records of the monopoly, shows that six shipments of goods of the value indicated were sent to Keowee between August, 1762, and March, 1764. There is a good discussion of the monopoly in Stuart to Amherst, March 15, 1763, Amherst MSS.

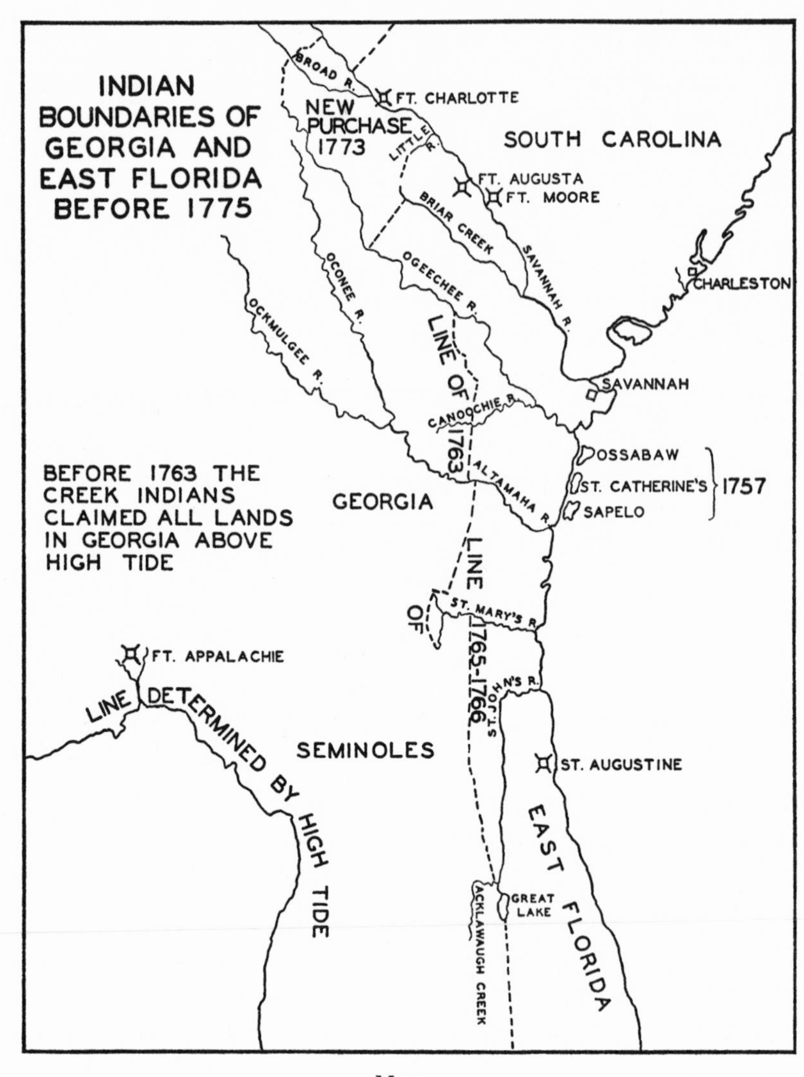

Map 3

attempts to persuade Georgia and Virginia to set up public monopolies failed,[4] the Cherokee trade situation had remained unsatisfac-

[4] Fauquier favored Boone's plan, but the burgesses did not take action, supposedly because of lack of funds. CJSC, xxix, 26–27. Amherst also approved of it. Amherst to Boone, July 8, Aug. 23, 1762, WO, 34/36, pt. 1.

tory. Moreover, encroachments of frontiersmen from Virginia on lands claimed by the Cherokees in the valley of the Kanawha River and increasingly rapid settlement by the whites west of Long Canes had added to the resentment felt by the Cherokees.[5]

The Catawbas were also dissatisfied, for they had failed to secure adequate protection for their lands. The attitude of the Choctaws was doubtful. Many of them were uneasy because of the impending loss of their French friends; and some of their chiefs feared that with the establishment of the English on the Gulf coast they would lose their influence. On the other hand, the Choctaws could hope for a flourishing commerce with the English; and a trading path from Mobile would be of more than merely economic value to them, because it would deprive their detested neighbors, the Creeks, of the power of cutting off their dealings with the English. In addition, the Anglophile party had been strengthened by a considerable supply of presents brought to them in the winter of 1762–63 by Captain James Colbert, who also carried a consignment from Boone to the Chickasaws.[6] In the spring of 1763 the Choctaws made a lasting peace with the Chickasaws.[7] The latter were as friendly as ever to the English, although they were displeased by disorder in the trade.

The years 1761–63 had not brought improvement in Anglo-Creek relations. In July, 1761, Governor Wright obtained some semblance of order in the Creek trade by strictly limiting the number of traders from Georgia and by allocating them to specific towns,[8] but friction was caused by the advance of white settlements along the banks of the Ogeechee River and on the south bank of the Savannah above Augusta. In February, 1761, Wright was authorized by the Board of Trade to purchase lands beyond the tide level from the Creeks, but he made no attempt to do so for fear of further alienating them.[9] Although the Indian allies of the Spanish in Florida were permanently driven off to Cuba by the Seminoles

[5] According to the *South-Carolina Gazette,* April 2, 1763, more than 1,000 families from colonies north of South Carolina settled in the region of Long Canes during the preceding year, and 400 additional families were expected.

[6] Minute of S. C. council, June 9, 1762, Public Records of South Carolina, iii, 516; CJSC, xxix, 65; CHJSC, xxxv, pt. 1, 145–48.

[7] Stuart to Amherst, June 2, 1763, Amherst MSS.

[8] Wright to Board of Trade, Aug. 27, 1764, *GCR,* XXVIII, pt. 2, 114–16.

[9] *GCR,* IX, 70 ff.; Wright to Board of Trade, Nov. 23, Dec. 23, 1763, *ibid.,* XXVIII, pt. 1, 810–11, 813–15. Wright testified that Georgia had made official grants of lands beyond the tide level before he became governor and that settlements had been made in consequence.

before the spring of 1762,[10] the entrance of Spain into the Seven Years' War as an ally of France and the English conquest of Havana gave French agents an excellent opportunity to inform the Creeks that the English planned to drive their European enemies from the South and subsequently to fall upon and destroy the Creeks. This story gained wide credence among the Creeks,[11] especially after the spring of 1763, when they learned that the English were about to take over Florida and the eastern half of Louisiana. Even the Creeks who did not believe this story were uneasy, for the impending withdrawal of the French and Spanish meant that the nation could no longer profit from a balance of power. The Mortar, who abandoned a settlement he had formed on the Coosa River [12] and returned to the Upper Creek towns, in the summer of 1763, was especially displeased by the situation. He feared that the expulsion of the French and Spanish would lessen his power and increase the prestige of the party in the nation which had favored the English. It soon became evident that The Mortar was not disposed to submit to misfortune but, rather, would attempt to retrieve his own position and that of his nation by organizing a southern Indian confederacy and attacking the English. In the summer of 1763 under his influence the Creeks refused outright to atone for the murder of the trader Spencer; and The Mortar assiduously disseminated French propaganda. Stuart believed that he was supported in his designs by French officials.[13]

Fortunately for the English, several factors worked against the success of The Mortar's intrigues and gave them time to prepare countermeasures. The Mortar was unable to command the undivided loyalty of the Creeks, and his chances of securing assistance

[10] *South-Carolina Gazette,* April 3, 1762.

[11] Minute of S. C. council, May 12, 1762, Public Records of South Carolina, iii, 493; Wright to Board of Trade, June 10, 1762, *GCR,* XXVIII, pt. 1, 635–41.

[12] *South-Carolina Gazette,* Aug. 27, 1762. Pressure of attacks by northern Indians forced The Mortar to remove from the Upper Coosa.

[13] Stuart to Amherst, March 15, June 2, 1763, Amherst MSS. Stuart reported that the commander of Fort Toulouse had urged Creeks, Choctaws, and Cherokees at the fort early in 1763 to make a simultaneous attack on the English; and he believed that the Baron des Jonnes, who was seized in the Cherokee country about the same time by Thomas Sumter, was a French agent. The baron admitted that he was a French officer and that he had held a lieutenancy in the French army, but declared that he had fled Fort Massac after killing a man in a duel and that he had been picked up by Ouconnostotah and brought to the Overhill country. Sumter carried him off to Charleston, and Boone put him out of the way of doing harm by shipping him to England. *South-Carolina Gazette,* May 7, 1763.

from other tribes were injured by various circumstances. All the other southern Indians were offended by the contemptuous manner in which they were treated by the Creeks, and they were also jealous of their increasing numbers. The Chickasaws and Choctaws, at peace with each other, were more disposed to wage war against the Creeks than to serve with them as allies. The Cherokees had a special reason to hate the Creeks, for they believed, not without cause, that the latter had persuaded them to attack the English in 1760 and had then deserted them in the hour of need.[14]

Strangely enough, Lord Egremont, who as secretary of state for the southern department (1761–63) sponsored a policy of economy toward the Indians in the northern district and who should bear part of the responsibility for the outbreak of Pontiac, recognized the need of conciliating the southern tribes. Following a plan of action proposed by Henry Ellis,[15] on March 16, 1763, he ordered Stuart and the southern governors to hold a congress with representatives of all the southern tribes to soothe any jealousies that might be created by the withdrawal of the French and Spanish and to remove grievances; and he indicated the procedure that should be followed. Stuart was to inform the Indians that the French and Spanish had been driven beyond the Mississippi merely to stop their deceitful propaganda and to insure Anglo-Indian friendship; he was to offer forgiveness of all past misdeeds, to promise a prosperous trade and redress of grievances, and to indicate that whatever forts were maintained in the southern Indian nations would be used only to aid the trade and not to coerce the savages. If the Indians asked that any fort be abandoned, Stuart was to declare that the royal government would graciously consider their request. Egremont also arranged for the shipment of £4,000 or £5,000 worth of goods to be distributed at the congress, and suggested Augusta as the most suitable place for the meeting.[16] On the same day he wrote to Amherst on the subject of the forthcoming congress. He indicated his belief that Forts Toulouse, Tombigbee, and Loudoun were of no military value to the English, and that they should be abandoned in such a way as to make it appear that relinquishment

[14] Stuart to Gage, May 22, 1764, Gage MSS.

[15] [Henry Ellis], "On the methods to prevent giving any alarm to the Indians by taking possession of Florida and Louisiana," Shelburne MSS, lx. The paper is neither signed nor dated, but Miss Edna Vosper has identified the handwriting as that of Ellis.

[16] Egremont to Stuart, March 16, 1763, Amherst MSS.

of the forts was carried out to please the Indians;[17] and he suggested that Amherst give advice on the matter of the forts and whatever other recommendations he might wish to Stuart and the southern governors.[18] Amherst himself believed that forts should be maintained along the Mississippi and in the Floridas,[19] but he left the question of the interior posts to the discretion of the officials who were to hold the congress.[20]

By the end of June Stuart knew that the governors could be present, and he therefore dispatched invitations to all the tribes to meet the English representatives at Augusta on October 15. Many difficulties arose, however, before a meeting place was definitely chosen. The Cherokees at first desired that the gathering be held at Saluda Old Town, because the Creeks had recently killed two of their number and because they feared they would be attacked en route to Augusta, but they finally agreed. The governors, except for Wright, preferred Dorchester in South Carolina. Stuart proceeded to Augusta, where he tried to persuade the arriving Indians to go on to Dorchester. When the Creek delegates positively refused, Stuart urged Boone, Dobbs, and Fauquier to come to Augusta. They arrived at that town on November 2 and found over 800 Indians there. Attakullakulla, the "Prince" of Choté, and Saluy headed the Cherokees, for Ouconnostotah sulked at home. Considerable numbers of Lower Creeks also attended, with several of their prominent chiefs, but the great leaders of the Upper Creeks, The Mortar and Emistisiguo,[21] failed to appear. In fact, The Mortar, who was guilty of the murder of two traders just before the congress,[22] was not specifically invited. The Choctaws were repre-

[17] As a matter of fact, Fort Loudoun had not been reoccupied. Apparently the cannon were removed, but the fortifications rotted away.

[18] Egremont to Amherst, March 16, 1763, Amherst MSS.

[19] Amherst to Secretary at War, April 26, 1763 (Extract), Amherst MSS.

[20] Amherst to Boone, June 15, 1763, Amherst MSS. J. C. Long, *Lord Jeffrey Amherst: A Soldier of the King* (New York, 1933), 184, erroneously states that the congress was called as a result of orders from Amherst to Atkin.

[21] Emistisiguo, chief of the town of Little Tallassies, had risen to rivalry with The Mortar for leadership among the Upper Creeks. He was well disposed toward the English, but for some years wielded less influence than The Mortar because of the fact that his mother was a slave. Eventually, through Stuart's support, Emistisiguo became as powerful as his rival. After the death of The Mortar in 1774 he was the outstanding chief among the Upper Creeks. With followers he attacked an American force under General Anthony Wayne in Georgia in 1782, engaged in a hand-to-hand conflict with "Mad Anthony," and was about to dispatch Wayne when he was slain by an American trooper. *Royal Gazette,* July 3, 10, 1782.

[22] Stuart to Amherst, Oct. 4, 1763, Amherst MSS.

sented only by two chiefs, who came through the Creek nation disguised as Chickasaws, all the other Choctaw chiefs remaining at home because of fear of a Creek attack while they were en route. The Chickasaws were well represented by a delegation led by Paya Mattaha. A few Catawbas were also present. Their leader was a chief known as Colonel Ayres, successor to "King" Hagler, who had been slain on September 4 by raiding northern Indians.[23]

The congress met formally on November 5 and made such rapid progress during the next five days that it was possible to sign a treaty on November 10. The speeches of Stuart, in behalf of himself and the governors, followed the lines laid down by Egremont and were well received. Since the Indians failed to bring up the subject of the interior forts, nothing was said regarding them by the English representatives. The Catawbas were satisfied by a promise that the survey of their reservation arranged by Atkin would be undertaken, a task which was completed in the following year.[24] The Creeks and Chickasaws complained about the trade and urged that it be strictly confined to the towns and that the number of traders be set at a reasonable figure. Stuart and the governors could do no more than recommend that they try to solve their difficulties by dealing with a few honest traders only. The Choctaws and Chickasaws were pleased by assurances that trade would be opened with them from Mobile, for their traders would then be free from danger of molestation by the Creeks.

The complaints of the Cherokees regarding intrusions on their lands and the inadequacy of the trade set up by South Carolina were less capable of appeasement. Attakullakulla, speaking for his tribe, protested against settlements made by Virginians west of the Kanawha River and asserted that the lands of the Cherokees extended to

[23] CJSC, xxix, 89–91. Colonel Ayres was formally elected "king" at the congress. He lost his popularity among the Catawbas and was succeeded early in 1765 by Captain Fron, who was elected and crowned "king" at the urging of Samuel Wyly, acting for Bull. CJSC, xxxii, 442–43, 504–5.

[24] The survey was completed by Samuel Wyly, whom Atkin had employed for the purpose. He was reëngaged by Bull and Dobbs, and was eventually paid by South Carolina. The reservation, an area roughly fifteen miles square, was laid out with the Catawba, or Wateree, River "centrical." Its northern boundary ran across the confluence of the main stream of the Catawba and its south fork. Wyly's bill was £1,000 (South Carolina currency). Bull to Gage, April 9, 1765, Stuart to Gage, Jan. 21, 1766, Gage MSS. Wyly drew a map of the reservation, which is to be found in Archer B. Hulbert, ed., *The Crown Collection of Photographs of American Maps,* Third Series, Plate 31. The reservation is well shown on Captain John Collet's "A Compleat Map of North Carolina from an actual Survey . . ." (London, 1770).

the Kanawha. Fauquier reminded Little Carpenter that Virginians had settled west of the river more than ten years before without protest from the Cherokees. He refused to negotiate regarding the establishment of a boundary between the Cherokees and Virginia because he was not instructed to do so. Attakullakulla promised that persons then residing on the left bank of the Kanawha and north of the Holston would not be disturbed; he declared that he had brought up the matter solely to obtain some assurance that his people would not be molested when hunting on the south bank of the upper Holston. The Cherokees also complained regarding the advance of the South Carolinians west of Long Canes Creek, for they still considered that stream the dividing line between themselves and the English. However, both Saluy and Attakullakulla indicated that settlers west of Long Canes Creek might remain, provided no further lands were seized. This stipulation required the English not to go beyond a line running across the Charleston-Keowee road between Templeton's and Swearingham's plantations, which were the most advanced settlements and which were then calculated to lie about sixty miles below Keowee. Stuart and Boone did not agree to this stipulation, for they contended that the clauses of the peace treaty of 1761 which provided that the Cherokees were not to go east of a line drawn across the road forty miles below Keowee constituted a boundary. But their stand was apparently not made clear to the Cherokees by the interpreters, and the problem therefore remained unsettled.[25] Criticism by the Cherokees of the South Carolina public trade was answered merely by an assurance that the matter would be referred to the king, since the English representatives thought that the system tended to maintain order among the Cherokees.

Much more serious were the discussions with the spokesmen for the Creeks. These claimed they represented the whole nation, although very few Upper townsmen were present. At first they assumed a very haughty attitude. They declared that the English were not to go beyond the tide level in West Florida, and that the territory of the English in East Florida was not to reach beyond the St. John's River in the neighborhood of St. Augustine. As late as June, 1763, the Creeks had asserted that the tide level should continue to serve as their boundary with Georgia,[26] but they now of-

[25] In addition to the journal of the congress see a "talk" from the Cherokee chiefs to Bull, July 11, 1765, also Captain Gavin Cochrane to Gage, Jan. 4, 1765, Gage, MSS.

[26] Wright to Egremont, June 10, 1763, *GCR*, XXXVII, 50–53.

fered a substantial cession to Georgia in return for the forgiveness of their past offenses. They proposed that the Georgia boundary run up Little River from its confluence with the Savannah, across to the headwaters of Briar Creek, down it for a few miles, thence in a southwesterly direction to the Ogeechee River, down the Ogeechee to a point near the mouth of Buckhead Creek, and thence southward to a point on the Altamaha near the mouth of Penholoway Creek. The course of the line below the Altamaha was to be left for future discussion. All the advanced settlements of Georgia were included within this line.[27] The Creeks declared that they would seize Negroes and cattle who might cross this boundary, although they were bound by earlier agreements to return both Negroes and cattle. The English representatives responded adroitly to the "talks" of the Creeks. They referred the question of boundaries in the Floridas to the governors who were soon to be appointed for those provinces, and they approved the boundary proposed for Georgia. By offering a reward for every Negro brought to the settlements they secured a promise from the Creeks to return all runaway blacks. They also succeeded in obtaining an agreement that neither the Indians nor the whites were to molest cattle or horses belonging to the other party. (The Georgia-Indian boundary of 1763 is shown on Map 3, p. 178.)

These agreements were all included in the treaty signed at the close of negotiations. Other articles of that document provided for the maintenance of peace between all the signatories; for the execution in the presence of two whites of an Indian murderer of a white man; and for the execution in the presence of the victim's relatives, after trial and condemnation, of a white murderer of an Indian.

Stuart and the governors were satisfied with their work, although they foresaw future difficulties arising from the trade and therefore recommended to Egremont that "the commerce with the Indians [be placed upon] a general, safe, equitable footing . . . which we are afraid will never be done by respective provinces." [28] Stuart was es-

[27] On negotiations regarding the Georgia line see Wright to Board of Trade, Nov. 23, Dec. 23, 1763, *GCR*, XXVIII, pt. 1, 810–11, 813–15.

[28] This account of the congress is based primarily upon Stuart to Board of Trade, Dec. 1, 1763, CO, 323/17; and the *Journal of the Congress of the Four Southern Governors, and the Superintendant of That District, with the Five Nations of Indians, at Augusta, 1763* (Charleston [1764]). Only fifty copies of this official journal were printed, one of which is in the William L. Clements Library. This little volume contains the proceedings, the treaty, and a letter from Stuart and the governors, dated Nov. 10, 1763, to Egremont.

pecially pleased, for he rightly believed that he had found a sound method of handling the Creeks: they could be isolated and rendered less dangerous by fanning the enmity already existing between the Creeks and their neighbors. As a result of his labors at Augusta, he believed that he could count on considerable moral support and even military aid from the other tribes if difficulties arose between the Creeks and the English.[29]

Stuart remained at Augusta until November 19 to cement friendships with the Chickasaws, Choctaws, and Cherokees, and also to distribute presents.[30] He reached Charleston on November 30, accompanied by the two Choctaws, whom he sent to West Florida by sea shortly afterward. A little later Stuart also sent the presents for the Choctaw nation to Mobile by sea.

Stuart soon learned that the Creeks were likely to test his plans before they had been thoroughly worked out. In December rumors began to come in that the Upper Creeks had murdered some traders; and these were quickly followed by authentic accounts of the murder of fourteen whites in the Long Canes area on December 24. Seven Lower Creeks acting upon instigation from The Mortar were responsible for the crime. Stuart feared that war might result if he demanded retribution in accordance with the treaty so recently signed at Augusta, but he felt that justice and the preservation of English prestige required such action. He informed the southern governors of the situation, and he sent messages to the Creeks requesting the execution of the culprits. Fearing an unfavorable reply, he also sent "talks" to the other tribes to solicit their help in the event that hostilities broke out. Aware that it might be impossible to coerce the Creeks without cutting off the trade, he asked the English military officers who had recently occupied Pensacola and Mobile to join in executing such a measure should necessity require it.[31]

Conciliatory replies from several Creek chieftains soon reached Stuart, but no response from the nation as a whole, supposedly because most of the headmen were absent from their towns. When

[29] Stuart to Amherst, Dec. 3, 1763, Amherst MSS.

[30] Stuart reported that he had distributed 59,808 lbs. of beef, 1,868 bushels of corn, and over 1,245 gallons of rum. "Return of Provisions Issued to the Indians at the Congress of Augusta from the 10th October to the 18th November Inclusive," Amherst MSS. He also gave out 1,077 guns, 36,500 gunflints, 7,216 lbs. of powder, 952 mirrors, and 73 "prettys." "Distribution of Presents to the Indians at the Congress, Fort Augusta, 19th November 1763," *ibid.*

[31] Stuart to Gage, Dec. 31, 1763, Feb. 2, 1764, Gage MSS; Stuart to Board of Trade, Jan. 16, 1764, CO, 323/17.

informed of this fact, Boone formally proposed to Wright and to the commanders at Pensacola and Mobile that the Creek trade be stopped immediately,[32] although such a step might well lead to war and although the South Carolina assembly, then in the midst of a hot quarrel with Boone regarding the prerogative, had refused to take any action to deal with the crisis.[33] In March, 1764, Stuart decided to employ Alexander Cameron [34] as a commissary and to send him to Choté to secure a definite promise of help from the Cherokees should the Creeks break out—a mission in which Cameron was successful. Stuart then hurried off to Georgia carrying Boone's proposal to Governor Wright.

According to Boone, Stuart indicated in private conversation before leaving Charleston that he was in favor of Boone's plan. But Stuart came to feel that further negotiations should first be attempted, since the Creeks had not refused satisfaction and since there was an excellent chance that they might be persuaded to give it. Even though such negotiations should fail, Stuart believed they would be of value because they would give time to complete his alliances with the other tribes and to make military preparations. He did not wish to cut off the trade except as a last possible resort. After his arrival at Savannah on March 17 he conferred with Wright.

[32] Boone to Wright, March 7, 1764, Gage MSS.

[33] Boone to Board of Trade, Jan. 21, 1764, CO, 5/377.

[34] Alexander Cameron was a native of Scotland. His real name was apparently MacLeod. Cameron to Stuart, Nov. 8, 1775, Sir Henry Clinton MSS. It is likely that he was a connection of Stuart by marriage. As General John Campbell testifies, he was neither well educated nor brought up to business. It is possible that he was the Alexander Cameron of Inverness, bond servant, who emigrated to Georgia with the Highlanders and who was a resident of Darien in 1737. See Campbell to Germain, Dec. 15, 1779, CO, 5/597, pt. 1; *GCR,* XXIX, 384. According to a statement made by his heirs, Cameron held a commission in "his Majestys Regiment" during the Seven Years' War, but the *British Army Lists* show only that he was created an ensign in the Independent Regulars on Feb. 25, 1761. Probably he served in the Cherokee War. He was stationed at Fort Prince George from September, 1762, to September, 1763, perhaps longer. When the Independent Regulars were disbanded Cameron began searching for the 2,000 acres of land to which he was entitled under the Proclamation of 1763. At that juncture he was employed by Stuart. He was promoted to deputy superintendent in or before 1768. He spent much time among the Cherokees during the following fifteen years, and became almost as much a Cherokee as his charges. Familiarly known as "Scotchie," he came to wield great influence among them. He died at Savannah on Dec. 29, 1781. He was the father of three children, probably half-breeds, who survived him. See *British Army Lists;* Stuart to Gage, April 11, 1764, Gage MSS; Wright to Germain, Jan. 2, 1782, *GCR,* XXXVIII, pt. 2, 558, also *ibid.,* 557; American Loyalist Transcripts, lv, 556–65. Other facts regarding Cameron appear elsewhere herein. See the index.

Wright, who had previously indicated that he was in favor of stopping the trade, was impressed by Stuart's arguments and urged Boone to take no action until a formal reply was received from the Creek nation. Since Boone could accomplish nothing without the aid of Wright, he was forced to acquiesce.[35]

The Lower Creeks had already admitted that the Long Canes murderers came from their towns. On March 26 a group of nineteen Creeks, including a few men of prominence, visited Augusta and spoke in very conciliatory fashion.[36] On April 10 some Upper Creeks led by Emistisiguo appeared at Augusta and called for peace and understanding. Emistisiguo claimed that his party represented all the Upper Creeks, including The Mortar.[37] But time passed without any punitive action on the part of the nation, and the culprits went into hiding. Captain James Mark Prevost, commander of the Royal Americans who replaced the Independent Regulars in South Carolina and Georgia after 1763,[38] sent a small reinforcement to Fort Augusta at Wright's request. To please Boone he also undertook to place twenty men on the Savannah River below Augusta.[39] However, neither South Carolina nor Georgia made any

[35] Wright to Boone, March 21, 1764, Stuart to Gage, April 11, 1764, Gage MSS; Boone to Board of Trade, April 7, 1764, CO, 5/377. Boone was exceedingly angry when he learned that Stuart had successfully opposed his plan. He had not formally consulted Stuart, and he claimed that the superintendent had changed his mind regarding methods of dealing with the Creeks merely because of this neglect, although such does not appear to have been the case. He protested energetically to the Board of Trade regarding Stuart's conduct and urged that the superintendent be compelled to operate under the orders of the southern governors when he was not engaged in executing instructions from the military commander. Such an arrangement would have reduced Stuart practically to the status of a provincial agent. The Board of Trade ignored Boone's protest.

[36] Stuart to Gage, April 11, 1764, Gage MSS.

[37] "Talk" from Upper Creek chiefs to Wright and Stuart, April 10, 1764, Gage MSS.

[38] Under orders from Amherst the Independent Regulars were formally disbanded on March 17, 1764. Those who were fit for duty and who desired to do so were permitted to enlist in the Royal Americans. Boone to Gage, March 28, 1764, Gage MSS.

[39] Wright to Gage, June 6, 1764, Gage MSS; CJSC, xxx, 85–92, 97–100. After 1763 small garrisons of Royal Americans were maintained at Forts Moore and Prince George in South Carolina, and at Forts Augusta and Frederica in Georgia. All these forts were supposedly supplied and maintained at provincial expense. A detachment was also stationed at Charleston, where the commander of all the regulars in the two provinces had his headquarters. Fort Prince George was once more repaired in 1765, but the South Carolina assembly decided in 1764 to abandon Fort Moore, since it no longer protected the frontier, and to replace it with another fort in a more useful situation. Lieutenant Governor Bull commissioned Captain Gavin Cochrane, Prevost's successor, to choose a new site, and

real preparation for a conflict. From Charleston, to which place he had returned on April 3, Stuart continued to press the Creeks for a favorable decision.

Meanwhile Stuart, Wright, and Boone had informed General Gage concerning the crisis. Gage believed an Indian war was fruitless unless it led to a permanent peace; and he was fully aware that the expenditures resulting from a war with the Creeks would meet with disapproval from the English statesmen then following a policy of economy. He would therefore in any case have counseled moderation in dealing with the Creeks, but the fact that he was already heavily burdened by the conflict with Pontiac furnished an overpowering argument for a conciliatory policy in the South, at least for the year 1764. Gage therefore urged the southern governors to maintain peace for the moment, even though the Creeks did not punish the murderers. He pointed out that he would be unable for some time to send reinforcements to the small bodies of regulars then stationed in the South. He also recommended that Stuart and the governors arouse animosity between the Creeks and their neighbors, so that the Creeks would have cause to fear a possible Anglo-Cherokee-Choctaw-Chickasaw alliance. He even suggested to Stuart that "it might not be very difficult to prevail upon some bold Cherokee to knock [The Mortar] on the head."[40]

Gage's support of Stuart's policy of moderation and caution compelled the southern governors to coöperate in executing that policy. Wright had been willing to give the Creeks ample time to comply with the English demand for satisfaction, but he felt that execution of the murderers must be secured. Nevertheless, Georgia was almost defenseless.[41] He finally concluded that the "artful man-

---

he selected one thirty-five miles farther up the river. The assembly voted £1,000 for the expense of construction. Fort Moore was evacuated by July, 1765. Fort Charlotte, as the new post was named by Bull, was completed early in 1767. It commanded a ford in the Savannah near the mouth of the Broad River of Georgia which had served in earlier times as an avenue for the invasion of South Carolina. Bull to Gage, Dec. 8, 1764, Bull to Gage, April 9, 1765, Cochrane to Gage, July 11, 1765, Lieutenant Ralph Phillips to Gage, March 24, 1767, Gage MSS. All the forts in South Carolina and Georgia were abandoned by the regulars in 1768.

[40] Gage to Stuart, Feb. 7, 1764, Gage to Wright, March 20, 1764, Gage to Boone, May 1, 1764, Gage to Stuart, May 1, 1764, Gage to Wright, May 2, 1764, Gage MSS.

[41] Wright to Gage, March 22, 1764, Gage MSS. In January, 1764, Georgia had only its 150 rangers on duty and some 200 or 300 militia available for service. Wright to Gage, Jan. 4, 1764, *ibid.* There were hardly 100 regulars at Forts Augusta and Frederica.

agement" which Gage and Stuart urged was preferable to a costly and possibly desperate conflict. The prudent William Bull, who succeeded Boone in May, 1764, came to the same decision.

While the English officials were debating the course they should follow, the Creeks were doing likewise. The Lower Creeks and Seminoles were not unfriendly,[42] and the Upper Creeks were not unanimously for war. Because of the continued moderation of the English, the inconveniences met by the Creeks through the interruption of trade resulting from the crisis, and the hostility of the other tribes, especially of the Cherokees, who actually secured a few Creek scalps, the attitude of the Creek nation as a whole slowly became more pacific. Even The Mortar's ardor cooled when the Chickasaws killed two of his brothers.[43] At length the Creeks formally announced to Stuart that they desired peace, although they failed to promise to punish the murderers.[44] By May the danger of war had passed for the time being because the English, probably wisely, refused to press them further. In August a "talk" from The Mortar himself declaring that he regretted joining the French against the English and that he desired the English king's forgiveness was delivered at Augusta. The Mortar also sent a string of white beads as a token that he desired peace, pledged himself to be friendly henceforth to the English, and asked that the traders return to his nation.[45] Wright accepted the white beads, and promised that the traders would come to the Creeks, but asserted that they would not remain unless they were well treated. The Mortar's "talk" did not mention the murders at Long Canes, nor did Wright's reply.[46]

At almost the moment when the Creeks formally engaged to keep the peace two Creek warriors engaged in a quarrel with two Long Canes settlers that resulted in the death of one Henry Benfield, on May 4. The warriors fled, then later returned to loot their victim's home. They appeared at the Cherokee town of Tugaloo, where they brazenly boasted of their exploits. Saluy, who was chief

[42] Major Francis Ogilvie reported from St. Augustine that the Creeks about that place were quiet, and that Cowkeeper was very friendly to the English. Major Francis Ogilvie to Gage, March 26, July 28, 1764, Gage MSS. Ogilvie belonged to the 9th Regiment, took part in the capture of Havana, and was the commanding officer at St. Augustine from 1763 to 1765.

[43] Stuart to Gage, May 22, 1764, Gage MSS.

[44] Stuart to Gage, May 20, 1764, Gage MSS.

[45] "Copy of a Talk from The Mortar in the Creek nation delivered by the Handsome Fellow at Fort Augusta the 13 of August 1764," Gage MSS.

[46] "Talk" to The Mortar by Wright, Aug. 25, 1764, Gage MSS.

of Tugaloo as well as of Estatoe, seized them and sent them off to Fort Prince George under the escort of Lieutenant Charles Tayler, an officer of the recently disbanded Independent Regulars.[47] One of the warriors escaped, but the other, appropriately named "the Evil Doer," was carried off to Charleston. The Creeks made no effort to protect him; and he was tried, condemned, and executed, meeting his fate with the stoicism of his race.[48]

The settlement of the Creek crisis of 1763–64 was obviously not a permanent one, for the Creeks were neither appeased nor thoroughly cowed. Nor had the fundamental problems in Anglo-Creek relations been touched upon. For some years at least the Creeks were certain to remain resentful over the loss of their bargaining position between the French, English, and Spanish. The establishment of boundaries between the Creeks and East and West Florida was also sure to cause trouble, for it was not to be expected that the new colonies would be content indefinitely with the lands recognized as open to settlement by the Creeks at the Congress of Augusta. The problem of the regulation of the trade, always a difficult one, was now rendered even more serious because of the participation in it of traders from the two new provinces. Nevertheless, the prudent diplomacy displayed by Stuart, Gage, and, to a lesser extent, the southern governors in the closing weeks of 1763 and the early months of 1764 scotched whatever hopes The Mortar and his clique may have had of forming a southern confederacy to act in unison with Pontiac.

[47] Tayler succeeded Lachlan McIntosh in command of Fort Prince George in 1762, and held that post until he was released from the service.

[48] CJSC, xxx, 185–87, 196; Bull to Gage, May 25, Nov. 3, 1764, Gage MSS; *South-Carolina Gazette,* Oct. 29, Nov. 5, 1764. Saluy was given £100 (South Carolina currency) in goods by South Carolina as a reward.

CHAPTER XII

STUART'S MISSION IN THE FLORIDAS, 1764–65

THE British occupation of the Spanish territories in Florida and of the French lands east of the Mississippi ceded by the Peace of Paris had begun before the Congress of Augusta. On August 6, 1763, Lieutenant Colonel Augustine Prevost occupied Pensacola, and on October 20 Major Robert Farmar [1] with a force sent from Havana took possession of Mobile. A month later a detachment led by Lieutenant Thomas Ford, under orders from Farmar, established itself as a garrison at Fort Tombigbee.[2] On February 20, 1764, Fort St. Mark (called by the English Appalachie) was taken over by Captain Jonathan Harries with a small body of troops.[3] Prevost and Lieutenant Colonel James Robertson also contemplated sending a garrison to Fort Toulouse, but the opposition of the Creeks prevented such a step, and that post was allowed to fall into ruins.[4] Captain James Campbell, ordered by Robertson to take over Fort Natchez, was forced to turn back because of an attack by the Small Tribes.[5]

Although the occupation met no armed opposition from the Creeks or Choctaws, it was evident that new Indian problems would arise from the presence of the English in the Floridas. From South Carolina Governor Boone urged Amherst to order the military of-

[1] There is a brief sketch of Farmar in Dunbar Rowland, ed., *Mississippi Provincial Archives, 1763–1766; English Dominion, Letters and Inclosures to the Secretary of State from Major Robert Farmar and Governor George Johnstone* (Nashville, 1911), I, 7–8, note. Only one volume was published, although others were projected. (This work is hereafter cited as *MPAED.*)

[2] Farmar to Secretary at War, Jan. 24, 1764, *MPAED,* I, 12.

[3] Captain Jonathan Harries to Gage, Feb. 25, 1764, Gage MSS.

[4] Robertson to [Colonel William Amherst?], Nov. 15, 1763, Amherst MSS; Farmar to Secretary at War, Jan. 24, 1764, *MPAED,* I, 12. Farmar gave permission to James Germany, a trader influential among the Creeks, to occupy and preserve Fort Toulouse. Wolf King promised to try to smooth over Creek irritation so that it might be occupied, but British officials eventually decided that Fort Toulouse was valueless to them.

[5] Captain James Campbell to Johnstone, Dec. 12, 1764, *MPAED,* I, 266. Campbell accompanied the Loftus expedition.

ficers in the Floridas to correspond with him at Charleston so as to secure a uniform Indian policy, and Amherst agreed.[6] Stuart, learning that South Carolina and Georgia merchants planned to establish trade with the Indians from Mobile and Pensacola, foresaw chaos if the trade was to be carried on from both the old and the new colonies, unless some measure of unity in regulation were obtained. He stressed the wisdom of taking steps to meet the evils certain to result from increased competition and intercolonial rivalry before those evils became deeply rooted, and he requested Amherst to give him exclusive power to license traders in the newly acquired areas in the South. But Amherst refused, on the ground that the privilege of engaging in the Indian commerce should be granted to "every British subject who conforms himself to the rules prescribed for carrying on trade in general." Amherst did, however, instruct the officers in the Floridas to encourage traders recommended by Boone and Stuart and to discourage and punish those guilty of fraud; [7] and Lieutenant Colonel James Robertson, who was sent by Amherst on a tour of inspection in the newly acquired territories, was specially ordered to prevent Indian traders lacking the approval of Stuart and the southern governors from entering the Indian country from the south.[8]

In response to a request from Stuart, General Thomas Gage, who succeeded Amherst in November, 1763, issued additional instructions to the officers, calling upon them to correspond with Stuart upon Indian affairs generally.[9] Stuart soon came to feel, however, that he needed his own agents at Mobile, Pensacola, St. Augustine, and other posts to keep him informed and to carry out his policies; and he asked Gage's approval of the appointment of such subordinates, preferably from that group of officers who had been placed upon half pay because of the Peace of Paris. These men would be of great value, as Stuart deftly put it, in assisting him to execute the plans of the ministry and of Gage.[10] The general's first reaction to this proposal was to counsel Stuart to delay such appointments

[6] Boone to Amherst, July 29, 1763, Amherst to Boone, Aug. 17, 1763, Amherst MSS.

[7] Stuart to Amherst, July 30, 1763, Amherst to Stuart, Aug. 17, 1763, "[Amherst] to the Commanding Officer of Whitmore's & Otways Regiments in Florida & the country ceded by Spain on the Continent of North America," Aug. 23, 1763, Amherst MSS.

[8] Stuart to Amherst, Oct. 6, 1763, Amherst MSS.

[9] Gage to Stuart, Feb. 7, 15, 1764, Gage MSS.

[10] Stuart to Gage, Feb. 2, May 22, 1764, Gage MSS.

until he could observe in person the situation in the Floridas,[11] but in August, 1764, Gage gave his approval, warning the superintendent that it would be unwise to permit officials in the Indian service to engage in the trade.[12]

Management of Indian affairs in the Floridas by the military officers in 1763–64 proved to be very unsatisfactory. Captain Harries at Fort Appalachie lived in constant fear of an Indian attack that never came, and asked for a grant of £250 per annum to conciliate the Creeks in the neighborhood of that post.[13] At the far more important post of Pensacola Major William Forbes was in command from December, 1763, to the summer of 1764. He distributed "huge" amounts of presents to the Creeks, and he invited some of them to meet him at Pensacola to decide upon a boundary between the English and their nation in the West Florida region. When these Creeks reached Pensacola, Forbes had gone, but Captain Robert Mackinnen, the senior officer, felt that it would be highly unwise not to hold the meeting. In a series of conferences that took place in September, 1764, the Creeks, most prominent of whom was Wolf King, made a small grant of land to the English, receiving in return a considerable quantity of presents. At this congress Wolf King asked for the establishment of a trade from Pensacola and urged that the sale of rum to his people be prohibited. The arrival of Governor George Johnstone relieved Mackinnen of the task of dealing with these requests. Moreover, the treaty made between Mackinnen and the Creeks, as he himself suspected, was void, for he had exceeded his powers and Wolf King did not represent all his nation.[14]

At Mobile Major Farmar was especially active in Indian affairs, in part at least from necessity. Before his departure for France Kerlérec had called into conference all the tribes about Mobile in order to present them with supplies long delayed by the war and to inform them of the withdrawal of the French. Jean Jacques Blaise

[11] Gage to Stuart, June 15, 1764, Gage MSS.

[12] Gage to Stuart, Aug. 10, 1764, Gage MSS.

[13] Captain Jonathan Harries to Gage, Feb. 25, March 11, 1764, Gage MSS.

[14] Proceedings of the Conference at Pensacola, Sept. 5–10, 1764, Captain Robert Mackinnen to Gage, Oct. 16, 1764, Gage MSS. The land grant was to be "ten miles in depth from Deer Point, opposite to the island of Saint Rose, quite round the Bay of Pensacola, and to extend along the sea coast, to the point of Mobile Bay, from thence up the east side of Mobile Bay, till it comes opposite the town of Mobile," and was to include "all the settlements formerly possessed by the Yamassas, and eight miles round." Stuart found no fault with Mackinnen's conduct, but severely criticized Forbes.

D'Abbadie, who had been sent out early in 1763 to govern the western half of Louisiana until the Spanish should take over, completed arrangements for the conference, and it was about to begin when Robertson and Farmar appeared upon the scene. Farmar insisted on participating, and D'Abbadie and Farmar presided jointly. Farmar and Robertson disbursed large amounts of provisions and presents. They promised the Choctaws that the English, as the French had long done, would hold annual congresses with them to distribute supplies, a promise that was to cause trouble for Stuart for many years. D'Abbadie and Farmar told the Choctaws that neither French nor English traders would be allowed to deal with them if they killed a white man. There is a piece of evidence indicating that certain Choctaws abandoned an idea of striking a blow at the English because of D'Abbadie's opposition.[15]

Farmar made strenuous efforts to establish some sort of order in the Indian country. He instructed his subordinates to drive from the Indian territories both thieving traders and Frenchmen who had not taken the oath of allegiance to Britain,[16] and he promised the Indians that justice would be done between them and the English on the basis of an eye for an eye and a tooth for a tooth.[17] Nor was Farmar content with words, for he destroyed a stock of liquor belonging to a merchant who sold rum to the Indians.[18] For cheating an Indian he had Daniel Ward, a merchant of Mobile, thrown into the "Black Hole" until amends should be made. The shopkeepers of Mobile attempted to compel Farmar to free Ward by closing their stores. When Farmar paid no heed, they reopened for business after two days. Farmar even contemplated banishing Ward from West Florida, but allowed him to resume business after he had satisfied his complaining customer.[19] Although these vigorous measures rendered Farmar extremely unpopular among the civilians in West Florida, they were performed in accordance with his orders from Amherst. Farmar's behavior in other respects was open to

[15] "A Counsel Held with the Chacta Nation by the Governour of Mobile, for the English Part of Louisiana; and the Governour of Orleans, for the French Part of the said Province," Nov. 14, 1763, Gage MSS; Farmar to Secretary at War, Jan. 12, 1764, D'Abbadie to Farmar, Oct. 4, 1763, *MPAED,* I, 11–12, 35; Robertson to [Colonel William Amherst], Nov. 15, 1763, Amherst MSS.

[16] Instructions by Farmar, Oct. 24, 1763, *MPAED,* I, 92–94.

[17] *MPAED,* I, 90–91.

[18] "The Case of Charles Conner," Jan. 2, 1764, Gage MSS.

[19] Farmar to Gage, Feb. 14, 1764, also "An Impartial Relation of the Behaviour of Major Robert Farmar, Commander of the Troops in Mobille with Regard to Daniel Ward, Merchant [1764 or 1765]," Gage MSS.

criticism, for he used his official status in 1764 to secure a very dubious title from the Upper Creeks to a strip of land running from the eastern shore of Mobile Bay to the Perdido River.[20]

Another phase of Indian affairs that constituted a sore problem for Farmar arose from his plans to occupy the French posts in the Illinois country by way of the Mississippi. Early in 1764 Major Arthur Loftus, acting under orders from Farmar, proceeded up the river with the 22nd Regiment. On March 20 Loftus was attacked by the Tonicas and other warriors of the Small Tribes,[21] and was forced to retreat.[22] Loftus, Farmar, and other English officers believed D'Abbadie was guilty of secretly instigating this attack.[23] Farmar immediately began laying plans for a second expedition. To insure success he sent Captain James Campbell and Lieutenant Philip Pittman to pacify the Small Tribes and the Illinois nations respectively. Farmar also planned a congress with the Choctaws and Chickasaws to persuade them to bring pressure upon any possibly hostile tribe on the river.[24] In addition, he asked permission from Gage to erect a fort at the confluence of the Iberville and the Mississippi to serve as a base.[25]

Although Gage had at first frowned upon the project to occupy the Illinois region by way of the Mississippi,[26] he gave general approval to Farmar's arrangements for the second attempt. Because

[20] According to Farmar, the Upper Creeks compelled him to accept these lands because he had reconciled them to the English! One doubts that the Upper Creeks generally made any such gift. Since Farmar himself admitted that the pretended gift was made after the issuance of the Proclamation of 1763, it was not only fraudulent, but presumably illegal. Johnstone refused to acknowledge the validity of the transaction, and Farmar urged the Board of Trade in 1770 to provide legal sanction for it, in all probability without success. Farmar also claimed that he bought Dauphin Island from its French possessor, but was illegally deprived of it by Johnston. Petition by Farmar to Board of Trade, May 7, 1770, CO, 5/577.

[21] Just below the present site of Fort Adams Landing.

[22] Major Arthur Loftus to Gage, April 19, 1764, Gage MSS. Four soldiers were wounded and six were killed. The Indians fired from ambush, and Loftus retreated for fear that they might be in overwhelming numbers.

[23] Accusations by the English officials brought forth a formal protest from the French government to the court of St. James's. Gage to Farmar, Sept. 29, 1764, Loftus to Gage, Dec. 6, 1764, Farmar to Gage, Dec. 27, 1764, Duc de Choiseul to Duc de Praslin, June 26, 1764, Gage MSS. Captain James Campbell, who accompanied Loftus, declared that French inhabitants of Point Coupée were responsible. Campbell to Johnstone, Dec. 12, 1764, *MPAED*, I, 267.

[24] Farmar to Gage, April 17, Aug. 7, 1764, Gage MSS.

[25] Farmar to Gage, April 17, 1764, Gage MSS.

[26] Gage to Stuart, Dec. 31, 1764, Gage MSS.

of the importance of securing control of the Illinois area he failed even to offer very strenuous objection to the erection of a fort at the Iberville, although he did not believe in maintaining posts not easily supported. He cautioned Farmar to avoid quarreling with the French at New Orleans, and warned him not to call upon Indians in the English interest for military aid against the Small Tribes or other nations on the French side of the Mississippi unless absolutely necessary.[27] D'Abbadie promised to help in clearing the path of the second expedition, but Farmar soon reported that Lieutenant Pittman had been compelled to turn back because of secret machinations on the part of D'Abbadie. Farmar then sent Lieutenant John Ross, acompanied by Hugh Crawford, a trader and interpreter, to do the job previously assigned to Pittman.[28] However, Captain Campbell was meeting with some success among the Small Tribes[29] when Stuart and George Johnstone, the first governor of West Florida, appeared in that province.

The necessity of establishing friendly relations between the Indians and the new English possessions in the Floridas was appreciated by Gage. Not long after he assumed office as commander in chief he became convinced that the military officers in the far South were making a mess of Indian affairs and that they were spending too much money. On March 31, 1764, when the crisis caused by the Long Canes murders had begun to subside, he urged Stuart to take passage on a supply ship going to the ports on the Gulf of Mexico via Charleston. Stuart should make a brief visit to all the forts on the coast, furnish the military officers with suitable Indian presents, inform them on the proper methods of dealing with Indians, and generally ensure peace in the Floridas until plans then being formed in London for the management of Indian affairs could be completed and implemented. On June 19 Gage requested that Stuart persuade the Cherokees to aid the expedition up the Mississippi and to stop French traders illegally operating on English territory and aiding Pontiac.[30] Stuart pointed out to Gage that help from the Chickasaws would be more valuable for these purposes, and promised to try to secure it.[31]

On May 22, since Gage's supply ship was crowded, Stuart sailed

[27] Gage to Farmar, March 31, May 20, 1764, Gage MSS.

[28] Farmar to Gage, Dec. 21, 1764, Gage MSS.

[29] Campbell to Farmar, Oct. 29, 1764, Gage MSS; Campbell to Johnstone, Dec. 12, 1764, *MPAED,* I, 266–67.

[30] Gage to Stuart, March 31, June 19, 1764, Gage MSS.

[31] Stuart to Gage, Sept. 29, 1764, Gage MSS.

from Charleston on the sloop *Sally*. The *Sally* was wrecked on the bar at St. Augustine, but Stuart was unharmed. In July he held a friendly conference with representatives of the Seminoles, headed by Cowkeeper, at St. Augustine.[32] There Stuart also met Lieutenant James Pampellone, who was about to supersede Captain Harries at Fort Appalachie. Stuart gave him a supply of presents and some advice on Indian affairs. His advice was no doubt similar to that given by the superintendent to other officers, and it throws much light on Stuart's policies in 1764. Pampellone should gain all possible information about the Creeks living near Fort Appalachie, especially about their chiefs; search out unfair traders and report them to Stuart; discover the relationships existing between the Indian tribes; and, above all, foment secretly jealousies or divisions existing between those tribes while assuming on the surface an attitude of good will to all.

> It will undoubtedly be detrimental to His Majesties service [he said], that too strict a friendship and union subsist between the different Indian nations within this department; it is therefore incumbent upon us by all means in our power to foment any jealousy or division that may subsist between them. But this must be done with great delicacy, and in such a manner as not to awaken the least suspicion in them that we have any end or view to answer by it.[33]

On July 28 Stuart departed from St. Augustine on the *Live Oak,* reaching Fort Appalachie on September 13 or 14, almost three months later.[34] There in the period September 25–28 he held a conference with the leaders of five Creek towns near the junction of the Chattahoochee and Flint rivers, again with satisfactory results.

On October 4 Stuart arrived at Pensacola, where he received a letter of May 12 from Lord Halifax, then secretary of state for the southern department. This letter, inspired by Gage's representations of the critical state of affairs in the Floridas, ordered Stuart to station himself in one of these provinces and to place a deputy in the other until conditions were improved. He was to follow Gage's advice in the matter of choosing St. Augustine or Pensacola as his headquarters, and he and his deputy were to assist Governors Johnstone and Grant in the distribution of large supplies of Indian presents that these officials were bringing out from England.[35] An

[32] Stuart to Gage, July 19, 1764, Gage MSS; Stuart to Halifax, Oct. 29, 1764, CO, 5/66.

[33] Stuart to Lieutenant James Pampellone, July 16, 1764, Gage MSS.

[34] No doubt the *Live Oak* sailed from St. Augustine to the West Indies and thence to Fort Appalachie.

[35] Halifax to Stuart, May 12, 1764, CO, 5/65; Stuart to Gage, Sept. 29, 1764, Gage MSS; Stuart to Halifax, Oct. 29, 1764, CO, 5/66; Gage to Halifax, March 10. 1764, *Gage Corr.,* I, 19–20.

accompanying letter from Gage suggested that Stuart establish himself at Pensacola, but left the choice of headquarters to the discretion of the superintendent.[36] At Pensacola Stuart met Lord Adam Gordon, a traveler who was on his way to New Orleans, and he decided to accompany Gordon thither in the hope of gaining D'Abbadie's assistance for the second expedition up the Mississippi. But when Stuart reached Mobile he realized that a journey to New Orleans might make it impossible for him to deal promptly with more pressing business, and he left the ship to consult with Farmar. Farmar, however, refused to give him an account of what he had done in regard to Indian affairs. Attacked by fever, Stuart returned hurriedly to Pensacola, where he arrived on October 27, to find that Johnstone had disembarked in his absence.[37]

From Pensacola Stuart sent official notice to Farmar that he was superseded in the management of Indian affairs, and asked Farmar's coöperation in the matter of congresses that Stuart and Johnstone had decided to hold with the Chickasaws, Choctaws, and Creeks.[38] Stuart and Farmar continued, however, to be on unfriendly terms for some time, for the officer thought Stuart's conduct was rather "cavalier."[39] Early in December Stuart returned to Mobile, and was met by Farmar as he left his ship. Farmar refused to shake hands, and a rather heated altercation between the two men took place on the street in Mobile on December 5. Two days later Farmar with some reluctance promised to give the superintendent all the information he possessed on Indian affairs and to furnish him with copies of his accounts and documents on the subject.[40] Henceforth Stuart and Farmar were to work together without serious friction.

Stuart and Johnstone agreed that a congress with the Choctaws and Chickasaws was absolutely necessary. Nothing of importance had been done in West Florida since the occupation to remove the resentment of the Choctaws caused by the withdrawal of the French. The Choctaws considered themselves neglected. They were alarmed by disorders caused by a swarm of unregulated traders who had moved into their country after the peace; and they were aroused by solicitations from the northern Indians and from The Mortar to join in assailing the English. Many of their chiefs still carried medals given them by the French, and Stuart believed that they medi-

[36] Gage to Stuart, July 22, 1764, Gage MSS.
[37] Stuart to Gage, Oct. 12, Nov. 19, 1764, Gage MSS.
[38] Stuart to Farmar, Oct. 31, Nov. 3, 1764, Gage MSS.
[39] Charles Stuart to Stuart, Nov. 10, 1764, Gage MSS.
[40] Stuart to Gage, Jan. 3, 1765, Gage MSS.

tated a blow against the English. In fact, both Stuart and Johnstone were convinced that Pontiac, The Mortar, and Alabama Mingo, old and influential Choctaw chief, were plotting a concerted attack.[41] They were eager to remove the grievances of the Choctaws and to bring them into such close friendship with the English that they could be used as a counterbalance to the Creeks. Johnstone especially desired a congress in order to obtain a boundary line between the Choctaws and West Florida that would give the province room for expansion. Such a meeting could also be used to cement the good understanding already existing between the English and the Chickasaws, and to bring aid from both the Choctaws and the Chickasaws for Farmar's Illinois expedition. Moreover, Stuart and Johnstone regarded a formal gathering as indispensable for launching a new general system of trade regulation that Stuart had conceived and that Johnstone heartily supported. They therefore decided upon their own initiative to convene the congress.[42] Gage warned Stuart that he would honor no resulting bills beyond those connected with the Illinois expedition, on the ground that this congress, as well as one planned for the Creeks, would deal largely with provincial matters.[43] Stuart, however, already had a considerable quantity of presents, for the large consignment that he had sent to the Choctaws after the Congress of Augusta still lay at Mobile undelivered, and he had bought more goods before and after his departure from Charleston.[44] In addition, Johnstone had brought out a supply worth £1,-500. They therefore proceeded with their plans, expecting, in view of the necessities of the situation, that Gage would furnish whatever funds were required beyond their resources. Gage was later persuaded that the congress had been essential, and a portion of the £6,000 [45] spent upon it came from the treasury through him.

Stuart and Johnstone hoped to meet the Choctaws and Chickasaws before the close of 1764 and the Creeks about March 1, 1765. They commissioned William Buckle, a prominent trader, and Captain James Colbert to secure the attendance of the Indians and their traders.[46] But the Indians did not wish to shorten their hunting

[41] Johnstone and Stuart to [secretary of state], June 12, 1765, *MPAED,* I, 184; Stuart to Gage, Sept. 20, 1765, Gage MSS.

[42] Stuart to Halifax, April 16, 1765, CO, 5/66.

[43] Gage to Stuart, Dec. 31, 1764, Jan. 7, 1765, Gage MSS.

[44] Stuart to Gage, April 11, 1765, Gage MSS.

[45] Estimate by the superintendent in Stuart to Germain, Aug. 23, 1776, CO, 5/77.

[46] Stuart to Captain Colbert, Nov. 3, 1764, Stuart to William Buckle, Nov. 6, 1764, Gage MSS.

season, and the traders were anxious to purchase the deerskins garnered during the season before presents were distributed to them. It was not until March 26 that the Choctaws (exclusive of those of the Six Villages) and the Chickasaws began conversations with Stuart and Johnstone at Mobile. Most of the traders to these nations were also present. The deliberations continued until April 4. The chiefs and warriors of the Six Villages, most Francophile of the Choctaws, delayed their appearance at Mobile until April 22; then they subscribed to a treaty made by their fellows, saying that they would be as reluctant to break their new friendship with the English as they had been slow to abandon their former alliance with the French.

Stuart followed at Mobile the policy that he had formed at Augusta: he continued to try to create a political combination that would hold the Creeks in check. He was more successful at Mobile than at Augusta. Regaled with beef, corn, potatoes, rice, beans, and rum,[47] and pleased by the prospect of receiving gifts, the Choctaws listened to the artful speeches of Stuart and Johnstone with almost as good grace as the Chickasaws. Their chiefs gave up the medals they had received from the French, and accepted English insignia instead. Henceforth Stuart was to have a voice in the selection of their leaders, for the possession of these copper decorations signified that the wearer had the confidence of "King George" and was responsible to him for the good behavior of his followers.[48] In a conference held on April 10 the Choctaws and Chickasaws promised Stuart and Farmar that they would send embassies to urge the Small Tribes and the Arkansaw nation not to oppose Farmar's expedition. Each tribe also pledged itself to furnish fifty men to serve as armed escorts for Farmar.

The good will of the Choctaws is even more strikingly shown in the formal Treaty of Mobile, dated April 27, in which that na-

[47] No doubt Stuart also enjoyed himself. Montaut de Monbéraut, who was closely associated with the superintendent in the early months of 1765, is represented as saying: "Drinking had a peculiar effect on the Superintendent. He often drank all night. Usually, he could hardly walk for the gout, but when the bacchic enthusiasm prevailed, he could dance long and violently to the music of instruments, and resembled a man bitten by a tarantula." John P. Brown, *Old Frontiers: The Story of the Cherokee Indians from Earliest Times to the Date of Their Removal to the West* (Kingsport, Tenn., 1938), 123, note.

[48] The French had long increased the prestige of their friends through the use of these decorations. Stuart gave out "great" medals and "lesser" medals to chiefs, according to the rank they held or the rank that he wished to confer on them.

tion made an extensive cession of territory to West Florida. The Choctaws ceded certain islands between the Mobile and the Tensaw rivers. They also gave up their rights to lands lying south of a line running up the Mobile and Alabama rivers to a point some distance above the Tombigbee-Alabama junction, thence westward and southwestward to the headwaters of the Buckatunna River, along the course of the Buckatunna and Pascagoula rivers to a point twelve leagues from the sea, and thence to the westward as far as the Choctaws had a right to grant. The western end of the line was not defined, because the Small Tribes had a stronger claim to the eastern banks of the Mississippi than the Choctaws. Nor was the opposite end of the line finally settled, for the Upper Creeks had pretensions to the eastern shores of the Mobile and the lower Tombigbee. (The Indian boundaries of West Florida appear in Map 4, p. 317.)

Like the Treaty of Augusta, that of Mobile also provided for the maintenance of peace between the parties, the punishment of murderers, the forgiveness of all past offenses, and future good conduct as neighbors. The final clauses of the treaty were perhaps the most interesting of all. In these the Indians promised that they would protect commissaries to be commissioned by Stuart to regulate the trade, that they would assist them in the execution of their duties, that they would abide by their decisions in altercations between the traders and Indians, and that they would aid them in transporting an offending trader to a province for trial. A price schedule to be observed by the Indians and traders alike was affixed to the treaty, and both parties pledged themselves to the rates contained therein. Stuart, Johnstone, and twenty-nine Indian chiefs signed the treaty.[49]

Stuart's activities before and during the Congress of Mobile helped materially in bringing about the English occupation of the Illinois country. Farmar had at first planned to give Loftus an opportunity to wipe out his failure of 1764, but Gage entrusted the command to Farmar himself, sending Loftus to England. Stuart spared no pains in carrying out Gage's instructions to aid Farmar. After consulting with Johnstone he sent Charles Stuart on November 1, 1764, to assist Captain Campbell in making peace with the Small Tribes, instructing him to proceed to his post by way of New Orleans, where he was to solicit the aid of D'Abbadie, M. Charles

[49] On the Congress of Mobile see Johnstone to Farmar, Nov. –, 1764, Stuart to Gage, April 11, May 6, 1765, and the proceedings of the congress, March 26–April 4, 1765, Gage MSS.

Philippe Aubry,[50] and M. Harpain de la Gauterais.[51] Disclaiming belief that the French governor had been secretly responsible for the failure of Loftus, Stuart urged D'Abbadie to assist Charles Stuart.[52] He also employed Pierce Acton Sinnott,[53] a Scotsman, and la Gauterais to procure provisions that Farmar could utilize as he advanced up the river and to persuade the Illinois Indians to accept the occupation.

The Choctaws and Chickasaws fulfilled their pledges to help Farmar. A party of eighty-five Choctaws under the leadership of Lieutenant Thomas Ford crossed the Yazoo in June and camped at Natchez [54] from July 12 to August 12, when Farmar reached that point. The presence of the Choctaws on the river insured the success of the diplomatic efforts of Campbell and Charles Stuart. They were able, with the assistance of Aubry, who succeeded D'Abbadie in February, 1765, to appease the Small Tribes and the Arkansaw nation. A body of 125 "breeds" led by John McIntosh met Farmar at the mouth of the Margot River. Judiciously managed by McIn-

[50] Aubry, veteran of the Seven Years' War, was commanding officer of the troops in Louisiana from 1763 to 1765.

[51] Instructions to Lieutenant Charles Stuart, Nov. 1, 1764, Gage MSS. La Gauterais had been a prominent citizen in the French settlements in Illinois, had at one time possessed considerable wealth, and, according to report, wielded great influence among the Indians along the banks of the Mississippi. He had been a captain in the French service over thirty years. He took the oath of allegiance to Britain in 1764. Stuart to Halifax, April 16, 1765, CO 5/66; Aubry to Haldimand, Jan. 27, 1768, Gage MSS; *MPAED,* I, 121–22.

[52] Stuart to D'Abbadie, Nov. 1, 1764, Gage MSS. But Stuart really thought D'Abbadie was guilty. He afterward declared that D'Abbadie had an interest in the fur trade of the Illinois region, and that he opposed the English occupation because he would suffer pecuniary loss as a result of it. Stuart to Gage, March 19, 1765, *ibid.* Lieutenant Colonel David Wedderburn, younger brother of the famous solicitor general, reported that D'Abbadie died possessed of £60,000, and hinted that a goodly portion of the estate was gained through the French governor's participation in the profits of the Illinois fur trade during the year preceding his death. David Wedderburn to Alexander Wedderburn, April 14, 1765, Alexander Wedderburn MSS, William L. Clements Library.

[53] Instructions to Sinnott, n.d., Gage MSS. Sinnott was later made assistant commissary by Stuart and stationed at Fort Appalachie until 1768. He sailed from Charleston for England in May, 1769. *South-Carolina Gazette,* May 18, 1769. In England he persuaded Lord Hillsborough that his services on this expedition had not been adequately recompensed, and Hillsborough gave him a sinecure appointment as lieutenant governor of Niagara. Captain James Campbell declared that Sinnott was "fractious and whimsical ... hated by every person on board ... a stranger to the art of pleasing ... [he] will not answer expectations." Campbell to Farmar, March 26, 1765, Gage MSS. Sinnott died in London on April 30, 1794. *Gentleman's Magazine,* LXIV (1794), pt. 1, 482.

[54] Lieutenant Thomas Ford to Stuart, June 21, July 16, 1765, Gage MSS.

tosh, they behaved splendidly and furnished the soldiers with fresh meat as the expedition moved slowly up the river. McIntosh and a small party of the Chickasaws accompanied Farmar all the way to Fort Chartres, and the presence of these warriors as English allies made a strong impression on the Illinois Indians.[55] A band of 100 Cherokees also went to the mouth of the Ohio, but failed to meet Farmar.[56]

It had been feared that the Illinois tribes would attempt by force to prevent the English occupation, but Farmar was not opposed. To what extent the agents sent out by Farmar and Stuart were responsible for the decision of the savages to accept British rule is not clear. Ross and Crawford reached the fort in safety and remained for some time, but were finally forced to flee down the river in order to save their lives.[57] La Gauterais and Sinnott underwent a similar experience, although they managed to secure a conditional acceptance of the British occupation from the Indians before they were compelled to seek safety in flight. George Croghan, proceeding westward from Fort Pitt, also obtained a pledge from the savages that the English would be allowed to take possession without molestation. In fact, a small force under Captain Thomas Stirling, following Croghan from Fort Pitt, was safely esconced within Fort Chartres before Farmar's arrival.[58]

Because it was necessary to hold the Choctaw-Chickasaw congress first in order to obtain help for Farmar, Stuart and Johnstone were unable to meet the Creeks until May, 1765. In the summer of 1764 the Upper Creeks had a new grievance, for they were offended by settlements made by the English on lands formerly occupied by French inhabitants at Tensaw in West Florida. Emistisiguo and The Mortar protested against these settlements; The Mortar, inspired by traders from South Carolina or Georgia, declared that no traders were to come from Pensacola or Mobile to the Creek nation.[59] Farmar, who first answered their "talks," although they were

[55] See Farmar to Gage, April 25, Dec. 16, 1765, Gage MSS. Farmar freely acknowledged that Stuart's services had contributed to his own success.

[56] Stuart to Board of Trade, July 10, 1766, CO, 5/67.

[57] Shortly after Ross and Crawford fled from Fort Chartres Lieutenant Alexander Fraser came to the Illinois country from Fort Pitt to procure the consent of the Illinois tribes to the occupation of Fort Chartres by troops from Fort Pitt. He was made prisoner by the Indians, and was released through the good offices of Pontiac. He also fled down the Mississippi.

[58] *Ill. Hist. Colls.*, X (1915), 483–84, 519, XI (1916), 59, 61, 67–68, 84, 88.

[59] "Talk" from Emistisiguo to Stuart, July 15, 1764, "talk" from The Mortar to Stuart, July 22, 1764, Gage MSS.

addressed to Stuart, pushed aside the complaints, asserting that the English settlers in question had purchased their lands of the French inhabitants and that those who had instigated The Mortar to protest against the establishment of a trade between the Creeks and West Florida were "vagabonds."[60] The Upper Creeks returned Farmar's undiplomatic reply unopened, a "lucky event," as Stuart characterized it.[61] The Mortar was again talking freely against the English in the fall of 1764. No doubt he was encouraged by the decimation of the English troops in West Florida by disease. In November of that year Stuart considered the situation serious enough to recommend to Gage that the force intended for the occupation of the Illinois country be retained at Mobile to assure the safety of West Florida.[62] At the same time Stuart and Johnstone sent a conciliatory message to the Upper Creeks. They stressed the value of Pensacola and Mobile as trade centers for the Creeks, and they asked why the Creeks should object to the English plantations at Tensaw when they had not caviled at the presence of the French in the same area.[63] They also sent a message of good will to the Lower Creeks.[64]

Emistisiguo sems to have been satisfied by the "talk" sent out by Stuart and Johnstone, but The Mortar remained sullen. Traders from South Carolina and Georgia who wished to prevent the opening of a trade from West Florida and the establishment of Stuart's regulations labored unceasingly to persuade The Mortar not to attend the congress that Stuart and Johnstone had decided to hold at Pensacola. They even informed him that Stuart planned to poison him when he came to that place. But Stuart sent out some friendly Creeks, a certain Tapulgee and his followers, to urge The Mortar to come to Pensacola; and he also employed Montaut de Monbéraut, whom he had just appointed as his deputy, for the same purpose. On May 22, when Stuart reached Pensacola, he found many of the Creeks awaiting him. Two days later The Mortar himself appeared.[65] On May 26 the congress was duly opened with several hundred Creeks present, including Emistisiguo for the

[60] "Talk" to Upper Creek nation by Farmar, Aug. 18, 1764, Gage MSS.

[61] Stuart to Gage, Nov. 30, 1764, Gage MSS.

[62] Stuart to Gage, Nov. 19, 1764, Gage MSS.

[63] "Talk" to Upper Creeks by Stuart and Johnstone, Nov. 19, 1764, Gage MSS.

[64] "Talk" to Lower Creeks by Stuart and Johnstone, Nov. 19, 1764, Gage MSS.

[65] The Congress of Pensacola and incidents preceding it are described in Stuart to John Pownall, Aug. 24, 1765, and Stuart to Halifax, Aug. 24, 1765, CO, 5/66.

Upper Creeks and Captain Aleck and Escotchabie for the Lower Creeks. Most of the Creek traders were present. Admiral Sir William Burnaby, Monbéraut, and Lieutenant Colonel David Wedderburn accompanied Stuart and Johnstone. Sessions of the congress continued until June 4.[66]

The Creeks proved to be more difficult to manage than their neighbors to the west. The Mortar, because he feared that the cession made by Wolf King in 1764 was too large and because he thought the English would strive to obtain a ratification of that cession, at first refused to discuss the land question, excusing himself on the ground that the whole Creek nation was not represented at the congress. However, after the narrow limits of the grant obtained by Captain Mackinnen had been explained to him in private by Monbéraut, he declared his willingness to ratify the cession and to make a further grant if peace continued between the Creeks and the English for four years. It was Stuart who finally won The Mortar over to a more conciliatory attitude by clever tactics based on Indian psychology. At the first of many private conferences that took place between the superintendent and the chief, The Mortar found Stuart sitting on a heap of French medals and gorgets abandoned to him by the Choctaws, a spectacle that greatly impressed the wily Creek. Soon he was hungering for one of Stuart's "great" medals; and the longer Stuart delayed gratifying his desire, the more eager The Mortar became. At length the superintendent gave him one, at the same time making it clear that possession of the medal carried with it responsibility for the good behavior of his followers. Stuart's success in persuading The Mortar to receive an English medal was the more noteworthy in that the chief had always refused to accept a similar badge from the French.[67]

Once The Mortar was pacified, the Congress of Pensacola proceeded to a successful conclusion, for Emistisiguo and the other chiefs leaned toward friendship with the English.[68] The terms of the formal treaty were identical with those of the Treaty of Mobile,

[66] The Gage MSS contain a copy of the proceedings of the congress.

[67] Stuart to John Pownall, Aug. 24, 1765, CO, 5/66. In this report Stuart paid a noteworthy tribute to The Mortar, declaring that he was "a sensible manly Indian, & seems to have been actuated in his opposition to us, more by principles of love to his country, & jealousy on account of their lands & independancy, than by love to the French, to whom he adhered for purposes of his own."

[68] Emistisiguo announced at the congress that he was about to journey to the Ohio, and that he intended to seize any French trader he discovered on English territory.

except for the boundary line provisions and the prices established for the trade, which were materially less favorable to the Creeks. The Mortar demanded for the Creeks the same rates that the other tribes were enjoying, but Stuart was unable to grant his request, because he did not have the power to lower the prices then in vogue with the traders from South Carolina and Georgia. Like the Choctaw and Chickasaw traders, the Creek traders agreed to conduct themselves according to Stuart's regulations. The question of the boundary between the Creeks and West Florida was a sore one, but the Creeks eventually ratified the cession made by Wolf King to Captain Mackinnen, and added a substantial area to it. They ceded to West Florida all territory south of a line running from the northern shore of Pensacola Bay in a northwesterly direction to a point above Tensaw on the Alabama River.[69] The tide level was to govern the boundary eastward around the Florida peninsula. The English settlements at Tensaw concerning which The Mortar and Emistisiguo had complained were thus included within the boundary. The Congress of Pensacola cost the crown £1,700.[70]

It has been noted that Stuart obtained promises from the Chickasaws, Choctaws, Creeks, and their traders to obey a set of trade regulations to be established by the superintendent. Almost from the moment of taking office Stuart had attempted to gain some share in the regulation of trade. Although the trade problem was serious before 1763, it had become even more difficult since the peace, for inhabitants of six provinces could engage in commerce with the Indians. The task of regulation was rendered hardly less burdensome because Virginia, North Carolina, and East Florida sent out but few traders after 1763.

Extraordinarily embarrassing as the trade situation was under the aegis of six separate colonial governments, the prospect became even darker as the result of the famous Royal Proclamation of October 7, 1763, one of the clauses of which stated that

> ...we do, by the advice of our Privy Council, declare and enjoin, that the trade with the said Indians shall be free and open to all our subjects whatever, provided that every person who may incline to trade with the said Indians do take out a license from the governor or commander in chief of any of our colonies respectively where such person shall reside, and also give security to observe such regulations as we shall at any time think fit, by ourselves or by our

[69] The text of the Treaty of Pensacola is printed in *MPAED*, I, 211–15. The date given to it is May 28, 1764.

[70] James Grant to Board of Trade, Dec. 9, 1765, CO, 5/540.

commissaries to be appointed for this purpose, to direct and appoint for the benefit of the said trade.[71]

The colonial assemblies might have continued to regulate the trade independently of these provisions on the ground that they were unconstitutional, but did not. Of course, the governors felt themselves to be bound by the proclamation. They interpreted these clauses to mean that they could not refuse a license to any person who offered bond and security and that they could neither confine the business activities of the traders nor limit the number of their employees until the home government should take further action regarding the trade problem.

Since the proclamation barred public monopolies and the use of traditional methods to regulate private trading, it was a staggering blow to those who placed the public welfare above the visionary ideal of free trade. Governor James Wright insisted that the evils which generally existed in the Indian commerce after 1763 arose largely from the proclamation, and he protested against it again and again to his superiors.[72] The council of West Florida registered a similar complaint,[73] and William Bull likewise,[74] but to no avail. The at least occasionally effective laws of Georgia were riddled with holes. The public trading system established by South Carolina in 1762 was also made ineffective; after receipt of the proclamation both Boone and Bull felt obliged to give licenses to all applicants,[75] and that portion of the act of 1762 upon which the public trading system rested was repealed in October, 1764.[76] The clauses of the proclamation ordering the traders to "give security to observe such regulations as we shall at any time think fit by ourselves or by our [Indian] commissaries to be appointed for this purpose, to direct and appoint for the benefit of the said trade" could serve as a basis

[71] The proclamation is printed in Adam Shortt and Arthur G. Doughty, eds., *Canadian Archives: Documents Relating to the Constitutional History of Canada, 1759–1791* (Ottawa, 1918, Second and Revised Edition, in two parts), Pt. I, 163–68, and in many other places.

[72] For examples see Wright to Board of Trade, Aug. 27, Dec. 11, 1764, *GCR*, XXVIII, pt. 2, 114–16, 158–59; Wright to Shelburne, Nov. 29, 1766, *ibid.*, XXXVII, 146–49.

[73] Representation of Council of West Florida to Board of Trade, Nov. 22, 1766, CO, 5/584, pt. 2.

[74] Bull to Board of Trade, Sept. 13, 1764, CO, 5/378.

[75] Bull to Board of Trade, Aug. 20, 1764, CO, 5/378.

[76] The directors of the South Carolina monopoly wound up their affairs in 1765. It had been conducted at a loss of over £3,932 (provincial currency) to the public. Journal of the Directors of the Cherokee Trade, 1762–1765, 45–46, 151–52.

for a system of trade regulation founded on coöperation between the Indian departments and the colonial governments, provided the home government gave its consent to the appointment of commissaries. However, it was not until the fall of 1766 that Lord Shelburne approved such appointments.

According to Stuart, the trade situation among the Chickasaws, Choctaws, and Creeks in 1764–65 was deplorable. He received incessant complaints about the conduct of the traders to these nations. There were only three licensed operators in the whole Choctaw nation, although there was at least one white man engaged in the commerce in every Choctaw town. The remainder were all subtraders employed by the three men named, who had obtained licenses from South Carolina and Georgia permitting them to trade where they would and to employ as many assistants as they wished. A comparable situation existed among the Creeks. The result was that the trade was virtually in the hands of a few uncontrolled principal traders, so far as these tribes were concerned, although the Proclamation of 1763 seemed to stress freedom of trade. Among the Chickasaws something like pandemonium reigned. Stuart reported that there were no fewer than seventy-two persons engaged in commerce with that tribe,[77] which had perhaps 300 hunters, for whom three traders would have sufficed. Worse yet, these traders had divided into two factions that quarreled so bitterly that several casualties resulted. One group even attempted to destroy the influence of Paya Mattaha, the loyal friend of the English, and to place Paya Mingo Euluxy, a bellicose young chief, at the head of the nation.[78]

Not long after he reached West Florida Stuart decided that something must be done to remedy the situation. In November, 1764, he received from the Board of Trade a copy of the "Plan for the Future Management of Indian Affairs."[79] This plan, based in part upon the recommendations of Stuart and Johnson, proposed to give the superintendents power to establish trading regulations and to enforce them through commissaries. Since Gage (though not the imperial government) had already given him permission to employ commissaries, Stuart determined to meet the emergency by temporarily establishing a similar system. But rules that Stuart

[77] But a list of the traders to the Chickasaws sent to Stuart early in 1766, probably by John McIntosh, names only thirty persons. "A List of Traders and Packhorsemen in the Chickasaw Nation," Jan. 22, 1766, CO, 5/67.

[78] There is an extensive analysis of the trade situation in Stuart to John Pownall, Aug. 24, 1765, CO, 5/66.

[79] This document is discussed in detail in Chapter XIV.

might promulgate would be scorned by the traders unless those rules had some legal sanction. Stuart hoped to secure this by persuading the southern governors to compel all those who were given licenses to promise obedience to his regulations under penalty of forfeiting license and bonds. He seems not to have given due weight to the fact that the powers of the governors over trade were severely limited by the Proclamation of 1763. However, Johnstone agreed to coöperate with Stuart; and the two men secured the approval of the Chickasaws, Choctaws, and Creeks, and their traders, as described above.

The regulations prepared by Stuart, derived largely from rules that the colonies of South Carolina and Georgia were accustomed to impose upon their traders, were detailed and carefully drawn. The sale of rum and of rifles to the Indians was forbidden, and also the purchase of green skins beyond a very small quantity. Trade was confined to the towns; provision was made for the use of just weights and measures; and the amount of credit to be given by a trader to an Indian was limited to thirty pounds of deerskins. Traders were forbidden to abuse or beat the Indians; to spread false reports among them; to hold general meetings with them; and to deliver to or receive messages from them except with the written permission of a commissary. They were not to employ Negroes, Indians, or half-breeds as assistants, and were not to entice employees of other traders from their masters. The names of all the assistants of a trader were to be written on his license. Traders were to attend all general meetings with the Indians at the call of the proper authorities; were to assist the commissaries in arresting and conducting from the Indian country all persons accused of infractions of the rules; and were to show proper respect for the medal chiefs. Attached to the regulations was a price list that each trader bound himself to obey. Failure to conform to the regulations was to be punished by forfeiture of license and bonds by the governor of the colony where the guilty person was licensed, on information given by Stuart or his aides.[80]

In accordance with instructions from Lord Halifax and Gage, Stuart engaged a number of assistants in the winter of 1764–65. On February 10, 1765, he chose Monbéraut [81] as deputy, partly because

[80] See Appendix A for a complete text of these regulations.

[81] Monbéraut was accused of extravagance by a Jesuit who served as chaplain and missionary at Fort Toulouse, and was recalled by Kerlérec in 1759. Because of difficulties with Kerlérec and a quarrel with D'Abbadie he found it wise not to return to New Orleans. He was the only Frenchman of gentle blood and

of Gage's recommendation of that gentleman and partly because Monbéraut seemed sensible and possessed of considerable influence with the French inhabitants about Mobile and the Creeks.[82] Monbéraut was of service at the Congress of Pensacola, but Stuart soon discovered that he was vain, sentimental, avaricious, and intriguing. Moreover, the Frenchman had not taken the oath of allegiance to England. On leaving West Florida Stuart informed his deputy that he must obey orders from Johnstone, or in the absence of the governor, from the commanding officer at Mobile, before embarking on any activities requiring the expenditure of money.[83] Stuart sailed from Pensacola for Charleston on June 15; he had been gone only four days when Monbéraut sent the first of a series of fourteen memorials and letters to Johnstone complaining of the restrictions placed upon him by Stuart and various other matters.[84] These lengthy epistles, characterized by insolence and childish egotism, aroused the easily inflamed Johnstone. He responded with a masterpiece of invective, comparing the Frenchman to a Yahoo and hinting that his son was a horse thief; he suspended Monbéraut from office and banished him from West Florida.[85] Stuart and Gage

---

influence who remained in West Florida after the English occupation. His residence was an old house on Pearl River, about twenty-seven miles from Mobile which he sold to Sir William Burnaby in 1764 for £600. He expressed a desire to Lieutenant Colonel James Robertson to enter British service; and at Gage's request Stuart and Johnstone negotiated with him. After his dismissal from the southern Indian department Monbéraut entered the service of Spain, receiving the rank of colonel. A complaint by Monbéraut regarding the treatment he had received from the British brought forth a formal protest from the French ambassador to the court of St. James's. See Lieutenant A. McLellan to Johnstone, Nov. 15, 1764, Stuart to Gage, Aug. 30, 1765, "Mémoire Justificatif De Mr. Le Chevalier De Montault De Monbéraut En Sa qualité De Deputé Superintendant . . . ," Feb. 1, 1766, and Haldimand to Gage, July 7, 1767, Gage MSS; Stuart to John Pownall, Jan. 24, 1765 (Abstract), CO, 5/72. Monbéraut apparently left Louisiana for France late in 1768 because he supported Francisco de Ulloa against the French inhabitants and found it uncomfortable in the province as a result. See a letter from Monbéraut to his brother, Oct. 31, 1768, ANC, C13A, 48. In this letter Monbéraut's title is given as "Comte."

[82] His salary was £200 per annum and £100 for house rent.

[83] Stuart's instructions to Monbéraut, n.d., Stuart to Gage, Aug. 30, 1765, Gage MSS. Stuart declared that when he stayed for a time at Monbéraut's home in Mobile he furnished most of the provisions for the table, but that Monbéraut charged him six dollars per day for "pepper, salt, vinegar oil & greens."

[84] Memorial by Monbéraut to Johnstone and Stuart, June 19, 1765, Johnstone to Stuart, July 16, 1765, Gage MSS.

[85] Johnstone to Monbéraut, June 26, 1765, Gage MSS. Johnstone also accused Monbéraut of intriguing with French officials at New Orleans. Johnstone to Lieutenant Colonel David Wedderburn, June 27, 1765, *ibid.*

supported Johnstone, although they thought he had acted with unnecessary harshness.[86]

Stuart was more fortunate in his other selections. Charles Stuart [87] was first appointed commissary to the Small Tribes, but was promoted to deputy on January 1, 1766, in the room of Monbérault.[88] To the Chickasaws Stuart sent as commissary John McIntosh,[89] who was to render long and faithful service with that tribe. Elias Legardere [90] was stationed at Fort Tombigbee to deal with

[86] As noted in Chapter IX.

[87] Charles Stuart served in the Seven Years' War in the 78th Regiment. He was commissioned as lieutenant on July 23, 1760. See *British Army Lists.* He left the service in 1763, and came to Charleston on October 30 of that year, no doubt in search of employment. *South-Carolina Gazette,* Nov. 5, 1763. Clarence W. Alvord, *Mississippi Valley in British Politics* (Cleveland, 1917), I, 289, erroneously states that he was a brother of the superintendent. Charles Stuart was a cousin of John Stuart. He was a son of John Roy Stuart. See Colonel David Stewart, *Sketches of the Character, Manners, and Present State of the Highlanders of Scotland: With Details of the Military Service of the Highland Regiments* (Edinburgh, 1822), II, 66; Montfort Browne to Lords Commissioners of the Treasury, Oct. 5, 1769, CO, 5/587, pt. 1. John Roy Stuart also had a daughter who married a Frenchman. Charles Stuart planned to make a journey to France in 1773, but was unable to carry out his purpose. John Stuart to Gage, Dec. 25, 1773, Gage MSS. He continued as deputy superintendent, first under Stuart and later under Alexander Cameron, until the end of his life. He was made prisoner when the Spanish captured Mobile in 1780, and died shortly after being released. Cameron to Germain, July 18, 1780, CO, 5/81.

[88] Johnstone appointed Jeremiah Terry, a prominent Indian trader, as a temporary deputy, but Stuart decided not to continue him in service, especially since his duty and his private interests would conflict. Charles Stuart was paid £200 per annum. Stuart to Gage, March 11, 14, 1766, Gage MSS.

[89] John McIntosh and his brother Roderick, later Stuart's commissary to the Creeks, were among the Highlanders from Inverness who settled at Darien in Georgia in 1736. They were sons of one Lieutenant John McIntosh, who was reputed to be the natural offspring of Brigadier William McIntosh, prominent leader in the rising of 1715. They were first cousins to John McIntosh (Moore), leader of the Highland emigration to Darien. Lachlan McIntosh, whose name appears at various places in the text and who is remembered for his fatal duel with Button Gwinnett, was a son of John McIntosh (Moore). In all probability the McIntoshes in Scotland were connected by blood, marriage, or close friendship with the Stuarts of Inverness. John McIntosh the commissary held his post under Stuart, except for a brief interval, until Stuart's death. He died in 1780. Cameron to Germain, July 18, 1780, CO, 5/81. He was the ancestor of both red and white men. Roderick McIntosh was a bachelor of choleric disposition familiarly known as "Old Rory." There is an interesting account of the McIntosh family in John Bartlett Meserve, "The MacIntoshes," *Chronicles of Oklahoma,* X (1932), 310–25. Meserve's genealogy of the family, although not documented, appears to be sound.

[90] Unfortunately, not much can be learned regarding Legardere. He resided in Charleston before the British occupation of West Florida. He was probably

the Choctaws, and William Struthers [91] was temporarily commissioned as commissary to the Creeks. Stuart also furnished each of these men with an interpreter, and stationed another interpreter, René Roi, at Mobile. Dugald Campbell and John Doigg were appointed commissaries of stores at Mobile and Pensacola respectively. In addition, Stuart promised blacksmiths to the Indians for the purpose of mending their weapons and tools.[92]

Stuart and his aides were unable to enforce the trade regulations. He wrote to the governors of East Florida, South Carolina, and Georgia requesting them to coöperate with him. He tried to exert pressure upon the governors through Gage and the Board of Trade. Gage approved of Stuart's plan, and expressed an opinion that the southern governors should assist in executing the scheme,[93] but he did nothing more. Because of the terms of the Proclamation of

---

a man of some education, since "Legardere and Crowly" advertised in 1759 that they were opening a school to teach among other things French, bookkeeping, navigation, and surveying. *South-Carolina Gazette,* Sept. 22, 1759. In July, 1762, he unsuccessfully applied to the directors of the South Carolina public trade for the position of factor at Keowee. Journal of the Directors of the Cherokee Trade, 1762–1765, 53. He was in West Florida as early as December, 1764, when he was made a justice of the peace. Minute of W. Fla. council, Nov. 25, 1764, CO, 5/625. Oddly enough, Legardere's wife resided with him at Fort Tombigbee, hardly a place for a white woman. James Adair, *History of the American Indians* (Williams ed.), 312, states that Legardere was "turbulent, proud, and querulous," that he was "as much unacquainted with the language, manners, and customs of the Indians, as his employer," and that he wrote "a considerable volume how to regulate Indian affairs in general, and particularly in the Choktah country." Unfortunately, no trace of this work has been discovered. Adair, *op. cit.,* 316, also says with reference to Legardere: "doubtless profitable family jobbs ought to be well minded." The meaning of this oblique remark is not clear. I have seen no evidence indicating that John Stuart and Legardere were connected by blood or by marriage, although it is quite possible that they were. Mrs. Legardere died at Savannah in March, 1770, and Legardere himself at the same place in April of the same year. *Georgia Gazette,* March 21, April 4, 1770.

[91] An Indian trader of considerable prestige among the Creeks. He served for a very short time.

[92] The salary of a commissary in the field was ten shillings per day. Stuart's secretary, or clerk, was William Ogilvie. Ogilvie was born in Scotland, and came to South Carolina in 1764. He sailed for England in March, 1775. Returning to America in May, 1776, he found Stuart at Pensacola, but Stuart failed to reemploy him, and he set himself up as a merchant at that place. He went to Charleston in 1780, and in the following year returned to Great Britain. American Loyalist Transcripts, liii, 200–20; *South-Carolina and American General Gazette,* March 24, 1775. Almost all the men employed by Stuart were Scots; and at least two of his aides were relatives. Sir William Johnson was likewise addicted to providing positions for his relatives.

[93] Stuart to Gage, March 19, 1765, Gage to Stuart, May 13, 1765, Gage MSS.

1763 Bull doubted that he could force the traders to obey Stuart's rules, and he refused to act, especially since it was expected at the time that some decision regarding the use of the "Plan for the Future Management of Indian Affairs" would soon be reached.[94] In August, 1765, Wright also returned a negative answer, for different reasons. Stuart's rules, except for those which related to the powers of the commissaries, were almost identical with rules that Wright had tried to impose upon Georgia traders since 1761. Wright indicated that he saw no object in requiring the Georgia traders to obey those of Stuart's regulations that were the same as his own; and he refused to impose the others upon the traders because they would increase the powers of the southern Indian department at his own expense. In fact, Wright placed the whole matter before the Board of Trade with a protest that "Lodging the supreme political power [in Indian affairs] in any other hands than the govr. or govrs. with the advice of the council may be attended with embarrassing & bad consequences."[95] Since unrestricted traders from South Carolina and Georgia continued their nefarious ways among the Chickasaws, Choctaws, and Creeks, Johnstone abandoned his attempts to enforce Stuart's regulations before the close of 1765.[96] By March, 1766, Wright had changed his attitude. At that time he was prepared to act in concert with Stuart in dealing with the trade problem.[97] But Stuart then was convinced that he could accomplish nothing without the intervention of the home government.

[94] CJSC, xxxii, 533-35, 541-42.

[95] Wright to Board of Trade, Aug. 19, 1765, Stuart to Wright, March 31, July 25, 1765, Wright to Stuart, Aug. 17, 1765, *GCR,* XXVIII, 250-51, 253-54, 256-61, 274-79.

[96] Johnstone to Legardere, Nov. 21, 1765, CO, 5/574.

[97] Stuart to Gage, March 14, 1766, Gage MSS.

CHAPTER XIII

POLITICS AND LANDS, 1765–68

TRAVELING with that amazing individual James Macpherson, the celebrated publisher of works on Fingal and Ossian, Stuart reached Charleston from West Florida on July 19, 1765,[1] to find that Anglo-Cherokee relations had taken a sharp turn for the worse during his absence. Early in 1764 the Cherokees had not only indicated willingness to aid in a war against the Creeks, but had undertaken at Stuart's behest to assist the English against Pontiac. Four parties of Cherokees, one of them headed by Ouconnostotah himself, had made forays on the Ohio in the spring of that year, and had brought in a total of eight scalps.[2] In the fall of 1764 a band of Cherokees led by Usteneka had attempted to intercept a large convoy of French goods en route to Pontiac's men via the Ohio, but had failed. They brought back only two French planters, although they were rewarded for their zeal by a gift of £900 (provincial currency) from the South Carolina assembly.[3] Another Cherokee party went to the Ohio in 1765 in an attempt to aid Farmar.

However, the friendship shown by the Cherokees in 1764–65 was seriously undermined in various ways. Frontier inhabitants, or "crackers" as they were known, irritated the Cherokees so greatly by poaching on their lands that Ensign George Price, commander at Fort Prince George,[4] urged the Indians to seize the traps and

[1] *South-Carolina Gazette,* July 19, 1765. Macpherson, holder of several offices in West Florida, had quarreled with Johnstone. He was born near Inverness. It seems likely that Stuart could have given useful evidence toward settling the Ossianic controversy.

[2] "Talks" by Ouconnostotah, Jan. 19, 1764, in CO, 323/17, and Feb. 18, 1764, in Gage MSS; Captain Gavin Cochrane to Gage, July 23, 1764, *ibid.*

[3] Bull to Gage, April 9, 1765, Gage MSS; *South-Carolina Gazette,* March 9, April 6, 1765.

[4] Price was commissioned ensign in the Royal Americans on February 18, 1761. He was in command of Fort Le Boeuf when the Pontiac rebellion broke out, and was forced to evacuate his post, but reached Fort Pitt in safety. He was ordered to Fort Prince George in January, 1764, and remained there until 1767.

skins of the offenders and to drive them from Cherokee territory.[5] Captain Gavin Cochrane, energetic commander of the Royal Americans stationed in South Carolina and Georgia,[6] finally ordered Price to arrest the offenders, and he actually seized three "crackers." When Lieutenant Governor Bull denied that he had authority to punish them, and urged that they be freed after solemn warning, Cochrane complied. At the same time he declared that in the future he would confine "cracker" trespassers until he could receive orders from Gage, if Bull and Wright refused to act.[7] Excessive sales of rum among the Cherokees resulted in brawl after brawl, and Bull's more or less forced inaction in regard to the whole problem of trade regulation heightened these disorders. When Alexander Cameron tried to make the traders behave, he was met by threats and was "collar'd" for attempting to force some traders to do justice to an Indian. Cochrane urged Bull, as did Stuart, to put a stop to the excessive trade in rum in the Cherokee country. Since Bull temporized, Cochrane himself assumed the responsibility, giving Price orders to limit the use of liquor in barter.[8] Because Georgia prohibited its traders from bringing rum to the Cherokees, the efforts of Cochrane and Price in this direction were of some importance, for they resulted in sobering up a portion of the nation.[9]

But Cochrane could do nothing to lighten the resentment felt by the Cherokees because of encroachments of white settlers upon their lands, a resentment that was all the greater because the encroachments had the approval of the governments of the Carolinas. North Carolina was freely granting lands as far back as the mountains without reference to Cherokee claims, while South Carolina was permitting occupation of part of the territory west of Long Canes Creek which the Cherokees believed they had succeeded in reserving for themselves at Augusta. Both Boone and Bull acted upon the assumption that the treaty of peace of 1761 set up a bound-

[5] Price to Captain Gavin Cochrane, Jan. 24, 1765 (Extract), Gage MSS.

[6] Cochrane saw service in the Seven Years' War as a captain of the 1st Battalion of Royal Americans. He commanded the royal troops in South Carolina and Georgia from May, 1764, to August, 1765. He later served at Crown Point, in the West Indies, and at Gibraltar. A "treatise" on the management of Indian affairs which Cochrane wrote at the end of 1763 and sent to Lord Halifax is an interesting rather than an important piece. There is a copy of it in the Newberry Library. Cochrane seems to have been an able officer.

[7] Cochrane to Gage, April 9, 1765, Gage MSS.

[8] Cochrane to Gage, April 26, 1765, Gage MSS.

[9] Cameron to Cochrane, June 6, 1765, Cochrane to Gage, Aug. 5, 1765, Gage MSS.

ary; and South Carolina permitted surveys to be made east of a theoretical line running from the mouth of the Keowee River to the junction of 40-Mile River and the Charleston-Keowee road, and thence in a direct northward direction. As a result, a hot debate arose between the frontier settlers and the Cherokees as to the true limits agreed upon. Finally, in April, 1765, Bull made an attempt to clarify the situation. He proposed to the Cherokees that a line which would include all the white settlements should be marked off. He appointed Lachlan McIntosh to act for him, but the Cherokee chiefs refused to negotiate until Stuart returned from West Florida, for they believed that Stuart would support their claim.[10]

The attitude of the Cherokees toward the English, although the Indians were not innocent of wrongdoing,[11] was on the whole prudent and moderate, a fact that made eventual rapprochement between them and the English possible. In the spring of 1765, before the Congress of Pensacola, The Mortar appeared once more in the Cherokee country in his rôle of prime intriguer. In a conference held with several Cherokee chiefs at Toqueh town The Mortar made a fiery address, charging that Stuart talked with two tongues, one asking for peace in West Florida and the other instigating the seizure of Cherokee lands. He declared that the English were planning to occupy all the territory between South Carolina and Fort Chartres. Ouconnostotah, still smarting from his imprisonment and defeat in the Cherokee War, supported The Mortar and called for an indiscriminate slaughter of the Cherokee traders, but Attakullakulla, also present at the conference, dissuaded his fellows from taking hostile measures against the English.[12] Attempts by The Mortar to win over Saluy, who had shown a marked dislike for the Creeks, likewise failed; in fact, the Creek chief was forced to avoid Saluy, for fear of being taken captive.[13] Then Ouconnostotah deserted The Mortar. Visiting Fort Prince George for the first time since the Cherokee War, he held a parley with Ensign Price and pledged his friendship to the English.[14] The Great Warrior and

[10] CJSC, xxix, 113–14, xxxii, 558–61; "talk" from Cherokee chiefs to Bull, July 11, 1765, Stuart to Gage, Aug. 6, 1765, Gage MSS; Stuart to Halifax, Aug. 24, 1765, CO, 5/66.

[11] Young Cherokee braves indulged themselves in stealing horses from the "crackers." One Cherokee party set fire to woods near a white settlement.

[12] Cochrane's "Account of What Intelligence relating to the Indians I have lately received from Fort Prince George," April 26, 1765, Gage MSS.

[13] Cochrane to Gage, June 3, 1765, Gage MSS.

[14] "Journal of Mr. Price's Proceedings with the Great Warrior . . . ," May 14, 1765, Gage MSS.

Usteneka claimed that the machinations of The Mortar were inspired by French intrigue.[15]

Luckily, the disturbance caused by The Mortar had subsided by June, for news then came to the Cherokees of the slaughter of nine of their fellows from the towns of Settico and Chilhowee by frontiersmen in Augusta County, Virginia.[16] On hearing an account of these murders, a group of Cherokees at Toqueh broke down Cameron's door in the night, but Cameron met them with pistols and smooth "palaver," and finally succeeded in calming them. Fortunately, the Cherokees had not had access to rum. A few traders were beaten in ensuing days, but none were killed.[17] Usteneka, Attakullakulla, and Willinawa strove to maintain peace, and managed to placate Ouconnostotah. Cameron called a meeting of the principal chiefs and succeeded in inducing all those who attended to smoke the peace pipe, although he was forced to push the pipe into the mouths of some of them.[18]

To apprehend the murderers of the nine Cherokees Fauquier sent out Major Andrew Lewis, who succeeded in capturing two of them. But a report spread that Cherokees who escaped the frontiersmen had slain a blind man and his wife in revenge; and 100 armed backsettlers freed the prisoners, breaking into a jail in order to accomplish their purpose.[19] The murderers were never punished, and Virginia failed to send sufficient presents to soothe the wounded feelings of the relatives of the slain Cherokees. The Settico and Chilhowee townsmen therefore continued to nourish a grudge against the frontier people, and especially against Virginians.

In spite of the Augusta County massacre the Cherokees were not unwilling to deal with the land question. Stuart was displeased because Bull had attempted to settle South Carolina's Cherokee boundary without consulting him or Cameron,[20] but he urged the Cherokees to negotiate a new line that would include all the fron-

[15] Price to Cochrane, June 26, 1765 (Extract), Cameron to Price, June 15, 1765 (Extract), Gage MSS. The Mortar may possibly have been inspired by individual Frenchmen in West Florida.

[16] Gage's reaction to this report is interesting. If war resulted, he hoped that it could be confined to Virginia, whose backsettlers, in his opinion, deserved chastisement. Gage to Stuart, Oct. 2, 1765, Gage MSS.

[17] Cameron to Price, June 15, 1765 (Extract), Gage MSS.

[18] Cameron to Cochrane, June 6, 1765, Gage MSS.

[19] Lewis to Fauquier, June 3, 5, 1765, CO, 5/43.

[20] Stuart complained sharply to the Board of Trade regarding Bull's attitude. He stressed the fact that difficulties arising from an unsatisfactory boundary would fall more upon his shoulders than upon those of Bull. Stuart to John Pownall, Aug. 24, 1765, CO, 5/66.

tier settlements, and they agreed. Cameron and Ensign Price met a Cherokee delegation at Fort Prince George on October 19, 1765, and secured the signature of an instrument by which the Cherokees ceded "all that tract of land (which previous to this time we deem'd our own) lying between a brook known to the white people by the name of Dervise's [Dewitt's] Corner, and to us by the Yellow water & another brook distant from the former about ten miles & known both by white and red people by the name of Long Canes." [21] Dewitt's Corner, which lay about six miles northwest of the present Due West, thereby became the limit of the South Carolina settlements on the road to Keowee. In the spring of 1766 Cameron, Edward Wilkinson, and Mr. Pickens, commissioner and surveyor respectively for South Carolina, and a party of Cherokees set out to survey and mark the boundary. The line as laid out by them differed slightly though not materially from that specified in the agreements of October, 1765. It began at a point on the Savannah River about ten miles above the mouth of Rocky Creek and ran in a direct course in a northeasterly direction through Dewitt's Corner to the Reedy River, a northern tributary of the Saluda River.[22] All along the line the Indians blazed the trees on both sides in a belt 50 feet wide, so that doubt as to its location was impossible. Even with this cession by the Cherokees Cameron informed Stuart that there were a few houses within four miles of the boundary.[23] At the close of 1768 one could travel toward the limit for thirty or forty miles without seeing a house; in its immediate vicinity, however, many families, especially from Virginia, had settled.[24] (The line is shown in Map 2, p. 102.)

On the whole, relations between North Carolina and the Cherokees were amicable for some years after the French and Indian War, in spite of the fact that the province was freely granting lands claimed by the Cherokees. In October, 1765, the Cherokees asked

[21] "Cession of Lands by the Cherokee Indians at Fort P: George," Oct. 19, 1765, Gage MSS. The agreement was invalid unless approved by Bull and Stuart. Their signatures were affixed on Oct. 10, 1765, and Jan. 10, 1766, respectively.

[22] The line stopped at Reedy River because Bull did not desire to continue it into territory that might eventually be determined to lie in North Carolina. The line still forms the boundaries of Anderson and Greenville counties on the southeast.

[23] Cameron to Stuart, May 10, 1766, CO, 5/66; Bull to Board of Trade, June 9, 1766, CO, 5/378. A map of the line, probably drawn by Pickens, is to be found in Archer B. Hulbert, ed., *The Crown Collection of Photographs of American Maps,* Third Series (London, 1914–16), Plate 43.

[24] Stuart to Hillsborough, Jan. 3, 1769, CO, 5/70.

that their boundary with the whites be continued in a straight line northward from Dewitt's Corner to the mountains and thence in a second straight line to Colonel John Chiswell's lead mine on the upper Kanawha River.[25] When Stuart placed this proposal before Governor William Tryon early in 1766, Tryon hesitated. He asserted that he was not familiar with the exact situation in the western part of his government and that he had no funds to cover the cost of negotiations and surveying. He also declared that he had had no instructions from home regarding the proposal. After Stuart sent him a copy of the Proclamation of 1763, in which there was a clause forbidding governors to grant lands reserved to themselves by the Indians, Tryon was convinced that it would be wise to come to an agreement with the Cherokees. In May, 1766, the Cherokees urged that the line be run from the end of their boundary with South Carolina directly to Chiswell's Mine. Such a line would have left parts of Rowan and Mecklenburg counties, already in the process of settlement, in the Cherokee country. Tryon therefore demanded that the boundary should follow the course originally suggested by the Indians.[26] A conference to be attended by Tryon, Stuart, and the Cherokees was arranged for September, but was postponed until April of the following year because of sickness in the nation and the imminent approach of the hunting season.[27] The North Carolina assembly granted the necessary funds, and in February, 1767, Tryon requested Stuart to call a meeting at Salisbury on May 16 to secure a formal agreement on the line and an immediate survey. He urged the superintendent to attend in person.[28]

Since the beginning of 1766 Stuart had been eager to hold a formal conference in order to soothe Cherokee unrest. He was especially anxious to call such a gathering because the Cherokees had not taken part in any congress since that of Augusta in 1763. Stuart was unable to carry out this design without authorization, but a letter from Lord Shelburne of September 13, 1766, instructed him to restore order in the Indian trade. This led Stuart to call a congress with the Cherokees in connection with plans for regulating that commerce, and he determined at the same time to attempt to settle all outstanding problems with the Cherokees.

[25] "A Meeting Held by the Cherokees," Oct. 20, 1765, Gage MSS.

[26] Tryon to Stuart, April 9, May 5, June 17, 1766, CO, 5/66; "talk" by Cherokees to Cameron, May 8, 1766, CO, 5/67.

[27] *NCCR,* VII, 244-45, 253-54; Stuart to Board of Trade, Dec. 2, 1766, CO, 5/67.

[28] Tryon to Stuart, Feb. 16, 1767, *NCCR,* VII, 437-38.

From May 18 to 21 at Hard Labor near the Savannah River Stuart and the Cherokees discussed the boundary of North Carolina, and more particularly the trade problem.[29] The Cherokees agreed to send a commission to join Tryon in drawing the line, and on May 21 Cameron and several chiefs left Hard Labor for that purpose.[30] Some days later they met Tryon, escorted by fifty armed men, near Reedy River. The discussion that ensued was reasonably satisfactory on both sides, and the delineation of the line was begun on June 4, the king's birthday, in accordance with Tryon's desire. Tryon did not remain until the boundary was completed, because of a lack of sufficient provisions, as he reported. However, his commissioners, John Rutherford, Robert Palmer, and John Frohock, accomplished the task in coöperation with the Cherokees.[31] In compliance with Tryon's wishes the line began

> ... at a Waughoe or Elm tree on the South side of Reedy River Standing on the Bank of the River where the South Carolina Line Terminates and Runs thence a North Course about Fifty Three Miles into the Mountains to a Spanish Oak marked with the Initial Letters of the Commissioners and several other Trees with the names and marks of Juds Friend [Usteneka] Sallowee [Saluy] Ecoy [Ecuy] [32] and others standing on the Top of a Mountain called by us Tryon Mountain on the head Waters of White Oak and Packet Creeks, White Oak running into Green River and Packet running into Broad River and as it was found Impracticable that a Line should be Run and marked through the Mountains to Colo Chiswell's Mines ... [the boundary shall follow] from the Top of Tryon Mountain aforesaid. Beginning at the marked tree thereon ... a direct line to Chiswell's Mines in Virginia ....[33]

In July, 1767, after completion of the boundary, Tryon issued a proclamation ordering any and all persons living beyond the line to vacate, and announcing that no land would be granted within one mile of the boundary.[34] The only untoward result of the negotiations regarding the line was a feeling of hostility toward Stuart on the part of Tryon, who complained to Shelburne of his conduct.[35] (The general course of the boundary may be followed on Map 2, p. 102.)

[29] The trade problem is discussed in Chapter XIV. An account of Stuart's movements in the spring of 1767 will be found there.

[30] "Journal of the Superintendant's proceedings," April 21—June 6, 1767, Gage MSS.

[31] *NCCR,* VII, 460–69.

[32] Ecuy, or the Good Warrior, was a chief of Estatoe.

[33] *NCCR,* VII, 470.

[34] *NCCR,* VII, 502–3.

[35] Tryon to Shelburne, July 8, 1767, *NCCR,* VII, 500–1. Tryon's complaints were not only trivial but unjustified. His vanity seems to have been hurt because Stuart did not reach him for a personal consultation. At the time Stuart was plunged in business.

Another problem in Anglo-Cherokee relations that perplexed Stuart sorely in the period 1765–68 arose from the incessant conflict that went on between the Cherokees and the Indians of the North and West after 1761. The peace between the Iroquois, the Cherokees, and the Catawbas made by the English in 1758 was broken by the Six Nations as soon as the conquest of Canada released their energies; and Johnson made no attempt to restrain them, for the conflict provided diversion and glory for the young braves at the expense of the Indians rather than the American frontiersmen.[36] But the raids of the Iroquois, Delawares, Shawnees, and other tribes from the Ohio valley proved so costly to the Cherokees that they were very anxious to make peace by 1765.[37] In the summer of that year, when Attakullakulla visited Williamsburg to consult Fauquier regarding the Augusta County massacre, Fauquier gave him a few trifles for the relatives of the victims, and also promised to try to arrange a peace between the Cherokees and their northern enemies.[38] When Fauquier requested Johnson to undertake mediation, the northern superintendent reluctantly consented, provided Stuart was not opposed to the measure.[39]

In a "talk" to the Cherokees of February 1, 1766,[40] Stuart informed them that he would ask Johnson to undertake mediation, if the Cherokees so wished, but this offer was no more than a hollow gesture. Stuart hesitated to take any action in the matter, for he realized that the southern frontier was safe from Cherokee attack as long as the conflict continued; on the other hand, the superintendent feared that if the war were not brought to a conclusion, the Cherokees would be so weakened that they could not be used as pawns against the Creeks. Of course, if the negotiations were successful, the Cherokees might be persuaded by the Creeks to join in an assault on the colonies. Stuart therefore appealed to Gage and the southern governors for their opinions.[41] Wright saw mediation as a generous policy, but an unwise one.[42] Gage advised Stuart not

[36] *Johnson Papers,* III, 988–89, IV, 67.

[37] The *South-Carolina Gazette,* Aug. 27, 1763, reported that no fewer than fifty-eight Cherokees had fallen before the onslaughts of northern Indians between May and August, 1763. Many other raids are mentioned in succeeding years. Several whites were also slain by marauders from the north.

[38] Fauquier to Board of Trade, Aug. 1, 1765, CO, 5/1331.

[39] Johnson to Stuart, Sept. 17, 1765, CO, 5/67.

[40] In CO, 5/67.

[41] Stuart to Bull, June 1, 1766, CO, 5/67.

[42] Wright to Stuart, July 10, 1766 (Extract), CO, 5/67. Wright stated that he personally would not instigate an Indian war, but that he would not attempt to end one which was of benefit to the English.

to encourage peace negotiations unless the Cherokees gave assurances of assistance to the English against the Creeks, because the English and the Upper Creeks were at the time on the verge of war.[43] Stuart finally decided that the Cherokees had suffered so severely from war and disease that no harm could arise from a peace between them and their enemies. With Gage's approval he planned to make peace first between the Cherokees and the Six Nations, and then between the former and the tribes about Fort Pitt.[44] To prevent further clashes, he made arrangements to send Cherokee emissaries northward by sea to New York, and thence to Johnson Hall. In November, 1767, after much delay, Attakullakulla and Ouconnostotah with their sons and a score of other Cherokees appointed as commissioners reached Charleston. Stuart permitted only eight persons to embark, including the two chiefs and their children.[45] John Watts accompanied them as mentor and interpreter.

The Cherokee party traveled on the sloop *Sally* to New York, where they were received by Gage with great ceremony on December 12. When the Indians evinced a desire to see a play in the theater, he obtained seats for them at a performance of *Richard III*. They were amused by the antics of Harlequin, and a great crowd that gathered at the theater was perhaps even more entertained by the Cherokees.[46] On December 29 they reached Johnson Hall. There in the following March, with the aid of Sir William, they succeeded in obtaining a peace with the Six Nations.[47] Most of the Cherokees, led by Ouconnostotah and accompanied by Watts, returned to New York, where they edified a theater crowd with a war dance, and then went on by sea to Charleston. But Attakullakulla, escorted by a party of Iroquois warriors, went toward Fort Pitt, where it was expected that George Croghan would arrange a peace between the Cherokees and the Shawnees, Delawares, Mingos, and Susquehannas. Croghan held a conference with the latter tribes that closed early in May, apparently before Attakullakulla could reach Fort Pitt, although some sort of treaty seems to have been made.[48] Gage viewed the successful results of these negotiations

[43] Gage to Stuart, Aug. 30, 1766, Gage MSS.

[44] Stuart to Gage, Dec. 19, 1766, Gage to Stuart, Sept. 18, 1767, Gage MSS.

[45] Stuart to Gage, Nov. 27, 1767, Gage MSS; Stuart to Shelburne, Feb. 10, 1768, CO, 5/69.

[46] *South-Carolina and American General Gazette*, Jan. 1, 8, 1768.

[47] *NYCD*, VIII, 36–53.

[48] The minutes of Croghan's conference, in the Gage MSS, merely show Croghan requesting the Indians present to see to it that Attakullakulla was not molested on his way home. Little Carpenter reached Paxton on May 2, and

with some misgivings, for he feared that the English might soon have cause to regret their friendly services,[49] but his forebodings proved to be unfounded.

Anglo-Creek relations did not improve greatly from 1765 to 1768. As many as ten whites suffered death at the hands of the Creeks during this period. East Florida and Georgia had various Indian troubles, chiefly with the Lower Creeks and the Seminoles. Much more dangerous to the peace of the southern colonies was a bitter quarrel between the English in West Florida and the Upper Creeks.

The Congress of Pensacola had been adjourned only a short time when relations between the English in West Florida and the Upper Creeks again entered upon a period of intense strain that came to a climax late in 1766. The Upper Creeks were jealous of the Choctaws and Chickasaws because of the presents given to those tribes for their assistance to Farmar, and they were dissatisfied because prices in the trade were not so low in their nation as in others. The Mortar, disgusted by the low prices offered the Creeks for deerskins, threw away his English medal. The Upper Creeks were responsible for the murder of one John Kemp near Pensacola not long after the close of the congress, and they labored energetically to increase the discontent of the Cherokees caused by the Augusta County massacre.[50] Their haughtiness toward the English was so excessive that it offended one of their own chiefs, Wolf King, who urged the English to reduce them to a proper sense of humility by suspending the trade for two years.[51]

But Stuart's policy of strengthening the Choctaws as a counterbalance to the Creeks bore fruit after the Congress of Mobile, and the English position in regard to the Creeks was therefore much stronger. Well supplied with implements of war and more united than they had been in the period of the French régime, the Choctaws began to answer in kind the insults and injuries heaped upon them by the domineering Creeks. When the Upper Creeks murdered a Choctaw near Fort Tombigbee in the spring of 1765, hostilities broke out that continued with greater or less intensity for eleven years, to the satisfaction of the English, who were thereby

probably remained there too long to attend Croghan's gathering, but he succeeded in his mission. *South-Carolina and American General Gazette,* June 3, 1768, Jan. 16, 1769.

[49] Gage to Stuart, April 10, 1768, Gage MSS.

[50] *MPAED,* I, 516–17, 529; Stuart to Board of Trade, July 10, 1766, CO, 5/67; Stuart to Gage, Aug. 2, 1766, Gage MSS.

[51] *MPAED,* I, 520–21.

partly relieved of fears of a Creek onslaught against the weak southern provinces. The war was formally inaugurated by a challenge from the Choctaws to Emistisiguo in the spring of 1766,[52] and was soon fanned into flame by Johnstone, Lieutenant Colonel William Tayler, Charles Stuart, Elias Legardere, and some of the traders. Charles Stuart thwarted attempts by the Upper Creeks and their opponents to reach a settlement (the Lower Creeks were not seriously involved); and Legardere used the strategic location of Fort Tombigbee to encourage the Choctaws and to supply them with ammunition. To aid Legardere in these tactics, Tayler, after consulting with Johnstone and Charles Stuart, sent a portion of the 21st Regiment under Captain Hope to reoccupy Fort Tombigbee,[53] which had been abandoned in the fall of 1764.[54] Choctaw auxiliaries led by John McIntosh escorted the garrison to the post. Tayler also sent a detachment to the Natchez, in part in order to prevent supplies from reaching the Creeks from across the Mississippi.[55] Wolf King, with a keen sense of the realities of the situation, then declared that the English were safe from attack by the Upper Creeks.[56]

The Upper Creeks were perfectly informed of the intrigues carried on by Legardere,[57] and in May, 1766, The Mortar, Emistisiguo, and other leaders boldly accused the English of inciting the Choctaws and Chickasaws against them.[58] A soft answer might well have turned away the wrath of the Upper Creeks, but Johnstone informed them he would as lief have war as peace.[59] In fact, the fiery Scot had made up his mind that it was time to put an end to their insolence; he had already urged Stuart to incite the Cherokees against them.[60] On June 23 in a formal report to Sir Henry Con-

[52] Stephen Forrester to Johnstone, May 25, 1766, B. M. Add. MSS, 21,671, pt. 1.

[53] Legardere to Johnstone, March 27, 1766, "Copy of Brigadier Genll Tayler order for a Party of the 21st Regiment to take possession of Fort Tombeckby ye 20th May 1766," B. M. Add. MSS, 21,671, pt. 1; John McGillivray to Charles Stuart, May 10, 1766 (Extract), Charles Stuart to Stuart, May 17, 1766 (Extract), Johnstone to Stuart, May 19, June 3, 1766, Tayler to Gage, June 1, Sept. 18, 1766, Gage MSS.

[54] See Farmar to Gage, Nov. 24, 1764, Gage MSS.

[55] Charles Stuart to Tayler, June 26, 1766, B. M. Add. MSS, 21,671, pt. 1.

[56] "Talk" by Wolf King to Johnstone, June 28, 1766, B. M. Add. MSS, 21,671, pt. 1.

[57] Lieutenant John Ritchy reported from Fort Tombigbee that Legardere made no attempt to conceal his intrigues. However, Ritchy hated Legardere.

[58] "Talk" by Upper Creek chiefs to Johnstone, May 16, 1766, *MPAED,* I, 526–31.

[59] "Talk" by Johnstone to Upper Creek chiefs, June 9, 1766, *MPAED,* I, 531–33.

[60] Johnstone to Stuart, May 19, 1766, Gage MSS.

way, secretary of state for the southern department, he called for a war of extermination against them, with the English joining the Choctaws, Chickasaws, and Cherokees in a general and simultaneous assault.[61] Claiming that 138 Englishmen had been slain by the Creeks without punishment and that the honor of England demanded vengeance, Johnstone called upon Stuart for coöperation.[62]

Stuart scoffed at Johnstone's figures; he pointed out that they included every Englishman killed by the Creeks since the two peoples had come into contact, and probably more. He took the sensible view that the honor of England could not be damaged by following a prudent policy in negotiating with an Indian tribe. He censured Johnstone for taking action leading toward an Indian war without conferring with him and with the governors of the other colonies that would be concerned in such a conflict. He himself now consulted the governors of those provinces, and they all counseled peace. Stuart was convinced that justice did not lie entirely on the English side, and that diplomatic means of settling Indian problems, costly as they might seem, could be financed for twenty years with the outlays necessary to wage such a war as Johnstone contemplated.[63] As in 1764, Stuart was of the opinion that a peaceful settlement could be reached, and that negotiations should be carried on until all hope of securing one was lost. While negotiations were in progress preparations for obtaining Indian assistance should be completed, so that allies would not be lacking in case war actually came.[64] Gage was in full agreement with Stuart. He urged the superintendent to incite the Choctaws to greater efforts against the Creeks, and expressed a hope that Stuart would be able to create an anti-Creek confederacy that, in the event of war, would be sufficiently strong to obviate the necessity of sending a large number of troops to the Floridas and Georgia.[65]

In September, 1766, two Chickasaw traders, Goodwin and Davis, suspected by the Upper Creeks of inciting the Choctaws against them, were slain, but this incident led to no change in Stuart's policy. He instructed his aides to try to secure Indian allies, and sent the Upper Creeks a demand for the execution of the murderers

[61] Johnstone to Conway, June 23, 1766, *MPAED,* I, 511–16. Johnstone's policy had the hearty support of James Adair. Adair to Johnstone, Sept. 16, 1766, B. M. Add. MSS, 21,671, pt. 2.

[62] Johnstone to Stuart, Sept. 30, 1766, Gage MSS.

[63] Stuart to Johnstone, Dec. 13, 1766, B. M. Add. MSS, 21,671, pt. 3.

[64] Stuart to Gage, Aug. 8, 1766, Gage MSS; Stuart to Conway, Aug. 8, 1766, CO, 5/67.

[65] Gage to Stuart, Aug. 30, 1766, Gage MSS.

of Goodwin and Davis. If satisfaction were refused, he proposed to try cutting off the trade. If this measure failed, he expected to be ready for the appeal to arms.[66] He was prepared to go to West Florida in person if the situation did not improve. He had long been searching for a man to serve as commissary among the Creeks; he had now found in Roderick McIntosh a man who seemed to be qualified.[67] In December he appointed McIntosh, who immediately left for his station.[68]

Johnstone's plans for energetic action against the Upper Creeks were never put into action. Johnstone joined Stuart in demanding the punishment of the leaders of the band who slew Goodwin and Davis, and Lieutenant Colonel William Tayler sent a special emissary to the Upper Creeks to announce that he wished peace, but would surround and crush them in the event of war. In succeeding "talks" he expressed himself to the same effect.[69] Meanwhile, at Fort Tombigbee, Elias Legardere and Lieutenant John Ritchy, commander at that post after its reoccupation, assiduously furnished the Choctaws with advice and ammunition, in accordance with instructions given by the superintendent and Charles Stuart. Embarrassed by the Choctaw forays, the Upper Creeks saw the wisdom of maintaining peace with the English. War was almost inevitable, Tayler believed, in mid-October; however, in November a delegation of Upper Creeks headed by Emistisiguo came to Pensacola, announcing that one of the leaders of the band who had slain the two traders had been executed. They spoke for peace, and tension then rapidly lessened. Tayler claimed that this happy result was due to his efforts,[72] and a report to Gage to that effect transmitted to Lord Shelburne secured him a few words of commendation from the minister.[73] Lieutenant Governor Montfort Browne, who succeeded Johnstone in January, 1767, supported Tayler's claim.[74] Stuart and Grant scoffed at it, Stuart asserting that

[66] Stuart to Board of Trade, Nov. 16, 1766, CO, 5/67.

[67] Regarding Roderick McIntosh's early history see p. 212 note.

[68] Stuart to Johnstone, Dec. 17, 1766, B. M. Add. MSS, 21,671, pt. 3.

[69] Tayler to Gage, Nov. 30, 1766, Gage MSS.

[70] Ritchy to Taylor, Nov. 5, 30, 1766, B. M. Add. MSS, 21,671, pt. 3.

[71] Tayler to Gage, Oct. 16, 1766, Gage MSS.

[72] Tayler to Gage, Nov. 30, 1766, Charles Stuart to Stuart, Nov. 23, 1766, Gage MSS; Stuart to Board of Trade, Dec. 2, 1766, CO, 5/67.

[73] Tayler to Gage, Aug. 11, 1767, Gage MSS.

[74] Browne to Shelburne, Feb. 25, 1767, CO, 5/577. Browne stated that he and Tayler worked together to avert the impending conflict, but that Tayler was chiefly responsible for the successful negotiations. The height of the crisis was past, however, when Browne became governor.

Tayler had had nought to do with the happy result of the negotiations.[75] There may have been some jealousy in Stuart's attitude, but there can be little doubt that his policy of inspiriting the Choctaws on the one hand and talking peace to the Creeks on the other was largely responsible for the success.

One interesting consequence of the West Florida–Upper Creek imbroglio of 1765–66 was the action taken by Lord Shelburne, Conway's successor, when he received reports concerning it. He immediately ordered the recall of Johnstone for proposing to begin a war upon his own initiative, instructed Stuart and the southern governors to inform the Creeks that the English were anxious to preserve peace because of their kindness of heart, and gave his permission for Stuart to hold a congress with that nation, if necessary. He expressed stern disapproval of those persons who had fomented quarrels among the Indians in order to prevent them from attacking West Florida, for he believed that, if the English were friends and protectors to all the tribes and acted as an arbiter in their quarrels, the Indians would conceive a fondness for the English that would assure the safety of the colonies from assaults by the red men.[76]

Gage and Stuart felt the sting of Shelburne's criticism. Gage deceitfully informed the minister that he had "never known Such a Policy adopted as your Lordship takes Notice of, That of Setting the Indians upon each other," [77] but Stuart prudently kept silent. Unquestionably, Gage's real opinion was that the fomenting of tribal conflicts was an excellent method to save himself from being involved in Indian wars such as had proved so damaging to Amherst's reputation. He had encouraged Stuart and officials in West Florida to follow that policy, and he had even officially assured Lord Halifax that it was vital to the preservation of Anglo-Indian peace.[78]

[75] Grant to Stuart, Aug. 22, 1767, Stuart to Grant, Oct. 3, 1767, CO, 5/73.

[76] Shelburne to Gage, Dec. 11, 1766, Feb. 19, 1767, *Gage Corr.*, II, 51–52; Shelburne to Stuart, Dec. 11, 1766, Gage MSS.

[77] Gage to Shelburne, Feb. 20, 1767, *Gage Corr.*, I, 120.

[78] In his very first letter to Stuart, Jan. 27, 1764, Gage MSS, the general said: "If we have not dexterity enough to turn that warlike spirit [of the Indians] from ourselves and derect it to other objects, I fear we shall often feel the effects of it. I therefore can't recommend it too strongly to you, so to foment the jars and bickerings of the several tribes against each other and excite that jealousy so natural to all savages, as shall be consistent with the peace security and welfare of His Majesty's subjects." See also Gage to Halifax, Jan. 21, 1764, *Gage Corr.*, I, 13. Gage had forgotten (!) that he once suggested to Stuart that the superintendent arrange for the assassination of The Mortar. His argument that it was inevitable that the Indians should fight, and that it was preferable that they combat each other instead of the English, had considerable sense behind it, whatever might be said regarding it on moral grounds.

Of course, Stuart also believed in that policy, although he was of the opinion that it should be employed with great caution. Stuart, always responsive to orders from home, abandoned all thought of such secret diplomacy while the altruistic and uninformed Shelburne was in power. Although both Stuart and Gage were discomfited by Shelburne's injunction to make peace among the Indian tribes, they obeyed, until Lord Hillsborough enjoined the resumption of the policy of *divide et impera.*[79]

The war between the Upper Creeks and the Choctaws continued to run a favorable course for the Creeks until 1768. In one notable clash in October, 1767, the Red Captain, a pro-English Choctaw, was slain with twenty-four followers.[80] It became increasingly likely, however, that the Chickasaws, as a result of the protracted intrigues of the English, would ally themselves with the Choctaws. The Upper Creeks were anxious to avert Chickasaw intervention and asked Stuart's aid, but a definite rupture and a bloody skirmish between the two tribes occurred in the spring of 1768. For some months peace overtures by the Upper Creeks failed, and they were made most uncomfortable by the vigorous attacks of the redoubtable Chickasaws.[81]

Relations between the Creeks and the colonies of East Florida and Georgia during the period 1765–68 brought forth several interesting problems. In the early years of his administration James Grant had large ideas about the rôle the new colony of East Florida should play in Indian affairs, ideas having approximately as much basis in fact as his optimistic hopes for the development of the province along other lines. He contended that East Florida had replaced Georgia as the English southern frontier, and asked Gage to trans-

[79] Professor Clarence E. Carter, in his essay, "The Office of Commander in Chief: A Phase of Imperial Unity on the Eve of the Revolution," in Richard B. Morris, ed., *The Era of the American Revolution,* (New York, 1939), 193, states that Gage "advised the encouragement of intertribal wars, notably in the case of the Creek-Choctaw war, even though he was aware that such a policy was generally opposed at home." To prove this point Professor Carter cites the Shelburne letter of Dec. 11, 1766, to Gage, referred to above. But the policy of divide and rule was not discountenanced by Shelburne's predecessors in the southern department, and there is no evidence to show that Gage followed that policy from the time he received this letter, February, 1767, until Shelburne fell from power. Thus, as mentioned earlier in this chapter, Gage viewed the Cherokee-Iroquois peace of 1768 with misgivings, but he made no attempt to prevent it.

[80] James Hewitt to Messrs. McGillivray and Struthers, Oct. 16, 1767, Charles Stuart to Stuart, Oct. 29, 1767 (Abstract), Gage MSS.

[81] Charles Stuart to Montfort Browne, March 14, 1767, B. M. Add. MSS, 21,672, pt. 5; Stuart to Gage, July 4, 1767, March 30, 1768, Gage MSS; Gage to Hillsborough, Aug. 17, 1768, *Gage Corr.,* I, 186.

fer the Georgia rangers to his colony, but the general refused. Grant believed that East Florida would wrest Georgia's share of the Indian trade from her; and he hoped that Fort Appalachie would become a greater center for the trade than Augusta. In 1764, on learning of Halifax's order that Stuart reside in one of the Floridas, Grant assumed that Stuart would choose East Florida.[82] Immediately after his arrival at St. Augustine on August 29, 1764, Grant urged Stuart to visit East Florida to hold a congress to establish a boundary between East Florida and the Creeks,[83] since the governor's high hopes for the future of the province could not be fully realized without extensive cessions of territory by the Lower Creeks and Seminoles. By April, 1765, Grant had become so impatient that he threatened to convene a congress on his own authority if the superintendent did not soon arrive in East Florida.[84] Meanwhile, the inhabitants of East Florida found their Indian neighbors friendly, so much so that the latter furnished the garrison at Fort Appalachie with provisions when food supplies ran low.[85]

Unable to comply with Grant's request until the autumn of 1765 because of more pressing business, Stuart sailed from Charleston on September 21 and reached St. Augustine on October 3. From the 12th to the 18th of November Stuart, Charles Stuart, and Grant parleyed with the chiefs of the Lower Creeks, including Sempoyasse of the Cowetas and Captain Aleck of the Cussitas, at Fort Picolata. At first the Lower Creeks were rather refractory, complaining about high prices in the trade and encroachments made on their lands near the Oconee River, west of the boundary established at Augusta. After the close of the Congress of Augusta they had indicated to Stuart rather specifically what they considered a satisfactory boundary between themselves and East Florida. At that time they desired that English settlements be confined to the eastern side of the St. John's River between Mosquito Inlet[86] and Fort Picolata. At the Picolata congress they proposed that the Augusta line be continued from the Altamaha to Picolata and thence eastward along the road to St. Augustine. Of course, Stuart and Grant were not satisfied. They treated the Indians with lofty indifference in public, and la-

[82] Grant to Gage, Oct. 2, Dec. 1, 1764, Aug. 30, 1767, Gage to Grant, Sept. 29, 1764, Gage, MSS.

[83] Grant to Stuart, Aug. 31, 1764, Gage MSS.

[84] Grant to Gage, April 4, 1765, Gage MSS.

[85] Lieutenant James Pampellone to Gage, Dec. 6, 1764, June 21, 1766, Gage MSS.

[86] Now known by the more enticing name of Ponce de Leon Inlet.

bored diligently with their leaders in private in order to secure a more generous offer. This strategy, coupled with the desire of the Indians for Grant's presents, soon rendered the Lower Creeks more pliant.[87] The line finally agreed upon ran from Lake George down the St. John's to the mouth of Acklawaugh Creek, thence in a straight line to the forks of Black Creek, and from that point in a straight line to a point near King's Ferry on St. Mary's River. The remainder of the Florida peninsula was open to occupation as far inland as the flowing of the tide in the bays. All the territory east of the St. John's and a goodly slice to the westward of that stream were abandoned to the English by the treaty.[88] In addition, the Lower Creeks commissioned Captain Aleck to cede to Georgia all territory east of a line drawn southward from the mouth of Penholoway Creek on the Altamaha to that part of the St. Mary's where the tide ceased. Since Captain Aleck faithfully executed this commission Georgia also received a slight addition of territory open to settlement as a result of the Congress of Picolata.[89] On January 1, 1766, Stuart landed once more at Charleston.[90] (Regarding these boundaries consult Map 3, p. 178.)

All was quiet on the East Florida frontier from 1765 to 1768 except for one affray in the fall of 1767 between the Seminoles of Alachua and some settlers, and Grant was able early in 1767 to assure Lord Shelburne that no person in East Florida had settled beyond the line set by the Proclamation of 1763.[91] Grant strove more energetically than any other southern governor of his time to maintain the peace between the "crackers" and their savage neighbors.[92] He was extremely anxious to avert an Indian war because of the effect one would have on his infant colony, and was willing, nay, eager,

[87] Proceedings of the Congress of Picolata, Nov. 12–18, 1765, Gage MSS.

[88] Treaty of Picolata, Nov. 18, 1765, Gage MSS.

[89] Treaty entered into by Captain Aleck and Governor Wright, Jan. 10, 1766, *GCR,* XXXVII, 343–46. Wright gave the Creek chief a Negro slave as a token payment. It seems very likely that this is the only case where land was obtained from Indians in exchange for a slave.

[90] Stuart to Gage, Jan. 11, 1766, Gage MSS, chronicles Stuart's journey to East Florida. Grant paid for most of the expense of the congress. It cost East Florida only £500. Grant to Board of Trade, Dec. 9, 1765, CO, 5/540. No doubt some Seminoles attended the congress, although they are not specifically mentioned. Cowkeeper, their head chief, was absent, but he concurred in the agreements that had been reached and received presents and a great medal shortly afterward. Grant to Gage, Jan. 13, 1766, Gage MSS.

[91] Grant to Shelburne, Feb. 22, 1767 (Abstract), Shelburne MSS, lii.

[92] Grant's attitude toward this problem is well shown in Grant to Gage, Aug. 27, 1767, Gage MSS.

to pay for peace with gifts. Since he had an annual grant of £1,000 for Indian expenses and other contingencies, he could well carry out this policy. Before the close of 1766 Grant was laying plans for a second congress, merely because he had received from the Board of Trade a large shipment of presents that seemed to require distribution. He appointed the spring of 1767 for this meeting, and asked Stuart to join him in holding it.[93] As Frederick Haldimand once put it, one could have a good time at Indian conferences, especially when the fishing was good, but Stuart was very busy and refused. Grant then decided to postpone the gathering until autumn and to proceed with his plans, whether Stuart attended or not.[94] Stuart again declined because of the pressure of business,[95] but he commissioned George Roupell [96] to act for him in the capacity of temporary deputy.[97] Ignoring Stuart's officers among the Creeks, Grant used traders to invite the Lower Creeks and Seminoles; [98] and a considerable number of Indians of no particular standing, except for Escotchabie, attended this second congress, held at Picolata from November 21 to 23. No business of importance was transacted, although the Indians promised satisfaction for two murders committed by the Seminoles on St. Mary's River a short time before. The Indians attending did not have enough influence, however, to make good this promise. Stuart was disgusted when Grant immediately began laying plans for still a third gathering.[99]

While Grant was throwing away money and disrupting the machinery of the southern Indian department, Stuart was making earnest efforts to bring the Creeks, especially those of the Lower towns, to realize the necessity of proper conduct on the Georgia frontier and to arrange for the surveying of the boundary between them and

[93] Grant to Gage, Nov. 15, 1766, Gage MSS; Stuart to Board of Trade, Dec. 2, 1766, CO, 5/67.

[94] Grant to Shelburne, April 19, 1767 (Abstract), Shelburne MSS, lii.

[95] Stuart to Gage, Sept. 26, 1767, Gage MSS.

[96] George Roupell had an office in the customs at Charleston in 1766, when he was invited by Grant to assume the duties of secretary of East Florida until the home government could fill the position, then vacant. Grant to Board of Trade, June 25, 1766, CO, 5/541. No doubt Roupell was in East Florida at the time Stuart appointed him. He later became deputy postmaster general for the southern district, and was Stuart's neighbor at Charleston after 1772.

[97] Stuart to Gage, Nov. 27, 1767, Gage MSS.

[98] Grant to Shelburne, Aug. 5, 1767, CO, 5/548.

[99] There is a journal of the congress in CO, 5/549, and another in B. M. Add. MSS, 14,034. See also George Roupell to Stuart, Dec. 10, 1767, Stuart to Gage, Dec. 26, 1767, Gage MSS. Wright's attitude toward this congress was the same as Stuart's. Wright to Stuart, Dec. 10, 1767 (Abstract), *ibid.*

that colony. Governor Wright reported early in 1767 that no person had established himself beyond the boundary with the Creeks; that not a single Indian had been slain by the whites on the frontiers of Georgia since 1765; and that three runaway Negroes who had killed a Creek had been convicted and executed. On the other hand, Georgia had grievances against the Indians. Three white vagrants hunting on Creek preserves beyond Augusta had been slain by a party of Creeks in September, 1765, and satisfaction had not been offered.[100] Moreover, the Creeks harbored fugitive slaves, a sore spot with all planters.

Stuart held a conference with the Creeks at Augusta late in the spring of 1767 in order to secure the establishment of a new set of trade regulations. At that time he brought up these other matters, and also the question of retribution for two homicides committed by the Creeks just before the conference opened. Stuart did not press the Creeks very energetically for fear of damaging his trade program.[101] The Creeks promised, however, to return the slaves. The Lower townsmen, refusing to recognize that their kinsmen had any interest in the Georgia boundary, also pledged themselves to send representatives to Augusta in the following September to assist in surveying that boundary.[102] Nevertheless, the Creeks made no effort during the summer of 1767 to redress grievances, and the Lower townsmen indulged in a cattle-stealing raid on the Georgia frontier. The Georgia backsettlers promptly took revenge by burning an outlying Creek village on the Oconee River. Although Wright and Roderick McIntosh were able to soothe the injured feelings of the Indians,[103] Stuart's patience was then almost at an end. He asked Gage whether he should recommend that the governors cut off the Creek trade,[104] but the general left the matter to Stuart's judgment.[105] Stuart's habitual caution soon regained its ascendancy.

[100] Wright to Shelburne, Jan. 5, 1767, *GCR,* XXXVII, 154.

[101] Activities at this conference in regard to trade are discussed in Chapter XIV.

[102] "Journal of the Superintendant's proceedings," April 21—June 6, 1767, Gage MSS; Stuart to Shelburne, July 28, 1767, CO, 5/68; *Georgia Gazette,* June 3, 1767.

[103] *GCR,* X, 246–48, 272–78, 302–3; Wright to Gage, Dec. 1, 1767, Gage MSS. Wright helped to assuage the hurts of the Creeks by giving them one keg of rum for each hut burnt.

[104] For Stuart's attitude see Stuart to Gage, Sept. 26, Oct. 2, Dec. 26, 1767, Gage MSS.

[105] Gage to Stuart, Nov. 14, 1767, Gage MSS.

The Lower Creeks failed to appear at Augusta in September to draw the Georgia boundary. After Stuart hurried from Charleston to Georgia to consult them in person, they would promise only to send deputies to Augusta in the following spring.[106] Again the Lower Creeks failed to keep their appointment.

One unfamiliar with Indian politics would have reason to infer from the fact that the English supported the Choctaws against the Upper Creeks that the English and the Choctaws were on very friendly terms from 1765 to 1768. Such an inference, however, would not be wholly consistent with fact. At least one Choctaw chief discarded his great medal within a few weeks after the Congress of Mobile,[107] and the tribe generally was disappointed when the annual congress promised by Farmar and Robertson failed to materialize.[108] The Choctaws accused English traders of causing the defeat and death of Red Captain by giving advance information of his motions to the Creeks,[109] and they charged that the English gave ammunition to the Upper Creeks as well as to themselves at Fort Tombigbee.[110] They committed depredations near that fort, and one party raided and sacked a plantation near Mobile itself.[111] Even in 1766 Tayler thought that a union of the Choctaws and the Upper Creeks against the English was not improbable.[112]

No doubt very friendly connections between the Choctaws and the English might have been established and maintained had it not been for the activities of the French and Spanish governments at New Orleans, and especially of French traders from Louisiana. The Peace of Paris by no means ended the interest of officials at New Orleans in the affairs of the southern Indians; and for some years that treaty had but little effect upon the profitable commerce carried on by the French merchants with those tribes. The French governors at New Orleans and the French commandant at the Illinois before 1765 were often accused of inciting Indians to attack the English, although the truth of these accusations has not been estab-

[106] Stuart to Shelburne, Oct. 3, 1767, CO, 5/68; Stuart to Shelburne, Feb. 10, 1768, CO, 5/69.

[107] Lieutenant Thomas Ford to Stuart, June 21, 1765, Gage MSS.

[108] Charles Stuart to Stuart, June 6, 1767 (Extract), Gage MSS.

[109] James Hewitt to Messrs. McGillivray and Struthers, Oct. 16, 1767, Gage MSS.

[110] Gage to Stuart, Jan. 26, 1768, Gage MSS.

[111] Tayler to Gage, Oct. 23, 1766, Lieutenant John Ritchy to Haldimand, Oct. 6, 1767, Gage MSS.

[112] Tayler to Gage, Sept. 25, Oct. 23, 1766, Gage MSS.

lished.[113] The French were also charged by Stuart with persuading Francophile Choctaws to murder chiefs of their own tribe who had English sympathies. It may be doubted that D'Abbadie and Aubry, and Don Antonio de Ulloa, the first Spanish governor, intrigued extensively among the southern tribes, but Stuart was sufficiently moved by reports of their activities to propose at the close of 1766 a congress with the Choctaws and the Small Tribes in order to confirm their loyalty to the English.[114]

There can be no question that French traders were very active commercially and politically on English soil after 1763. There was, to be sure, an ordinance in Louisiana forbidding inhabitants of the colony to trade on English territory, but it was ignored.[115] Prices for furs and deerskins at New Orleans were estimated to be as much as 10 to 25 per cent above those paid by English merchants at Mobile and Pensacola,[116] and even greater than those offered at London.[117] French traders inevitably sought to profit from this favorable circumstance and from their ancient friendship with the tribes east of the Mississippi. Captain Harry Gordon was told at Mobile in 1766 that the French enjoyed the greater part of the Choctaw trade.[118] In the Illinois country George Morgan keenly felt the competition of the French as late as 1768. At that time he contemplated recommending to his employers, Baynton and Wharton, the great fur-trading company of Philadelphia, that they make a present of £1,000 to Stuart or Sinnott to put a stop to it.[119]

English traders in the Illinois area and among the Choctaws, ignoring *patria* for profit, also sold their garnerings at New Orleans. Johnstone was quite unable to restrain the Choctaw traders from carrying their skins to Tangipahou on Lake Ponchartrain and

[113] Gage exonerated Aubry of the charge. Gage to Shelburne, Jan. 23, 1768, *Gage Corr.*, I, 160. The best authorities on the early history of Illinois believe that the French officials were not guilty of such subversive activities in that area. Clarence W. Alvord and Clarence E. Carter, eds., *Ill. Hist. Colls.*, X (1915), Introduction, xliii, xlix.

[114] Stuart to Gage, Dec. 19, 1766, Gage MSS. Ulloa appeared in the colony in 1766, but failed to assume complete control because of the opposition of the French inhabitants. In part he governed through Aubry.

[115] Haldimand to Gage, June 4, 1768, Gage MSS.

[116] Gage to Shelburne, Feb. 22, 1767, *Gage Corr.*, I, 121-25; Captain Forbes, "State of the Commerce and Country of the Illinois &ca," Jan. 6, 1769, Gage MSS.

[117] Johnstone to John Pownall, Dec. 29, 1765, CO, 5/574.

[118] "Journal of Capt. Harry Gordon," N. D. Mereness, ed., *Travels in the American Colonies* (New York, 1916), 485.

[119] *Ill. Hist. Colls.*, XVI (1921), 361-62.

thence to the old French capital.[120] English officials were eager to prevent French traders from operating on English territory, and also to stop English merchants from selling skins and furs at New Orleans. They were especially anxious to bar the French merchants because they displayed their national sympathies among the savages. The desire to save the trade of the Choctaws and the Small Tribes for West Florida, to cut off French influence at its source, and to force English merchants coming down the Mississippi to carry their goods to West Florida was a major cause for the erection of Fort Bute in 1765, at the junction of the Iberville and Mississippi rivers.[121] At that time a garrison was not stationed at the fort, but Lieutenant John Thomas was left at the post by Farmar to guard Indian presents that he lodged there as he progressed up the Mississippi. A motley band of Indians, largely Alabamas and Small Tribesmen, plundered and wrecked Fort Bute. Late in 1765, however, Captain James Chisholm was ordered by Johnstone to the Iberville to repair it or, if necessary, to build a new post,[122] and from January, 1766, to 1768 a garrison was maintained there. Considerations of Indian policy similar to those which, in part, motivated the erection of Fort Bute were important factors in the establishment of a garrison at the Natchez. Fort Panmure, as this post was known to the English, was occupied by a force commissioned for the purpose by Tayler in 1766, and a garrison was also maintained there until 1768. Stuart heartily approved of the establishment of these outworks on the Mississippi. His recommendation was in part responsible for the sending of a garrison to the Natchez.[123]

But the two forts on the lower Mississippi failed to accomplish the purposes of their sponsors, so far as Indian affairs were concerned. The garrisons could not prevent Indians from going to

[120] Johnstone to John Pownall, Dec. 29, 1765, April 2, 1766, CO, 5/574. The English traders claimed they could not sell their skins at Mobile because of lack of shipping facilities and excused themselves from disposing of them at Charleston or Savannah on the ground that the skins would become wormy during the long journey.

[121] Johnstone to John Pownall, May 4, 1765 (Extract), *MPAED,* I, 478–80. Johnstone also claimed that the post would serve as a military outwork against the Spanish, and as a center of English influence among the Indians.

[122] Archibald Robertson to Stuart, Sept. 14, 1765, Gage to Stuart, Jan. 21, 1766, Captain James Chisholm to Gage, March 13, 1766, Gage MSS. Johnstone assumed command of the troops in West Florida in the interim between Bouquet's death in 1765 and Lieutenant Colonel William Tayler's arrival in 1766.

[123] Stuart had also recommended the reoccupation of Fort Tombigbee in 1766. See Tayler to Gage, Sept. 18, 1766, Gage MSS.

New Orleans, and traders passing up and down the Mississippi apparently went by the posts without difficulty. Moreover, the forts proved to be useless for the purpose of keeping French traders out of West Florida. These gentry continued to reach the Choctaws, notably the Six Villages, by means of the Pascagoula and Pearl rivers. English merchants used the same routes to travel between West Florida and New Orleans. Charles Stuart and the superintendent were convinced that the French traders incited the Choctaws to commit depredations upon the English; and Stuart recommended to Gage that a small post be erected on the Pascagoula River to cut off commercial intercourse between West Florida and New Orleans.[124] Montfort Browne urged Tayler and, later, Frederick Haldimand, who replaced Tayler early in 1767, to set up a post at Tangipahou for the same purpose.[125] Gage, dubious about the wisdom of building such a post, referred the matter to Tayler and afterward to Haldimand. Although both officers approved of the idea,[126] the post was never built.

From the time he had assumed the supreme command in America Gage had frowned upon the maintenance of forts in the interior or in exposed places where they could not be supported. He had not liked the occupation of Natchez; he had approved of the erection of Fort Bute only on the condition that the Iberville River should prove to be satisfactory for passage from the Mississippi to the Gulf of Mexico;[127] and he had approved of the reoccupation of Fort Tombigbee in 1766 only as a temporary measure to inspirit the Choctaws against the Upper Creeks.[128] Farmar and Tayler had not paid much heed to Gage's opinions on these matters, but Haldimand did. In the summer of 1767 he decided to withdraw the garrison from Fort Tombigbee, and by the close of the year the task was completed. The Choctaws and Creeks were separately and diplomatically assured that it was dismantled to please them, since each of these tribes had complained that the fort had been em-

[124] Stuart to Gage, Aug. 2, 8, 1766, Patrick Strachan to Tayler, Jan. 28, 1767, Charles Stuart to Stuart, June 6, 1767 (Extract), Gage MSS; Stuart to Board of Trade, Dec. 2, 1766, CO, 5/67.

[125] Haldimand to Gage, Aug. 5, 1767, Gage MSS.

[126] Gage to Stuart, Aug. 30, 1766, Gage to Haldimand, April 26, 1767, Haldimand to Gage, Sept. 1, 1767, Gage MSS.

[127] For many years various English officials entertained a hope that the Iberville could be so used, and thus make it unnecessary for English shipping to pass through French (Spanish) territory.

[128] Gage to Tayler, June 26, Aug. 11, 1766, Gage MSS.

ployed to aid the other.[129] In September, Haldimand still believed that the rest of the garrisons should be continued.[130] By November 30 Haldimand had become convinced that Forts Panmure and Bute should be abandoned, and by December that Appalachie deserved the same fate; he thought at that time that Tangipahou might have a small patrol to replace the forts at the Iberville and on the Natchez.[131] A letter from Gage of November 15, 1767, indicating that he was reluctant to erect a post at Tangipahou or any other place on the route used between the Choctaw country and New Orleans, and expressing a hope that West Florida would do the job, gave Haldimand his cue in that matter also. He ordered an engineer to choose the best site on the route for a post, but planned to delay action as long as possible, in the hope that West Florida would solve the problem for him.[132] Finally, Gage referred the question to the home government for decision.[133] The project was not approved at home, and no action was taken.

Whether or not such a post or patrol would have stopped commercial and political intercourse between New Orleans and the Choctaws and Small Tribes is doubtful. In 1768 Haldimand undertook to arrest all French traders among the Choctaws, and he persuaded Aubry to issue a proclamation forbidding them to trespass on English soil under pain of severe punishment.[134] That this measure induced the French traders completely to forsake carrying on their business on the English side of the lower Mississippi is improbable. When Panmure, Bute, and Appalachie were abandoned in 1768 the defenses of the Floridas were confined to Mobile, Pensacola, and St. Augustine.

Although it was never put into effect, a curious scheme evolved by Stuart in 1766 to meet the problems of defense, trade, and Indian affairs generated by the presence of the French and later the Spanish on the western banks of the Mississippi deserves mention. This project was to build a barrier of friendly Indians on the eastern shores of the river. The Pascagoulas, numbering about 130 gun-men, had crossed the river into French jurisdiction in 1763, but were longing to return to their old homes; there were still 150

[129] Haldimand to Gage, Jan. 16, 1768, Gage to Stuart, Jan. 26, 1768, Gage MSS.

[130] Haldimand to Gage, Sept. 1, 1767, Gage MSS.

[131] Haldimand to Gage, Nov. 30, Dec. 6, 1767, Gage MSS.

[132] Gage to Haldimand, Nov. 15, 1767, Haldimand to Gage, Jan. 16, 1768, Gage MSS.

[133] Gage to Haldimand, June 27, 1768, Gage MSS.

[134] Gage to Shelburne, April 24, 1768, Gage to Hillsborough, Aug. 17, 1768, *Gage Corr.*, I, 169, 183.

or 200 Natchez, who, though scattered among the other southern tribes, retained their tribal customs and language, their inveterate hatred of the French, and a love for their former homes; the Arkansaw tribe, with over 200 warriors, was friendly to the English and might easily be persuaded to cross the Mississippi; and, furthermore, the Alabama tribe, which had been associated with the Creeks before 1763 and had then moved to the valley of the Tombigbee, was anxious to settle farther to the westward because the Creeks and Choctaws each suspected them of aiding the other. If these friendly tribes were allowed to settle on the river, they would owe the English their homes and could be expected to serve as a defense against attacks from New Orleans and as counterchecks to the Choctaws and Small Tribes, if they became hostile. With the Chickasaws they would give England a force of 1,000 Indian allies on an exposed frontier and ensure the free navigation of the Mississippi to the English. When Stuart placed this proposal before the Board of Trade,[135] it met with no response.

[135] Stuart to Board of Trade, Dec. 2, 1766, CO, 5/67.

CHAPTER XIV

IMPERIAL MANAGEMENT OF THE INDIAN TRADE IN THE SOUTH, 1767–68

ON MAY 5, 1763, the Earl of Egremont submitted to the Board of Trade some suggestions regarding the government of the territories in America acquired from France and Spain as a result of the Peace of Paris. The major part of these suggestions was embodied in a report of the Board of Trade of June 8, which became the basis for the Proclamation of October 7, 1763.[1] This celebrated document established civil governments in Quebec and the Floridas and temporarily set aside the remainder of the acquisitions as an Indian reservation, omitting provision for any sort of government there. English settlement beyond the Allegheny divide, except within the bounds of the new governments, was forbidden. An even more drastic curb on western expansion was included in clauses that denied the colonial governors the privilege of granting any land claimed by the Indians. Furthermore, purchases of lands from the Indians were declared illegal unless made by a governor at a public meeting attended by representatives of all the Indian claimants.[2] Another significant portion of the proclamation, that which

[1] Professor Verner W. Crane has demonstrated that the document "Hints relative to the Division and Government of the Conquered and Newly Acquired Countries in America" is the key document leading to the proclamation and that it was presented by Lord Egremont on the date given. He points out that the author of the paper is unknown, but that in all probability it represents Egremont's views. Professor Clarence W. Alvord has suggested that the author was Henry Ellis. See *Miss. Vall. Hist. Rev.*, VIII (1922), 367–73. R. A. Humphreys, "Lord Shelburne and the Proclamation of 1763," *Eng. Hist. Rev.*, XLIX (1934), 241–58, gives the best account of Lord Shelburne's connection with the proclamation. His article should be read as a corrective to Professor Alvord's accounts in "Genesis of the Proclamation of 1763," *Mich. Pioneer and Hist. Colls.*, XXXVI (1908), 20–52, and in *Mississippi Valley in British Politics*, (Cleveland, 1917), I, Chapters V–VII.

[2] These clauses prevented settlement in large areas east of the Allegheny divide in the Carolinas and Georgia. They were also operative in the regions west of the divide. It has often been assumed that when English politicians spoke of enforcing the proclamation they referred merely to the rough geo-

dealt with the subject of the Indian trade, has already been discussed. It undoubtedly was the work of Lord Halifax, who succeeded Egremont as secretary of state for the southern department.[3]

In considering plans for governing the new territories British officials rather carefully examined the existing arrangements for the management of Indian affairs, especially in regard to trade. As we have seen, Lord Halifax had expressed an opinion as early as April, 1754, that the trade should be placed directly under the control of royal officers, but that regulation of the trade was left to the colonial governments when the superintendents were appointed. In November, 1757, however, the Board of Trade declared:

> ...as any plan [for trade regulation] formed by any particular province however proper in itself must from the nature of it be partial and probably will be counteracted by the measures of another province.... We cannot but be of the opinion that the only effectual method of conducting Indian affairs as well with respect to this as all other transactions with them will be to establish one general system under the sole direction of the Crown and its officers. The obtaining proper materials with which to form such a plan was one of the principal objects in view in the appointment of the agents to the northern and southern districts, and we hope soon to be enabled in the lights and facts which we expect they will furnish us with, to enter upon the consideration of such a plan. But without such lights and from the very imperfect information we have at present with respect to almost every point necessary to be attended to in so important a business we cannot form a proper judgement upon it.[4]

The board failed for some years to take action, probably because of the pressure of other business, possibly also because it did not desire to offend the colonies during the war with France. In 1762, however, the board strongly commended Governor Boone's scheme of securing order in the trade by the establishment of similar public monopolies in all the southern colonies, and asserted that

> ...those mischiefs and inconveniences which have followed from different provinces, connected with the same Indians passing partial acts, for regulating

graphical limit to expansion established therein. Actually, they sometimes intended to refer to these clauses.

It is an interesting fact that a plan for establishing an Indian boundary was being considered in official circles as early as January, 1763. At that time Egremont stated that "His Maty [has] it much at heart to conciliate the affection of the Indian nations, by every act of strict justice, and by affording them his royal protection from any incroachment on the lands they have reserved to themselves, for their hunting grounds, & for their own support & habitation: and I may inform you that a plan, for this desirable end, is actually under consideration." Egremont to Amherst, Jan. 27, 1763, CO, 5/214.

[3] The ideas the proclamation expresses on trade are to be found in Halifax to Board of Trade, Sept. 19, 1763, Shortt and Doughty, eds., *Documents Relating to the Constitutional History of Canada, 1759–1791* (1918 ed.), Pt. I, 153.

[4] Board of Trade to Lyttelton, Nov. 9, 1757, CO, 5/403.

the trade, not only differing from, but frequently obstructing and counteracting each other [have] undoubtedly been one principal source of that jealousy and discontent amongst the Indians, which has of late years been attended with such terrible consequences, and we are inclined to think, that our interest with respect to the Indians never can be settled with stability, but by the interposition of the parliament of Great Britain, in making some general regulations for the management of Indian affairs, upon some general plan under the sole direction of the Crown & its officers.[5]

In August, 1763, the board began actively to seek information upon which to build that general plan. On the fifth of that month the board instructed the superintendents henceforth to report to it and requested suggestions for improving the administration of Indian affairs.[6] In October Lord Halifax roughly outlined the "Plan for the Future Management of Indian Affairs," which was completed the following year.[7] In January, 1764, Halifax expressed a belief that the Proclamation of 1763 would dispose of the Indian land problem and that this plan would solve the trade question.[8] It was first formally considered by the board on December 6, 1763, again in January, 1764, and finally in June, 1764.[9] On July 10 it was completed and sent for criticism to all those who supposedly were cognizant of Indian affairs.

The "Plan for the Future Management of Indian Affairs" or, as it is commonly designated, the "Plan of 1764," contained an elaborate set of provisions.[10] Political relations with the Indians were to be controlled by the superintendents; all colonial laws dealing with Indian matters were to be repealed; and the power to regulate the Indian trade was to be placed exclusively in the Indian departments. The superintendents were to be empowered to appoint deputies, commissaries to serve as inspectors of trade, interpreters, and blacksmiths, all of whom were to be subject to the orders of the agents. To insure adequate supervision, trade was to be confined to the Indian towns in the South and to the military posts in the North. In the South the savages from each town were to elect a "beloved man" to protect English interests; and an assembly of the "beloved men" was to choose a chief from the tribe to reside near and to work with the commissary of the district. All In-

[5] Board of Trade to Boone, June 3, 1762, CO, 5/404.

[6] Board of Trade to Stuart, Aug. 5, 1763, Gage MSS.

[7] Halifax to Amherst, Oct. 19, 1763, *Gage Corr.*, II, 5.

[8] Halifax to Gage, Jan. 14, 1764, *Gage Corr.*, II, 10.

[9] *Journal of the Commissioners for Trade and Plantations from January 1764 to December 1767* (London, 1936), 70–71.

[10] The document has been printed in *NYCD,* VII, 637–41, and in various other places.

dian officials were to be required to take an oath of office before a governor or chief magistrate, and were not to carry on trade for themselves or others or to purchase Indian lands. Military officers were to be forbidden to engage in trade or to interfere with the Indian officials, but were to be instructed to render to the latter all possible assistance. Merchants were to secure licenses from the colonial governors; licenses were to be annual, to name the purchasers and their employees, and to bear the names of the places where trade was to be carried on. Permits were to be entered in the offices of the secretaries of the colonies, and each trader was to show his permit immediately upon arrival at a trading station. Bond was to be required for observance of all regulations, and also a surety possessing property equal to twice the amount of the bond. Failure to secure a license in proper fashion or to obey regulations could be punished by forfeiture of license, seizure of trading goods, fines, and imprisonment. Merchants were forbidden to sell rum or rifle-barreled guns to the Indians, and were to give no credit beyond fifty shillings, all debts above that amount to be uncollectible. Trade rules and fixed prices were to be established by the commissaries. All disputes between merchants and Indians concerning weights and measures were to be settled by the commissaries.

The plan also provided for the establishment of a judiciary system; the agents, their deputies, and the commissaries were to be empowered to act as justices of the peace with all the powers of those officials.[11] The commissaries should try all civil cases arising in the Indian country involving not more than £10, appeal to be had to the superintendent, whose judgment was to be final. Testimony of Indians was to be admitted under proper regulations. The provisions of the Proclamation of 1763 regarding lands reserved to themselves by the Indians were repeated. Moreover, it was set forth "That proper measures be taken with the consent and concurrence of the Indians to ascertain and define the precise and exact boundary and limits of the lands which it may be proper to reserve to them and where no settlement whatever shall be allowed." For the purposes of administration the Indians were placed under the jurisdiction of the superintendents according to tribes. Stuart was given control of those residing southward from the Blue Grass region of Kentucky, and Johnson of the remainder. Expenses for the Indian departments operating under the plan were estimated at £20,000, and it was suggested that they be defrayed by an export

[11] After 1707 Indian agents in the South were usually made justices of the peace. Atkin, Stuart, and many of the latter's aides held such commissions.

tax on furs and deerskins—beaver excepted—sent from America, or by levies on furs and deerskins collected at the posts. Finally, it was proposed that the superintendents have the privilege of sitting as special members of the colonial councils within their districts in order to secure coöperation from the colonies.

It is difficult to give credit or blame to any one individual for the authorship of the "Plan of 1764," because various officials had a share in shaping it. In its general structure and in certain specific details it represents views on Indian affairs that Lord Halifax had expressed in April, 1754; [12] and there can be no question that Halifax and Lord Hillsborough, who was at that time Halifax's man and president of the Board of Trade, were its chief sponsors. Many of the details came from Johnson and Stuart. The more significant recommendations made by the former were conveyed orally to the board by George Croghan, who appeared before that body in person as Johnson's representative. Not all the suggestions made by Croghan were reduced to writing, but it is clear that they called for the establishment of more powerful and more independent Indian departments.[13] Stuart's recommendations undoubtedly exercised considerable influence, as the inclusion in the plan of provisions to meet problems peculiar to southern Indian affairs clearly shows. It is odd that the most vital proposal made by Stuart was ignored. It was obvious to him that any system of trade regulation enforced by the superintendent was likely to encounter great difficulties unless the superintendents exercised authority in licensing, for the licensing power was the very basis of regulation. While Stuart did not ask that that power be given to him, he did urge that the governors be required to seek his advice or that of his aides in regard to issuing trade permits.[14]

In answer to the board's request for criticism of the plan Johnson forwarded a careful point-by-point analysis with a scheme for raising the necessary funds. On the whole, he was very enthusiastic, commending vigorously the clauses restricting the trade in the northern district to the posts and giving the commissaries the power to set prices. In his opinion, rum was an indispensable article of

[12] For a summary of Halifax's ideas on Indian policy in April, 1754, see John R. Alden, "The Albany Congress and the Creation of the Indian Superintendencies," *Miss. Vall. Hist. Rev.*, XXVII (1940), 200.

[13] Croghan to Johnson, July 12, 1764, *Johnson Papers*, IV, 462–63.

[14] Stuart's proposals are largely contained in Stuart to Board of Trade, March 9, 1764, CO, 323/17. As Professor Verner W. Crane has pointed out in *The Southern Frontier, 1670–1732* (Durham, N. C., 1929), 137, the influence of Johnson and Croghan has been overestimated by earlier writers.

trade. He felt that the sale of liquor at a few large posts would not produce untoward results. Johnson also suggested exact penalties to be levied upon violators of the regulations. His scheme to finance operations under the plan was a tax to be levied upon the goods sold by the traders. He estimated that £10,850 would be necessary for the expenses of his department. He calculated that the value of the goods sold to the Indians in his department could be set at approximately £200,000, a figure based on the cost of the goods on reaching America, and that profits of the merchants would average 100 per cent, the export value of the furs being therefore at least £400,000. On a basis of £200,000 worth of imported goods, a levy of five per cent on all goods sold to the Indians would bring in about £10,000. He further suggested an additional levy of five per cent on liquor, firearms, and ammunition to collect some £800, so that the total revenue would be raised to approximately the sum judged sufficient for the northern department under the plan.[15]

Stuart, of course, also strongly favored the plan. But again he laid stress upon the importance of the licensing power; and he urged that licenses be issued by the superintendents or by the superintendents in coöperation with disinterested colonial officials. Estimating the expenditures of his department at £15,000 under the plan, of which £3,000 was to be used for salaries, Stuart proposed that an export tax of ten per cent on deerskins and furs sent from his district be levied, calculating that it would bring in £8,000. Evidently he expected the imperial government to furnish the additional £7,000 needed to cover his estimated expenses.[16]

The comments of other colonial officials were generally favorable, although some of them offered minor criticisms and a few displayed hostility on major grounds. Cadwallader Colden, who was considered an expert on Indian affairs, voiced hearty approval, although he insisted that the prohibition of the sale of rum would be very unwise, and even impossible of execution.[17] Governor Grant could find no fault with the proposed plan.[18] Benjamin Franklin, however, was skeptical, if not definitely opposed. He claimed that colonial regulation ought to be fairly satisfactory, since the colonies had had long experience. He contended that it would be difficult to set prices in the trade and that liquor could not be kept from the

[15] Johnson to Board of Trade, Oct. 8, 1764, *Ill. Hist. Colls.*, X (1915), 321–42.

[16] Stuart's observations have been presented by Clarence E. Carter in *Am. Hist. Rev.*, XX (1915), 817–27.

[17] Colden to Board of Trade, Oct. 12, 1764, *NYCD*, VII, 667–70.

[18] Grant's opinion has been presented by Carter, *op. cit.*, 827–31.

Indians. Suggesting that the plan be tried out in a few places to observe its effect in practice, he declared that export taxes on trade goods leaving England and import taxes on furs brought to England would be the best means of obtaining the necessary revenue.[19] Richard Jackson, colonial agent for Pennsylvania and Connecticut, was much more forthright in his criticism. He found fault with many details, and argued that minute regulation of trade was impossible in the wilderness. He believed that the only means of ending the Indian problem was to form settlements in the West to bring the "infirmities" of civil life to the Indians and to lead them into the paths followed by the white man. Fully aware of the hardships that such a policy would bring upon the Indians, he could see no way to avoid them.[20]

The plan certainly had weaknesses. Jackson's contention that the very nature of the people and the territory involved would operate against its success was well founded. The support of the colonies was also vital, and it was to be doubted whether that support would be obtained. But perhaps the most serious difficulty in the eyes of those concerned with the problem was the matter of finance. As a result of the Seven Years' War Great Britain was deeply in debt, and there was little likelihood that Parliament would add to the already heavy burden of taxation by increasing the costs of colonial administration. It was necessary, therefore, that the colonists assume the responsibility; and, as Franklin had intimated by suggesting that revenue should be raised by taxes collected in Great Britain, a direct levy would not be popular in America. The sponsors of the plan, foreseeing these difficulties, therefore moved slowly. During February and March, 1765, when the Board of Trade discussed the plan in the light of criticisms that had been received, no action was taken.[21] In January, 1766, with the Earl of Dartmouth sitting as president of the board, consideration of the problem was

[19] Albert H. Smyth, ed., *The Writings of Benjamin Franklin* (New York and London, 1905–7), IV, 467–71.

[20] Richard Jackson, "Remarks on the Plan for the Future Management of Indian Affairs," Nov. —, 1766, *Ill. Hist. Colls.,* XI (1916), 422–30. For the observations of Governor James Murray of Canada and a list of other papers containing comments regarding the plan see R. A. Humphreys, ed., "Governor Murray's Views on the Plan of 1764 for the Management of Indian Affairs," *Can. Hist. Rev.,* XVI (1935), 162–69. The observations of Governor Horatio Sharpe of Maryland are not listed in this article. They are to be found in W. W. Browne, C. C. Hall, B. C. Steiner, J. H. Pleasants, eds., *Archives of Maryland* (Baltimore, 1883—), IX, 179–80.

[21] *Journal of the Commissioners for Trade and Plantations from January 1764 to December 1767,* 149–62.

resumed. In view of the Stamp Act controversy the members of the board agreed that "it would be advisable in the present state and situation of American affairs to postpone any representation thereupon.[22] Two months later Sir Henry Conway, then secretary of state for the southern department, declared that responsible officials would come to a decision on policy regarding the Indian trade.[23] However, nothing was done until the Rockingham ministry fell and Shelburne succeeded Conway.

In 1768 Stuart declared that the "Plan of 1764" was the light "by which I have steered my course," [24] in which statement there was perfect justice. But it should be emphasized that the plan was never more than a convenient arsenal of weapons that might be employed only when authority from some other source was procured. In July, 1766, Stuart earnestly urged the Board of Trade that he should be empowered to exercise a measure of control over the trade through his commissaries; and in the following month he made the same request to Sir Henry Conway.[25] Stuart pointed out in his letter to Conway that Johnson had already undertaken to lay restraints upon the traders with the help of the northern governors, but that only Johnstone, among all the southern governors, had actually coöperated with him. Stuart therefore requested that the home government either give him the power of licensing or divide the southern Indian country into several districts, in each of which one colony and only one colony should have the power of licensing, enforcement of whatever regulations were established to be in Stuart's hands.

Before this letter reached London, however, Shelburne had succeeded Conway. On September 13 he wrote a significant letter to Stuart. Inspired by numerous reports from Johnson, Stuart, and other officials of fraud and irregularities in the trade and of illegal settlements on Indian lands, Shelburne instructed Stuart to

> . . . take every measure that prudence can suggest to appease for the present, the too just resentment of the Indian tribes . . . till more regulated measures can be taken, it is hoped that your prudence in the department entrusted to you, facilitated by the commander in chief, & the civil governments in the provinces will be able to suspend the ill-consequences of those irregularities which must very speedily be finally prevented.[26]

---

[22] *Ibid.*, 244.

[23] Conway to Johnstone, March 13, 1766, *MPAED,* I, 296.

[24] Stuart to Hillsborough, July 14, 1768, CO, 5/69.

[25] Stuart to Board of Trade, July 10, 1766, Stuart to Conway, Aug. 8, 1766, CO, 5/67.

[26] Shelburne to Stuart, Sept. 13, 1766, CO, 5/225.

Orders to enforce the Indian boundary lines and to rectify the wrongs of the Indians were also sent to the governors in America on the same day.[27] On December 11, after receiving Stuart's letter of the preceding August to Conway, Shelburne sent further instructions:

> I cannot therefore recommend it too strongly to you to take every measure possible to conciliate the affections of the Indians in general, to restrain the traders as much as possible from going among them until the proper regulations shall take place, to find out who the delinquents are who fill the minds of the savages with prejudices and lyes to our disadvantage, and to take care if they cannot be severely punished, that they shall be excluded from license, and all privileges of trade for the future.

After doling out some severe criticism of the "Plan of 1764" and of Stuart for attempting to enforce parts of that document in 1765, Shelburne informed Stuart that he expected the superintendents, Gage, and the governors to "supply the want of fixed regulations, and obviate all temporary inconveniences" until a new plan could be formed.[28]

In view of Shelburne's strictures on Stuart's plan of 1765 for trade regulation it is not at all certain that Shelburne intended these instructions as a basis for another formal plan of regulation. Nevertheless, Shelburne certainly did not believe that the Proclamation of 1763 gave the traders absolute freedom of trade.[29] In any case Stuart, Johnson, and Gage[30] construed the instructions to mean that the minister actually did desire a general regulatory scheme, with the superintendents taking the lead. Stuart used Shelburne's orders for that purpose, explicitly informed the minister that he was doing so,[31] and was permitted to continue until 1768.

Peculiarly enough, the trade plan which Stuart formed in 1766–67 was virtually identical with that which he had evolved in 1765 and which had met the censure of Shelburne. It is true that one of the chief criticisms of Stuart's plan of 1765 made by Shelburne was the expense supposedly involved, an objection that might be

[27] Shelburne to governors in America, Sept. 13, 1766, CO, 5/67.

[28] Shelburne to Stuart, Dec. 11, 1766, Gage MSS.

[29] Shelburne believed activities of the traders were the chief cause of the Creek crisis of 1766 and that precautions in licensing would help to remove the difficulty. He instructed Lord Charles Montagu, governor of South Carolina, to use extreme caution in granting licenses. Shelburne to Montagu, Oct. 25, 1766, CO, 5/390.

[30] See Gage to Stuart, Aug. 13, 1767, Gage MSS.

[31] Stuart to Shelburne, April 1, 11, July 28, 1767, CO, 5/68.

removed, since it was based on a misconception.[32] The governors were to give licenses only on the conditions that each trader furnish a bond and responsible surety to the amount of £300 and that he promise obedience to trading rules laid down by Stuart, his commissaries, or the governors, on pain of forfeiting his license. Again the consent of the traders was to be gained at public meetings, and the various tribes were to be solemnly informed of the new rules promulgated by Stuart. These "Regulations for the better carrying on the Trade With the Indian Tribes in the Southern District" were similar to those that Stuart had attempted to establish in 1765, the only change of any importance lying in the fact that the sale or gift of rum to the Indians had been absolutely forbidden in 1765, while the new rules forbade only the exchange of rum for skins or furs.[33]

The possibilities of success in 1767 were greater than they had been two years previously. The new plan had a legal basis, for in his letters cited above Shelburne had given tacit approval to Stuart's employment of commissaries. Stuart was therefore able to quote to all and sundry the Proclamation of 1763 as legal sanction for his assumption of control over trade in 1767. This argument, coupled with Shelburne's letter to the governors of September 13, 1766, could serve to bludgeon indolent or recalcitrant governors into participation in Stuart's scheme. Another factor in favor of Stuart's new plan was the added evidence of the need for centralized management of the trade accumulated since 1765. Not only the governors but also the wealthier and more responsible traders, especially those who had been in business before 1763, were convinced that something had to be done to remove anarchic conditions existing in the trade. Thus sixteen of the principal traders to the Creeks

[32] Shelburne informed Stuart that expenses under the "Plan of 1764" as employed in West Florida were incommensurate with services performed and that some of the articles of the plan were of a very "dubious" nature. Stuart pointed out that the heavy expenses resulting from his mission to West Florida were due in large part to the necessity of rendering the English occupation pleasing to the Indians and to the efforts he made at Gage's behest to aid Farmar's expedition. Stuart to Shelburne, April 11, 1767, CO, 5/68. No doubt Stuart hoped that this argument would remove the financial objections advanced by Shelburne. Stuart's expenses for 1765, exclusive of his salary, seem to have been in the neighborhood of £10,000. Bills which he drew upon Gage during that year and which were presented for payment before Feb. 24, 1766, totaled a little over £16,400 (New York currency). Gage to Stuart, March 15, 1766, Gage MSS. Stuart probably spent more money during 1765 than in any other year before the Revolution.

[33] Printed copy in Gage MSS. Other copies were sent to Shelburne, the southern governors, and the officers of Stuart's department.

urged Stuart to restrict the number of participants in the commerce and to set up a fair price schedule that would prevent excessive undercutting.[34]

In November and December, 1766, Stuart began to communicate his plan to the southern governors, asking for suggestions and amendments, and for coöperation in putting it into effect.[35] Early in January Wright acceded to Stuart's request and sent out instructions to the Georgia traders to obey Stuart's new regulations.[36] By June Lord Charles Montagu, governor of South Carolina, had also agreed to coöperate; [37] Montfort Browne followed suit in July. Tryon's first response was that he could not force observance of the regulations without an act of the North Carolina assembly, and that he knew of no trader operating from his colony. In July, however, he issued a proclamation ordering all traders from North Carolina to secure licenses in conformity with Stuart's wishes.[38]

But the coöperation of these officials had not been obtained without "literary altrications," and Stuart met with annoying difficulties in his negotiations with Grant and Fauquier. Apparently because Stuart's first communication on the subject failed to reach Grant newspaper advertisements announcing that Stuart would not recognize as valid after October 1 any license not issued in accordance with the Proclamation of 1763 appeared before the governor was officially informed of Stuart's plan. Already jealous of the superintendent, Grant was piqued. He declared that he had great personal respect for Stuart, but he put forth a host of objections to his scheme, in spite of the fact that only two or three traders were licensed in East Florida. He reminded the superintendent that the power of licensing these men lay exclusively in his hands, and objected that Stuart was trying to cram his scheme down the throats

[34] "Memorial of the Merchants and Traders of the Province of Georgia Trading from Augusta to the Creek Nation" [early in 1767], Gage MSS. On trade conditions see also the *South-Carolina and American General Gazette,* May 22, 1767.

[35] Minor changes in Stuart's regulations were made as a result of suggestions from the governors, notably Wright. Compare two copies of the regulations submitted to Shelburne on April 1, 1767, and July 28, 1767, in CO, 5/68.

[36] Stuart to Wright, Dec. 17, 1766, Wright to Stuart, Jan. 5, 1767, *GCR,* XXXVII, 162, 162–66.

[37] Stuart to Shelburne, April 11, 1767, CO, 5/68; Montagu to Shelburne, April 14 [1767], CO, 5/390; CJSC, xxxiii, 69–72, 75–76, 168–69. Early in 1767 Montagu adopted new trading rules very similar to Stuart's. Later he adopted Stuart's rules in their entirety.

[38] Montfort Browne to Shelburne, Aug. 6, 1767, CO, 5/584, pt. 1; *NCCR,* VII, 437–38, 502–3.

of the governors. He criticized Stuart for setting up price schedules, accused some of Stuart's commissaries of engaging in the trade, and positively refused to compel the East Florida traders to obey certain of Stuart's rules without specific instructions from home. He also made it clear that he would continue to send and receive "talks" from the Indians without reference to Stuart's department.[39] Stuart responded that he had attempted to consult Grant; that price schedules were necessary to lower the Creek trading prices (as Shelburne had ordered); and that South Carolina and Georgia had long given out such price lists with licenses, a fact Grant very well knew. He denied that any of his aides were engaged in trade.[40] The superintendent indicated that he could not consider "any person as properly authorized to trade in the Indian countries, who is not licensed in the manner in which his Majesty has been pleased to point out; without disobeying his orders which have been repeatedly signified to me by the principal secretary of state." [41] Grant continued obdurate, although Stuart hoped in May, 1768, that he was about to see the light.[42]

Stuart's negotiations with Fauquier were even more awkward because of Fauquier's pretended ignorance of official business. In May, 1765, the House of Burgesses, in the belief that a prosperous trade would pacify the Cherokees, revived the act of 1757 establishing a public trading company.[43] Like Atkin, Stuart pointed out that, if goods were sold at prime cost plus expenses, the company would be able to undersell and ruin all private traders to the Cherokees; and that the company would probably operate only for a short period. Moreover, lower Cherokee trade prices would also bring demands from the other tribes for similar favor. Stuart therefore protested to the Board of Trade against the act as a potential source of serious discord among the southern tribes.[44] He urged Fauquier to support his own trade plan, in accordance with the Proclamation of 1763. Fauquier replied that he did not have any discretionary power in issuing licenses and that he had had no or-

[39] Grant to Stuart, Aug. 22, 1767, CO, 5/73. Stuart's advertisement had appeared in the *South-Carolina and American General Gazette* on July 3, 1767, and in the *Georgia Gazette* on Aug. 5, 1767. Later it appeared in other papers.

[40] Stuart asserted that he would discharge any person in his department who traded.

[41] Stuart to Grant, Oct. 3, 1767, CO, 5/73; Stuart to Gage, Dec. 26, 1767, Gage MSS.

[42] Stuart to Gage, May 17, 1768, Gage MSS.

[43] Private trading was not outlawed by the act.

[44] Stuart to Board of Trade, July 10, 1766, CO, 5/67.

ders from home upon the subject. Stuart then sent him pertinent extracts from the proclamation and a copy of Shelburne's letter of September 13, 1766.[45] On receipt of these papers Fauquier informed the superintendent that he had hitherto been completely ignorant of them, and again denied that he had power to limit the number of traders or to compel them to obey Stuart's regulations. Because of the terms of the proclamation Fauquier even thought that he lacked authority to punish a trader operating without a license.[46] Stuart was never able to secure Fauquier's help, and hope of obtaining the coöperation of John Blair, his successor, was ended by the abolition of Stuart's system in 1768. But Stuart's protest to the home government regarding the Virginia act did bear fruit. Although the statute was approved by Matthew Lamb, law officer of the crown, the Privy Council disallowed it.[47] As a matter of fact, the Virginia assembly itself made no real effort to enforce the act.[48]

Since Virginia and East Florida had actually but a trifling share in the southern Indian trade after 1763, the refusals of Grant and Fauquier to assist Stuart were not of vital consequence; and Stuart's failure to get their help was partly compensated for by hearty support from Gage and Haldimand. When the superintendent requested Gage to use his influence in Stuart's cause with the governors, Gage replied that officials who ignored a circular letter from home could hardly be expected to heed the advice of the military commander.[49] But he approved of Stuart's system and of his regulations, and he ordered the military men in the South to give all possible assistance to Stuart.[50]

In order to put his system in motion Stuart planned to secure the coöperation of the Indians and their traders in general conferences. He invited the Creeks to a meeting at Augusta at the close of April, 1767, and the Cherokees to another at Hard Labor on May 8. When the superintendent reached Augusta on April 30, he

[45] Stuart to Fauquier, Nov. 24, 1766, CO, 5/67; Stuart to Shelburne, July 28, 1767, CO, 5/68.

[46] Fauquier to Stuart, Sept. 17, 1767, CO, 5/69. Fauquier's statement that he had not received a copy of the proclamation is astonishing, for he had. It seems hardly possible that he had forgotten the proclamation, in view of the effect of it upon the interests of various Virginians and of the colony as a whole. See Chapter XV.

[47] Order in Council, June 26, 1767, CO, 5/1332.

[48] See W. Neil Franklin, "Virginia and the Cherokee Indian Trade, 1753–1775," *The East Tennessee Historical Society's Publications,* No. 5 (1933), 25–27.

[49] Gage to Stuart, Aug. 13, 1767, Gage MSS.

[50] Gage to Stuart, May 16, Aug. 12, 1767, Gage to Haldimand, April 26, 1767, Gage MSS.

found the Creek traders there, but not their clients. On May 5 Stuart held a conference with a number of the more prosperous traders to the Creeks, including George Galphin. These declared that they were gratified by Stuart's plans and agreed to substantial reductions of prices in the trade. On May 10 the Creeks were still missing; and Stuart hurried off to Hard Labor, under the escort of a number of Cherokee chiefs. There he conferred with 300 Cherokees, headed by Attakullakulla, Ouconnostotah, Usteneka, and Saluy, from May 18 to 20. The Cherokee traders also attended, and both they and their clients readily agreed to conform to the new rules. Stuart then quickly returned to Augusta. When he arrived at that place on May 24 he found 120 Lower Creeks awaiting him. They promptly acquiesced in the new arrangements, rejoicing because of the lower rates offered by the traders through Stuart. A large delegation of Upper Creeks led by Emistisiguo that appeared at Augusta on June 4 also greeted with pleasure the new plan and the reduction in prices. Charles Stuart informed the Choctaws and Chickasaws of the change. Stuart's arrangements were thus as complete as he could make them.[51]

The system of regulation established in this fashion was not without good results. Toward the close of 1767 Stuart reported that the new rules were being placed in force and that they were having a beneficial effect.[52] In May of the following year, however, Stuart was obliged to confess that the traders in the more distant parts of the Indian country were still very disorderly and that the commissaries were almost helpless, because it was impossible to bring suit successfully in South Carolina and Georgia against the bond of a trader carrying on his business hundreds of miles in the interior.[53] Emistisiguo asserted that the regulations were frequently disobeyed among the Creeks and that many traders to that nation did not even purchase a license.[54] There can be no question that the rules were often evaded,[55] but it is equally certain that something was accom-

[51] Stuart to Shelburne, April 1, July 28, 1767, CO, 5/68; Stuart to Gage, July 4, 1767, "Journal of the Superintendant's proceedings," April 21—June 6, 1767, Gage MSS; Stuart to Haldimand, June 25, 1767, B. M. Add. MSS, 21,672, pt. 5.

[52] Stuart to Gage, Dec. 26, 1767, Gage MSS.

[53] Stuart to Gage, May 17, 1768, Gage MSS.

[54] *GCR*, X, 580–82.

[55] Romans, *A Concise Natural History of East and West Florida* (New York, 1775), 69, states that the commissaries could do little to remedy abuses, that one who tried too persistently to execute his orders might have lost his life, and that the commissaries eventually came to be ridiculed by traders and Indians alike.

plished in the way of restoring order in the trade.[56] Wright and Elias Durnford expressed keen disappointment because Stuart's system was soon abandoned.[57]

Much of the burden of enforcement fell, of course, on the shoulders of the commissaries and other minor officials in Stuart's department. In the period 1766–68 Stuart therefore made several additions to his staff. As has been mentioned, Roderick McIntosh was sent to serve as commissary to the Creeks generally. Pierce Acton Sinnott was appointed at the beginning of 1767 assistant commissary with instructions to live at Fort Appalachie and to conduct departmental business with five Lower Creek towns near the junction of the Chattahoochee and Flint rivers and with the Seminoles.[58] Stuart first chose Lieutenant Charles Tayler, who had become a Cherokee trader after his service in the Independent Regulars, as commissary to the Six Villages of Choctaws and the Small Tribes. When Tayler decided that it was more profitable to continue his trading, Stuart gave the position to Harpain de la Gauterais, in March, 1768.[59] At the same time he employed Lieutenant James Henderson to replace Elias Legardere among the East and West Parties of the Choctaws.[60]

[56] In 1771 the leading Creek and Cherokee traders declared that Stuart's system had worked very satisfactorily. "The Memorial of the principal Traders to the Creek and Cherokee Nations [to Stuart]," Sept. 10, 1771, CO, 5/73.

[57] Wright to Hillsborough, Aug. 5, 1768, *GCR*, XXXVII, 334–41; Durnford to Hillsborough, Feb. 7, 1770, CO, 5/587, pt. 1. Wright had often quarreled with Stuart regarding their respective powers, but he declared that he would much prefer to place trade regulation absolutely under Stuart's control rather than go back to colonial regulation under the Proclamation of 1763. Durnford was provincial engineer of West Florida for some years, and later secured a commission as lieutenant governor of the same province. He was acting governor for a short time in 1770.

[58] A complete list of the persons Stuart expected to employ during 1767 is given in an "Estimate of Annual Expences for Officers Sallarys & other Contingencies in the Southern Department of Indian Affairs/general Meetings & Congresses Exclusive," n.d., Gage MSS.

[59] Stuart to Gage, Jan. 21, 1766, March 30, 1768, Gage MSS. La Gauterais had encountered great difficulties since 1765, chiefly because of charges of financial corruption in connection with the Illinois expedition of that year brought against him by Farmar. Haldimand had the matter investigated by a court of enquiry, and La Gauterais was exonerated. Haldimand was impressed by his conduct, and urged that he be given an appointment as commissary. Stuart entertained a hope that he could counter the influence of the French traders and more particularly of Monbéraut in the Six Villages, but la Gauterais was not in office long enough to show his mettle. After 1768 he settled down on a plantation in West Florida.

[60] Stuart to Haldimand, March 24, 1768, B. M. Add. MSS, 21,671, pt. 7. Henderson was probably a friend of Charles Stuart, since he had served in the 78th Regiment. Perhaps he was a relative of the Stuarts.

However, Henderson died not long afterward.[61] Several interpreters and blacksmiths were also added to the staff during this period.

Much depended upon the caliber of the commissaries, for a man possessing firmness of character and genuine influence among his charges could overcome to some extent the legal weaknesses of Stuart's system. That all of Stuart's commissaries had these qualities may well be doubted. John McIntosh was capable and had had experience in Indian affairs, but he was bitterly opposed by a clique of traders among the Chickasaws and was unable to accomplish much. He did not, in fact, set a splendid example as a law-abiding servant of the crown, for he had a plantation well stocked with Negroes and cattle twelve miles from the council place of the Chickasaws, in violation of the spirit, if not the letter, of the Proclamation of 1763.[62] Legardere seems to have been made of inferior stuff. He was haughty and insolent to the Choctaws; and he was accused of carrying on trade with them. His continual quarreling with Lieutenant John Ritchy created for the military and Indian officials an annoying problem that was solved only by recalling Ritchy. In the later months of 1767 or early in 1768 Legardere either resigned or was discharged.[63]

At least one commissary, Roderick McIntosh, made an honest effort to enforce the regulations. He succeeded in cutting down the traffic in green skins; and he drove from the Creek nation one trader operating without a license. But McIntosh was plunged into difficulties when a party of Upper Creeks burst into a traders' hangout called Buzzard's Roost on Flint River and destroyed skins acquired both legitimately and illegitimately. The traders charged that McIntosh urged the Indians to despoil them. McIntosh claimed that he had given them permission to destroy green skins, and that he had given that permission only because he was certain he could

[61] Montfort Browne to Stuart, Sept. 30, 1768, CO, 5/71. When Charles Stuart went on leave of absence in 1768 Henderson undertook to act as temporary deputy, but he died some time later, before the letter cited was written. Browne then appointed one Lionel B. Westropp to serve as temporary deputy. Stuart neither recognized nor paid Westropp.

[62] On McIntosh see Romans, *op. cit.,* 68–69, 313–14; Lieutenant Alexander Fraser to Haldimand, May 4, 1766, *Ill. Hist. Colls.,* XI (1916), 231; James Adair, "A Memorandum of some material Heads of what was lately transacted in the Chickasaw Nation," Feb. 26, 1766, Gage MSS.

[63] Many references to Legardere's conduct at Fort Tombigbee are to be found in the Gage MSS and the Haldimand MSS. The most pertinent are: Ritchy to Tayler, Sept. 10, 1766, B. M. Add. MSS, 21,671, pt. 2; Ritchy to Haldimand, June 10, 1767, B. M. Add. MSS, 21,672, pt. 5; Tayler to Gage, Jan. 25, 1767, Gage to Haldimand, March 20, 1767, Haldimand to Gage, June 17, 1767, Gage MSS.

not stop the Indians. The traders claimed £1,500 to £2,000 damages. Emistisiguo defended his brethren on the ground that Stuart had authorized the Creeks to plunder illicit traders. Although Stuart denied the truth of this statement,[64] the affair caused ill feeling between Stuart and Lord Charles Montagu, who had given licenses to some of these traders. They appealed to the governor for support, and he complained that Stuart's department was not showing due respect to South Carolina licenses. Concerning Montagu, Stuart angrily remarked: "It is too much the fashion in this province to attempt calling the superintendt down & disputing his authority on every occasion."[65]

Whatever the merits of Stuart's plan for regulating the trade—and his plan was perhaps as good as experience could devise and the situation would permit—the superintendent never had an opportunity to give it a proper test, for in the summer of 1768 came orders from home placing the trade under control of the colonial governments.

Lord Shelburne had been more or less familiar with the Indian problem since 1763. Soon after his appointment to the office of secretary of state for the southern department, he began to collect information concerning it preparatory to a reconsideration of western policy. In the course of his investigation he learned of Stuart's attempt to regulate the Indian trade in 1765, and also of similar endeavors on the part of Johnson to establish order in the trade in the northern district from 1764 to 1766. Because Johnson's activities had considerable effect on the formulation of British policy by Shelburne and others in 1767–68 a brief account of them will be useful.

Trade in the northern district in 1764 had proceeded without great difficulty under the supervision of the colonies because of the fact that Pontiac's uprising limited it to a relatively small area. In preparation for the stream of traders that was certain to pour into the northern Indian country in the spring of 1765 Johnson, after consulting with Gage, persuaded the governors to issue passes, by the terms of which the merchants bound themselves to obey the regulations contained in the "Plan of 1764" should that instrument be

[64] Affidavit by William Fraser, March 16, 1768, Wright to Stuart, April 4, 1768, Roderick McIntosh to Stuart, April 14, May 29, 1768, Stuart to Gage, July 2, 1768, Gage MSS.

[65] Stuart to Gage, July 4, 1768, Gage MSS. Montagu's interference was especially displeasing to Stuart because the governor knew nothing regarding Indian affairs.

implemented. He drew up a set of rules embodying some features of the plan, and Gage ordered the officers at the posts to enforce these under Johnson's direction.[66] The trade was accordingly opened in 1765, but the officers met difficulties in trying to enforce the regulations.[67]

Early in 1765 Johnson began to urge Gage to permit the establishment of a trade system to be managed by the northern superintendent through members of his own department. Gage at first refused because a treasury order of November 28, 1764, forbade any increases in Gage's expenses except in case of emergency, and reserved to treasury officials the right to judge whether such an emergency existed.[68] If Gage should authorize Johnson to expend sums beyond what he had formerly had, Gage would become liable for them in the event that the treasury disapproved of his action. However, Johnson insisted, even threatening to resign if his request were not approved; [69] and Gage finally gave reluctant consent to the temporary establishment of a system similar to that which Stuart later set up in the South.[70] In the early months of 1766 Johnson added five commissaries to his department, and somewhat later two more. Expenses in the northern department for salaries alone mounted to some £3,500.[71]

Johnson hoped to enforce most of the provisions of the "Plan of 1764" regarding trade. Each commissary was furnished with a copy of it,[72] and instructed to follow it so far as possible. Traders were to obtain licenses under bond from the colonial governors, business was to be confined to the forts, and the commissaries were

[66] "Orders for the Regulation of Trade," Jan. 16, 1765, *Ill. Hist. Colls.,* X (1915), 400–1.

[67] For an example see Gage to Johnson, Aug. 18, 1765, Gage MSS.

[68] Gage to Johnson, Feb. 2, March 10, 1765, Gage MSS.

[69] Johnson to Gage, Aug. 16, 1765, Gage MSS; Johnson to Daniel Claus, Aug. 17, 1765, *Johnson Papers,* IV, 829.

[70] Johnson to Board of Trade, March 22, 1766, *Ill. Hist. Colls.,* XI (1916), 193–95. C. W. Alvord and C. E. Carter, *ibid.,* Introduction, xxxvi, express surprise that Stuart was allowed to employ commissaries in 1764–65 while Johnson was forced to wait until 1766. The treasury order undoubtedly explains Gage's attitude. Before he received this instruction Gage's conduct in regard to financing the Indian departments was probably governed by a private letter from Halifax of January, 1764, warning him not to follow Amherst's policy. See Halifax to Gage, Jan. 14, 1764 (Private), *Gage Corr.,* II, 10.

[71] The organization of the northern department in 1766 is described in *Johnson Papers,* V, 442–43. Commissaries serving at Michilimackinac and Halifax were added after this document was written.

[72] Johnson to Gage, July 4, 1766, Gage MSS.

to insure honest weighing and measuring.[73] But no means of compelling obedience to their orders were furnished the commissaries. Johnson's system remained in force until the close of 1768, though it was never very effectively executed. It proved to be impossible to restrict trade to the posts, and attempts by the commissaries to enforce the rule brought forth protests from Guy Carleton, then lieutenant governor of Canada, which led Shelburne to order Johnson to relax it in Canada. The commissaries were unable to stop the flow of liquor, and many traders did not even bother to obtain licenses. From the misbehavior of unscrupulous traders arose not only administrative difficulties but also protests from honest merchants who felt that they lost by observing the rules.[74]

During the period 1766–68 the expenses of the northern department steadily mounted. From September, 1766, to September, 1767, Edward Cole, commissary at Fort Chartres, incurred obligations amounting to more than £10,700 (New York currency). Expenditures at other posts were smaller than those made in the Illinois country, but the total, in Gage's opinion, was staggering.[75] Expenditures of Johnson's assistants were certified by military officers at the posts, and Gage therefore instructed them to scrutinize all accounts with extreme care. Although Gage's efforts to reduce these outlays had little effect, his protests regarding the expenses of the Indian departments,[76] coupled with complaints from merchants and reports by Johnson and Stuart that their regulations were often evaded, resulted in creating serious doubts in England concerning the wisdom of imperial management of Indian affairs, particularly in regard to trade.

As early as December, 1766, Lord Shelburne believed that the

[73] Johnson's instructions are contained in *Johnson Papers,* V, 337.

[74] This brief summary of Johnson's endeavor to establish imperial control of the trade from 1766 to 1768 is based on documents too numerous to cite. They are to be found in the Gage MSS, *Johnson Papers,* V and VI; *Ill. Hist. Colls.,* XI (1916); *NYCD,* VII and VIII; and *Gage Corr.,* I. No study of the northern Indian department has thus far been published.

[75] Gage to Johnson, April 4, 1768, Gage MSS.

[76] A few examples of Gage's letters deploring expenses for the Indian departments are: Gage to Shelburne, April 4, 1767, Gage to Charles Lowndes, Nov. 24, 1765, Gage to Barrington, April 24, 1767, *Gage Corr.,* I, 129–31, II, 317, 413–14. Parliament called for financial estimates from the Indian departments early in 1766. Gage to Johnson, Oct. 5, 1766, Gage MSS. Stuart submitted an estimate of £5,431 odd, provided departmental supplies were purchased in England. "Estimate of Annual Expences for Officers Sallarys & other Contingencies in the Southern Department of Indian Affairs/general Meetings & Congresses Exclusive," n.d., *ibid.*

"Plan of 1764" gave too much authority to the superintendents, that partial execution of the plan had proved to be expensive, and that the careful supervision laid down in that document was impossible. He was therefore inclined to favor returning control of the trade to the colonies "under some general rules and restrictions."[77] Shelburne decided to move slowly, however, for he soon discovered that many difficulties were to be met,[78] and that those he consulted had various opinions. In spite of Gage's criticisms of expenses of the Indian departments the commander in chief continued officially to urge that management of the trade be retained under imperial control.[79] But by the fall of 1767 Shelburne had settled upon a plan of action. In a report to the cabinet he suggested setting aside the "Plan of 1764," abolishing the office of superintendent, returning control of the trade to the colonies, and forming new colonies in the Mississippi valley.[80] His final suggestion was the vital element in Shelburne's policy. By this time he had become convinced that the fur and skin trade was not worth the care and expense which management of it involved; that the Indian country would be more valuable to England as an agricultural region buying manufactured goods from the mother country than as a hunting ground; and that new colonies would serve to draw the attention of the colonists from their quarrels with England. Shelburne's report did not meet with the full approval of his colleagues, and the cabinet decided to refer his proposals to the Board of Trade for advice. The board received the report and many memorials concerning Indian affairs on October 5.[81] It also heard the opinions of several officials and received from the merchants trading with North America a petition that supported Shelburne's policy.[82] The view of Johnson and Stuart that the Indian departments should be rendered more powerful through legislation was also considered.

Finally, on March 7, 1768, the board made its representation. On the grounds that it was difficult to restrict the trade to the forts in the northern district and that England alone could not bear the

[77] Shelburne to Gage, Dec. 11, 1766, *Gage Corr.*, II, 47–51.

[78] Shelburne's "Reasons for Not Diminishing American Expense This Year," March 30, 1767, *Ill. Hist. Colls.*, XI (1916), 536–41.

[79] Gage to Shelburne, Feb. 22, April 4, Aug. 20, 1767, *Gage Corr.*, I, 123–24, 129–30, 144–45.

[80] The report appears in *Ill. Hist. Colls.*, XVI (1921), 12–21. Its date is given as Sept. 11, 1767, although doubt as to its accuracy is indicated.

[81] *Ill. Hist. Colls.*, XVI (1921), 77–81.

[82] "Advice of the North American Merchants to the Board of Trade, About the Indian Trade," Oct. 30, 1767, *Ill. Hist. Colls.*, XVI (1921), 102.

costs of regulation, control of the trade should be entrusted to the colonies. The board admitted that colonial management in the past had been rather disastrous, but indicated that assurances had been given of the ability and the desire of the colonies to manage the trade. It reported against the formation of new colonies, because they would be expensive and would not create a market for British manufactures, and urged that all garrisons in the interior of North America be withdrawn unless there existed special reasons for maintaining some of these. Political relations with the Indians should remain under the superintendents. A new boundary line to protect lands reserved by the Indians should be drawn, and treaties directed toward that end should be negotiated by the superintendents with the consent of the governors of the colonies concerned. The board also recommended that the Indian departments be placed upon budgets of £4,000 per annum.[83] On March 18 the report was adopted by the cabinet without change.[84] Undoubtedly the chief reason for transferring control of the Indian trade to the colonies was the cost of the imperial establishment rather than the policy of Shelburne or any other statesman. As a matter of fact, Shelburne was rapidly losing prestige in the cabinet in 1767, and the colonies were actually separated from his department in January, 1768.[85] On April 15 Lord Hillsborough, who had become secretary of state for the newly created colonial department, informed the various colonial officials concerned of the new arrangements, adding that the salaries of the Indian agents should henceforth be £1,000 per annum.[86]

In conformity with Hillsborough's instructions Stuart issued orders for the discharge of all his commissaries and most of the inferior employees in his department on November 1,[87] and abandoned his trade restrictions. Until 1775 he operated under the

[83] "Representation of the Board of Trade on the State of Indian Affairs," March 7, 1768, *NYCD*, VIII, 19–31.

[84] Cabinet minute, March 18, 1768, *Ill. Hist. Colls.*, XVI (1921), 219–20.

[85] On Shelburne's rôle in the formation of western policy from 1766 to 1768 see R. A. Humphreys, "Lord Shelburne and British Colonial Policy, 1766–1768," *Eng. Hist. Rev.*, L (1935), 257–77.

[86] Hillsborough to Gage, April 15, 1768, *Gage Corr.*, II, 61–66; Hillsborough to colonial governors, April 15, 1768, Hillsborough to Johnson, April 15, 1768, *NYCD*, VIII, 55–56, 57–59. Both Johnson and Stuart had asked for increased salaries. Johnson's budget was increased to £5,000 in 1769.

[87] Stuart to Hillsborough, Sept. 15, 1768, CO, 5/69. The commissaries in the more distant parts of the southern department actually served several months beyond the date given. Stuart to Hillsborough, May 2, 1770, CO, 5/71.

budget laid down by the Board of Trade, which was enlarged in 1771 by Hillsborough, because it was found necessary to reëmploy John McIntosh as commissary to the Chickasaws and to engage Lieutenant John Thomas as agent to the Small Tribes.[88] In consequence of Hillsborough's instructions Gage ordered the royal troops in South Carolina and Georgia evacuated.[89] In order to remove uneasiness among the Indians caused by the abandoning of Forts Prince George, Charlotte, Augusta, and Frederica, and to explain the change made in trade regulation, Stuart thought it wise to call congresses with the Cherokees and Creeks. He was also anxious to meet the Cherokees because it was necessary to deal with them regarding their boundary with Virginia. In August, 1768, he therefore requested them to meet him once more in conference at Hard Labor in September.[90]

[88] The budgets for the Indian departments did not include allowances for congresses. If funds above the budgets were needed, it was necessary to obtain a special grant.

[89] Gage to Captain Valentine Füser, June 25, 1768, Gage MSS. Both Bull and Wright vainly protested against the withdrawal. Neither province had any royal protection after the summer of 1768, for Gage had ordered the Georgia rangers disbanded the previous year. The governors made some attempt to preserve the various forts, but without much success.

[90] Stuart to Gage, Aug. 22, 1768, Gage MSS.

CHAPTER XV

THE VIRGINIA-CHEROKEE FRONTIER, 1765–75

THE year 1768 undoubtedly marked high tide in the prestige and power of the southern Indian department before the War of Independence. With the loss of support from home in regard to trade regulation Stuart's activities in that sphere were henceforth limited in whatever degree the various southern governors deemed advisable. Loss of control over the trade also probably led to a slight diminution of political influence, but the superintendent's authority in the political sphere was to suffer more severely in the seven years before the Revolution because the honest execution of his office required that he struggle against a rising tide of land speculation and westward emigration that could not be stayed. Although he was not opposed to all colonial expansion, he was all too well aware that excessively rapid extension of settlements led directly to Indian wars. He was also duty-bound to attempt to enforce the Proclamation of 1763 and the various Indian boundary lines in the South. A faithful servant of the crown, he therefore opposed every land grant which to him seemed unduly large, until he received a hint or a positive order from home to desist. As a loyal officer he was compelled not only to oppose the speculative projects of English and American speculators, but also to try to counteract the influence and actions of royal officials such as Sir William Johnson, Sir James Wright, and Lord Botetourt, who lent their aid to the speculators. His lot was not made easier when the home government, after encouraging him to continue in a strenuous fight against the "New Purchase" on the boundary of Georgia between 1771 and 1773, abandoned him and gave its approval to the purchase. Although his authority was frequently flouted during this period, Stuart nevertheless on the whole retained the affections of the southern Indians. It is greatly to his credit that the steadily increasing hostility between them and the colonists, caused in large part by the rapid advance of white settlements, was prevented from breaking out into open warfare.

Perhaps the most vexing problems Stuart ever met were those

resulting from the conflicting interests of the Cherokees and of the whites on the Virginia frontier in the period 1765–75, especially those connected with the delineation of the Virginia-Cherokee boundary line. (Map 2, p. 102, should be consulted in connection with this chapter, Chapter XVI, and Appendix B.)

If relations between the Cherokees and Virginia were not too happy before 1765, they were more friendly than they were in the last ten years of British rule. In no southern colony before the War of Independence were the frontiersmen more aggressive and less trammeled by authority. They became so obnoxious that the southern Indians came to apply the term "Virginian" to any person who encroached on their lands along the old southeastern frontier. While some of the pioneers may have been democratic, hardy, independent spirits, others were shiftless debtors who fled to the wilderness to evade court action.[1] The Virginians and their fellows from the backwoods of North Carolina killed large quantities of game on hunting grounds that the Cherokees looked upon as exclusively their own, causing the Cherokees at length to adopt the policy of depriving such hunters of their weapons and their spoils. Unfortunately for the cause of peace on the frontier, many of these backwoodsmen also acted on the well-known principle that a good Indian was a dead one. The Cherokees retaliated, eye for eye and tooth for tooth.

As increasing numbers of frontiersmen moved westward along the Holston River and over the Cumberlands into Kentucky the Cherokees may have slaughtered many hunters and settlers whose fate was never known, but reports of slayings by the Cherokees came occasionally to Stuart. In 1772 a war party from that nation slew seven Virginians and a Negro, offering to Stuart the palpably false excuse that they thought their victims were Frenchmen. Stuart was convinced that the Cherokees should be punished, but at a time when relations with the Creeks were severely strained he was unable to demand the execution of the culprits because of similar deeds on the part of the Virginians and because of the necessity of preserving peace with the Cherokees.[2] In 1773 an attack by the Cherokees on another group of Virginians resulted in several casualties, among them James Boone, son of Daniel Boone, and Stuart was able eventually to secure the execution of only one of the aggressors. The Virginians officially and unofficially complained loudly about this

[1] Fauquier to Board of Trade, May 22, 1766, CO, 5/1331.

[2] Cameron to Stuart, Aug. 9, 1772, Stuart to Gage, Sept. 7, 1772, Aug. 8, 1774; Stuart to Haldimand, June 21, 1773, B. M. Add. MSS, 21,672, pt. 2; Stuart to Dartmouth, June 21, 1773, CO, 5/74.

and other attacks, unjustly suspecting that Stuart's endeavors to obtain redress from the Cherokees were halfhearted. Their own hands were not too clean. Isaac Crabtree, a border ruffian who survived this assault, slew an inoffensive Cherokee at a race track on the Watauga River soon afterward, and his action was condoned by many Virginians. At least one other bloody onslaught by Virginians upon innocent Cherokees immediately before the Revolutionary War has been recorded,[3] and it is not improbable that an occasional Cherokee fell before the long rifles in the "Dark and Bloody Ground" without the knowledge of his nation. It is notable that both Fauquier and John Blair failed to keep promises that the relatives of the Augusta victims would receive the value in goods of 500 pounds of deerskins for each of the slain.[4]

The most serious cause of dispute between Virginia and the Cherokees arose, however, from Cherokee claims to lands west and south of the Kanawha River.

It is now well known that many Virginians were deeply interested before 1754 in lands located beyond the Alleghenies. Hundreds of thousands of acres lying "on the waters of Mississippi" were granted by the governors of Virginia after 1745, a large part of which was given in grants of great size. One of these grants, that made to James Patton in 1746 of 100,000 acres in the valleys of the Kanawha River and two other streams farther west flowing into the Ohio, was partly surveyed and sold to persons who made settlements between the Kanawha and the Holston before the outbreak of hostilities with the French. Other persons moved into the same area at the same time as the result of smaller patents. This movement toward

[3] Dunmore to Stuart, April 5, 1774, Arthur Campbell to Cameron, June 20, 1774, Stuart to Gage, Aug. 8, 1774, Gage MSS; Reuben G. Thwaites and Louise P. Kellogg, eds., *Documentary History of Dunmore's War, 1774* (Madison, 1905), 2, 38–39, 73, 373–77. To his credit, Andrew Lewis wanted justice done on both sides and promised his coöperation. "Talk" by Lewis to Cherokee chiefs, June 9, 1774, Gage MSS.

[4] Blair purchased goods for the Cherokees to be given out at Chiswell's Mine in 1768, but the meeting at which they were to be disbursed was postponed, and the goods were discovered to be unsatisfactory. Botetourt not long afterward requested Stuart to purchase and disburse the proper amount of supplies, with the understanding that he would be repaid. Stuart, on the basis of information from Fauquier, had long before promised the Cherokees that this redress would be offered and had suffered some criticism from the Cherokees because Fauquier had not executed his promise. He therefore refused to assist Botetourt. Botetourt to Stuart, Dec. 20, 1768, Botetourt to Thomas Walker and Andrew Lewis, Dec. 20, 1768, John P. Kennedy, ed., *Journals of the House of Burgesses of Virginia, 1766–1769* (Richmond, 1906), xxxi-xxxii, xxxii-xxxiii; Stuart to Botetourt Jan. 19, 1769, CO, 5/1347. I have seen no further mention of this affair.

and beyond the Kanawha had the full approval of the British imperial government, which believed that the new settlers would serve as a bulwark against the French, and that Indian titles to these lands had been extinguished by treaties signed at Lancaster and Logstown in 1744 and 1752 with the Six Nations and Ohio valley tribes. In 1754 the imperial government, at the urging of the Virginia burgesses, forbade the issuance of further grants by Virginia beyond 1,000 acres to a person, but the major grants previously made were still valid, provided they were surveyed and developed.[5] The great grantees, with the exception of Patton and his heirs, seem, however, to have failed to meet these specifications, no doubt partly because of the war.

As late as 1760 additional minor grants of lands beyond the mountains were issued,[6] although the settlers in that area had been for the most part driven from their homes by Ohio valley Indians. As long as the French held Fort Duquesne, projects for reoccupation were necessarily held in abeyance, but Duquesne had hardly fallen when Fauquier reopened the question of exploiting the territory beyond the Alleghenies. In spite of the fact that his own son had become affiliated with one of the great land companies Fauquier considered the major grants lapsed, except Patton's, because they had not been developed; and he urged the Board of Trade not to permit their renewal or to permit renewal only under restrictions that would favor the settler as against the speculator.[7] The reply of the board, in June, 1760, was a severe blow to those interested in western lands, since it foreshadowed the Proclamation of 1763 and other measures calculated to restrain expansion in America. The board declared it had encouraged settlement in the West before 1754 because it had believed that Indian claims to the southern bank of the Ohio had been abandoned, but that it had since learned the contrary was true. In view of this consideration and the fact that the French were still entrenched in America, the board instructed Fauquier to make no further grants upon the Ohio or its tributaries.[8] When Fauquier argued that this prohibition should

[5] Representation of Board of Trade to committee of privy council for plantation affairs, June 20, 1754, Board of Trade to Dinwiddie, July 3, 1754, additional instruction to Lord Albemarle, Aug. 6, 1754, CO, 5/1367.

[6] John Robinson and John Chiswell were each granted 1,000 acres in May, 1760, the grants to be contiguous and to be located on both sides of the Kanawha. Minute of Va. council, May 6, 1760, CO, 5/1429.

[7] Fauquier to Board of Trade, Jan. 30, 1759, CO, 5/1329; Fauquier to Board of Trade, Dec. 1, 1759, CO, 5/1330.

[8] Board of Trade to Fauquier, June 13, 1760, CO, 5/1367.

not apply to persons who were then returning to their homes on the Greenbrier and Kanawha Rivers and who were seeking renewal of their patents, the board heartily agreed; at the same time he was told not to grant more land on those rivers until all Indian claims had been extinguished and the board had given its approval.[9]

In November, 1761, Fauquier tried to secure the consent of the Board of Trade to the making of new grants in the Kanawha region, alleging that no Indian rights to the area existed and arguing particularly against any possible pretensions on the part of the Cherokee nation. Fauquier pointed out that the Cherokees had failed to assert ownership when they met Randolph and Byrd in congress in 1756. In fact, he declared, they had never made any claim.[10] However, a special instruction, based on an order in council of November 23, was sent on December 11 to all the American governors enjoining them, under pain of immediate removal from office, from granting Indian lands. Private persons were forbidden to purchase land from them except with special royal consent. Every governor was to publish a proclamation ordering all persons illegally settled on soil claimed by the savages to remove, and was to notify the Indians resident in or near his colony of this instruction.[11] It is curious that, although Fauquier had denied the existence of any Cherokee pretensions within the colony of Virginia, he undertook to inform a great Cherokee chief of the import of this special instruction.[12] In April, 1762, the Board of Trade repeated to Fauquier its prohibition of grants "on the waters of Mississippi."[13]

Probably Fauquier continued to the end of his life to be hostile to Virginia speculators in western lands, although he seems to have tried to pursue a course that would displease neither his constituents nor his superior officers. In 1763 he refused, in accordance with his instructions, it is true, to give his assent to a petition from Dr. Thomas Walker for a renewal of the Loyal Company grant of 1749 for 800,000 acres north and west of the boundary between North Carolina and Virginia.[14] In July of the same year he reported that Virginians were illegally settling in the valley of the Kanawha and that this had caused the Ohio River tribes to renew their attacks on

[9] Fauquier to Board of Trade, Dec. 6, 1760, CO, 5/1330; Board of Trade to Fauquier, Feb. 17, 1761, CO, 5/1368.

[10] Minute of Va. council, Nov. 7, 1761, CO, 5/1435; Fauquier to Board of Trade, Nov. 30, 1761, CO, 5/1330.

[11] See *NYCD,* VII, 472–76, 477–79.

[12] Fauquier to Board of Trade, April 16, 1762, 5/1350.

[13] Board of Trade to Fauquier, April 8, 1762, 5/1368.

[14] Minute of Va. Council, May 25, 1763, 5/1435.

the frontier; and he declared that peace could not be maintained on the frontier "unless this enthusiasm of running backwards to hunt for fresh lands can be stopped." At that time he desired regulation to assure settlement of western lands in orderly and compact fashion.[15] On the other hand, at the Congress of Augusta Fauquier cautiously avoided negotiating with the Cherokees regarding the establishment of a boundary between that tribe and his colony, on the ground that he was not instructed to do so.[16]

Until 1764 Fauquier successfully defended to the home government the cause of those who had occupied and were occupying the Kanawha valley under legal patents. When he received a copy of the Proclamation of 1763 he once more took up the cudgel in their behalf, urging that the proclamation should not apply to them, but the Board of Trade responded that it forbade all settlement beyond the mountains, without exception.[17] Since Fauquier sympathized with the pioneers who had complied with Virginia law and since he lacked power even to prevent squatters from occupying the Kanawha region, he prudently let the matter drop. The pioneers remained, but at the same time declined to pay quitrents, because their titles were in serious doubt. Such was the status of the Kanawha valley settlements until 1766, when John Stuart reopened the whole question.

As we have seen, the Cherokees had urged in October, 1765, that their eastern boundary be made to follow a line run northward from Reedy River to Chiswell's Mine. In so doing they repudiated the informal agreement made by Attakullakulla and Fauquier at the Congress of Augusta. Stuart believed that the creation of a boundary between Virginia and the Cherokees was both expedient and required by the Proclamation of 1763. He therefore placed this proposal before Fauquier and wrote to the governor regarding it on three separate occasions in 1766, but Fauquier failed to make any reply.[18] In November of the same year, however, Fauquier reminded Lord Shelburne of the persons legally settled (according to Virginia law) in the Kanawha region. On the thirteenth of the following month the burgesses took a much more drastic step; they voted an

[15] Fauquier to Board of Trade, July 8, 1763, 5/1330; Fauquier to Earl of Egremont, July 27, 1763, 5/1345.

[16] Fauquier to Shelburne, Feb. 2, 1767, CO, 5/1345.

[17] Fauquier to Board of Trade, Feb. 13, 1764, 5/1330; Board of Trade of Fauquier, July 13, 1764, 5/1368.

[18] Feb. 10, Nov. 24, Dec. 17. Stuart to Fauquier, Feb. 10, 1766, CO, 323/23; Stuart to Fauquier, Nov. 24, 1766, CO, 323/24; Stuart to Botetourt, Jan. 19, 1769, CO, 5/1347.

address to the crown setting forth the claims of these settlers and requesting that the territory between Pennsylvania on the north, the Ohio on the west, and North Carolina on the south be thrown open to occupation. The burgesses asserted that no Indians resided in this loosely defined but vast area and that only a few used it for hunting.[19] On December 18 Fauquier suggested in a letter to Shelburne that a Virginia-Cherokee boundary might exercise a good effect. In February, 1767, he repeated the suggestion. He asserted that the Cherokees had abandoned their claims north of the Holston at the Congress of Augusta, and he asked for specific directions regarding the course of such a line should it be deemed advisable to establish one.[20] It is hardly to be doubted that Fauquier requested specific directions because as a free agent he would be subjected to pressure from those interested in western lands.

By December 11, 1766, Shelburne, in response to reports from Stuart, had already decided that a boundary should be drawn, and he instructed Stuart to undertake the task, in coöperation with Fauquier.[21] In 1767 Stuart wrote four times to Fauquier regarding the matter, but Fauquier continued until the end of his life to refuse to join Stuart in dealing with the Cherokees. He declined to act for lack of more precise instructions; he suggested that Stuart negotiate a line on his own authority; and he failed to indicate to the superintendent that the Cherokee offer of 1765 was unsatisfactory to Virginia.[22]

Although Stuart was irritated by Fauquier's attitude, he informed Shelburne in July, 1767, that he did not believe the Cherokee-Virginia boundary question to be of prime significance so long as the Proclamation of 1763 prevented occupation of the trans-Allegheny region.[23] Shelburne learned, however, that George Mercer, who

[19] Fauquier to Shelburne, Nov. 18, 1766, 5/1345; *Journals of the House of Burgesses of Virginia, 1766–1769*, 69–70.

[20] Fauquier to Shelburne, Dec. 18, 1766, Feb. 21, 1767, CO, 5/1345.

[21] Shelburne to Stuart, Dec. 11, 1766, Gage MSS. Professor Thomas P. Abernethy, *Western Lands and the American Revolution* (New York, 1937), 61, states incorrectly that Shelburne sent these instructions "in the spring of 1767."

[22] Stuart to Fauquier, April 11, 1767, CO, 5/68; Fauquier to Stuart, Sept. 17, Nov. 21, 1767, Gage MSS; Stuart to Botetourt, Jan. 19, 1769, CO, 5/1347. Professor Thomas P. Abernethy, *op. cit.*, 60–61, expresses an opinion that Fauquier may have refused to coöperate with Stuart because he believed a Virginia-Cherokee line negotiated in 1766 or 1767 would be detrimental to Virginia speculators. It would appear, however, that Fauquier really desired to avoid raising a thorny question as long as possible and to place the burden of it when raised upon the home government or upon Stuart.

[23] Stuart to Shelburne, July 28, 1767, CO, 5/68.

appeared before the Board of Trade in the early summer of 1767 on behalf of the Ohio Company of Virginia, had declared that the burgesses were considering measures to encourage settlement beyond the Alleghenies; and in October the minister informed Fauquier of his disapproval of any such action on the part of the burgesses.[24] On November 14 he sent to Fauquier the instructions the governor had desired on the Virginia-Cherokee boundary.[25] Fauquier was to join Stuart and the Cherokees in running a line from Chiswell's Mine behind the Virginia settlements to "that point from whence [the Indian boundary of] the northern provinces sets out." What was that point? One authority states that it was interpreted at the time to be the southwestern corner of Pennsylvania, but that its location is yet to be determined.[26] Indeed, it will never be determined, for Shelburne, although he has been described as a great student of the American West, on receiving reports of the completion of the Mason-Dixon line, concluded that Indian boundaries had been drawn for Maryland and Pennsylvania! John Blair, who assumed the acting governorship of Virginia on March 4, 1768, did at first believe that the southwestern corner of Pennsylvania was the intended northern terminus of the Virginia Indian boundary, until Sir William Johnson explained Shelburne's grotesque error to him.[27]

Further directions regarding the Virginia boundary were forthcoming. Since 1764 Johnson had been urging the establishment of a northern Indian boundary to run down the Ohio as far as the mouth of the Tennessee River. Shelburne referred this matter to the Board of Trade, which on December 23, 1767, recommended that the northern boundary be drawn, but that it should terminate at the Kanawha River because the Cherokees justly claimed the territory west of that stream and used it for hunting. On January 5, 1768, Shelburne ordered Johnson to execute this report.[28] It is clear that Shelburne and the Board of Trade intended that the Kanawha should serve as the line between Virginia and the Cherokees. It is equally certain that Shelburne's instructions favored the Cherokees as against Virginia because the Indians placed their pretensions before the home government through Stuart and because Virginia

[24] Board of Trade to committee of privy council for plantation affairs, June 26, 1767, CO, 5/1368; Shelburne to Fauquier, Oct. 8, 1767, CO, 5/1345.

[25] Shelburne to Fauquier, Nov. 14, 1767, CO, 5/1345.

[26] Thomas P. Abernethy, *op. cit.*, 61.

[27] Johnson to Blair, April 23, 1768, *Johnson Papers*, VI, 202–4. See also Blair to Gage, June 17, 1768, Gage MSS.

[28] Board of Trade to Shelburne, Dec. 23, 1767, Shelburne to Johnson, Jan. 5, 1768, *NYCD*, VII, 1004–5, VIII, 2.

made no specific objection, either to Stuart or to officials in London.

In the spring of 1768 Blair, Johnson, and Stuart corresponded regarding Shelburne's instructions. Johnson assured Blair that he would comply with them [29] and laid plans for a congress with the interested northern tribes for the following summer. Stuart ordered Alexander Cameron to arrange a meeting of Cherokee representatives, Cameron himself, and commissioners to be appointed by Virginia to undertake the survey of the Virginia-Cherokee line as laid down in the instructions, that is, from Chiswell's Mine to the Kanawha, a very short distance, and thence along the Kanawha to its mouth. Cameron accordingly planned to begin the survey at Chiswell's Mine on October 25.[30] Although Stuart wrote thrice to Blair regarding the survey and indicated that the Cherokees expected the Kanawha to serve as the line, Blair, like his predecessor, failed to tell the superintendent that Virginia was not satisfied. No doubt he saw no reason for protesting to the superintendent, for it could hardly be expected that Stuart would do other than obey Shelburne's instructions. Blair was not satisfied, but he could only appeal to London. He did appeal to London. However, on June 15 he appointed Dr. Thomas Walker and Andrew Lewis to act for Virginia at Johnson's congress and to coöperate with Cameron in surveying the Cherokee line.[31]

[29] Johnson to Blair, April 23, 1768, *Johnson Papers,* VI, 202–4.

[30] Minute of Va. council, June 30, 1768, CO, 5/1435.

[31] Minutes of Va. council, June 15, 30, July 29, Sept. 7, Oct. 19, 1768, CO, 5/1435; Stuart to Botetourt, Jan. 19, 1769, CO, 5/1347. Abernethy, *op. cit.,* 64–65, confuses this survey and the Cherokee congress held by Stuart at Hard Labor from October 14 to 17, 1768. He thinks the Hard Labor congress was originally scheduled for Chiswell's Mine on October 25; that Blair accordingly collected gifts to present to the Cherokees in exchange for any land cession they might make; and that Stuart deliberately held his congress at Hard Labor eleven days before the date he had set so as to prevent Virginia from being represented. But the minutes of the Virginia council cited show clearly that Walker and Lewis were ordered to coöperate with Cameron in the survey, not to meet Stuart and negotiate for lands. The minute of October 19 also shows that Blair ordered a hat, shirt, blanket, and a small quantity of powder and lead for each Cherokee participating in the survey, and another supply of goods to compensate the relatives of the nine Cherokees murdered in Augusta County in 1765. Professor Abernethy has mistaken the purpose of these presents. October 25 was, of course, the date set by Cameron for the survey, not the date set by Stuart for his congress. Aside from the fact that Stuart never held a congress in the Indian country, it should be noted that it would have been a most remarkable arrangement to have Stuart meet the Cherokees at Chiswell's Mine, a site very inconvenient for Stuart and almost equally so for many of the Cherokees. Stuart's actual plans for the congress are dealt with elsewhere.

Even before Blair and Stuart had made substantial progress in the matter of the survey the thoroughgoing reconsideration of British western policy initiated by Shelburne in 1767 led to still further instructions from London in regard to the Virginia-Cherokee boundary. In its famous report of March 7, 1768, the Board of Trade urged that Stuart obtain from the Cherokees formal recognition of the Kanawha as the boundary; or, since the Cherokees had abandoned any pretension to lands below Chiswell's Mine,[32] of a straight line running from the mine to the mouth of the Kanawha. As noted above, this report was approved by the cabinet, and on April 15 Lord Hillsborough sent a copy of it to Stuart, with a command to execute it.[33] Other copies were sent to Johnson, Gage, and the American governors. In early summer the question was again reopened in London because of the receipt of an address from the Virginia burgesses urging that the settlers beyond the Alleghenies be permitted to remain and that the issuance of additional grants in the same area be approved.[34] The Board of Trade, in a report of June 10, sanctioned by Hillsborough, denied the petition of the burgesses; it again declared that the Proclamation of 1763 precluded all settlement beyond the mountains. However, the board indicated that the region east of the line laid down in its representation of March 7 might be occupied after the formal ratification of that line.[35] Nor did a proposal made by Stuart in July, that the Virginia-Cherokee boundary follow a straight line from Chiswell's Mine to the mouth of the Kentucky River, meet with favor from Hillsborough. On September 15 he informed the superintendent that the line described in the report of March 7 should be ratified and that he believed that any further cession on the part of the Chero-

[32] Apparently the board assumed the Cherokees had given up this pretension because in 1765–66 the Indians wished to end their line with North Carolina at the mine.

[33] *NYCD,* VIII, 22, 33–34, 53–54.

[34] This address appears to be similar to that voted by the burgesses in December, 1766, mentioned in the text above. More likely it was another in similar terms. The *Journals of the House of Burgesses of Virginia, 1766–1769,* contain no address by the burgesses in these terms for 1767 or the early part of 1768.

[35] See Hillsborough to Board of Trade, May 17, 1768, CO, 5/1332; Board of Trade to Hillsborough, June 10, 1768, Hillsborough to Blair, July 9, 1768, CO, 5/1346. The report implies that the cabinet could modify the geographical limit laid down by the Proclamation of 1763 by instructions issued through the secretary of state for the colonies. In 1774, as described in the following chapter, lands reserved west of the Alleghenies by the proclamation were actually ordered by Lord Dartmouth to be opened to settlement. Some might question whether an order in council could be set aside in this fashion.

kees would be highly unwise.[36] Twelve days later Blair wrote to Hillsborough expressing a hope that the Virginia-Cherokee line when finally settled would legalize all the existing settlements in western Virginia, in accordance with the representation of the Board of Trade of June 10.[37]

The congress that Stuart planned to hold with the Cherokees at Hard Labor in September, 1768, in order to explain the changes in British military and Indian policy arising from the report of March 7 [38] was necessarily postponed to October 10.[39] Although the home government seems to have expected that the colonies concerned would take part in negotiations with the Indians regarding boundary changes authorized by that report, Stuart did not invite Virginia to send a representative to Hard Labor. Possibly he did not realize that he was expected to do so, especially since his orders required a mere ratification of the line as agreed upon by his charges and by the home government. This was an unfortunate omission on his part, for it gave to Virginia an opportunity to levy unfair accusations of misconduct against him after the close of the congress. Stuart made no effort, however, to conceal his plans. They were announced not only to Hillsborough and Gage, but also in a circular letter of September 15 to the southern governors, including, of course, Blair.[40]

At Hard Labor from October 13 to 17 Stuart conferred with representatives of the Cherokees. They readily agreed to cede their claims east of the straight line drawn from Chiswell's Mine to the mouth of the Kanawha. Because of the fact that Johnson's congress had been delayed Blair had already secured Stuart's consent to a postponement of the survey to November 10. The Cherokees now requested that it be further postponed—until May 10, 1769. The reason for this request, a sensible one, was that the line agreed upon would be too difficult to mark in November because of the nature of the terrain through which it would pass and the season of the year. Stuart agreed with the Cherokees. On October 17 he wrote to Blair to inform him of what had occurred at Hard Labor.[41]

[36] Stuart to Hillsborough, July 14, Aug. 16, 1768, Hillsborough to Stuart, Sept. 15, 1768, CO, 5/69.

[37] Blair to Hillsborough, Sept. 27, 1768, CO, 5/1346.

[38] See p. 261.

[39] Stuart to Gage, Sept. 12, 1768, Gage MSS.

[40] Stuart to southern governors, Sept. 15, 1768, CO, 5/69. If Stuart's letter was not delayed in transit it would have been possible for a commissioner from Virginia to reach Hard Labor in time for the congress.

[41] Minute of Va. council, Sept. 7, 1768, CO, 5/1435; Proceedings of the Con-

Although Fauquier had refused to renew the patent of the Loyal Company in 1763, that company began selling the lands it claimed to settlers on a large scale after 1764. Both Dr. Thomas Walker and Andrew Lewis were financially interested in it, and they actually made some profit from it.[42] Lewis was also head of another group of speculators, the Greenbrier Company. They were therefore greatly interested in removing all bars to the settlement of western Virginia. In July, 1768, Walker and Lewis reached Shamokin, Pennsylvania, where they learned that Johnson's congress had been postponed to the following fall. However, they proceeded to Johnson Hall, where they had much time for consultation with the northern superintendent before delegates from the Six Nations began to appear. Johnson suddenly discovered that the Six Nations would "insist" on selling to the crown their claim to the south bank of the Ohio as far west as the mouth of the Tennessee. But such a sale would not be of much value to Walker and Lewis if the Cherokees continued to assert ownership of the area between the Kanawha and the Tennessee. Johnson therefore wrote to his southern colleague to persuade him to take no action that would recognize Cherokee pretensions to that area, but his letter never reached Stuart.[43] To the same end, since Johnson's congress, held at Fort Stanwix, was delayed until November, Lewis left his companion in the north and hurried south toward Chiswell's Mine. And Lewis hurried! He quitted Fort Stanwix on October 12 and was in Augusta County, Virginia, on the

---

gress of Hard Labor, Oct. 13–17, 1768, Gage MSS; Stuart to Blair, Oct. 17, 1768, CO, 5/1347. Abernethy, *op. cit.,* 64–65, declares that Stuart was instructed to obtain the ratification of the Kanawha River as the line; that the Hard Labor line was therefore unauthorized; and that Stuart may have disobeyed his instructions to placate Virginia. Aside from the fact that there was no reason why Stuart should placate Virginia Professor Abernethy has ignored the provisions of the well-known representation of March, 1768, relating to the line. Curiously enough, he has reprinted a map prepared to illustrate the report; it clearly demonstrates his errors. He is unquestionably and unwarrantedly greatly biased against Stuart. He may have acquired this attitude from Professor Clarence W. Alvord, who declares without justice in his *Mississippi Valley in British Politics* (Cleveland, 1917), II, 64, that Stuart "dictated" the line settled upon at Hard Labor. As we shall see, both he and Professor Alvord exhibit a marked anti-Stuart bias in dealing with later developments in connection with the Cherokee-Virginia boundary.

[42] Fauquier to Board of Trade, Feb. 13, 1764, CO, 5/1330; William Nelson to Hillsborough, Oct. 18, 1770, CO, 5/1348.

[43] Johnson to Blair, Sept. 25, 1768, Johnson to Stuart, Sept. 25, 1768, Stuart to Johnson, April 14, 1769, *Johnson Papers,* VI, 406–7, 407–8, 693–94; Johnson to Hillsborough, June 26, 1769, *NYCD,* VIII, 172–73.

26th of the same month. Then, fearing that he lacked power singly to represent Virginia, he wrote to Blair asking him for further instructions.[44]

On November 4 Stuart's letter of October 17 to Blair was brought by its recipient to Lord Botetourt, who had just taken office as governor of Virginia. A meeting of the Virginia council was quickly arranged for the following day, and it was decided to send an express to inform Lewis that the survey had been postponed once more. Botetourt and his council were aware that Stuart had merely executed his instructions. When writing to Hillsborough and Stuart shortly afterward Botetourt therefore offered no strictures upon Stuart's conduct.[45] But Walker soon reached Virginia with the information that Johnson, in absolute disregard of his orders, had purchased from the Six Nations for the crown the south bank of the Ohio as far as the mouth of the Tennessee.[46] The deep disappointment felt by Walker and Lewis when they learned of the Treaty of Hard Labor may be imagined; they made some very energetic representations when they presented their report to the Virginia council in December.[47] Botetourt suddenly discovered that Stuart should have invited Virginia to express her need for westward expansion at Hard Labor. He urged the superintendent to undertake negotiations for the purpose of changing the line just arranged by Stuart so as to include the settlements made west of the Kanawha before the French and Indian War, which still lay outside the boundary, and also all the territory ceded by the Six Nations at Fort Stanwix. He requested that surveying of the Hard Labor line be delayed until Virginia had had an opportunity to petition the king for the establishment of the Tennessee as the line. To achieve these objects, on December 20 he sent Walker and Lewis to Charleston to consult Stuart.[48] Four days later he wrote to his friend Hillsborough setting

[44] Minute of Va. council, Nov. 1, 1768, CO, 5/1435.

[45] Minute of Va. council, Nov. 5, 1768, CO, 5/1435; Botetourt to Hillsborough, Nov. 10, 1768, CO, 5/1347.

[46] On dealings between Walker and Lewis on the one hand and Johnson on the other regarding the Indian boundary see Alvord, *op. cit.*, II, 69–73; Abernethy, *op. cit.*, 61–64. There is good reason to believe that Walker and Lewis sold out Virginia's interest in the Pittsburgh area in order to help their own cause.

[47] Walker and Lewis to Botetourt, Dec. 14, 1768, also minute of Va. council, Dec. 17, 1768 (Extract), CO, 5/1347.

[48] Botetourt to Walker and Lewis, Dec. 20, 1768, Botetourt to Stuart, Dec. 20, 1768, *Journals of the House of Burgesses of Virginia, 1766–1769,* xxxi-xxxii, xxxii-xxxiii.

forth Virginia's desires and denying that the Cherokees had any real claim to the region west of the Kanawha.[49]

While on their way to Charleston Walker and Lewis met Governor Tryon, who arranged a conference at Fort Johnston between them and a number of Cherokees who happened to be in North Carolina. The Virginians persuaded Usteneka and Saluy, who were in this group, to accompany them to Charleston by sea. On January 11, 1769, the party landed and immediately sought out Stuart. Stuart pointed out that Johnson had disobeyed his instructions. He was incensed by the charge of unfair dealing levied against him by Botetourt,[50] and he was reluctant to consider any immediate change in the boundary. However, he permitted the Virginians to ask the Cherokees in his presence whether they would agree to a rectification that would bring the settlements between the Kanawha and the Holston within the boundary. The chiefs indicated that they would give their consent. Stuart cautiously refused to continue negotiations unless he received the demands of the Virginian commissioners in writing. They suggested as a boundary the line 36 degrees, 30 minutes! Stuart declared that he was unable to reopen the question with the Cherokee nation except under orders from Hillsborough. He was irritated by what he considered the excessive demands of Virginia, especially after that colony had been so long silent regarding her desires, but he undertook to put the proposal of the commissioners before the ministry. In February Stuart wrote to place the matter before Hillsborough. To Hillsborough he made a counterproposal that the boundary should be made to run from the northern end of the North Carolina Indian boundary directly west to the Holston and thence in a straight course northeast to the mouth of the Kanawha. All Virginia settlements existing in 1768 and legal according to Virginia law would lie within this line. He indicated that a congress would be necessary to secure the consent of the Cherokees.[51]

Hillsborough was completely satisfied with Stuart's conduct at Hard Labor.[52] He did not know, however, until early in 1769 that there were settlements beyond the Kanawha considered lawful in Virginia. In March, 1769, he informed Botetourt that he was re-

[49] Botetourt to Hillsborough, Dec. 24, 1768, CO, 5/1347.

[50] See Stuart to Botetourt, Jan. 19, 1769, CO, 5/1347; Stuart to Johnson, April 14, 1769, *Johnson Papers,* VI, 693–94.

[51] Walker and Lewis to Botetourt, Feb. 2, 1769, CO, 5/1347; Stuart to Hillsborough, Feb. 12, 1769, CO, 5/70.

[52] Hillsborough to Johnson, Jan. 2, 1769, *NYCD,* VIII, 144; Hillsborough to Gage, March 24, 1769, *Gage Corr.,* II, 86.

ferring the whole matter of the Virginia-Cherokee line once more to the Board of Trade and that he personally was willing that Virginia purchase Cherokee claims east of the mouth of the Tennessee. He thereby roused great hopes in Virginia.[53] But Stuart's counterproposal appealed to Hillsborough and the Board of Trade, and on May 13 Hillsborough ordered Stuart to hold the necessary congress. If Virginia refused to bear the expense of the congress Stuart was to have the Hard Labor line surveyed. Because of pressure from other members of the cabinet the minister was forced to announce on the same day that the purchase made from the Six Nations by Johnson was approved, but the cabinet attempted to prevent any difficulties that might arise from that approval by forbidding new settlement beyond the Hard Labor line.[54]

The Cherokees were not unwilling to concur in this additional cession, although they insisted on being well paid for it.[55] At the same time they were highly displeased by new squatter settlements made by Virginians and North Carolinians on the Watauga, the Holston, and the Nolachucky rivers in 1768, and in the valley of the Powell River in 1769;[56] and they became more and more restless as news of the expansionist schemes of Virginia officials seeped into the Cherokee country. They were also dissatisfied because of bands of white hunters who infested their hunting grounds along the Holston.[57]

Although the Cherokees were willing to accept the revised boundary ordered by Hillsborough, Botetourt was not. The Virginia council decided in August to call the burgesses into session to consider the situation. The burgesses responded as Botetourt had hoped. On December 18 in a formal address that body denied the right of the Cherokees to the lands between the Kanawha and the Tennessee; asserted that the Treaty of Fort Stanwix settled the own-

[53] Hillsborough to Botetourt, March 1, 1769, Botetourt to Hillsborough, May 10, 12, 1769, CO, 5/1347. It should be remembered that the colonial secretary was also president of the board.

[54] Report of Board of Trade, April 25, 1769, Hillsborough to Johnson, May 13, 1769, *NYCD,* VIII, 158–63; Hillsborough to Stuart, May 13, 1769, CO, 5/70.

[55] Stuart to Hillsborough, May 13, 1769, C.O., 5/70.

[56] Some of these settlements lay below the line of 36 minutes 30 degrees, and actually were located in North Carolina. They remained illegal in British eyes, while the lands occupied above the line were ceded by the Cherokees in 1770–71. Cameron tried to force the illegal settlers to remove, but the pioneers succeeded in obtaining a deed from the Cherokees by chicanery and defied him. See *NCCR,* X, 768–69; Thomas P. Abernethy, *From Frontier to Plantation in Tennessee: A Study in Frontier Democracy* (Chapel Hill, 1932), 2–8.

[57] "Talk" from Cherokee chiefs to Stuart, July 29, 1769, Gage MSS.

ership of that territory; and called for the extension of the North Carolina–Virginia line to the Ohio as the Cherokee boundary. Other reasons of little weight for this proposed extension of territory open to settlement were offered, and a grant of £2,500 was made for the expense of negotiations with the Cherokees. Botetourt wrote to Hillsborough in support of this address and warned Stuart to take no further action until the minister could consider it. He testily informed Stuart that he saw no reason for opposing a scheme that would increase the Virginia quitrents.[58]

A heated debate between Stuart and the Virginia expansionists followed. Stuart pointed out a fact that some Virginians must have known—that the line proposed by the burgesses was impossible, since by following latitude 36 degrees 30 minutes it would never strike the Ohio. He argued with considerable justice that it would pass too near the Cherokee towns and that it would deprive both the Cherokees and the Chickasaws of their best hunting grounds. He recalled to Botetourt the fact that the Virginia frontiersmen as hunters and Indian haters were peculiarly obnoxious to the Cherokees, and he contended that it was bad policy to bring the backwoodsmen and Cherokees into closer proximity than was necessary. He further averred that the Cherokees would never consent to such a large grant. He warned Botetourt, moreover, that the Indians generally would resent such an extension of Virginia settlements and that a confederacy of the Shawnees, Delawares, Cherokees, Creeks, and Chickasaws against the whites might well result. He also argued that such a huge cession would not benefit the commerce of the mother country.[59] Botetourt retorted that Virginia would fight the matter through. On July 5 the Committee of Correspondence of the burgesses heatedly and incoherently denounced Stuart's attitude to Edward Montagu, agent for Virginia at London, and instructed him to complain about Stuart's conduct.[60] But the

[58] Minute of Va. council, Aug. 8, 1769, CO, 5/1440; memorial by burgesses to Botetourt, Dec. 18, 1769, Botetourt to Stuart, Dec. 18, 1769, CO, 5/71.

[59] Stuart to Botetourt, Jan. 13, 1770, CO, 5/71. Gage heartily supported Stuart's stand at this juncture. He likewise feared that acquiescence in Virginia's demands would lead to a general Indian war. Gage to Stuart, March 26, 27, May 17, 1770, Gage MSS.

[60] The Committee of Correspondence assumed that Indians had no rights whatever to land. While offering no objection to the policy of drawing boundaries, the authors of this document nevertheless criticized Stuart severely because he had informed the Cherokees that settlers beyond them would not be protected by English officials. The attitude of the committee was that settlement was always proper, whether within or without the boundary, and that purchase was merely a sop to remove Indian discontent.

burgesses had actually capitulated before this protest was sent. On June 15 that body requested Botetourt to take the necessary measures to draw and survey the boundary in accordance with Hillsborough's orders, and granted £2,500 for the purpose, saying that it did so because longer delay would endanger the lives of those who were settled beyond the line of 1768. On June 21 the governor asked Stuart to undertake the necessary negotiations. Three weeks later the superintendent responded that he planned to meet the Cherokees once more at Hard Labor on October 5 and that £2,900 was needed to defray expenses. Botetourt was so eager to finish the business that he took the extraordinary step of drawing the sum needed from the Virginia quitrent fund. He sent Colonel John Donelson, surveyor of Pittsylvania County in Virginia after 1769, as his official representative to attend the congress.[61]

It is not entirely clear why the burgesses abandoned their quarrel with Stuart in the middle of June, 1770. Possibly that body was anxious to obtain as solid a grip as possible over Virginia's western lands in order to combat the designs of the Grand Ohio Company. This company had been formed in the previous year by Samuel Wharton, of the firm of Baynton, Wharton, and Morgan of Philadelphia, and Thomas Walpole, an English banker. Included in its membership were a number of English nobles and officials. The company was striving to obtain a proprietary grant to be bounded on the north by the Ohio, on the west by a line drawn from the mouth of the Scioto River to Cumberland Gap, on the south by the Cumberland range and the Greenbrier River, and on the east by the western boundaries of Maryland and Pennsylvania.[62] Perhaps a letter from Hillsborough to Botetourt of April 14 [63] indicating that the minister still supported Stuart's stand reached Virginia before June 15 and exercised an effect. It seems likely, however, that Botetourt was moved to quit the struggle because of the persuasion of Sir William Draper, the hero of the capture of Manila in 1762. Draper landed at Charleston late in 1769 [64] and attended with many other officials and gentlemen a conference that Stuart held with the Cherokee chiefs at the Congarees in April, 1770. At this meeting the Cherokees declared that they were strongly opposed to settlement

[61] John P. Kennedy, ed., *Journals of the House of Burgesses of Virginia, 1770–1772* (Richmond, 1908), xii-xiv, 76–77; *Virginia Magazine of History and Biography,* XII (1905), 355–64.

[62] For accounts of the early history of the Grand Ohio Company see Alvord, *op. cit.,* II, Chapters IV and V; Abernethy, *op. cit.,* Chapter III.

[63] In Co, 5/1348.

[64] South-Carolina Gazette, Jan. 4, 1770.

beyond the line suggested by Stuart and urged Draper to present their case to Botetourt, for he was acquainted with the Virginia governor and planned to visit Virginia. Stuart persuaded Draper that he was in the right, and Draper consented.[65] Since he reached Williamsburg at the end of May [66] and since Botetourt had a very high opinion of him,[67] it would appear that Draper's influence led to a change in the governor's attitude. Certain it is that Botetourt was henceforth unwilling to give his support to Walker and Lewis. In the summer of 1770 Jacob Hite,[68] their agent, forged a letter from Ouconnostotah to Botetourt. This forgery urged the governor to ignore Stuart and to arrange a congress with the Cherokees on behalf of Virginia, at which gathering Ouconnostotah would see to it that Virginia obtained all the lands she desired. The Virginia speculators also arranged for the appearance of Saluy before the governor and his council on August 17 to support this forged "talk"; and Lewis urged Botetourt to comply with the supposed request of the Great Warrior. But Botetourt refused to listen.[69]

When Stuart, Cameron, Donelson,[70] and about 1,000 Cherokees headed by Ouconnostotah met at Lochaber,[71] South Carolina, during the period October 18–22, no major difficulties appeared. Because of the fact that the Cherokees objected to giving up the Long Island in the Holston River, since they feared it would be used as

[65] Proceedings of the Congarees conference, April 10–12, 1770, Gage to Stuart, May 17, 1770, Gage MSS; Daniel Claus to Johnson, Sept. 12, 1770, *Johnson Papers,* VII, 897.

[66] *Virginia Gazette* (Rind), May 31, 1770.

[67] Botetourt to Hillsborough, Feb. 25, 1770 (Private), CO, 5/1348. Said Botetourt regarding Draper: "Good use of him may be made for the publick —— Men like him shoud never be neglected, in times like these they are invaluable."

[68] A minor Virginia speculator.

[69] Stuart to Hillsborough, Nov. 28, 1770, Minute of Va. council, Aug. 17, 1770, "talk" by Botetourt to Ouconnostotah, Aug. 18, 1770, Botetourt to Lewis, Aug. 18, 1770, CO, 5/72; proceedings of the Congress of Lochaber, Oct. 18–22, 1770, Gage MSS. Hite and Richard Pearis were agents among the Cherokees for Walker and Lewis.

[70] Professor Archibald Henderson thinks it significant that Walker and Lewis represented Virginia at Lochaber, but they were not at the congress. See "Dr. Thomas Walker and the Loyal Company," *Proceedings of the American Antiquarian Society,* New Series, XLI (1931), 79, and "A Pre-Revolutionary Revolt in the Old Southwest," *Miss. Vall. Hist. Rev.,* XVII (1930), 198.

[71] Lochaber was Alexander Cameron's plantation, located on Penny Creek, a stream flowing into Long Canes Creek from the northwest. It contained about 2,600 acres, 2,000 of which were granted to Cameron in 1765 by virtue of his service in the Seven Years' War. Memorial Book, ix, 131, Historical Commission of South Carolina.

a site for a fort, a change was necessarily made in the line ordered by Hillsborough. Stuart reported to the minister that

> ... The Indians offered, by way of compensation for the land they refused to grant to run the line a more western course to the Ohio, which would have given a good territory upon that river; but I declined accepting it, not being within the limits of my instructions; and if I had been certain that your Lordship would have forgiven it, I should not have done it; as the precedent would possibly have exposed me to future solicitations.

The line was described in the Treaty of Lochaber, dated October 18, as

> ... beginning where the boundary line between the province of North Carolina and the Cherokee hunting grounds terminates, and running thence in a west course to a point six miles east of Long Island in Holsten's River, and thence to said river six miles above the said Long Island, and thence in a direct course to the confluence of the Great Conhoway and Ohio rivers.

A provision was inserted in the treaty to the effect that no alteration should be made in the line except at a general meeting of the nation with the superintendent or another royally authorized person in attendance.[72]

The treaty was received with mixed sentiments in the Cherokee nation. Ever since the Treaty of Fort Stanwix the Shawnees and Delawares, because their claims to the south bank of the Ohio had not received much consideration, had harbored a grudge against the Six Nations and more particularly against the English. Delegations from these tribes had been constantly among the Cherokees and Creeks urging them to join in a general assault on the English, and their intrigues could hardly fail to cause discontent. Fortunately for the peace of the southern frontier, the treaty negotiated between the Cherokees and the Six Nations proved to be of great value. In 1770 the parties to that peace, with Stuart's blessing, formed an alliance.[73] Aided by this circumstance Stuart and Johnson managed to keep the Cherokees and the Six Nations hostile to the western tribes until the Revolution, but Stuart, Johnson, and Gage suffered many an anxious moment because of the widespread machinations of the Shawnees and Delawares.[74] In the winter of 1770–71 the

[72] Proceedings of the Congress of Lochaber, Oct. 18–22, 1770, Gage MSS; Stuart to Hillsborough, Nov. 28, 1770, CO, 5/72.

[73] Proceedings of the Congarees conference, April 10–12, Gage MSS; *NYCD,* VIII, 227–44.

[74] Many references might be cited on the activities of the Shawnees and Delawares and on efforts to combat them. Johnson's part in dealing with this problem is rather clearly shown in *NYCD,* VIII, *passim.* Informative documents on Stuart's part are: Gage to Stuart, March 27, 1770, Feb. 5, 1771, proceedings of the

Cherokee traders were so frightened at the prospect of an alliance between the western tribes and the Cherokees that they prepared to flee the nation. Through Cameron, Stuart maintained a careful watch on the Cherokees. They, of course, denied that they were listening with approval to the messages of the Shawnees and Delawares.[75] More confusion arose from the action of the Overhill tribes in negotiating a deal with the Cherokee traders whereby the latter were to receive an extensive cession of land belonging to the Lower Cherokees and the Creeks in exchange for canceling the trading debts of the Cherokees.[76] Intrigues of Richard Pearis and others for further private cessions did not pour oil on the troubled waters. The Cherokees actually refused at first to ratify the Lochaber cession and Ouconnostotah was sharply criticized because he had taken the leading rôle at Lochaber, but at Cameron's insistence they finally agreed to join in surveying the line.[77]

Congarees conference, April 10–12, 1770, Gage MSS; Stuart to Cameron, Feb. 23, 1771, CO, 5/72; Stuart to Germain, Aug. 23, 1776, CO, 5/77.

[75] "At a Convention of the over Hill Cherokee Chiefs & Beloved Men &ca. at Toqueh on the 3 March 1771," Gage MSS.

[76] This problem will be discussed in Chapter XVII.

[77] Cameron to Stuart, March 9, 1771 (Abstract), Stuart to Gage, April 23, 1771, Gage MSS. For agreeing to make the survey the Cherokees asked 1,000 pounds of powder, but Stuart and Virginia officials refused their request.

CHAPTER XVI

THE VIRGINIA-CHEROKEE FRONTIER, 1765–75 *(Continued)*

ALTHOUGH he had opposed the line of 36 degrees 30 minutes as a Cherokee-Virginia boundary, Stuart believed in 1770, as he did in 1768, that no harm could result from the expansion of Virginia settlements to the Kentucky River, provided the Virginians did not attempt to press southward down the valleys of the Holston and neighboring streams. Since the Cherokees had indicated at Lochaber that they were willing to cede their claims to all, or at least most, of northeastern Kentucky in exchange for Long Island and since the Lochaber line would not be surveyed until the spring of 1771, Stuart suggested to Virginia officials immediately after the congress that they petition Hillsborough for permission to accept the offer of the Cherokees. He also sent orders to Cameron to make the necessary arrangements with the Cherokees if Hillsborough gave his assent. When Donelson, who had worked with the superintendent at Lochaber in friendly coöperation, brought this suggestion to Williamsburg, Botetourt was dead. On December 12 the Virginia council appointed Donelson to coöperate with Cameron in surveying the Lochaber line. William Nelson, who had assumed the reins of government, failed to push Stuart's proposal energetically to Hillsborough, but he forwarded it to the minister, declaring that "it is a pity, that this addition to His Majesty's territory, which is so easy to be obtain'd, should be refused."[1]

Hillsborough failed to make a direct answer to Nelson's appeal. In a letter to Nelson of February 11, 1771, he said merely that "I hope that when the line shall have been ascertained in the manner proposed by the council [on December 12] in their resolutions upon that subject, it will be followed by some regulation that shall have the effect to prevent any contravention of the treaty." [2] Here cer-

[1] Stuart to Botetourt, Oct. 25, 1770, William Nelson to Hillsborough, Dec. 15, 1770, CO, 5/1349; minute of Va. council, Dec. 12, 1770, CO, 5/1440.

[2] Hillsborough to William Nelson, Feb. 11, 1771, CO, 5/1349.

tainly was no explicit negative. Perhaps Hillsborough did not even notice the appeal. In any case, this statement was all that could have been known officially by Donelson and Cameron regarding the minister's attitude when they began the survey in the following May. Hillsborough also wrote to Stuart on February 11:

> The final conclusion of the boundary line between Virginia and the Cherokee country . . . is much approved by the King.
>
> The reasons you assign for leaving Long Island to the Indians, & for not accepting their proposition of giving a compensation by an extension of our limits upon the Ohio, appear to be satisfactory; but you will allow me to observe, that it would have been very usefull in a case of this nature, where the judgement is so much to be guided by precise ideas of the geography of the country, if your report had been accompanied with such a map as you promised in your letter of 30th July 1769 to transmit to me.

Since this dictum reached Stuart after July 29 at Pensacola—Stuart was on a mission in West Florida between May, 1771, and May, 1772—neither Cameron nor Donelson had any knowledge of it when they began their task.[3] The fact that they did not know that the minister was positively opposed to accepting the offer made by the Cherokees at Lochaber may have encouraged them to use their own judgment regarding the course that the line should follow.

On May 27, 1771, Cameron, Donelson, Donelson's deputy surveyor of Pittsylvania County, two interpreters named Will Emery and Joseph Vann, Attakullakulla, and a number of Cherokees began the survey. They were gone about five months, and they traversed territory through which few Englishmen had previously traveled. Even as the surveying party reached the Holston the Cherokees agreed to a slight change in the line in order to accommodate certain settlers on the western bank of that river.[4] Shortly afterward, according to Stuart and Donelson, the Cherokees proposed that the line be run over the Cumberlands to the headwaters of the Kentucky and along that stream to the Ohio. That the Cherokees made such an offer is not unlikely, since the delegates of the nation at Lochaber had presented a somewhat similar proposal. Stuart states that they made the offer because they did not wish to travel through the rough country between the Holston and the mouth of the Kanawha and because ownership of the south bank of the Ohio was still disputed by the Shawnees and Delawares. The statements of Stuart and Donelson are also borne out by the fact that the Overhills, who would be principally affected by the change,

[3] Hillsborough to Stuart, Feb. 11, 1771, Stuart to Hillsborough, Sept. 24, 1771, CO, 5/72.

[4] "Talk" by Attakullakulla to the governor of Virginia, n.d., CO, 5/1350.

were represented in the party only by Attakullakulla. According to John Filson, however, Donelson suggested the change at the instance of pioneers living in the valleys of the Powell and Clinch rivers. At all events Donelson and the Cherokees agreed to run the line down the Kentucky, no doubt with the approval of Cameron, and Donelson promised presents worth £500 to the Cherokee nation for its compliance.[5]

In accordance with this agreement, the Donelson-Cameron group struck northwestward across the Powell River, the Cumberlands, and the North Fork of the Cumberland River until they came upon a tributary of the Kentucky. From that point the line was allowed to follow that stream and the Kentucky itself to the Ohio. The line was blazed and marked in other ways throughout its course.[6] At the

[5] The most significant documents on this agreement are a quotation from an affidavit by Donelson cited in James Hall, *The Romance of Western History; or, Manners in the West* (Cincinnati, 1885), 155; Attakullakulla's "talk" cited in the preceding note; Stuart to Dartmouth, Feb. 25, 1773, CO, 5/74. Corroborative evidence regarding the Donelson purchase is to be found in Colonel William Preston to Dunmore, March 10, 1775, Reuben G. Thwaites and Louise P. Kellogg, eds., *The Revolution on the Upper Ohio* (Madison, 1908), 3; Willard R. Jillson, ed., Filson's *Kentucke* (Filson Club Publications, No. 5, 1930), 9; deposition by Charles Robertson, Oct. 3, 1777, W. P. Palmer, S. McRae, and W. H. Fleurnoy, eds., *Calendar of Virginia State Papers, 1652–1869* (Richmond, 1875–93), I, 291; deposition by Dr. Thomas Walker, March 15, 1777, *Proceedings of the American Antiquarian Society,* New Series, XLI (1931), 48–50. Preston states that he was informed that the Cherokees, in March, 1775, contended that the lands north and east of the Kentucky were still their property, because Virginia had failed to pay the promised £500 in goods. Robertson testifies to the same effect. Filson, with a peculiar mixture of truth and error, asserts that Donelson made the purchase from the "Five Nations" at a price of £500. Walker states that he saw a copy of a message from the Cherokee nation to Lord Dunmore in which the Cherokees "disavowed the sale of the Lands lying between Cumberland mountain & the Ohio." On the composition of the Cherokee group in the surveying party see Stuart to Gage, Aug. 31, 1771, Gage MSS.

[6] Donelson affidavit and Stuart's letter of Feb. 25, 1773, cited in the preceding note; John Donelson [Map of the Virginia-Cherokee boundary as laid down in the Donelson survey], 1771, Public Record Office. Donelson's map was formerly in the Colonial Office Library at London. After I had made an unavailing search for it Professor Verner W. Crane suggested that I consult C. Atchley's *Catalogue of the Maps, Plans and Charts in the Library of the Colonial Office* (London? 1910). Donelson's map was listed under the title "Virginia." The William L. Clements Library purchased a photograph of it, which I have used. Earlier writers on the Donelson survey, notably Professor Clarence W. Alvord and Professor Thomas P. Abernethy, did not have access to this map. For this reason and for others their accounts of the survey and following events are inaccurate. Professor Alvord has tried to prove that Donelson actually ran the line down the Louisa–Big Sandy watercourse, but Donelson's map, which is unquestionably authentic, shows the line running down the Kentucky. Doubt later arose in the

end of October Cameron and the Cherokees returned to the Cherokee country and informed the nation of what they had done. The Cherokee chiefs gave their approval, and one of them, probably Attakullakulla, set out about the first of November for Virginia to remind Donelson of the presents that had been promised by him.[7] But Virginia failed to furnish the presents.

On March 20, 1772, Lord Dunmore, who had recently become governor of Virginia, wrote to Hillsborough regarding the cession made by the Cherokees to Donelson and enclosed a map of the new line drawn by Donelson. This map was well calculated to persuade a casual inspector that no great change had been made in the boundary as a result of Donelson's negotiations with the Cherokee representatives, for the Kentucky as shown upon it lay a considerable distance to the eastward of its true course. Moreover, for some unexplained reason Donelson designated the Kentucky as the "Louisa River." Since the Kentucky was commonly designated on the maps of 1771 as the "Catawba" or "Cuttawa"[8] River and since the term "Louisa" was used on the maps to indicate a supposed western tributary of the Kanawha, Donelson's map was certainly not drawn in such a fashion as to give a very accurate idea of the new line. Nor did Dunmore indicate that the Cherokees had ceded a large territory to Donelson. He reported that the

> ... commissioners ... found the country, thro' which the proposed line was to run, so mountainous, rugged and difficult of access, that they could not have accomplished it in many months, nor without an expence that would have been enormous, but they have, nevertheless, conducted it as nearly as possible, conformable to their orders, have only deviated from them, as your Lordship will see by the map, by continuing from the point on Holstein's river, where it is intersected by the division line of this colony and North Carolina, down that river a small distance, to a place from whence they had an easier access, than was any where else to be found, to the head of Louisa river; which they follow to its conflux with the Ohio.
>
> Thus, except where they cross from Holstein's to Louisa river, which being of no great distance and the country passable, they have been able to be particularly careful in marking, they have established a natural boundary, that can never be mistaken.

---

minds of interested Virginians whether Donelson ran the line to the Kentucky or the Cumberland, but a party of scouts sent out to investigate in 1774 actually followed the blazed line left by Donelson to the Kentucky. See Colonel William Preston to Washington, May 27, 1774, and deposition by Richard Stanton, Edward Sharp, Ephraim Drake, and William Harrel, May 7, 1774, *Letters to Washington,* V, 1–3.

[7] Cameron to Cherokees, Feb. 5, 1772, Papers of the Continental Congress, No. 71, Vol. ii, Division of Manuscripts, Library of Congress.

[8] "Catawba" and "Cuttawa" are corruptions of "Kentucky."

He strongly urged the ratification of the new line on the grounds that it would save much confusion and bloodshed, and considerable expense, and he begged that Hillsborough act quickly. He claimed that there were settlers who would be left in the Indian country if the Lochaber line were allowed to stand. At the same time Dunmore urged that Hillsborough rescind an order sent out in July, 1770, forbidding all further grants of lands by the Virginia council beyond the Alleghenies until the fate of the Grand Ohio Company's project should be determined.[9] Indeed, Dunmore was exceedingly anxious to open western Virginia to settlement. With Captain Andrew Snape Hamond and others he soon asked for a considerable grant in the area between the Lochaber and Donelson lines.[10] A little later he was to petition the king without success for 100,000 acres in western Virginia for himself and his sons.[11]

Hillsborough had had too much experience with problems connected with Indian boundaries, especially in regard to western Virginia, to accept Dunmore's report and Donelson's map without question. Perhaps he took the trouble to compare Donelson's map with one of John Mitchell's and correctly concluded that Mitchell's "Cuttawa" or "Catawba" and Donelson's "Louisa" were one and the same stream. In any case, he knew that Donelson and Cameron had not performed their task "as nearly as possible, conformable to their orders." He repeated his injunction of 1770, that the Virginia council was to grant no lands beyond the Alleghenies until further notice, and he declared:

> The deviation in the Indian boundary line made by the commissioners who were appointed to mark it out in consequence of the treaty with the Cherokees, at the same time that it very much surprises, appears to me to be a matter of very great moment, and to require the most serious attention; and as that treaty was the result of the unanimous opinion of His Majesty's confidential servants, that it was expedient for the true interest of this country, that the settlements of His Majesty's subjects should be confined to the limits prescribed by that treaty, it will be my duty, before I submit my own opinion to His Majesty upon the alteration which has been made, to receive their sentiments upon this proceeding.[12]

---

[9] Dunmore to Hillsborough, March [20], 1772, CO, 5/1350; Hillsborough to Botetourt, July 31, 1770, CO, 5/1348.

[10] Clarence W. Alvord, *Mississippi Valley in British Politics* (Cleveland, 1917), II, 86, note.

[11] Petition by Dunmore to the king, n.d., Order in Council, Nov. 19, 1773, CO, 5/1334; Board of Trade to committee of privy council for plantation affairs, June 20, 1774, CO, 5/1369.

[12] Hillsborough to Dunmore, June 6, 1772, CO, 5/1350.

Since Hillsborough was then engaged in a struggle with the Grand Ohio Company and since the grant requested by that company included part of the lands ceded by the Cherokees to Donelson, it was necessary to consider the question of accepting the cession in connection with the desires of the company. In August Hillsborough resigned, and the problem fell to his successor, the pious Lord Dartmouth, who was much more friendly to the Walpole group. Dartmouth was also aware that the territory ceded by the Cherokees to Donelson was extensive. On assuming office he prepared a memorandum to the effect that the "sense of the cabinet" should be obtained because "A much larger district (several million acres) is taken into Virginia, than was stipulated for by the treaty [of Lochaber] made in the king's name with the Cherokees." [13] Dartmouth and the cabinet failed to reach an immediate decision regarding the Donelson-Cherokee agreement, in part no doubt because precise knowledge of the area included by the agreement could not be obtained. On the 14th of August the Privy Council formally gave its approval to the grant requested by Walpole, Wharton, and their associates, and to the establishment of a new colony to include all the territory within the grant and also the region between the grant and the North Carolina–Virginia border. But the Privy Council, in order to prevent Indian discontent arising from an immediate and large-scale expansion of English settlements, also prohibited the speculators from occupying the territory between the Lochaber line and the western boundary of the proposed new colony.[14] On September 2 the Indian superintendents were notified of the action of the Privy Council. Before the close of the same month Dartmouth urged Stuart to send in a large map of the southern Indian nations and their boundaries that Stuart had promised in 1769,[15] but had been unable to forward because of inaccuracies in existing maps.

For a reason or reasons not perfectly clear there is no discussion in Stuart's correspondence of the problem raised by the Donelson survey until February 25, 1773. Then Stuart informed Dartmouth that the cession made by the Cherokees arose from their own initiative. He indicated that the cession did not displease him, and sent in a map of the southern Indian district drawn for him by Joseph Purcell and a chart that gave a fairly accurate conception of

[13] Alvord, *op. cit.*, II, 89, note 139, quoting Dartmouth MSS.

[14] There is a copy of the order in council in the Gage MSS.

[15] Dartmouth to Johnson, Sept. 2, 1772, *NYCD*, VIII, 311; Dartmouth to Stuart, Sept. 2, 27, 1772, CO, 5/73.

the extent and situation of the cession. At the same time Stuart indicated that Donelson's "Louisa" was the same stream as Mitchell's "Catawba" or "Cuttawa." [16] On May 5 Dartmouth declared his complete satisfaction with the new Virginia-Cherokee boundary.[17] On the following day the Board of Trade suggested that the proposed new colony be named "Vandalia" and extended to the Kentucky River, but that the grant to be made to the Walpole group remain unchanged. However, the board recommended that the proprietors be allowed to make use of all their grant, since it was believed that its western limits lay well within the new Cherokee boundary.[18] At the beginning of June, at a congress held with the Cherokees and Creeks at Augusta, Stuart informed the Cherokees of the prohibition of settlement (already removed, although he was not aware of that fact). His interpretation, undoubtedly an erroneous one, was that the clause forbade settlement by the Walpole group between the original western boundary of Vandalia and the Kentucky River.[19] Of course, his error was unimportant, since the prohibition had already been removed. It has been contended by two recent writers that Stuart's behavior in connection with various questions arising from the Donelson survey is open to severe criticism. The evidence indicates, however, that Stuart honestly executed his office and that he looked upon the Donelson line as a reasonably satisfactory solution to the conflicting claims of Virginia and the Cherokees.[20]

The instructions laid down in 1770 by Hillsborough forbidding Virginia to grant lands beyond the Alleghenies until the fate of the Walpole project was determined did not prevent Lord Dunmore from making extensive grants beyond the mountains. In spite of these instructions and in spite of orders from Hillsborough to make no grants to Virginia provincials claiming lands under the Proclamation of 1763, Dunmore and his council gave warrants to survey 200,000 acres for Washington's Virginia regiment and some 13,000 acres for other persons who had served in the recent conflict. Al-

[16] Stuart to Dartmouth, Feb. 25, 1773, CO, 5/74; Joseph Purcell's "A Map of the Southern Indian District of North America Compiled under the Direction of John Stuart Esqr. His Majesty's Superintendant of Indian Affairs." There is a MS copy of the map in the Ayers Collection, Newberry Library. I had access to a photostatic copy in the William L. Clements Library.

[17] Dartmouth to Stuart, May 5, 1773, CO, 5/74.

[18] Report of Board of Trade, May 6, 1773, CO, 5/1369.

[19] Proceedings of the congress, Gage MSS; Stuart to Ouconnostotah, n.d., Papers of the Continental Congress, No. 71, Vol. ii, and enclosed map by Stuart.

[20] See Appendix B.

though the Cherokees had not been paid for the cession they made to Donelson, Dunmore unscrupulously permitted the surveyors to lay out these lands as far west as the Donelson line. Nor was the governor at all concerned because some of these lands lay within the territory sought by the Grand Ohio Company.[21] Moreover, Dunmore searched energetically to find means to justify further grants. In 1773 he brought to the attention of Lord Dartmouth two statutes of Virginia enacted before 1754 which stated that lands which had been granted, but later forfeited, could be granted again. Dunmore argued that these statutes could be repealed only in the same fashion they were established or by act of parliament.[22] If carried to the extreme, this line of argument would have permitted the governor and his council to regrant a vast amount of territory within and beyond Vandalia, in spite of the restrictions laid down by the imperial government. However, Dunmore indicated to Dartmouth in the spring of 1774 that he would be satisfied with power to make grants freely within the Donelson line.[23] In April, 1774, Dartmouth peremptorily forbade the governor to make further grants to the Virginia provincials.[24] In the following July, probably without full understanding of the implications of his decision, the minister finally informed Dunmore that the Virginia statutes passed before 1754 could be regarded as still in effect; Dartmouth insisted, however, that regrants should not be made within the area asked by the Grand Ohio Company. On second thought he added a further restriction two months later: Dunmore was to make no regrants beyond the Lochaber line.[25] In effect, he permitted the governor and his council to make regrants between the Greenbrier River and the Virginia–North Carolina border.

The Vandalia project languished.[26] In the spring of 1774, with Dunmore's approval Virginia surveyors were actually engaged in laying out land claims on *both* sides of the Kentucky and as far down the Ohio as the present site of Louisville. Dunmore was not disposed to permit Dartmouth's orders to interfere with the occu-

[21] Dunmore to Dartmouth, June 9, 1774, CO, 5/1352.

[22] Dunmore to Dartmouth, July 4, 1773, CO, 5/1351; Dunmore to Dartmouth, March 20, 1774, CO, 5/1352.

[23] Dunmore to Dartmouth, April 2, 1774, CO, 5/1352.

[24] Dartmouth to Dunmore, April 6, 1774, CO, 5/1352.

[25] Dartmouth to Dunmore, July 6, Sept. 8, 1774, CO, 5/1352.

[26] There is some very interesting correspondence in the Gage MSS between Gage and Lord Barrington regarding the Walpole project. Both men were strongly opposed to it.

pation of all Kentucky under Virginia auspices.[27] But the last pre-Revolutionary purchase of Cherokee claims in the Ohio valley was made by private speculators. Between 1768 and 1773 a number of private persons had purchased lands from the Cherokees in spite of the Proclamation of 1763 and colonial statutes that forbade such purchases.[28] By 1774 it was patent that the Cherokees were utterly unable to resist the suasion, the goods, and the rum of the speculator. A group of Virginians including Patrick Henry, William Byrd, Ralph Wormley, Samuel Overton, John Page, and William Christian sought to take advantage of this situation. They associated themselves in a plan to purchase a large section of territory lying on the upper reaches of the Clinch, Holston, and Powell rivers; and they sent William Kennedy to open negotiations with the Cherokees. Kennedy learned that they were willing to sell because they were suffering from a shortage of goods. The scheme fell through, however, for reasons not clearly established, but apparently not because of opposition by Stuart.[29]

Certainly Stuart had no success whatever in his attempts to prevent the cession by the Cherokees of a much more extensive territory to a speculative combination headed by Judge Richard Henderson of North Carolina.[30] On August 25, 1774, Henderson, Nathaniel

[27] See Thomas P. Abernethy, *Western Lands and the American Revolution* (New York and London, 1937), Chapter VII.

[28] See the following chapter.

[29] Henry afterward testified that he lost interest because he saw that a conflict would develop as a result of this speculation between his duties as a member of the first Virginia convention and the first Continental Congress and this private interest. If sovereignty over these lands were wrested from the king, Henry could foresee that American governmental organizations would assume the rôle in opposition to such purchases formerly played by the imperial government. Deposition by William Christian, June 3, 1777, deposition by Patrick Henry, June 4, 1777, deposition by Arthur Campbell, Oct. 21, 1778, *Cal. Va. St. Papers,* I, 288–89, 289–90, 303–4. Professor Abernethy, *op. cit.,* 123, suggests that Stuart may have prevented the success of this scheme, but there is no mention of it in Stuart's letters. Abernethy is inclined to believe that a letter from Dunmore to Stuart of April 5, 1774, CO, 5/1353, was intended to inform Stuart of the plan of Henry and his friends. But Dunmore was really warning Stuart of the activities of Judge Richard Henderson. See Dunmore to Dartmouth, Feb. 7, 1775, *ibid.*

[30] The following account of Henderson and his activities is based in general on various writings of Archibald Henderson, including: "The Creative Forces in American Expansion: Henderson and Boone," *Am. Hist. Rev.,* XX (1914), 86–107; "Richard Henderson and the Occupation of Kentucky, 1775," *Miss. Vall. Hist. Rev.,* I (1914), 341–63; *The Conquest of the Old Southwest . . .* (New York, 1920); and "A Pre-Revolutionary Revolt in the Old Southwest," *Miss. Vall. Hist. Rev.,* XVII (1930), 191–212.

and Thomas Hart, John Luttrell, John Williams, and William Johnston met at Hillsborough in that colony and formally organized the Louisa Company, the purpose of which was either to rent or purchase lands from the Cherokees and to settle upon them. Like Patrick Henry and his friends, the Henderson group displayed utter lack of respect for the Proclamation of 1763, colonial statutes, and the Indian boundaries established through the efforts of Stuart. They prepared for quick action.

When Stuart learned that the Henderson crowd had invited the Cherokees to meet them on Holston River to negotiate regarding a land grant, he sent Cameron to endeavor to prevent the consummation of a sale and supplied him with gifts so that the Cherokees would not sell territory because they lacked goods.[31] Cameron failed to achieve success in this mission. In November, 1774, Henderson and Nathaniel Hart met several Cherokee chiefs and secured a preliminary agreement whereby the Cherokees undertook to sell them all the territory south of the Ohio lying between the mouth of the Kanawha and the Tennessee River; and Attakullakulla returned with the speculators to North Carolina to advise in regard to the sort of supplies desired by the Cherokees in payment. Cameron reported that Henderson openly declared that the Proclamation of 1763 could not prevent the consummation of this purchase.[32] As early as Christmas Day, 1774, the Henderson group publicly advertised their intentions.

On January 6, 1775, after the admission of three additional members into the company and the formation of new articles of agreement, the title of the organization was altered to that of "Transylvania Company." Governor Josiah Martin of North Carolina issued a proclamation warning the speculators to desist from their activities. Martin declared that the execution of the project would violate the Proclamation of 1763 and also a North Carolina statute that required the consent of the governor and council to private purchases from the Indians. He threatened prosecution under the provincial law if the speculators did not abandon their plan.[33] The Transylvania Company ignored the proclamation and completed its purchase from the Cherokees at a great conclave at the Sycamore Shoals on the Watauga River between March 14 and 17. The Cherokees tried unsuccessfully to sell Henderson land lying

[31] Stuart to Dartmouth, Sept. 3, 1774, CO, 5/75; Stuart to Gage, Sept. 14, 1774, Gage MSS.

[32] Cameron to Stuart, March 2, 1775, CO, 5/76.

[33] Printed copy in Gage MSS.

east of the Kentucky River; they eventually sold him a magnificent domain stretching from the Ohio and the Kentucky to the southern edge of the Cumberland River watershed. They also granted Henderson and his associates a strip of territory between the Watauga River and the Cumberland range, so that settlers traveling from North Carolina would not be forced to go through Cherokee territory. It has been contended that the negotiations at Sycamore Shoals were characterized by frankness and honesty on the part of Henderson and that he gave the Indians goods valued at £10,000,[34] but documents on the subject show that Henderson's transactions were by no means above suspicion.[35]

The interpreter at Sycamore Shoals was none other than Joseph Vann, who was at that time in the employ of the southern Indian department because of his knowledge of the Cherokee tongue. That fact does not indicate, however, that Henderson's project had received sanction from Stuart, for Vann was acting without instructions and contrary to his duty.[36] Stuart was unable to give much attention to Henderson's activities, because he was busily engaged in settling a dangerous quarrel that had arisen between the Creeks and Georgia in 1774. In all likelihood he could not have prevented the sale in any case. When he learned of it, he was very angry and bitterly censured the Cherokees for ceding their lands so freely,[37] but the coming of the Revolution restrained him from attempting to invalidate the grant. Dunmore issued a proclamation against the activities of the Transylvania Company; [38] and he blandly informed Lord Dartmouth that the surveyors whom he had sent out in the spring of 1774 into the area sought by Henderson had been put in

[34] By Archibald Henderson. But Professor Henderson also states that the goods were contained in one cabin.

[35] Depositions in *Cal. Va. St. Papers,* I, 271 ff.

[36] Depositions cited in the preceding note make it clear that Vann was not authorized to act in this capacity by Stuart. Vann took care at Sycamore Shoals to secure evidence that he was merely translating. That Henderson did not trust him is shown by the fact that several Indian traders were present to check on his translating. Vann had been an employee of Andrew McLean, a merchant of Augusta, and was appointed interpreter among the Cherokees after the death of John Watts in 1770. He proved to be unreliable and was discharged. As noted above, he was employed by Virginia for the Donelson survey. Pressure of business, coupled with a promise by Vann to behave, moved Cameron to reëngage him in 1774. Cameron to Stuart, March 4, 1771 (Abstract), July 4, 1774 (Abstract), Gage MSS.

[37] "Talk" by Stuart to Cherokees, Aug. 30, 1775, CO, 5/76.

[38] Peter Force, ed., *American Archives,* Fourth Series (Washington, 1837–46), II, 174.

motion in order to dispose of the territory before Henderson could act![39] But Dunmore was really helpless. Henderson proceeded to form settlements on the basis of the Treaty of Syracuse Shoals. He thereby caused further disgruntlement among the Cherokees, and contributed to the enmity felt by them toward the American colonists and to the decision of the Cherokees to attack the colonists when the Revolution came.

* * * * *

Professor Archibald Henderson, a descendant of the famous judge, has steadily maintained that the actions of his ancestor were not unlawful. He quotes the well-known Camden-Yorke opinion as part proof and insists that Lord Mansfield assured Henderson, before he took positive measures, that a private purchase from the Indians was legal, in spite of an order in council to the contrary. Other scholars have been unable to agree with Professor Henderson. It may well be doubted that the Camden-Yorke opinion, which supported the legality of private purchases from sovereign native princes in India, would have served as an unassailable argument in a case involving a similar purchase from an Indian tribe in America. See a review by Dr. St. George L. Sioussat, *Miss. Vall. Hist. Rev.*, VII (1921), 378–83. One authority—and with good reason—characterizes the supposed analogy between a Hindu prince and an American Indian tribe as a thoroughly spurious one. Abernethy, *op. cit.*, 363. There is some question whether Mansfield actually gave the opinion credited to him; if he did, the opinion was nevertheless informal and should not be given too much weight. The legality of Henderson's purchase is open to doubt not only because of the Proclamation of 1763, but also because it was secured in violation of the North Carolina law that forbade private negotiations regarding lands between citizens of the colony and Indians. The legality of the transaction is open to still further objection, on the ground that it constituted a treaty violation, although this fact has not been noted by historians. The Treaty of Lochaber, like many other treaties negotiated by Stuart, contained a clause requiring that no further land cessions be made by the signatory Indians unless the superintendent or another royally authorized representative conducted the negotiations. It may well be argued that any cession made by the Cherokees in contravention of this stipulation was void, in spite of the fact that the Donelson survey changed the Virginia-Cherokee line without strict conformance to it.

[39] Dunmore to Dartmouth, March 14, 1775, CO, 5/1353.

CHAPTER XVII

THE OLD SOUTHEASTERN FRONTIER, 1768–75

PROBLEMS similar to those that arose between the Cherokees and Virginia from 1768 to 1775 also developed on the borders of South Carolina, Georgia, and East Florida during the same period, although in the lower South the Indian trade added some other complications. But there, as on the Virginia frontier, the major motif was westward expansion. The Indians chiefly involved were the Creeks and, in a lesser degree, the Cherokees.

Early in 1768 Stuart and Wright resumed their efforts to secure the demarcation of the Georgia-Creek boundary. The Georgia frontier was less disturbed than during the preceding year, probably because the Creeks felt it to be necessary to be moderate in that area, since on their western borders the Chickasaws were on the verge of joining the Choctaws. Roderick McIntosh took advantage of this situation and managed to persuade the Creeks to return a number of runaway slaves, an achievement that greatly pleased Stuart, especially since he was himself a planter.[1] Toward the close of May representatives of the Lower Creeks met McIntosh at Augusta for the purpose of drawing the line. Wright failed to send commissioners to act for Georgia, but the task was begun on June 6.[2] McIntosh and the Indians marked the line as far south as the Canoochie River. There the Creeks discovered that the presents furnished by Wright to compensate them for their trouble were of inferior quality; and they departed for home, leaving about forty miles of the boundary unmarked. Stuart went to Savannah in July, expecting to meet the Lower Creek representatives and to ratify the line. When he discovered what had occurred, he joined Wright in sending conciliatory "talks" to the Creeks; and Wright dispatched goods to replace those that had been found unsatisfactory. Stuart then laid plans to return to Georgia in the fall to participate in the final ratification of the line and to explain to the Creeks that their

[1] Roderick McIntosh to Stuart, April 14, 1768, Stuart to Gage, July 2, 1768, Gage MSS.

[2] Stuart to Hillsborough, July 14, Sept. 15, 1768, CO, 5/69.

trade was henceforth to be regulated by the colonial governments.[3]

After the Congress of Hard Labor Stuart, Cameron, and Pierce Acton Sinnott held a brief conference with the Lower Creeks[4] at Silver Bluffs on the Savannah River.[5] This meeting led to the signing of a treaty on November 12 that confirmed the line as laid down in previous agreements and provided for the completion of the survey.[6] Wright commissioned Captain James Mackay to join in the survey, and Stuart appointed Lachlan McGillivray as his representative. By the end of December the boundary was completely marked, the actual work of surveying being done by Samuel Savery.[7] Both Gage and Stuart foresaw that this boundary, as well as other Indian boundaries in the South, would not long be respected.[8]

Although Stuart's plans had called for surveying the East Florida Indian line immediately after completing that of Georgia, he found it expedient to give up the idea. Grant was willing to concert in the work of demarcation; however, he desired first to obtain the cession by the Lower Creeks of the peninsula between the St. John's River and the Acklawaugh Creek. But in 1768 the Creeks considered the hunting grounds in East Florida their most valuable lands, since they were remote from their enemies, and they would have refused to make such a cession. Aware of this fact, Grant urged that demarcation be postponed until the Creeks could be brought to consent to his wishes. Stuart saw no harm from postponing the survey, and Hillsborough therefore gave his approval to this course.[9]

When London officials sanctioned the representation of the Board of Trade of March 7, 1768, they expected that the American colonies would deal with the Indian trade problem and that they would pass legislation to enforce the several Indian boundaries. It was obvious that the southern provinces could not meet the trade

[3] Stuart to Hillsborough, Aug. 16, 1768, CO, 5/69; Stuart to Gage, Aug. 22, 1768, Gage MSS.

[4] The Upper Creeks were too busy with the Choctaw war to send delegates. Since they had no villages near the line the boundary question did not directly affect them.

[5] Where George Galphin maintained his headquarters.

[6] Treaty of Augusta, Nov. 12, 1768, Gage MSS; "Journal of the Superintendant's proceedings," CO, 5/70.

[7] *GCR*, XV, 402–3; Lachlan McGillivray to Stuart, Dec. 14, 1768, CO, 5/70. McGillivray saw to it that all doubts regarding the course of the line were resolved in favor of Georgia. Savery drew a map of the line in 1769. There is a copy of it in the William L. Clements Library.

[8] Gage to Grant, April 24, 1769, Gage MSS.

[9] Stuart to Hillsborough, July 14, 1768, CO, 5/69; Stuart to Hillsborough, April 14, 1769, Hillsborough to Stuart, July 15, 1769, CO, 5/70.

problem except by common action. Stuart therefore urged the governors to employ the method of regulation he had striven to establish in 1765, but the reaction of the governors, except for Montfort Browne of West Florida, was unfavorable.[10] Wright proposed, instead, a division of the Indian country among the several colonies for purposes of trade. Since, as Hillsborough pointed out, it was unlikely that the colonies would agree to the partition, Wright abandoned his scheme.[11] In 1769–70 the South Carolina assembly approached the problem from another angle, suggesting that the southern provinces pass similar trade laws and coöperate in maintaining the peace.[12] South Carolina did not advocate this plan very earnestly, and failed to enact new legislation either to control the trade or to enforce her Indian boundary. Georgia finally passed an act to regulate the trade and also to protect her Indian boundary, but it was disallowed, because the Board of Trade felt that the clauses regarding the boundary were not germane to the general purpose of the statute.[13] The result was confusion in Indian affairs on the old southeastern frontier.

Even if the legislation of Georgia to maintain her Indian boundary had been approved, it would have been of little avail, for Wright himself showed utter lack of respect for the line that he had helped to draw. By the summer of 1771 he had granted lands as far as forty miles beyond it, although he could not possibly have done so by mistake.[14] Protests inevitably came from the Creeks against these grants as well as against settlements beyond the line by squatters, and also against incursions of hunters into the Creek reserves.[15] At a private conference held at the request of The Mortar at Augusta in October, 1769, both The Mortar and Emistisiguo complained to Stuart regarding abuses in the trade.[16] Particularly displeasing to the Creeks were little stores on the Georgia frontier that flourished by bartering rum to young braves for stolen horses.[17]

[10] See Stuart to Bull, Dec. 2, 1769, CO, 5/71.

[11] Wright to Hillsborough, Aug. 5, Oct. 5, 1768, Hillsborough to Wright, Dec. 10, 1768, *GCR*, XXXVII, 334–41, 369–70, 374–75.

[12] CHJSC, xxxviii, 140–41, 281, 317–18, 329.

[13] Stuart to Gage, Sept. 7, 1772, Gage MSS.

[14] Stuart to Gage, Aug. 31, 1771, Gage MSS.

[15] For example, Gun Merchant and other chiefs to Stuart, May 1, 1771, Gage MSS.

[16] Stuart to Hillsborough, Dec. 2, 1769, CO, 5/71.

[17] "Talk" from Escotchabie to Stuart, April 26, 1770, CO, 5/71. These stores were so productive of trouble that Stuart planned to investigate them in person. He was prevented from doing so by illness. Stuart to Hillsborough, July 16, 1770, *ibid.*

There was little Stuart could do to remove their grievances. When he sent David Taitt [18] to the Creeks in January, 1772, in the capacity of commissary, he instructed him to force traders operating without licenses to leave the nation, but Taitt could see no way to execute his orders.[19] Under the circumstances frontier strife was inevitable. In the spring of 1770 several fracases along Little River angered the frontiersmen so greatly that they armed themselves and traveled to Augusta, where they declared they would not permit traders to carry ammunition into the Indian country. At Augusta they unloaded several packhorses and threatened to slay the drivers.[20] In August of the same year Oakfuskie tribesmen slew two backsettlers, Thomas Jackson and George Buck. Wright sent out a body of militia to investigate the matter. The troops carried out their instructions, and also burned down a Creek village on the Oconee River, despite efforts on the part of their officers to restrain them. Fortunately, the Creeks, who considered outlying villages a source of weakness to their nation, exhibited no resentment. In 1771 frontiersmen on Briar Creek evened the score with the Oakfuskies by slaying one warrior of that town and whipping another.[21] In the following year John Carey, a backsettler, was slain by a Lower Creek. His murderer, however, was duly executed by the Indians.[22]

Relations between the Creeks and East Florida were much more satisfactory, partly because of lack of contact between whites and reds and partly because of Grant's determination that quarrels between the "crackers" and the Creeks should not menace the peace

[18] David Taitt, a Scot, was first given temporary appointment, but Stuart was so well pleased with his work that he employed him permanently. Stuart to Gage, May 23, Sept. 7, 1772, Gage MSS. He was paid out of Stuart's regular allowance. Taitt was assistant surveyor of West Florida from 1764 to 1767, and went to England in the latter year because of ill health. He returned to West Florida before May, 1769. Stuart considered him an excellent mathematician and surveyor, and employed his services in making maps of parts of West Florida and the Creek country. He continued in the southern department until 1779, when he was discharged by the West Florida commissioners for Indian affairs. Cameron failed to reëngage him. Taitt saw some service in the artillery at Charleston in 1779. When Mobile fell to the Spanish in 1780, he was made prisoner. Eventually released, he sailed for England from Charleston in January, 1782. In England he petitioned for new employment in the Indian service or, failing that, for an appointment in Senegambia, where he thought his experience in Indian affairs would be of value!

[19] David Taitt to Stuart, Oct. 19, 1772, Gage MSS.

[20] Stuart to Gage, Dec. 12, 1770, Gage MSS.

[21] Wright to Hillsborough, Oct. 8, 1770, *GCR*, XXXVII, 484–85; James Habersham to Hillsborough, Oct. 31, 1771, and enclosure, *ibid.*, 569–81.

[22] James Habersham to Hillsborough, April 24, 1772, *GCR*, XXXVII, 609–15.

of his province. Grant acted with military promptness when a colonist slew a Creek on St. John's River in 1769. The aggressor was seized, tried, and executed within three weeks of the crime, although careful precautions were necessary even in East Florida to ward off attempts at rescue on the part of other "crackers." Grant was equally opposed to breaches of the peace by the Creeks,[23] and they tried to coöperate. In response to insistent demands from Grant and Stuart for the punishment of those who had committed the two murders on St. Mary's River in 1767, the Creeks finally made a pathetic reply. An uncle of one of the slayers had attempted to execute him, but had lost his own life instead. Would not Grant consider his death adequate satisfaction? [24]

No doubt it was in part the relatively satisfactory state of relations between the Creeks and the colonies bordering upon the Atlantic that led Hillsborough to congratulate Stuart in June, 1772, because Indian affairs in the southern district seemed to go more smoothly than in past years.[25] But another Creek crisis was in the offing, caused in large part by a too-clever attempt on the part of the Cherokees to rid themselves of their trading debts at the expense of the Creeks.

As early as the summer of 1768 certain Cherokee chiefs had evinced willingness to make cessions of land to private individuals, in spite of the Proclamation of 1763. At that time Ouconnostotah and Saluy attempted to persuade Stuart to permit the Cherokees to give a piece of land twelve miles square in the valley of the Saluda River beyond the South Carolina Indian line to a son of Cameron by a Cherokee woman. When Stuart pointed out that their proposal was contrary to the proclamation, the chiefs adroitly argued that the proclamation did not apply, since Cameron's son was an Indian. At the Congress of Hard Labor the Cherokees importuned the superintendent so forcefully that he placed the matter before Hillsborough. The Cherokees actually measured off the land they desired to give, although Stuart prevented the completion of the cession, before Hillsborough could reply.[26]

[23] See Grant to Gage, March 5, 1769, Gage MSS.

[24] Grant to Hillsborough, July 10, 1770, CO, 5/551. The uncle was suspected of instigating the slayings.

[25] Hillsborough to Stuart, June 6, 1772, CO, 5/73.

[26] Stuart to Cameron, Dec. 11, 1770 (Abstract), Cameron to Stuart, Jan. 23, 1771 (Abstract), Stuart to Hillsborough, April 27, 1771, CO, 5/72; Stuart to Hillsborough, Feb. 9, 1772, CO, 5/73. To what extent Cameron was involved in the transaction it is impossible to say. He insisted "upon the word of a gentleman" that he had done nothing to motivate the action of the Cherokees—that he had actually tried to restrain them.

In the winter of 1768–69 another scheme to circumvent the proclamation came to light. When Dr. Walker and Andrew Lewis came to Charleston in January, 1769, Walker carried to Cameron a letter from David Ross, formerly a factor in the Virginia public trading company. Ross proposed to Cameron that they persuade the Cherokees to earmark for them some desirable lands and to insist that the grant be consummated at the next formal treaty negotiated by Stuart. Cameron reported Ross's overture to the superintendent, who placed the matter before Hillsborough. The minister instructed Stuart not to permit the inclusion of any provision giving approval to such a deal in the Treaty of Lochaber. Ross's scheme therefore fell through.[27] But though his project failed, Ross's technique offered too great possibilities to be ignored by land speculators in the South.

The next attempt to consummate a private purchase—in the final analysis a successful one—was made by Richard Pearis. According to Cameron, whom we may well believe, Pearis was a finished scoundrel; Cameron claimed that Pearis even managed to cheat Walker and Lewis while acting as their agent among the Cherokees. Certainly Pearis's activities in behalf of Walker and Lewis did not occupy all his energies. In 1769 he secretly and fraudulently secured the consent of a number of Lower Cherokees to a cession twelve miles square in the valley of the upper Saluda for his half-breed Cherokee son. In the following year with the aid of Saluy, whom he promised maintenance for life in return for his services, Pearis strove to secure the approval of the whole nation. He obtained signatures to a deed by representing to the Cherokees that it was a petition for the establishment of a trade with Virginia. Ouconnostotah opposed his scheme, and Stuart quashed his attempt to have the grant approved at Lochaber.[28] Pearis was not dismayed. With Jacob Hite, to whom he had sold part of the land, he simply assumed that the cession was complete and legal; and the superintendent was unable to stop him from making use of it. Because the land was within the jurisdiction of South Carolina Stuart finally appealed to the governor and council of that province for help. He was referred to the acting attorney general, James Simpson. Simpson unearthed the South Carolina act of 1739 forbidding private purchases and prosecuted Pearis and Hite. Late in 1773 in the

[27] Ross to Cameron, Dec. 20, 1768, Hillsborough to Stuart, April 14, 1770, CO, 5/71; Stuart to Hillsborough, April 27, 1771, CO, 5/72.

[28] John Watts to Stuart, May 17, 1770 (Abstract), Cameron to Stuart, June 27, 1770, Gage MSS; Stuart to Hillsborough, Nov. 28, 1770, April 27, 1771, CO, 5/72; CJSC, xxxvi, pt. 2, 174–77.

newly established circuit court at Ninety-Six, both were found guilty of violating the act. They were forced to renounce their titles, and were also fined. But Pearis placed the grant in his son's name in the winter of 1774–75, had it surveyed, and persuaded Edward Rutledge to make out titles for the son in the same court.[29] Pearis settled upon the land, was driven from it by the patriots at the onset of the Revolution, and was later compensated for its loss by the British Loyalist Commission![30]

Another attempt to carry through a private purchase was engineered by Edward Wilkinson, who had established himself as a Cherokee trader after the collapse of the South Carolina public trade. In 1770 Wilkinson made an agreement with the Cherokees providing for the cession to him of a large strip of land contiguous to those reserved for the sons of Cameron and Pearis, in exchange for the cancellation of their debts to him of over £8,000, but Stuart objected to the deal. He thereby placed Wilkinson in a very awkward position, for the Cherokees considered the debts already paid. Wilkinson then asked Stuart to arrange for a sale of the land by the Cherokees to the crown, Wilkinson to be repaid from the proceeds of the sale or to have the use of the land for ten years free of taxes and quitrents. Early in 1773 Stuart placed the Wilkinson problem before Dartmouth, indicating his disfavor and pointing out that Wilkinson would share in the proceeds of the "New Purchase," a project then just coming to fruition whereby all the Cherokee traders would secure cash in return for canceling trading debts. Although Wilkinson went to England in the spring of 1773 to attempt to gain the approval of Dartmouth, the minister merely ordered that he be given an appropriate sum from the money received by the sale of the "New Purchase."[31]

[29] Stuart to Haldimand, Aug. 20, 1773, B. M. Add. MSS., 21,672, pt. 3; Stuart to Gage, Dec. 25, 1773, Stuart to Haldimand, April 23, 1774, Gage MSS; Cameron to Stuart, Feb. 23, 1775, CO, 5/76.

[30] American Loyalist Transcripts, ii, 256, xxvi, 362–85. Pearis sold 30,000 acres to Hite for £2,500 (Virginia currency), but Hite failed to pay, and Pearis therefore claimed title to the whole tract. After a number of adventures at the beginning of the Revolution Pearis made his way to Pensacola late in 1776. There Stuart appointed him captain of one of four companies of Loyalists raised by the superintendent. At the close of the Revolution Pearis emigrated to the Bahamas. He asked over £15,000 in compensation from the Loyalist Commission. The Saluda tract constituted almost two thirds of his claim. He was actually given £5,624.

[31] Stuart to Dartmouth, Jan. 8, 1773, and enclosures, Dartmouth to Stuart, April 10, 1773, Stuart to Dartmouth, June 30, 1773, CO, 5/74; Dartmouth to Wright, April 10, 1773, *GCR*, XXXVIII, pt. I, 50–51.

Stuart's endeavors by legal action to enforce the South Carolina Indian line [32] were accorded full approval by Dartmouth and Gage, although both these officials had little hope that the courts could or would protect the Indian reserves.[33] But in his attempts to prevent the "New Purchase" Stuart was deserted by the home government.

For some years before 1770 Governor Wright had been eager to open up to settlement all the territory east of the Oconee and Broad rivers. On learning of the Wilkinson deal he conceived the idea of purchasing the south bank of the Savannah above Little River from the Cherokees in return for the cancellation of their trading debts.[34] Because of the reduction in prices resulting from the South Carolina public trading act of 1762, increased and vicious competition, and rather scanty returns of skins the Cherokee traders had suffered heavy losses since the peace of 1763. Poor yields had led the traders to give much more liberal credit than before, and by 1770 the Cherokees were heavily in debt. The traders therefore welcomed Wright's proposal. They offered to cancel the debts and to give the Cherokees all their stock on hand in return for such a cession, and the Indians, including even Ouconnostotah, happily

[32] Another land deal in which Stuart was involved concerned the Catawba reservation. After the reservation was definitely determined to lie entirely within South Carolina, in 1772, William Henry Drayton tried to obtain a twenty-one-year lease upon it from the government of South Carolina. By the terms of the proposed lease Drayton was to pay each Catawba warrior goods to the value of one guinea per annum, and the Indians were to retain full use of their towns and fields and the privilege of hunting as they wished. It was claimed that Drayton's purpose was to protect the reservation from speculators and squatters, and one modern authority has expressed an opinion that Drayton's intentions were unselfish. One may doubt, however, as Stuart did, that Drayton proposed to expend fifty to seventy guineas per annum without hope of reimbursement. Stuart protested to the governor and council on the ground that the proposed lease was in violation of the Treaty of Augusta of 1763, and it was denied. Stuart to Dartmouth, Dec. 27, 1772, CO, 5/74; St. George L. Sioussat, "The Breakdown of the Royal Management of Lands in the Southern Provinces, 1773–1775," *Agricultural History,* III (1929), 86, note 34.

[33] Dartmouth to Stuart, March 3, 1773, CO, 5/74; Gage to Stuart, March 27, 1773, Gage MSS.

[34] Wright later offered in justification of his project an argument that Stuart had given his "approbation and assistance" to Wilkinson. A recent writer has also indicated that Stuart favored Wilkinson. Sioussat, *op. cit.,* III, 84. Evidence other than Wright's charge is lacking to support this assertion. Stuart did inform Dartmouth that Wilkinson had not used the unscrupulous methods employed by Pearis, but he made it clear that Wilkinson's grant was legally in the same category as that of Pearis. See Stuart's reports to Dartmouth on the Wilkinson affair, cited above.

approved the bargain. A deed was signed on February 22, 1771, the accounts of the traders were destroyed, and their goods were distributed. When Cameron, who was absent from the nation at the time of this transaction, protested, the Cherokees refused to listen to him.

Although all seemed well for the traders, difficulties soon developed. The Cherokees had ceded a district about sixty miles square north of Little River and west of the Savannah. Part of this district, the area between Little River and Broad River, the Creeks claimed by virtue of conquest in the first half of the century. Moreover, the cession was, of course, in contravention of the Proclamation of 1763. Immediately before Stuart's departure for West Florida, in the spring of 1771, representatives of the traders approached the superintendent in an attempt to remove the latter difficulty. He condemned the cession as illegal, and insisted that the traders cease their intrigues with the Indians, but placed before Hillsborough the problem created by them.[35]

Meanwhile Wright was also trying to remove objections to the sale. He inspired the Cherokees to ask the crown for permission to grant the lands in question to the king for the benefit of the traders. At the same time he deceitfully informed the Creeks that he had had no share in the deal between the Cherokees and their traders, and suggested that the Creeks join in the cession; in fact, Wright also urged the Creeks to cede all their claims east of the Oconee River. In July, 1771, he sailed for England on leave of absence. In England he labored energetically to secure permission to purchase officially both the Cherokee cession and the left bank of the Oconee.[36]

As Stuart had foreseen, the Creeks were greatly angered by the attempt of the wily Cherokees to sell Creek lands. When the Cherokee traders arranged a meeting between delegations from the two nations in an effort to placate the Creeks, the Cherokees asserted their ownership of the disputed territory in such haughty language that the Creek emissaries indignantly left the conference. The Cherokee traders, probably at the urging of Wright, then changed their tactics. They approached the Creek traders with a proposal to divide the grant and to secure the consent of the Creeks by can-

[35] Cameron to Stuart, Jan. 23, 1771 (Abstract), Stuart to Gage, April 29, 1771, Gage MSS; Stuart to Hillsborough, April 27, 1771, CO, 5/72.

[36] In regard to Wright's part in the early development of the "New Purchase" see his "List of Papers Relative to My Memorial about Indian affairs &c With Some Notes and Remarks thereon," *GCR*, XXVIII, pt. 2, 786–90.

celing their trading debts. The Creek traders agreed. In the fall of 1771 they began to bring heavy pressure upon their clients.[37]

Stuart was opposed to the transactions of the Cherokee traders, not only because of their seeming illegality, but also because the deal, if completed, would lessen his own prestige, since he had had no share in it. If the Cherokee traders were permitted to execute their agreement, private negotiations between Indians and traders regarding lands would seem to meet the approval of government. Moreover, he feared trouble would result because of the fact that the Cherokees were trying to sell Creek lands. He therefore urged Hillsborough that the deed obtained by the Cherokee traders be rendered invalid.[38] Hillsborough approved of Stuart's attitude and ordered him to oppose the Cherokee traders. However, Wright, with the support of merchants trading to Georgia, including Stuart's son-in-law, James Graham,[39] persuaded the minister of the desirability of expansion in Georgia. In January, 1772, Hillsborough instructed James Habersham, president of the Georgia council and acting governor in Wright's absence, to aid in preventing the execution of the private cession made by the Cherokees. At the same time he informed Stuart that he could see no objection to a large cession south of the Savannah, provided it was made to the crown by both the Cherokees and Creeks, with part of the proceeds of the sale of the land going to the traders.[40] Hillsborough resigned his office before a decision was reached concerning the proposal advanced by Wright, but he recommended it to his successor.[41]

By the spring of 1772 the Creek traders had succeeded in winning over most of their clients, although they were opposed by The Mortar and Emistisiguo. In the following fall the traders held a general conference with the Creeks, who offered, in exchange for the cancellation of their debts, to cede all the lands to which the Cherokees had abandoned their rights, and even more.[42] But David

[37] Stuart to Hillsborough, Feb. 9, June 12, 1772 (Private), memorial by Creek and Cherokee traders to Stuart, Sept. 10, 1771, memorial by George Galphin, Robert Mackay, James Jackson, and Andrew McLean to Stuart, Nov. 13, 1771, CO, 5/73.

[38] Stuart to Hillsborough, Sept. 23, 1771, CO, 5/72.

[39] Memorial by Wright to Hillsborough, read Dec. 12, 1771, memorial by merchants trading to Georgia to Hillsborough, read March 25, 1772, *GCR*, XXVIII, pt. 2, 765–84, 851–53.

[40] This fact is an indication that Hillsborough was not an implacable enemy to westward expansion in America in 1772.

[41] Stuart to Gage, Sept. 7, Nov. 24, 1772, Gage MSS.

[42] Stuart to Hillsborough, June 13, 1772, CO, 5/73; David Taitt to Stuart, Oct. 19, 1772, Gage MSS.

Taitt arrived at the conference in time to prevent ratification of this agreement. He then opened negotiations with the Creeks as a royal official and intermediary. They reconsidered the matter. Finally, they offered to sell a strip of territory about thirty miles wide south of the Savannah between Little River and Tugaloo Old Town, a strip that included Cherokee territory above Little River which had not been sold to the Cherokee traders! Interested Georgians desired Stuart to accept this offer.[43] Since he foresaw trouble ahead unless the Cherokees agreed, he reserved the matter for future consideration.

At length, on December 9, 1772, Lord Dartmouth, in accordance with a report of the Board of Trade of November 9, sent Stuart instructions to make a purchase from the Cherokees and Creeks at a general congress. But the minister refused to authorize the purchase of all the territory desired by Wright; he ordered Stuart to negotiate only for the lands already privately ceded to the traders. The customary presents were to be furnished by the traders, who were to be paid for these and for canceling the trade debts from the proceeds of the sale of the ceded lands.[44] Stuart invited the Creeks and Cherokees to a general congress to be held at Augusta on May 25, 1773. Then new difficulties arose. Wright returned to Georgia early in 1773. Soon afterward, no doubt with his blessing, the Georgia assembly formally urged that all Creek claims east of the Oconee should also be bought. Stuart, however, feared that the Creeks, already extremely uneasy at the prospect of losing lands, might go to war rather than agree; and he refused to act upon this request without specific instructions from home.[45] Furthermore, although the traders had put in claims for three times as much money as Wright had expected, they failed to furnish the requisite presents, which Stuart was forced to supply.[46]

The congress actually opened in June, with representatives of the Creeks, Cherokees, and Catawbas present.[47] Ouconnostotah,

[43] "Talk" from Lower Creeks to Stuart, Sept. 19, 1772, Stuart to Gage, Nov. 24, 1772, Gage MSS.

[44] *GCR,* XXXVIII, pt. 1, 15–26; Dartmouth to Stuart, Dec. 9, 1772 (Separate), CO, 5/73.

[45] *GCR,* XV, 425–26; Stuart to Dartmouth, April 8, 1773, CO, 5/74; Stuart to Gage, April 22, 1773, Gage MSS.

[46] Stuart to Haldimand, Feb. 10, April 23, 1774, Gage MSS.

[47] The object of the Catawbas was to obtain the services of a missionary. Stuart referred their request to Dartmouth, who declared that the question was one to be decided by the governments of the Carolinas. Dartmouth to Stuart, Oct. 28, 1773, CO, 5/74. On missionary activities among the southern Indians from 1754 to 1775 see Appendix C.

however, remained at home to confer with The Mortar, a suspicious circumstance, especially since emissaries from the Shawnees were expected to join in their discussions. The Creeks had only consented to any sort of a cession because of the influence of George Galphin and Lachlan McGillivray.[48] Although the Cherokee delegation offered to cede all the territory desired by Georgia, the Creeks refused to abandon more than the left bank of the upper Ogeechee, and Wright was forced to accept their offer. The Cherokees, however, ceded part of their lands lying north and east of the Broad River. In all, over 2,100,000 acres were thrown open to settlement. This boundary problem was at length decided, though not without misgivings on the part of Stuart and Wright, who received private information during the congress that the Creeks were preparing to attack Georgia. When presents were distributed, Stuart and Wright prudently gave out no ammunition.[49] (Regarding the "New Purchase," see Map 3, p. 178.)

As Stuart had foreseen, the "New Purchase" promptly brought on a new crisis. The surveying of the line was quickly completed, but immediately afterward two Cherokees who had aided in this task were slain by backsettler Hezekiah Collins [50] near Broad River; and a white man was murdered by the Cherokees about the same time. Nevertheless, Ouconnostotah was still peace-minded. He had refused to join The Mortar and the Shawnees in an attack on the English, and at the close of 1773 he came in person to Charleston to assure Stuart of his pacific intentions.[51] There Stuart entertained him royally, even securing his election to membership in the St.

[48] David Taitt to Stuart, March 16, 1772, CO, 5/73; *GCR*, XII, 439.

[49] Stuart to Dartmouth, June 21, 30, 1773, CO, 5/74; Stuart to Gage, July 5, 1773, Gage MSS. It is an interesting fact that the "New Purchase," characterized by chicanery from its inception, had repercussions as late as 1850, and that suspicions (though not proof) of corruption accompanied negotiations regarding George Galphin's claims arising from it until these were finally settled. The British government in 1790 compensated all the traders who had remained loyal to the crown, but Galphin served as Indian agent for the Continental Congress, and therefore was not included among these. He and his heirs sought redress of Georgia and failed; and then his heirs approached the federal government. Robert Toombs, the advocate of the Galphin heirs, succeeded in persuading Congress to pass an act permitting Zachary Taylor's secretary of the treasury to hear the claim. The claim, of almost £10,000, was paid; and in 1850 the heirs were also given $191,000 in interest. Oddly enough, George W. Crawford, then secretary of war, was attorney for the Galphin heirs at the time the interest was awarded, and he received one half of the sum granted.

[50] Collins was apprehended in South Carolina, but escaped.

[51] Stuart to Dartmouth, Aug. 5, 24, 1773, CO, 5/74; Stuart to Haldimand, Jan. 5, 1774, B. M. Add. MSS, 21,672, pt. 4.

Andrew's Society.[52] The more serious problems created by the cession inevitably arose from resentment among the Creeks. The traders had acted in part under pressure from their merchants; they had been compelled to turn over their claims to the latter in order to meet their own debts; and as a result they obtained nothing substantial for themselves.[53] They now communicated their own discontent to the already resentful Creeks, and their influence proved to be very disturbing.[54] The continued lack of trade regulation also increased the dissatisfaction of the Creeks.[55]

In December, 1773, a Lower Creek murdered one of his fellows near the head of Ogeechee River. Since there were no witnesses, he persuaded his people that a settler named William White dwelling near the scene of the crime had in fact committed the murder. On Christmas Day a body of Lower Creeks led by the real murderer attacked and slew White and his family; and on January 14, 1774, a second body of seventeen Lower Creeks murdered William Sherrill, a neighboring settler, and his family. Thirteen persons in all were killed by the two parties, although the Creeks also lost five men at Sherrill's. A posse of Georgia militia set out in pursuit of the second group, but was attacked on January 23 and forced to retreat. Two or three militiamen were killed, and one was captured.[56] The frontier was immediately plunged into an uproar, and many settlers left their homes to escape further attacks.[57]

Stuart was fully aware of the gravity of the situation thus created. He immediately revoked a leave of absence he had given Charles Stuart, and ordered him to hurry back to West Florida [58] to incite the Choctaws to greater efforts against the Creeks; and he instructed John McIntosh to prevent mediation by the Chickasaws between the Creeks and the Choctaws and, if possible, to secure Chickasaw

[52] Ouconnostotah's certificate of membership is to be found in the Papers of the Continental Congress, No. 71, Vol ii.

[53] David Taitt to Stuart, March 16, 1772, N. D. Mereness, ed., *Travels in the American Colonies* (New York, 1916), 524–25; David Taitt's Journal, *ibid.*, 542–43.

[54] Stuart to Haldimand, Feb. 3, 1774, B. M. Add. MSS, 21,672, pt. 4.

[55] David Taitt to Stuart, Feb. 25, 1774, B. M. Add. MSS, 21,672, pt. 5.

[56] Wright to Bull, Jan. 27, 1774, CJSC, xxxviii, 15–17. The unfortunate white captive was afterward tortured to death.

[57] Stuart offered some severe strictures upon the valor of the frontiersmen. "[The backsettlers] in this part of America although insolent and savage when they may be so with impunity, behave like the most dastardly of mankind whenever they apprehend danger." Stuart to Gage, May 12, 1774, Gage MSS.

[58] Charles Stuart was at Charleston on his way to Europe.

aid in case of war. Cameron was ordered to keep a watchful eye upon the Cherokees.[59] Both he and Wright informed Haldimand[60] and Dartmouth of the critical state of affairs. Wright, whose policy was largely responsible for the crisis, now, at the urging of the Georgia assembly, begged Haldimand for a force of regulars to protect Georgia, asserting that the Georgia militia was useless and that 500 persons had already fled the province.[61] The Georgia council also petitioned the king for troops. The council alleged that the frontier would have been made safe by populating the "New Purchase," but that the Creeks had prevented Georgia from taking this excellent measure for defense![62]

After completing his arrangements to meet a possible conflict Stuart went to Savannah in April to join Wright in a general conference with the Creeks. There he discovered that David Taitt had safely escorted the traders out of the Creek villages at the first reports of the murders and that he had succeeded in persuading most of the Creek chiefs to meet Stuart and Wright at Savannah to discuss the situation. But the Cherokees, jealous of the Creeks, now saw an opportunity to involve their neighbors in a war with the English. They informed the Creeks that the chiefs who went to Savannah would suffer the fate of the Cherokees who visited Lyttelton at Charleston in 1759; and they succeeded in persuading most of the Creek chiefs to remain at home. Emistisiguo and Neathlacco despised the Cherokee warning and proceeded to Savannah. Before they could complete their "talks" with Wright and Stuart a new outrage occurred. Mad Turkey, an Oakfuskie chief, was so indiscreet as to visit the English settlements; and he was treacherously slain by Thomas Fee, a cowardly blacksmith. Although Fee was seized and imprisoned in the jail at Ninety-Six, the jail was forced by a body of frontiersmen, and the slayer was released. About the same time one of the Creek murderers suffered death at the hands of an avenger. Emistisiguo continued negotiations in spite of these events. He agreed with Wright and Stuart that five Lower Creeks must die to balance accounts; and he assured them that he would call a grand council of the whole Creek nation to secure the consent

[59] Stuart to Haldimand, Feb. 3, 1774, B. M. Add. MSS, 21,672, pt. 4; Stuart to Haldimand, Feb. 10, 1774, Gage MSS.

[60] Acting commander in chief in America from June, 1773, to June, 1774, in the absence of Gage.

[61] Wright to Haldimand, Feb. 15, 1774, B. M. Add. MSS, 21,672, pt. 5; Wright to Haldimand, March 10, 1774, Gage MSS.

[62] *GCR,* XVII, 769–70.

of his people.[63] Stuart then returned to Charleston, but held himself in readiness for an early return to Georgia. He stationed David Taitt at Augusta to keep close watch upon the situation.

Soon afterward, to bring pressure upon the Creeks, Stuart, the governors, and the military officials in the South undertook to cut off the flow of trade to the Creeks and to prevent supplies from reaching them through the Cherokees. Their efforts, although at first not completely successful, had an effect, especially since they were coupled with renewed activity on the part of the Choctaws and threats of war by the Six Nations if the Creeks should attack the English. The Upper Creeks, though they desired the life of a prominent white man in exchange for that of the Mad Turkey, were not wholly in sympathy with their quarrelsome brethren of the Lower towns. Even The Mortar was not unfriendly during the spring and summer of 1774. The Seminoles were not hostile, and the Lower Creeks were divided. The Cowetas, who were chiefly responsible for the original outbreaks, were, of course, opposed to complying with the demands of Stuart and Wright; other Lower towns were willing to make a settlement.[64] When Emistisiguo called the grand council representatives from twenty-six towns appeared. On May 26 they collectively informed Wright that they had decided upon the execution of five ringleaders in the attacks on the Georgia frontier, and also of two other Creeks responsible for the killing of two whites a short time before near St. Joseph's Bay in East Florida. The condemned warriors attempted to flee, but Ochtulkee, who was the leading figure in the Georgia murders, was caught and executed, as well as the two men responsible for the East Florida slayings.[65] Then the Creeks urged that their traders be sent back to the nation, for they were told that George Galphin believed they had given adequate satisfaction.[66]

Wright was unwilling to abate his demands. He sent a messenger to require the execution of the four murderers still unpunished, but the courier was afraid to deliver the message. In July Stuart

[63] Wright to Haldimand, April 18, 1774, Stuart to Gage, May 12, 1774, Gage MSS; Stuart to Haldimand, April 23, 1774, B. M. Add. MSS, 21,672, pt. 6; Stuart to Dartmouth, May 6, 1774, CO, 5/75.

[64] Taitt to Stuart, June 3, 1774, Captain Fordyce to Haldimand, June 9, 1774, Stuart to Haldimand, June 25, 1774, Andrew McLean to William Ogilvie, May 13, 1774, William Ogilvie to Haldimand, June 8, 1774, Gage MSS.

[65] Wright to Stuart, June 13, 1774, "A Talk from the Pumpkin King, The Head Men of the Hitchitaws, Pallachocolas Occonees & Oakmulgees," June 23, 1774, Stuart to Gage, July 3, 1774, Gage MSS.

[66] Taitt to Stuart, July 4, 1774, Gage MSS, also "talk" cited in preceding note.

returned to Georgia and sent another courier with a "talk" to the same effect. He set a time limit of forty days for an answer. Thereupon the Creeks informally agreed to comply. On August 20 a number of chiefs conferred with Wright, Stuart, and James Habersham, and they promised complete satisfaction.[67] Wright continued, however, to plague Gage with appeals for troops.[68]

Upon hearing of the outbreak on the Ogeechee Haldimand seriously considered hurrying to Georgia in person to concert measures with Stuart and the southern governors to meet the crisis.[69] But after the initial shock had passed and an accommodation seemed fairly probable, Haldimand came to believe that the principal cause of Wright's demands for troops was his desire to have their pay spent in Georgia. In fact, both Haldimand and Gage were disgusted by Wright's repeated calls for aid, for they were well aware that his difficulties were largely occasioned by his own conduct. Busily engaged with a much more serious crisis in Massachusetts, Gage remarked sarcastically that Wright believed the safety of America lay in maintaining troops on the Georgia frontier. He was positively opposed to sending the regulars where they would be exposed to Indian attacks brought on by the activities of land speculators and the lawless conduct of American frontiersmen.[70] For months he ignored Wright's pleas, and his reply, which came after the Creek crisis was over, was a flat refusal, coupled with advice to accept the overtures of the Creeks.[71] Dartmouth informed Stuart that no troops could be sent to Georgia. He left the management of the crisis to the superintendent, counseled by Wright, in the hope that Stuart would secure a peaceful settlement. However, he approved of cutting off the Creek trade.[72]

Wright's fears were partly justified, for the time limit set by

[67] "Talk" by Stuart to Chiefs of Upper and Lower Creeks, July —, 1774, Wright to Gage, Aug. 21, 1774, Gage MSS; Stuart to Dartmouth, Dec. 15, 1774, CO, 5/76.

[68] Wright to Gage, Aug. 19, Sept. 9, 1774, Gage MSS.

[69] Haldimand to Stuart, March 13, 1774 (Extract), Gage MSS; Haldimand tc Lord Barrington, March 2, 1774, calendared in Douglas Brymner, *Report on Canadian Archives, 1885* (1886), 229.

[70] Haldimand to Gage, April 6, Aug. 6, 1774, Gage to Haldimand, Aug. 18, 1774, Gage MSS.

[71] Gage to Wright, Aug. 18, 1774, Gage MSS. The letter failed to arrive at its destination. A copy of it reached Wright in a later letter from Gage. Wright also asked Stuart to enlist Choctaw parties openly against the Creeks, but Stuart refused. Stuart to Gage, Sept. 14, 1774, *ibid.*

[72] Dartmouth to Stuart, May 4, July 6, 1774, circular letter from Dartmouth to Bull, Tonyn, and Chester, July 6, 1774, CO, 5/75.

Stuart expired without formal action by the Creeks. The failure of the Indians to respond was undoubtedly caused largely by certain traders who furnished the Creeks with goods and ammunition at this dangerous juncture, in spite of the trade embargo and considerations of public welfare. Governor Patrick Tonyn of East Florida seized a whole shipload of ammunition intended for the Creeks, but he allowed a supply of goods worth £1,400 to slip through to the nation.[73] Georgia traders both secretly and openly defied Wright's embargo. It was not until midsummer that Wright called into service rangers who more or less effectively restrained the traders.[74] Fortunately, the Creeks were unable to procure ammunition from the Cherokees, for Cameron so strictly limited the supplies carried up by the Cherokee traders that the Cherokees themselves were embarrassed for lack of powder and lead.[75]

That the Creeks were not unanimously for peace in the fall of 1774 is clearly shown by the last activities of that indefatigable intriguer The Mortar. Although the French were gone, there were still French officers in the service of Spanish Louisiana! The Mortar conceived an amazing plan to secure a trade with Louisiana and military aid from France through these officers. With eighty Upper Creek warriors he set out for New Orleans. However, his party was fired upon by thirty Choctaws as it traveled down the Alabama River. The Creeks landed and pursued their enemies to William Strother's plantation opposite Mobile. Driving off the Strother family, the Choctaws intrenched themselves in the house and an outlying kitchen. After a three-day siege The Mortar's party burned down the buildings, and the Choctaws took refuge in a garden surrounded by a picket fence. Sure of their prey, the Creeks renewed their assault, but The Mortar fell fatally wounded before the fire of the desperate Choctaws. His companions returned home in disappointment. A body of a hundred Lower Creeks which passed Pensacola to assist The Mortar likewise abandoned their mission.[76]

Nevertheless, the Creeks had good reason to come to terms with Stuart and Wright. In spite of clandestine trading they suffered from a lack of ammunition and other goods. They were well aware

[73] Tonyn to Dartmouth, Aug. 5, 1774, CO, 5/554; Stuart to Gage, Sept. 14, 1774, Gage MSS; *GCR*, XII, 405–10.

[74] Taitt to Stuart, July 7, Aug. 29, 1774, Gage MSS.

[75] Cameron to Stuart, July 4, 1774, Gage MSS.

[76] Taitt to Stuart, Dec. 17, 1774, Stuart to Gage, Jan. 18, 1775, Gage MSS; Charles Stuart to Stuart, Dec. 12, 1774, CO, 5/76; *South-Carolina and American General Gazette,* Jan. 6, 1775.

that the Cherokees were encouraging them to fight because the Cherokees desired their destruction; [77] moreover, they were suffering rather severely from attacks by the Choctaws, who maintained superiority over them during 1774. With such a discouraging outlook the more warlike factions were compelled to listen to the prudent Emistisiguo.[78]

In September Stuart learned from Taitt that the Creeks had bowed to his ultimatum. From the Creeks themselves came "talks" declaring that two more murderers had been executed, and that two others named Houmachta and Sophia had fled to the Cherokees for refuge. They promised to return all fugitive slaves and stolen cattle, and informed Stuart that they were sending emissaries to Savannah to make a formal peace. Wright dispatched militia to escort the Indian representatives,[79] and they arrived safely. At Savannah on October 20 the Creeks concluded a treaty of friendship with Stuart and Wright in which they repeated the promises made in their "talks." They pledged themselves again to try to apprehend Houmachta and Sophia, and promised to refrain from stealing horses and cattle and from molesting white settlers in any way. In return, the English were to reopen the trade. The treaty also provided for the establishment of a quasi-neutral zone on the Georgia frontier.[80]

The Creeks thereafter made honest efforts to execute the treaty. They gave up thirteen fugitive slaves. In 1775 they sent out a party to hunt down Houmachta and Sophia, but the two warriors were protected by the Cherokees.[81]

Amazing as it may see, the crisis which arose from the "New Purchase" did not prevent either private speculators or the southern governors from seeking further cessions from the Creeks. Even before the signing of the Treaty of Savannah Jonathan Bryan, a Georgia colonist, obtained through fraud a ninety-nine-year lease

[77] Cameron reported that the Cherokees "would be very glad to see the Creeks brought down to their marrow bones" and that Saluy's followers offered to take up arms against them. Cameron to Stuart, July 4, 1774 (Abstract), Gage MSS.

[78] Stuart to Haldimand, Nov. 20, 1774, B. M. Add. MSS, 21,672, pt. 6.

[79] Stuart to Gage, Oct. 6, 1774, Gage MSS; Stuart to Dartmouth, Oct. 6, 1774, CO, 5/75.

[80] Treaty of Savannah, Oct. 20, 1774, Stuart to Gage, Nov. 19, 1774, Gage MSS. The Creeks promised not to build villages on the banks of the Oconee and the Ockmulgee, and Stuart and Wright engaged themselves to prevent whites from hunting on the northern bank of the Oconee.

[81] Stuart to Dartmouth, May 20, 1775, "talk" by Stuart to Cherokee chiefs, Aug. 30, 1775, CO, 5/76.

from seven or eight Creeks of all the lands of their nation in East Florida. At Savannah Stuart upbraided the Lower Creeks for making this grant. They explained how the situation had arisen and declared the lease void. Bryan then waylaid twenty Lower Creeks on their way home from Savannah, plied them so energetically with liquor that one of them died, and obtained a second lease carrying the same stipulations.[82] Governor Tonyn fruitlessly searched for legal means to quash Bryan's lease.[83] However, it was rendered ineffective by the Revolution.[84]

No doubt inspired by Bryan's action, both Wright and Tonyn tried to obtain new cessions from the Lower Creeks. Tonyn sought the complete removal of the tribe from East Florida, while Wright desired to obtain the left bank of the Oconee in exchange for a pardon to Houmachta and Sophia. Stuart disapproved heartily of Tonyn's proposal, but was at a loss regarding Wright's.[85] Gage urged him to oppose it, for he thought that such an exchange would create a very bad precedent. When Stuart informed Tonyn that his scheme was impracticable, Tonyn dropped it. Wright also abandoned his plan.[86]

As Stuart's attitude toward Wright's last land scheme indicates, he had given up hope before the Revolution of maintaining the Indian boundary lines in the South under the conditions then existing. Early in 1775 he despairingly informed Dartmouth that satisfactory provincial enactments to protect the lines could not be secured and that an act of Parliament was necessary. As Stuart no doubt expected, Dartmouth replied that such an act could not be considered at so critical a time in Anglo-American relations.[87]

The Creek crisis of 1774 produced one interesting result. It brought about the resurrection of Stuart's trade scheme of 1765. Wright adopted Stuart's regulations as his own and entrusted en-

[82] Samuel Thomas to Taitt, Dec. 10, 1774, Taitt to Stuart, Dec. 29, 1774, Stuart to Gage, Jan. 18, 1775, Gage MSS; Stuart to Dartmouth, Jan. 3, 1775, CO, 5/76. William Drayton, attorney general of East Florida, was affiliated with Bryan in this project, but he proved to Stuart's satisfaction that he had acted with Bryan on the assumption that any grant which might be obtained would conform to the Proclamation of 1763. Drayton to Stuart, July 14, 1775, and enclosed apologia, Stuart to Dartmouth, July 27, 1775, *ibid.*

[83] Tonyn to Dartmouth, Dec. 18, 1774, CO, 5/555.

[84] Bryan became a patriot.

[85] Tonyn to Dartmouth, Dec. 18, 1774, CO, 5/555; Wright to Stuart, Jan. 12, 1775 (Abstract), Stuart to Gage, Jan. 18, 1775, Gage MSS.

[86] Gage to Stuart, March 11, 1775, Stuart to Gage, May 26, 1775, Gage MSS.

[87] Stuart to Dartmouth, Jan. 3, 1775, Dartmouth to Stuart, March 3, 1775, CO, 5/76.

forcement of them to Stuart's department. Governor Peter Chester of West Florida followed suit, and William Bull looked favorably upon the idea.[88] Dartmouth gave hearty approval and urged Stuart to do everything possible toward executing it.[89] At last a workable plan to control the trade had received freely given support from the governors of the colonies chiefly concerned. After striving for twelve years to obtain a sound and general system of regulation Stuart was on the verge of success. The onset of the Revolution put an end to this scheme, as it did to many another.[90]

[88] Stuart to Dartmouth, Dec. 15, 1774, CO, 5/76; Chester to Dartmouth, Jan. 22, 1775, CO, 5/592.

[89] Dartmouth to Stuart, Feb. 1, 1775, CO, 5/76.

[90] It is by no means certain that the plan would have been completely successful. Taitt reported that George Galphin ignored Wright's rules and declared openly that he would not obey them. Taitt to Stuart, Dec. 17, 1774, Gage MSS.

CHAPTER XVIII

INDIAN AFFAIRS IN THE WEST FLORIDA AREA, 1768–75

ALTHOUGH the Indian relations of West Florida were never so strained as those of the older southern colonies during the period 1768–75, they nevertheless constituted an important phase in the activities of the southern Indian department. Here also boundary disputes and questions of trade regulation were of major importance. Other problems arose from the presence of the Spanish west of the Mississippi.

Perhaps the most significant factor in Indian affairs in the western portion of the southern district during this period was the Upper Creek–Choctaw war. The entrance of the Chickasaws into the war in 1768 marked a turning point in the tide of battle, for thereafter fortune slowly veered toward the Choctaws.[1] In August, 1768, the Upper Creeks actually made peace overtures. By Shelburne's altruistic instructions of 1766 Stuart was bound not to oppose such a peace, but he was determined, for reasons of prestige, that negotiations should be conducted only through his department.[2] This policy was sanctioned by Hillsborough in 1769.[3]

Although the Upper Creeks decided in the fall of 1768 to continue the struggle, they were again willing to make an accommodation by 1770. Stuart then ordered Charles Stuart to undertake mediation.[4] However, before any action was taken by the agent, the Chickasaws had dropped out of the conflict. In June, 1770, representatives of the Upper Creeks and Choctaws met Charles Stuart at Mobile to discuss peace terms. These negotiations were on the verge of success when a party of Lower Creeks murdered four Choctaws. Since the Choctaws considered the Lower and Upper Creeks one

[1] The Chickasaws also tried to secure the Cherokees as allies, but Stuart prevented this move from succeeding. Stuart to Hillsborough, May 7, 1768, CO, 5/69.

[2] Stuart to Gage, Aug. 22, 1768, Gage MSS.

[3] Hillsborough to Stuart, July 15, 1769, CO, 5/70.

[4] Stuart to Hillsborough, June 8, 1770, CO, 5/71.

people, they were convinced that they had been tricked and broke off the negotiations. The traders continually incited the Indians to attack each other, and the war therefore continued.[5] Moreover, in the course of 1770 Hillsborough came to fear that the two tribes might attack West Florida if they were at peace with each other; and he ordered Stuart to cease his efforts at mediation.[6] Stuart contended that failure to offer mediation would have united the antagonists against the English by convincing them that the English were still following the policy of "divide and rule."[7] But the superintendent, of course, obeyed.

Charles Stuart had continued negotiations between the Creeks and the Choctaws during the fall of 1770; indeed, he had arranged for a final ratification of peace when news of Hillsborough's changed attitude gave him pause. He then proceeded to undo his own labors and to foment discord so adroitly between Creek and Choctaw representatives meeting at Mobile in December that the war was continued.[8] In 1771, and again in 1772, Handsome Fellow tried to secure Chickasaw mediation, but failed; from 1771 until 1776 the war went on without interruption. Charles Stuart himself contributed materially to its continuation by insidiously persuading the Choctaws that all peace overtures on the part of the Creeks were intended merely to collect useful information.[9] During these six years the Choctaws seem to have had the best of the fighting. Emistisiguo was severely injured in one affray in 1773,[10] and The Mortar, as noted elsewhere, was fatally wounded in the following year. The war was finally ended by Stuart because he desired the full support of both tribes in the Revolution.[11]

The Creek-Choctaw war was not the only cause of unrest among the Indians of the hinterland of West Florida during the period 1768–70, for the lack of trade regulations was certainly very disturbing. From July, 1769, to August, 1770, West Florida did not even bother to issue licenses. In 1770 Charles Stuart estimated that four fifths of the skins brought in by the traders were purchased

[5] Charles Stuart to Stuart, Aug. 26 (Abstract), Sept. 27, 1770 (Abstract), Gage MSS.

[6] Hillsborough to Stuart, Feb. 11, May 4, 1771, CO, 5/72.

[7] Stuart to Hillsborough, Dec. 2, 1770, Sept. 24, 1771, CO, 5/72.

[8] Charles Stuart to Stuart, Dec. 26, 1770, Stuart to Hillsborough, March 5, 1771, CO, 5/72.

[9] Charles Stuart to Chester, April 10, 1771, March 10, 1773 (Abstract), Gage MSS.

[10] Stuart to Haldimand, Jan. 5, 1774, B. M. Add. MSS, 21,671, pt. 4.

[11] Chester to Germain, Oct. 25, 1776, CO, 5/593.

with rum.[12] Moreover, an attempt by a group of merchants to monopolize the Choctaw and Chickasaw trade created dissension that communicated itself to the Indians. The Chickasaws had a special grievance in that eighteen of their traders took to hunting for themselves. There were also difficulties over land. Settlements made in the Tensaw area beyond the boundary of 1765 irritated the Upper Creeks, while the Chickasaws were displeased because of plantations established by traders in their hunting grounds. The Upper Creeks, Choctaws, and Chickasaws were all clamoring for presents.[13] And, finally, Spanish intrigues among the Indians and attempts by Shawnee emissaries to form a general alliance against the English added to the confusion.

Disorder consequently increased on the borders of the settled area in West Florida, especially after the discharge of the commissaries. In 1769 reports came to Pensacola of depredations committed upon the property of French settlers on Pearl River and near Lakes Ponchartrain and Maurepas, and of pranks perpetrated by the Indians upon soldiers on wood-gathering details.[14] In January, 1770, Lieutenant Governor Durnford declared that only Pensacola and Mobile were free from Indian incursions.[15] It is quite probable that Durnford exaggerated the gravity of the situation in order to persuade Gage to send troops to West Florida, because they would bring money into the province.[16] On January 21 a band of eighteen Choctaws plundered the store of John Bradley, a trader at the Natchez. Bradley, with a group of friends pursued the Choctaws and attacked them, killing two and wounding one. Bradley and his friends then fled down the Mississippi to New Orleans, warning other traders that the Choctaws were about to take the warpath. But Durnford and Haldimand were not alarmed.[17] The Choctaw chiefs declined to consider the casualties resulting from the Bradley attack an affront to their nation. They expressed a desire for peace and saw to it that most of Bradley's goods were returned.[18] Never-

[12] Charles Stuart to Stuart, June 17, Aug. 26, 1770, CO, 5/72.

[13] Stuart to Hillsborough, Dec. 2, 1770, Charles Stuart to Stuart, Dec. 26, 1770, Chester to Stuart, Sept. 10, 1771, CO, 5/72.

[14] Captain Patrick Innes to Gage, Aug. 19, Oct. 10, 1769, Gage MSS; Montfort Browne to Hillsborough, Oct. 8, 1769, CO, 5/587, pt. 1.

[15] Durnford to Gage, Jan. 27, 1770, Gage MSS.

[16] After 1763 the governors of Georgia and the Floridas commonly exaggerated Indian unrest for this reason.

[17] Durnford to Gage, Feb. 7, 1770, and enclosures, Haldimand to Gage, April 11, 1770, Gage MSS.

[18] Durnford to Gage, May 4, 1770, Gage MSS.

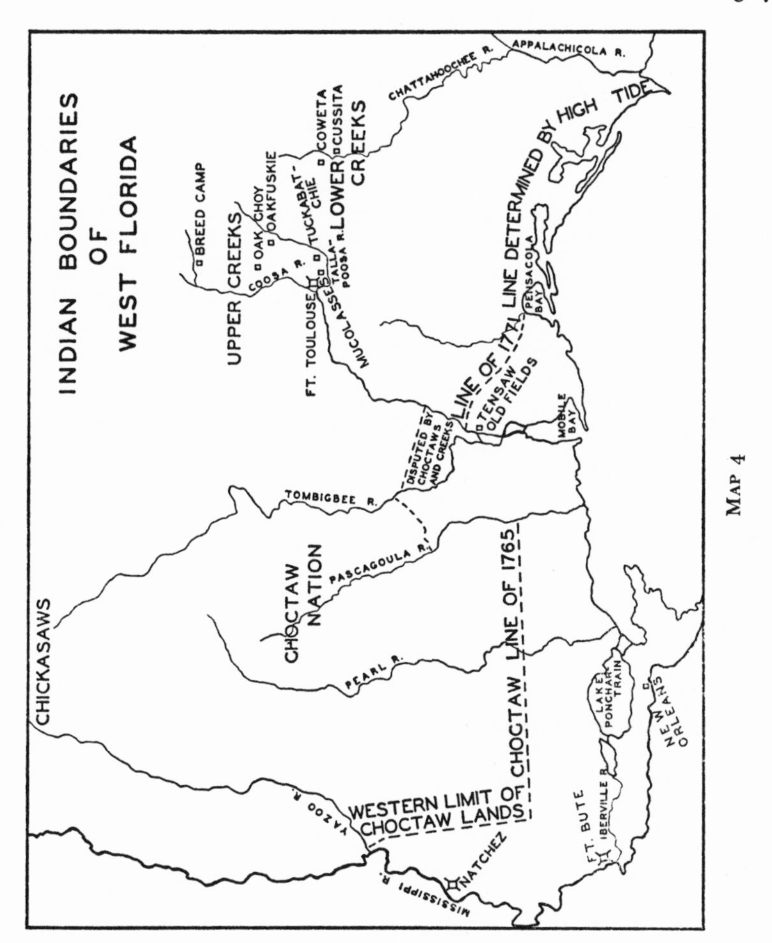

MAP 4

theless both the Choctaws and the Creeks continued to raid outlying plantations.[19]

Montfort Browne, in his period of office as chief executive of West Florida from 1767 to 1770, did nothing toward bringing order in the Indian trade,[20] and he also conferred grants of land beyond the Creek boundary near Tensaw.[21] Elias Durnford, however, who was acting governor of West Florida for a short time in 1770, made

[19] Durnford to Hillsborough, July 14, 1770, CO, 5/587, pt. 2.

[20] See Haldimand to Gage, April 11, 1770, Gage MSS.

[21] As Stuart later remarked, it is quite unlikely that Browne did not know the true course of the line.

sincere efforts to deal with the Indian problem. He proposed that the southern Indian country be divided into areas controlled by adjacent colonies and that enforcement of trading rules be placed in the hands of commissaries responsible to the governors. He placed this project before Gage and Hillsborough because West Florida could not afford to maintain the commissaries.[22] Gage promptly indicated that he had no faith in the plan, since the colonies would not pass identical trade laws.[23] Even before Durnford could learn of the attitude of Gage and Hillsborough he secured the passage of a law by the newly organized West Florida legislature that enacted most of Stuart's regulations of 1767–68. The act made it illegal to carry skins to New Orleans or to sell them to non-British subjects, and provided that the traders must obey orders from the commissaries in the event that such officers were appointed. It was to be in force for two years.[24] At the same time Durnford offered to put control of the West Florida trade in the hands of Charles Stuart until an official decision regarding his plan was reached, but Stuart refused on the ground that he might not be continuously in the province.[25] At the same session the West Florida assembly also passed an act that forbade private purchases from the Indians and settlements beyond the boundary lines set up in 1765.[26]

As a result of urging from West Florida and from the Indian superintendent, Hillsborough gave his approval to the appointment of two additional Indian officials, but Hillsborough wisely attached both of these to Stuart's department. In June, 1770, Charles Stuart had appointed John McIntosh as commissary without salary, in the hope that McIntosh's influence would be sufficient to remove the worst trade abuses in the Chickasaw and Choctaw nations until the West Florida act should go into force.[27] John Stuart gave McIntosh his old post as commissary to the Chickasaws in 1771. In December, 1770, at Hillsborough's recommendation, he chose Lieutenant John Thomas as deputy superintendent for the Small Tribes. This ap-

[22] Durnford to Gage, Feb. 27, 1770, and Durnford's enclosed "Plan for the Indian trade," Gage MSS; memorial of council of W. Fla. to Hillsborough, in Durnford to Hillsborough, July 9, 1770, CO, 5/587, pt. 2.

[23] Gage to Durnford, May 16, 1770, Gage MSS.

[24] "An Act for the better Regulation of the Indian Trade in the Province of West Florida," in Stuart to Gage, Aug. 2, 1770, Gage MSS.

[25] Charles Stuart to Stuart, Aug. 26, 1770 (Abstract), Gage MSS.

[26] "An Act for punishing all persons who may infringe any of the Treaties that are made with the Indians," in Stuart to Gage, Aug. 2, 1770, Gage MSS. Another act to prevent the building by the whites of huts or homes on Indian lands was passed in 1771.

[27] Charles Stuart to Stuart, June 12, 1770, Gage MSS.

pointment was made for the same purposes as that of McIntosh, and also to counteract Spanish influence with the Small Tribes.[28]

Peter Chester, who took over the reins of office from Durnford in August, 1770, held views on Indian affairs very similar to those of Durnford. When he discovered that the West Florida Indian trading act was evaded because provincial authority was limited by the boundaries of the province, he recommended to Hillsborough that all the southern colonies be urged to pass similar trade laws or that the boundaries of West Florida be extended so as to cover the adjacent Indian tribes.[29] Although this proposal made no progress, Stuart attempted to help Chester. In October, 1771, he issued orders to John McIntosh to enforce the laws of West Florida within the jurisdiction of that province and to apply Stuart's regulations of 1767–68 in the extraprovincial areas. This measure, however, was only a temporary expedient,[30] and disorder continued in the trade. After the expiration of the act of 1770 Chester reported that it had not done all that had been hoped, but that it had limited to some extent the sale of rum and that it had had a moderating effect upon the traders.[31]

Nor was the land problem in West Florida easy to handle. Early in 1769 Stuart requested the Upper Creeks and the Choctaws to concert with him in surveying their respective boundaries with the province, but no action was taken.[32] Later in the year he learned that West Florida officials desired congresses to secure additional cessions of territory from the Indians and to arrange for the surveys. Durnford wished to acquire four miles of land on each side of the rivers (with their chief tributaries) flowing from the Creek country through West Florida, for a distance from 80 to 100 miles from the sea, and in addition to buy from the Choctaws the eastern bank of the Mississippi between the Yazoo and the Iberville. To protect new settlements recently made on the Mississippi he also hoped that Fort Bute would be reoccupied.[33] Stuart, of course, referred the question

[28] Both appointments had Gage's approval. Stuart to Hillsborough, Dec. 2, 1770, Hillsborough to Stuart, Feb. 11, 1771, CO, 5/72; Gage to Stuart, May 17, 1771, Gage MSS; Hillsborough to Gage, Feb. 11, 1771, *Gage Corr.*, II, 127.

[29] Chester to Hillsborough, March 9, 1771, CO, 5/578.

[30] "The Notice given by John Stuart Esqr. Relative to the Trade in the Chactaw & Chickisaw Nations," Oct. 9, 1771, Stuart to Gage, Dec. 14, 1771, Gage MSS.

[31] Chester to Hillsborough, July 8, 1772, CO, 5/579.

[32] Stuart to Montfort Browne, Feb. 7, 1769, CO, 5/71; Browne to Hillsborough, July 26, 1769, CO, 5/577.

[33] A number of pioneers had traveled down the Ohio and the Mississippi to the fertile lands about Natchez. Durnford and Chester were anxious to encourage

of congresses to Hillsborough, for he could not call these without special authority.[34] In July, 1770, the council of West Florida accordingly placed Durnford's proposals before Hillsborough. As a supporting argument, the council alleged that in 1765 Stuart and Johnstone had promised a congress to the Chickasaws and Choctaws within three years.[35] When Stuart learned of this petition he advised Hillsborough that the Choctaws could not cede the eastern bank of the Mississippi above the Iberville because they did not own it, and that the Creeks would not abandon further territory in West Florida while the "New Purchase" was in progress. He quite correctly denied that he had ever promised the Choctaws and Chickasaws a congress.[36]

Hillsborough was greatly concerned in the fall of 1770 by repeated reports of the disturbed state of Indian affairs in the West Florida region, especially because of the Anglo-Spanish crisis that had arisen from the Falkland Islands controversy. On October 3 he therefore ordered Stuart to proceed to West Florida immediately upon receipt of his letter unless better news were forthcoming from that province.[37] But on the same day he informed Chester that further consideration was necessary before any decision could be reached regarding the stationing of garrisons on the Mississippi. In other words, Hillsborough was opposed to this step, and nothing was done in the matter.[38] In February, 1771, the minister expressed a hope that congresses would be unnecessary; in July he hinted that he would have no objection, provided Stuart and Chester agreed that they were necessary. He also declared that a further cession of land by the Upper Creeks would not be displeasing to him.[39]

---

them and to secure more settlers. Both Fort Bute and Fort Panmure were in ruins in January, 1771. See Edward Mease, "Narrative of a Journey through Several Parts of the Province of West Florida in the Years 1770 and 1771," Dunbar Rowland, ed., *Publications of the Mississippi Historical Society,* Centenary Series (Jackson, Mississippi, 1925), V, 68–77.

[34] Durnford to Hillsborough, July 24, 1769, and enclosures, CO, 5/114; Stuart to Hillsborough, Oct. 3, 1769, and enclosures, CO, 5/70; Durnford to Stuart, Sept. 11, 1769 (Abstract), CO, 5/72; Stuart to Durnford, Jan. 4, 1770, Durnford to Hillsborough, Feb. 17, 1770, CO, 5/587, pt. 2; Stuart to Haldimand, March 2, 1770, B. M. Add. MSS, 21,672, pt. 1.

[35] Memorial by W. Fla. council to Hillsborough, in Durnford to Hillsborough, July 9, 1770, CO, 5/587, pt. 2.

[36] Stuart to Hillsborough, Dec. 2, 1770, April 27, 1771, CO, 5/72.

[37] Hillsborough to Stuart, Oct. 3, 1770, CO, 5/71.

[38] See Hillsborough to Chester, Oct. 3, 1770, CO, 5/587, pt. 2; Gage to Haldimand, Oct. 31, 1770, Gage MSS. Early in 1773 the Board of Trade recommended the reoccupation of Forts Panmure and Bute, without result.

[39] Hillsborough to Stuart, Feb. 11, July 3, 1771, CO, 5/72.

Stuart was very ill with gout early in 1771 and was therefore unable to go immediately to West Florida.[40] It was not until May 4 that he embarked for Jamaica, and he did not reach Pensacola until July 29. Stuart and Chester then opened a discussion regarding boundaries and congresses. Stuart held that West Florida had sufficient land open to development under existing conditions and that a demand for more would unnecessarily alienate the Creeks. Chester did not believe, however, that a request for lands from the Creeks would cause trouble. He desired a strip on each side of the Escambia River and, if that could be obtained without difficulty, a similar cession in the valley of the Alabama. He did accept Stuart's opinion that the Choctaws had no valid claims to the eastern shore of the lower Mississippi and that no attempt should be made to purchase in that area, since the Small Tribes had made no objection to white settlements there. Chester was convinced that congresses should be held, one with the Upper Creeks to negotiate for lands and another with the Choctaws and Chickasaws to counteract supposed Spanish intrigues.[41] Stuart himself was anxious to settle the boundary line with the Creeks and Choctaws, and he decided that the congresses were indispensable.[42]

Although Stuart at first hoped to meet the Upper Creeks at Pensacola in September, they were too busily engaged in their war with the Choctaws at that time, and the congress was therefore postponed. It was actually held from October 29 to November 2, with Stuart, Haldimand, Chester, Durnford, Charles Stuart, and other officers present. Emistisiguo was the chief speaker for the Creeks.[43] As usual, various grievances were brought forth. The Creeks complained about trade conditions, concerning persons who drove cattle from Georgia through their country to West Florida,[44] and regarding various individuals who had established plantations and cowpens in their hunting grounds. Stuart and Chester, of course, enlarged upon disorderly acts committed by the Creeks. But the important subject at the congress was land.

[40] Stuart to Hillsborough, March 5, 1771, CO, 5/72. Stuart was in a very low state of health during all of 1771. In the expectation that he was about to die Dartmouth later offered his position to one of his own relatives.

[41] Stuart to Chester, Aug. 30, 1771, Chester to Stuart, Sept. 10, 1771, CO, 5/72.

[42] Stuart to Gage, Aug. 31, 1772, Gage MSS; Stuart to Hillsborough, Sept. 24, 1771, CO, 5/72. Stuart also cited the promises made by Robertson and Farmar as reasons for holding a congress with the Choctaws and Chickasaws.

[43] The Mortar was not present.

[44] Notably George Galphin.

Chester opened the discussion of the land question. He informed the Upper Creeks that all persons who had settled beyond the boundary line of 1765 along the east bank of the Alabama River had removed at his request; and he adroitly remarked that he was able to give but few presents because the Creeks had failed to cede sufficient territory to West Florida to enable the province to flourish. Haldimand made a supporting "talk," and Stuart requested the Creeks to cede to West Florida five miles of land on each side of the Escambia River as far as it was navigable [45] and to join in surveying a new line. Emistisiguo promised to assist in the survey, but was willing to cede only four miles of the Escambia valley beyond the line of 1765. He also complained that the triangular bit of territory between the Alabama and the Tombigbee rivers ceded by the Choctaws in 1765 really belonged to the Upper Creeks. Stuart remarked that the land offered by Emistisiguo was very little and that the soil was very poor. The chief then resorted to a time-honored subterfuge: the Creeks present, he said, did not represent the whole nation and could not make a more extensive grant in the Escambia valley. He announced that he and his brethren would depart for home, but Stuart persuaded the Creeks to remain. He declared that he would not accept their offer, not because he disdained it, but because he hoped that the nation as a whole would agree to his request. The Indians responded by promising to support it before a great council of their nation. In regard to the Alabama-Tombigbee triangle, Stuart pointed out that no settlements had been made in that area and suggested that the Creeks and Choctaws would have to decide whether or not the Choctaws had a right to cede it. This matter was then dropped. Finally, the Upper Creeks agreed to cede all their rights to a strip of land about thirty miles in length along the eastern bank of the Alabama River beyond the old boundary at Tensaw. They also abandoned their claims to the islands between the Mobile and Tensaw rivers previously ceded by the Choctaws.[46]

About the beginning of December Stuart, Chester, Haldimand, and Charles Stuart arrived at Mobile. On December 31 they opened discussions with the Chickasaws and with over 1,500 Choctaws. Paya Mattaha was the most prominent chief at the congress, which lasted until January 6, 1772. Delegates from the West Party of the Choc-

[45] Stuart estimated that the strip would extend thirty-five miles from the Gulf of Mexico.

[46] Proceedings of the Congress of Pensacola, Oct. 29—Nov. 2, 1771, Stuart to Gage, Dec. 14, 1771, Gage MSS; Stuart to Hillsborough, Nov. 2, 1771, CO, 5/73.

taws did not reach Mobile until January 21, but in conferences with Stuart lasting from January 23 to 29 they concurred in all that had been arranged by their fellows. Negotiations with the Choctaws regarding land were quickly completed, for they freely consented to assist in surveying their boundary with West Florida. However, both the Choctaws and the Chickasaws complained about conditions in the trade. Stuart conceded that they had grievances. He counseled them to support McIntosh against unscrupulous traders and to despoil traders carrying rum into their towns in excess of fifteen gallons every three months. He also scolded both tribes because of their own misbehavior.

Stuart's most important achievement at this congress lay in insuring the continuance in power of chiefs friendly to the English. Many of the Choctaw leaders honored with medals by Stuart in 1765 had died. By giving out new medals he virtually selected new chiefs for the nation. He also settled a conflict over leadership among the Chickasaws. One Mingo Ouma, instigated by unscrupulous traders, had set himself up as "king" of the Chickasaws, insisting that he ranked above Paya Mattaha. Stuart informed the Chickasaws that he and other English officials would continue to recognize Paya Mattaha as their head as long as he lived.[47] He warned Mingo Ouma that he must behave himself if he desired honors from English officials. Stuart thus crushed his pretensions, but made him a small medal chief by way of consolation.[48] The cost of the congress was £6,000.[49]

On January 16 Charles Stuart and a group of Choctaws set out to survey the Choctaw–West Florida line. The party did its work as far as the Buckatunna River, where the Choctaws refused to continue because the line ran through morasses, but Charles Stuart went on, marking the boundary to the mouth of the Buckatunna. When Chester refused to pay anything toward the necessary expenses for completing the line except those of the surveyor,[50] John Stuart let the matter drop, and it was not completely marked until 1779. Chester also declined to bear any part of the expense for surveying

[47] Paya Mattaha was so pleased at this turn of events that he made himself drunk for three days and delayed the congress for that length of time.

[48] Proceedings of the Congress of Mobile, Dec. 31, 1771—Jan. 6, 1772, Stuart to Gage, Feb. 16, 1772, Gage MSS; Stuart to Hillsborough, Jan. 7, 1772, CO, 5/73; Stuart to Haldimand, Jan. 20, 1772, B. M. Add. MSS, 21,672, pt. 1.

[49] Stuart to Germain, Aug. 23, 1776, CO, 5/77.

[50] Chester to Hillsborough, Feb. 20, 1772, CO, 5/579; Chester to Charles Stuart, June 24, 1772, Gage MSS.

the Creek boundary except to pay the surveyor.[51] Although the Creeks agreed in 1772 to send delegates for the purpose, Stuart delayed action indefinitely, in the hope that the Creeks would agree to cede the valley of the Escambia.[52]

Early in 1772 Stuart instructed David Taitt to carry on further negotiations with the Upper Creeks regarding the Escambia valley.[53] Partly as a result of Taitt's urging they offered to cede a strip of land along that river stretching eight miles beyond the existing boundary and a small bit of territory east of Pensacola Bay.[54] This offer was not satisfactory, and Chester continued to hope for a more extensive cession. He urged the colonial secretary not to countenance the "New Purchase" because it would damage the Escambia project,[55] though to no avail. As Stuart and Chester foresaw, the completion of the "New Purchase" necessitated the abandonment of the Escambia scheme.[56]

After 1768 it was necessary for the English to counter the efforts of the Shawnees and Delawares to form a hostile Indian confederacy, not only in the Cherokee country, but also in the Creek and Choctaw nations. Such an alliance could never materialize, so far as the Choctaws and Creeks were concerned, as long as these tribes

[51] Charles Stuart to Chester, June 23, 1772; Chester to Charles Stuart, June 24, 1772, Gage MSS. Stuart requested Gage to furnish the funds, but Gage refused. Gage to Stuart, Sept. 30, 1772, *ibid.*

[52] Stuart to Hillsborough, June 13, 1772, Stuart to Dartmouth, Sept. 23, 1772, CO, 5/73.

[53] "Instructions to Mr. David Taitt [by Stuart]," Jan. 20, 1772, CO, 5/73.

[54] Stuart to Hillsborough, June 13, 1772, CO, 5/73. This new offer was likewise conceived in part to compensate for a murder or two committed by the Upper Creeks.

[55] Chester to Hillsborough, Aug. 13, 1772, CO, 5/579.

[56] The West Florida Indian boundary was completed to the Mississippi during the Revolution. In a treaty signed at Mobile by Stuart with the West Party and the Six Villages of the Choctaws in May, 1777, the Choctaws renounced any possible pretensions to lands west of a line drawn from the western end of the Choctaw boundary of 1765 to the mouth of the Yazoo River. In 1779 Joseph Purcell surveyed the Choctaw line. Board of Commissioners for Exercising the Office of Superintendant of Indian Affairs in the Southern District of North America to Germain, July 13, 1779, CO, 5/81. Since the Small Tribes had never objected to English settlements and since their numbers were steadily decreasing, there was no Indian bar to occupation of the eastern bank of the Mississippi between the Yazoo and New Orleans after 1777. Farquhar Bethune, Stuart's commissary to the Choctaws after the beginning of the Revolution, with Joseph Purcell and others, concluded on January 9, 1779, an agreement with the West Party of the Choctaws whereby the latter promised to sign a formal treaty that would have ended any Choctaw claims to the banks of the river at the Yazoo. Agreement of Huma Chitto, Jan. 9, 1779, *ibid.*

continued at war with each other, although continual rumors of the machinations of the Shawnees and Delawares in the far South caused much uneasiness in the minds of Stuart, Gage, and other British officials.[57] For a time in 1772 there was a real danger that the alliance might be consummated, as a result of an unfortunate affray that occurred at Kaskaskia between a party of Chickasaws and a detachment of British troops at that place. The Chickasaws, led by Paya Mingo Euluxy, lost two warriors, and the chief himself was wounded.[58] Returning home, Paya Mingo Euluxy tried to persuade his people to drive out their traders and to undertake mediation of the Creek-Choctaw conflict. He hoped to bring the Creeks, Choctaws, and Chickasaws into an alliance with the Shawnees and Delawares. Success in this project might have brought on a great Indian war in America, but Paya Mattaha and Mingo Ouma refused to support the scheme, and the danger passed.[59]

Some aspects of Indian affairs in the southern district after 1768, involving relations between England and Spain, were of international importance. From 1768 until the conquest of West Florida by Don Bernardo de Galvez the Spanish carried on intrigues among the southern tribes, from both Havana and New Orleans. These intrigues, not overly important before the American Revolution, aroused concern among English officials. On the other hand, the English meddled with the Indians of Louisiana, also on a relatively small scale.

Spanish fishing vessels continued to frequent the west coast of the Florida peninsula after 1763,[60] and the Spanish fishermen unavoidably came into contact with the Lower Creeks, whose best hunting grounds lay in that region. They made presents to the Creeks and also carried off several of them to Havana.[61] For some

[57] There are many references to Shawnee emissaries in the Creek and Choctaw nations in the Gage MSS and the Haldimand MSS. For example, see Stuart to Haldimand, Jan. 23, 1771, B. M. Add. MSS, 21,672, pt. 1.

[58] Capt. Hugh Lord to Stuart, May 30, 1772, Gage MSS.

[59] Deposition by Henry Le Fleur, Aug. 27, 1772, John McIntosh to Charles Stuart, Sept. 3, 1772, Stuart to Gage, Sept. 7, 1772, Gage MSS. Paya Mingo Euluxy was killed by northern Indians in 1774. Cameron to Stuart, July 26, 1774, *ibid.*

[60] Grant reported that these vessels were licensed by officials at Havana as if the Florida Keys were Spanish property. Grant to Hillsborough, Dec. 12, 1770, CO, 5/552.

[61] W. Bartram, *Travels through North and South Carolina, Georgia, East and West Florida*... (London, 1792), 225–26, asserts that English traders bought goods from such vessels and that some of the Lower Creeks went to Havana to trade. These activities were probably not extensive.

years Governor Grant believed that the fishermen offered presents merely so that they would not be molested, and that such Indians as were borne to Cuba went at their own request. In fact, both Grant and Haldimand were pleased as late as 1769 by the presence of those vessels on the Gulf coast, for they believed that the ships might serve as a means of opening a trade with Spanish ports.[62] But by 1768 rumors were current that Spanish agents were actively engaged in intrigues with the Lower Creeks, and there was even a report circulated that the Creeks were attempting to sell the Spanish lands on the Appalachie River. Hillsborough was sufficiently worried by these rumors to order them investigated.[63] Upon inquiry Stuart declared that the Spanish were actually negotiating with the Lower Creeks. He noted, however, that for the most part the Creeks retained their former dislike for the dons.[64]

In May, 1769, Escotchabie, who was more friendly to the Spanish than any other Creek chief, told Stuart that a conference between the Spanish and representatives of the whole Creek nation was planned for September of that year and that it was to be held at the mouth of the Appalachicola River. Stuart was so greatly upset by this report that he ordered Charles Stuart to the spot to prevent the meeting and suggested to Montfort Browne that a warship be stationed off the coast for the same purpose.[65] Browne requested Captain William Philipps of the *Tryal,* then in the harbor at Pensacola, to patrol the coast, and Philipps agreed. Accompanied by Charles Stuart, he sailed up and down the shores of Florida during September. At the end of the month Philipps left for Jamaica, but another warship took Charles Stuart aboard and continued the vigil for some days longer, without success.[66] Charles Stuart finally came to the conclusion that the rumor of a conference grew out of reports of the approach of General Alexander O'Reilly's force toward New Orleans.[67]

Although the deputy superintendent's search for Spanish envoys

[62] Haldimand to Gage, Oct. 13, 1769, Gage MSS; Grant to Hillsborough, May 15, 1769, CO, 5/550; Grant to Hillsborough, Nov. 6, 1769, March 27, 1770, CO, 5/551.

[63] Hillsborough to Stuart, July 12, 1768, CO, 5/69.

[64] Stuart to Gage, Dec. 6, 1768, Gage MSS; Stuart to Hillsborough, Dec. 28, 1768, CO, 5/70.

[65] "Talk" by Escotchabie to Stuart, May—, 1769, Stuart to [Browne], June 30, 1769, CO, 5/70.

[66] Brown to Philipps, Aug. 18, 1769, Philipps to Philip Stephens, Aug. 18, Oct. 9, 1769, Charles Stuart to [Philipps], Aug. 22, 1769, Stuart to Hillsborough, Oct. 3, 1769, CO, 5/70.

[67] Reports by Indians could and did contain such gross mistakes.

was fruitless, English officials continued to be apprehensive of Spanish activities in the Lower Creek towns, especially after news of the Falkland Islands quarrel reached America. Both Gage and Stuart were very anxious to prevent negotiations between the Creeks and Havana because they might endanger the English hold on the Floridas if England and Spain went to war.[68] One reason for the appointment of David Taitt as commissary to the Creeks in January, 1772, was the hope that he could counter Spanish machinations. Nor were the fears of Gage and Stuart without some justification. In 1770 and 1771 small parties of Lower Creeks visited Cuba and returned with presents.[69] In the following year Escotchabie received another invitation to a conference with Spanish emissaries. Stuart again suggested that a ship of war be stationed off the Gulf coast to prevent such meetings,[70] but no action was taken; and the Spanish continued to cast their nets for both fish and the Lower Creeks.[71] During the Anglo-Creek crisis of 1774 Charles Stuart was told that the Lower Creeks were receiving ammunition from the Spanish and that some of them were displaying Spanish commissions. At that critical juncture the Lower Creeks asserted that they could obtain powder and lead from the Spanish whenever they desired,[72] but it is unlikely that Spanish officials gave them much encouragement. When Escotchabie was picked up in 1775 by a Spanish fishing vessel and carried to Cuba,[73] he returned without "talks" or presents.

The complete establishment of Spanish control over Louisiana by General Alexander O'Reilly in 1769 caused changes in Indian relations in the lower Mississippi valley. Intrigues by French traders among the Small Tribes and the Choctaws lessened, because the Spanish gave a monopoly of the Louisiana Indian trade to the military officers. But Stuart, Gage, the governors of West Florida, and the secretaries of state for a time entertained suspicions that Spanish officials in New Orleans were trying to win the affections of Indians on English territory. These suspicions apparently had little basis in fact, although they were supported by the rumors of similar activities

[68] In 1768 Haldimand and most of the troops in West Florida were sent to St. Augustine. When the Falkland Islands controversy arose Haldimand was ordered back to West Florida, and reinforcements were sent to that province. Gage to Haldimand, Feb. 26, 1770, Gage MSS.

[69] Stuart to Gage, May 23, 24, 1772; N. D. Mereness, ed., *Travels in the American Colonies* (New York, 1916), 548.

[70] Stuart to Gage, Sept. 7, 1772, Gage to Stuart, Sept. 30, 1772, Gage MSS.

[71] Lieutenant Governor John Moultrie to Dartmouth, Feb. 21, 1774, CO, 5/554.

[72] Charles Stuart to Haldimand, May 12, 13, 1774, Gage MSS.

[73] Stuart to Dartmouth, May 20, 1775, CO, 5/76.

on the part of the Spanish in East Florida. In view of the exposed position of West Florida all interested British officials were fully aware of the importance of preventing understandings between the Spanish and the Choctaws, Small Tribes, and the Chickasaws. They therefore kept close watch on the activities of O'Reilly and Don Luis de Unzaga y Amezaga, who succeeded O'Reilly in March, 1770.[74]

When shortly after O'Reilly's landing the Choctaws and Small Tribes committed depredations upon English plantations, Browne and Stuart thought it possible that the Spanish were partly responsible.[75] In 1770 Charles Stuart reported that the dons were offering medals to Indians on English territory, although some Choctaws who had gone to New Orleans were coldly received.[76] In the spring of 1771 Haldimand declared that the Spanish were giving presents to Indians east of the Mississippi. Some months later a trader reported that several Choctaw chiefs had gone to New Orleans at Unzaga's invitation.[77] As has been noted, Governor Chester gave as one reason for holding the second Congress of Mobile supposed tampering with the Choctaws by the Spanish. Stuart was told at the congress by the Choctaws that the Spanish had sent representatives to them with presents.[78]

Reports of intrigues carried on from New Orleans became less and less common during the governorship of Unzaga. Even in 1770 Haldimand and Charles Stuart were inclined to believe that the Spanish were not very aggressive.[79] After visiting New Orleans and its vicinity in 1772 Charles Stuart decided that the Spanish could make no trouble. He reported that they were unpopular both with the French inhabitants of Louisiana and with the Indians, and that they had no desire to follow an active policy.[80] In April, 1773, Stuart believed that it was wise to keep a commissary in service among the Small Tribes, but only because he might be useful in case of war. At that time Gage was so thoroughly convinced that the Spaniards

[74] Both O'Reilly and Unzaga informed Gage that they desired peace on the Mississippi. O'Reilly to Gage, Sept. 21, 1769, Unzaga to Gage, April 27, 1770, Gage MSS.

[75] Browne to Hillsborough, Oct. 8, 1769, CO, 5/587, pt. 1; Stuart to Hillsborough, Dec. 2, 1769, CO, 5/71.

[76] Charles Stuart to Stuart, June 12, Aug. 26, 1770, Gage MSS.

[77] Haldimand to Gage, April 14, 1771, Gage MSS; Alexander McIntosh to Chester, Sept. 12, 1771 (Extract), CO, 5/578.

[78] Stuart to Gage, Feb. 16, 1772, Gage MSS.

[79] Haldimand to Gage, April 11, 1770, Charles Stuart to Stuart, Aug. 26, 1770, Gage MSS.

[80] Charles Stuart to Stuart, Dec. 2, 1772, Gage MSS.

intended to remain quiet that he thought it might be well to dispense with the commissary.[81] The fact that reports are not found of Spanish maneuverings in the Choctaw nation during the Anglo-Creek crisis of 1774 indicates that Louisiana officials continued to pursue a cautious policy in Indian affairs on the lower Mississippi until the Revolution. Such dealings as they had with the Choctaws and the Small Tribes were probably for the purpose of maintaining peace with them rather than because of any real intention to incite them against the English.

On the other hand, major British officials were prudent in dealing with Indians on Spanish territory. As related above, Stuart had contemplated in 1766 an attempt to persuade the Arkansaw tribe to remove to English soil, since that nation had shown a friendly attitude toward the English. Stuart did not abandon this idea for some years, but he never actually tried to put it into effect, although it would have been relatively easy at any time after 1768 to execute it.[82] An Arkansaw chief visited Haldimand at Mobile in 1771 and asked for an alliance with the English. Haldimand, careful not to refuse the request, did not give a definitely favorable reply.[83] Some Arkansaw warriors accompanied the Chickasaws to the second Congress of Mobile. In 1774 thirty-five Arkansaw braves proposed an alliance to Governor Chester at Natchez. They were referred to John Thomas, who definitely declined the offer because of specific instructions from Stuart.[84]

One English official—and he a member of the southern Indian department—undoubtedly was guilty of intriguing with the Louisiana tribes. In April, 1770, Hillsborough was personally solicited by Lieutenant John Thomas for an appointment as commissary to the Small Tribes. Since Thomas had spent several years on the Mississippi, Hillsborough believed that he might be able to perform useful service, and he gave him a letter of introduction to Stuart, but did not urge Stuart to appoint him.[85] Stuart, however, who was

[81] Gage to Stuart, June 21, 1772, June 3, 1773, Stuart to Gage, April 22, 1773, Gage MSS.

[82] The Arkansaws were very much dissatisfied with trade conditions under the Spanish régime and were eager to ally themselves with the Chickasaws. See Charles Stuart to Chester, April 10, 1771, Gage MSS; Romans, *A Concise Natural History of East and West Florida* (New York, 1775), 61.

[83] Haldimand to Gage, June 12, 1771, Gage MSS.

[84] Deposition by John Duesbuge, Dec. 18, 1774, Gage MSS.

[85] Hillsborough to Stuart, April 14, 1770 (Separate and Private), CO, 5/71. Thomas was an officer in the royal artillery. After Fort Bute was pillaged in 1765 Thomas went to Pensacola, but returned to the Iberville with Captain

always responsive to suggestions from the colonial secretary, tendered Thomas an appointment as deputy superintendent.[86] At Pensacola in August, 1771, he instructed Thomas to keep a watchful eye upon the Indian trade and also to try to persuade the Indians who had moved westward across the Mississippi after 1763 to return. He was strictly enjoined not to exceed his budget of £600 and not to meddle with permanent Indian residents on the western banks of the Mississippi.[87] Late in the same month Thomas went on board ship to proceed to his new post.

Before leaving for his station Thomas showed that he was dominated by visionary and impractical ideas. On the one hand, he offered to Hillsborough to bring the Arkansaws upon English soil and to capture New Orleans by means of an Indian confederacy headed by the Chickasaws and Arkansaws whenever the colonial secretary should give the word; [88] and, on the other, he hinted to Gage that he carried secret instructions from the minister to guide him in the conduct of his office.[89] On his way to the Iberville Thomas interviewed Unzaga at New Orleans and was led to believe that the Spanish governor would not object to the return of the tribes that had crossed the Mississippi after 1763 to English territory.[90] Thomas immediately set to work to carry out his instructions regarding these tribes. By December, 1771, he had persuaded some 300 Indians to consider favorably a return to their old homes. But Unzaga then complained of his activities.[91]

Meanwhile Thomas had become convinced that Captain Balthasar de Villiers, commander of the Spanish post opposite Point Coupée, was intriguing among the Tonicas and was attempting to persuade them to remove to Spanish territory. He complained of Villiers's activities to Unzaga; he declared that, if the governor did not put a stop to them, he would feel free to try his own diplomatic

---

Chisholm's detachment. He remained there until January, 1768, and then returned once more to Pensacola. Thomas to Gage, Dec. 31, 1768, Gage MSS. He died in 1776 at his post on the Mississippi. Stuart to Germain, Sept. 16, 1776, CO, 5/79.

[86] Thomas's appointment was at first temporary, because Stuart's budget was not large enough to cover his salary and expense account, £150 and £600 respectively. Stuart to Gage, Dec. 13, 1770, Gage MSS. Hillsborough later approved the necessary addition to Stuart's budget.

[87] Stuart's instructions to Thomas, Aug. 17, 1771, CO, 5/73.

[88] Thomas to Hillsborough, Dec. 1, 1770, CO, 5/72.

[89] Thomas to Gage, Aug. 29, 1771, Gage MSS.

[90] Thomas to Stuart, Dec. 12, 20, 1771, CO, 5/73.

[91] Unzaga to Thomas, Nov. 23, 1771, CO, 5/73.

talents with the Spanish tribes.[92] When he reported these matters to Stuart, he was again strictly enjoined not to interfere with the Spanish Indians and not to exceed his budget.[93] However, before he heard from Stuart, Thomas again visited New Orleans. There he made an agreement with Unzaga by the terms of which Thomas and Unzaga were personally to manage Indian relations, the English and Spanish were to receive all Indians in friendly fashion, and tribes desiring to move to their former homes east of the Mississippi should be permitted to do so.[94]

This agreement between Unzaga and Thomas lasted only a very short time. Soon Thomas was informed that French officers in the Spanish service were trying to form an alliance of Arkansaws, Chickasaws, Shawnees, and Cherokees to attack the Osage tribe, which had been responsible for the death of some Frenchmen in 1771. Thomas suspected that Unzaga supported the French officers. Ignoring his instructions, he conferred with a number of Arkansaw chiefs early in 1772 and entered into an agreement with them. He hoped to use the Indian alliance planned by the French officers, not against the Osages, but against the Kickapoos, who had been unfriendly to the English! In the spring of 1772 Thomas asked Stuart for more funds, for he had exhausted his budget. He also requested that a few troops be sent to the Iberville because he had had troubles with English traders. Thomas hinted to Stuart, as he had to Gage, that he was acting in accordance with private instructions from Hillsborough.[95]

By February, 1772, Stuart was disgusted with Thomas.[96] When Unzaga complained to Chester regarding him and the traders on the lower Mississippi petitioned for his removal, Chester wrote to Unzaga disavowing him and urged Stuart to suspend him from office.[97] Since Thomas had committed a multitude of official sins, Stuart did suspend him. He demanded that Thomas explain his conduct and

[92] Affidavit by William Richardson, Nov. 21, 1771, Captain Balthasar de Villiers to Thomas, Nov. 25, 1771, Thomas to Unzaga, Dec. 3, 12, 1771, CO, 5/73. Thomas persuaded Lattanash, chief of the Tonicas, to accept an English medal, although the warrior already had a Spanish one. According to Thomas, Villiers tried to force Lattanash to give up his English medal; according to Villiers himself, he merely told the chief that he must give up the Spanish medal if he would keep the English one.

[93] Stuart to Thomas, Jan. 10, Feb. 19, 1772, CO, 5/73.

[94] Thomas to Stuart, Jan. 27, 1772, CO, 5/73.

[95] Thomas to Stuart, March 11, 12, 1772, CO, 5/73.

[96] Stuart to Haldimand, Feb. 26, 1772, B. M. Add. MSS, 21,672, pt. 1.

[97] Minute of W. Fla. council, April 7, 1772, CO, 5/73; Chester to Unzaga, April 11, 1772, Chester to Hillsborough, April 11, 23, 1772, CO, 5/579.

reveal the alleged secret instructions from Hillsborough which supposedly justified his actions.[98] Stuart also disavowed Thomas to Unzaga.[99] Then came news that Thomas had slain George Harrison, a trader. Chester immediately directed his arrest on a charge of murder, and the Spanish governor ordered him seized and sent to Pensacola if he appeared on Spanish soil.[100]

Thomas surrendered to West Florida authorities and was acquitted of the murder charge on the ground of self-defense.[101] He offered Stuart a very inadequate apologia for his official conduct. He denied that he had disobeyed orders, cried to the heavens for justice, and declared once more that he had acted in accordance with confidential instructions from Hillsborough.[102] He tried to persuade Gage to give him a new appointment at the Iberville, but the general refused. Both Gage and Haldimand agreed with Stuart that Thomas was probably insane, and that he should be discharged,[103] although the superintendent refrained from taking the final step until Hillsborough had considered the case. In January, 1773, after learning that the minister thought Thomas's conduct was "very exceptionable," Stuart dismissed him and gave him his pay to May 31, 1773, so that he could transport his family to England or some other destination distant from the southern Indians.[104] Then Thomas finally admitted that he had had no secret instructions from Hillsborough.[105]

Thomas came to Charleston in the summer of 1773 to plead for reinstatement, and Stuart learned that he was stupid rather than insane. When Stuart discovered that Dartmouth and John Pownall favored reëmploying Thomas, Stuart did reëngage him, although he had no faith in the man. But the superintendent laid him under the strictest injunction to refrain from meddling in the Indian affairs of Louisiana.[106]

[98] Stuart to Thomas, April 10, 1772, Gage MSS.

[99] Stuart to Unzaga, April 10, 1772, Gage MSS.

[100] Haldimand to Gage, May 14, 1772, Gage MSS.

[101] Chester to Hillsborough, Oct. 27, 1772, CO, 5/579.

[102] Stuart to Hillsborough, Sept. 24, 1772, and enclosures, CO, 5/73.

[103] Thomas to Gage, Nov. 18, 1772, and enclosures, Dec. 20, 1772, Gage MSS; Stuart to Haldimand, Sept. 13, 1772, B. M. Add. MSS, 21,672, pt. 2.

[104] Stuart to Thomas, Jan. 8, 1773, Gage MSS. Stuart said that he would have retained Thomas if his defense had been made in decent terms, because of his wife, whom the superintendent respected. Stuart to Gage, June 21, 1773, *ibid.*

[105] Thomas to Gage, March 8, 1773, Gage MSS. Thomas said that in his interview with the minister Hillsborough was silent when he proposed bringing the Arkansaws to English territory, and that he had construed silence to mean approval.

[106] Dartmouth to Stuart, Dec. 9, 1772, May 5, 1773, CO, 5/74; Stuart to Haldi-

Although Chester believed that Unzaga was satisfied by the suspension of Thomas and the disavowals of Thomas made by Stuart and Chester,[107] the superintendent labored energetically to remove any possible suspicion lingering in the mind of the Spanish governor. Henry Le Fleur, who had acted as interpreter for Thomas, was sent to tell the Arkansaws that a conference planned by Thomas for the fall of 1772 was not to be held,[108] and the superintendent ordered Charles Stuart to the Mississippi to smooth over the whole affair. Charles Stuart proceeded to New Orleans, where he had a friendly discussion with Unzaga. He also held a conference with the rapidly diminishing Small Tribes, and reported that he had found no evidence of Spanish intrigues among them.[109] Affairs on the Mississippi then quieted down, although a few Arkansaw warriors moved to the English side of the river in 1773.[110] In 1775 Stuart urged Dartmouth to increase Thomas's allowance by £150 because he had to compete with the Spanish.[111] This move, however, was intended merely to uphold English prestige with the Small Tribes.

In 1775 came a protest from the Spanish ambassador at the court of St. James's regarding English tampering with the Indians of Louisiana, a delayed repercussion from the Thomas affair.[112] But the Spanish really had little about which they could justly complain. On the other hand, the English had small reason to criticize the Spanish because of the Indian diplomacy of the dons in the lower Mississippi valley before 1775. If war had been declared between England and Spain in 1775, very few of the southern Indians would have favored Spain. That some of the Choctaws supported Spain when war actually broke out between the two powers was due to the activities initiated by Bernardo de Galvez after the American Revolution had begun.

---

mand, Aug. 20, 1773, B. M. Add. MSS, 21,672, pt. 3; Stuart to Haldimand, Oct. 18, 1773, B. M. Add. MSS, 21,672, pt. 4. Characteristically, after returning to his post, Thomas persuaded the Tonicas to grant him some lands. Thomas to John Pownall, May 12, 1775, CO, 5/77. He died before he could make use of the grant.

[107] Chester to Hillsborough, July 7, 1772, CO, 5/579.

[108] Henry Le Fleur to Charles Stuart, Sept. 3, 1772, Gage MSS.

[109] Proceedings of conference between Charles Stuart and the Small Tribes, Oct. 14, 1772, Charles Stuart to Stuart, Sept. 24 (Abstract), Dec. 2, 1772, Gage MSS.

[110] Stuart to Haldimand, Oct. 17, 1773, B. M. Add. MSS, 21,672, pt. 4.

[111] Stuart to Dartmouth, March 28, 1775, CO, 5/76.

[112] Dartmouth to Chester, Sept. 1, 1775, Chester to Germain, July 7, 1776, CO, 5/592.

CHAPTER XIX

RETROSPECT

EXCEPT perhaps for Attakullakulla the "noble savage" seems to have been nonexistent among the southern Indians during the period 1754–75. Whether Cherokee or Chickasaw, Choctaw or Creek, the southern Indian was often temperamental and untrustworthy; occasionally he was dishonest and vicious. With all his faults, however, he compares favorably with the white man with whom he had most frequent contact, the outlaw, the ne'er-do-well, the rum seller, the squatter, and the land speculator. If he had the faults of the barbarian, he had his virtues also. In any case he could not be ignored by responsible English officials.

Because England, France, and Spain did not engage in large-scale military operations in the South, rivalry in that area during the Seven Years' War consisted largely of strokes and counterstrokes in Indian diplomacy. On the whole, the French were somewhat more successful than the English. Mismanagement of relations with the Cherokees by the governments of South Carolina and Virginia, coupled with astute French propaganda, led to the harassing and costly Anglo-Cherokee war of 1760–61. The inability of South Carolina and Georgia to restrain their traders and to assuage the fears of the Creeks for their lands gave the French another excellent opportunity. They made good use of it, but the need of the Creeks for English goods and the prudence of English officials, notably William Bull and Henry Ellis, prevented an Anglo-Creek war. Between 1763 and 1775, although English leaders feared for the safety of the southern colonies because of the presence of the French and Spanish in Louisiana and Cuba, the continental powers had no great influence with the southern Indians. But problems arising from the Indian trade and the covetousness of the whites for Indian lands continued.

The imperial office of superintendent of Indian affairs was created at the beginning of the Seven Years' War, thanks to provincial mismanagement of Indian relations and the need of countering French efforts to win the support of the Indians. While the office quickly became one of importance in the North owing to the ability and energy of Sir William Johnson, the southern superintendency gained little influence during the Edmund Atkin régime, partly because of his own shortcomings. Under John Stuart, however, the southern superintendency acquired powers equal to those possessed by its northern counterpart under Johnson.

Upon the shoulders of the military commander and, more directly, upon those of the superintendents, fell most of the burden of executing British western policy between 1763 and 1775. The primary aims of that policy undoubtedly were the maintenance of peace on the frontier and the winning and holding of the loyalty of the Indians east of the Mississippi. Another objective cherished by some British politicians was to restrict the American colonies to the seaboard, so that the Americans would continue to produce raw materials and to serve as consumers of finished products from England. This objective should not be overstressed, for the expansionists had their supporters at home. Even Lord Hillsborough, who has been described as a champion of restriction, was not opposed to moderate expansion into the continental interior. There were three ways in which these basic aims of British policy might be achieved: through the prevention of encroachments on the lands of the red men, through the establishment of order in the Indian trade, and through Indian diplomacy. With varying success, but with complete loyalty to the program as a whole, Stuart pursued each of these objectives.

It is clear that Stuart's views upon the western problem in general coincided with those of the home government, although he was not always in agreement with his superiors regarding the methods to be employed, notably in regard to trade regulation. His attitude toward expansion into the interior was much the same as that of Lord Hillsborough—or should we say that the minister's attitude was much the same as that of Stuart? Stuart approved only of moderate expansion in areas contiguous to existing settlements, because a too-rapid advance into the trans-Appalachian region seemed to him certain to lead to Indian conflicts. On two occasions he did argue against expansion on the ground that English interests would suffer, but in perfunctory fashion.

In the main, and largely through the efforts of Stuart, the primary aims of British western policy were achieved within his district. After much negotiation he eventually managed to set up Indian boundaries behind the southern colonies from the Ohio to the Mississippi, lines which by 1773 gave the colonies considerable room for development, so far as the Indians were concerned. He was unable effectively to prevent the Americans from making settlements beyond those lines, but his failure in that respect was almost inevitable. Nor did his attempts to bring order into the trade bear rich fruit. In part, this is explained by the opposition of the Indian traders and their merchants, of colonial assemblies, and of other royal officials; in part, it is explained by the fact that his regulatory plans, because of their nature and because of the expense they involved, did not gain the approval of the home government. That Stuart accomplished as much as he did in harmonizing the conflicting interests of the colonists and the Indians regarding land and in removing abuses in the trade is remarkable, especially since his very office was a novel experiment and remained something of an anomaly in the imperial system.

It was in the field of diplomacy that Stuart won his greatest triumphs. His dignified and generous behavior, his gifts to the Indians, and his adroit manipulation of Indian politics brought him great prestige with his charges—prestige that suffered only slightly during the years immediately preceding the Revolution. Under his management the Creeks steadily became more docile, as is shown by the several crises in relations with them after 1763, the results of which were successively more favorable to the English. The Cherokees and Choctaws, especially the former, came rather thoroughly under English influence. That Stuart's policy was based on sound premises and was well executed is demonstrated by one striking fact: from 1763 to 1775 peace was maintained on the southern frontier. No doubt fortuitous circumstances helped to bring about this result, but the superintendent's caution and address certainly contributed to it. It is interesting that the expenses of the southern Indian department during those twelve years were less than the cost of the Cherokee War of 1760–61.[1]

Because Stuart labored diligently to execute his instructions, he was unpopular with some of the American frontiersmen. They detested him because he tried to maintain the Indian boundaries and because they believed—unjustifiably—that he furnished the Indians with arms and ammunition to be used against them. He was also viewed with cordial dislike by some land speculators because, unlike Johnson, he fought their schemes; and his trade regulations made him *persona non grata* to many of the traders, although most of

[1] William Bull and James Grant estimated the cost of the war to the public alone at £100,000.

these gentry in the South eventually stood, like Stuart himself, for the king. But he remained consistently loyal to his trust. Indeed, fidelity and prudence were perhaps his outstanding characteristics as superintendent. While he scrupulously obeyed orders from London, he was not lacking in initiative. In spite of poor health he performed many arduous labors. He traveled thousands of miles on official business, although he never entered the southern wilderness after his appointment as superintendent. He liked his job; he was jealous of his dignity; he quarreled with other British colonial officials; he was no saint. On the whole, his conduct of Indian affairs in the South before the American Revolution must be regarded as a bright spot in the uneven record of British administration of the American colonies in the later eighteenth century.

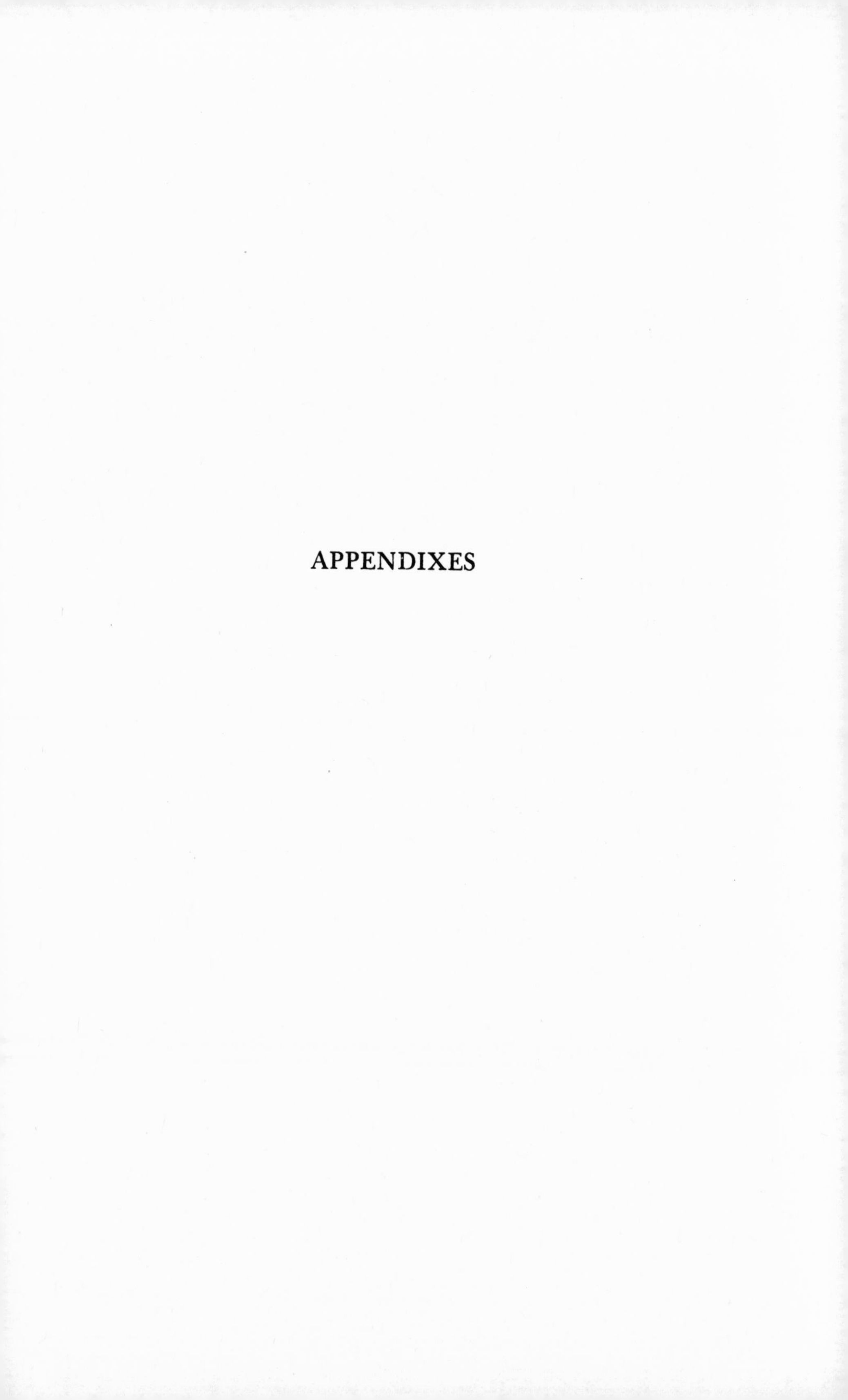

APPENDIXES

APPENDIX A

STUART'S TRADE REGULATIONS OF 1765

REGULATIONS SETTLED AS NECESSARY FOR THE BETTER CARRYING ON THE TRADE WITH THE INDIAN NATIONS SURROUNDING THE PROVINCE OF WEST FLORIDA, BY HIS EXCELLENCY GEORGE JOHNSTONE ESQUIRE. AND THE HONOURABLE JOHN STUART ESQUIRE AND ALSO WITH THE CONSENT OF THE TRADERS THEMSELVES, AND TO WHICH THE SEVERAL BONDS & LICENCES REFER.[1]

1st.—That no Indian trader by himself or substitute, or servant, shall sell or give to any Indian any spirituous liquor of any kind whatsoever—

2d.—That in case any Indian trader by himself substitute or servant shall send more than ten gallons of rum at any one time into the nation or in case there shall be found in the possession of any one person above that quantity in the Indian country such persons or the principal shall be considered as having forfeited his bond & licence.

3d.—That no trader shall employ any person or clerk, packhorseman or factor in their service before an agreement is first entered into in writing between them specifying the time, and conditions of service, and also his or their names indorsed on the back of the licence which may be given to such trader whereby the principal trader shall then be deem'd answerable for his or their conduct.

4th.—That every Indian trader on employing any clerk factor or packhorseman as aforesaid shall give notice within ten days thereafter to the commissary residing in the nation, and whose permission for his continuance must/be also obtained otherwise in case of not obtaining such permission in the space of six weeks, and such clerk factor or packhorseman still continuing in the service of the

[1] This copy of Stuart's trade regulations of 1765 was taken from CO, 5/66. There is another draft in the Gage MSS, entitled "Heads of Instructions to the Traders."

said trader after the said six weeks, then upon such fact being proved the bond & licence to be forfeited

5th.—That no Indian trader shall employ any negro or Indian or half breed, who from his manner of life shall in the conscience of a jury be considered as living under the Indian government as a factor or deputy to trade in any town or village on account of the said trader

6th.—That no trader shall employ in his service any clerk factor or packhorseman who may have been before engaged with another trader untill a regular discharge from such former master shall have been had and produced to the party hireing the said servant &ca. showing the former contract had been disolved by mutual consent or else untill the said servant shall have produced an authentick certificate from the commissary shewing that the former contract is disolved for good & sufficient reasons have been shewn before him the said commissary—

7th.—That no Indian trader shall harbour in his house any white person exceeding eleven days unless under the foregoing regulations, except in case of sickness

8th.—That whatever Indian trader clerk packhorseman or factor shall refuse or neglect to be aiding and assisting to the commissaries on a legal demand being made for the apprehending any offender such conduct shall be considered as a forfeiture of the bond & licence given by the principal—

9th.—That no Indian trader by himself substitute or servant shall sell any swann shott or riffled barrell guns to the Indians—

10th.—That all goods shall be sold according to the following tariff, and if any trader by himself or servant shall sell any goods cheaper or dearer than in the following tariff, then such fact is to be considered as a forfeiture of their bond and licence.

11th.—That the weights and measures of every Indian trader shall conform exactly to the standard weight and measure lodged with the commissary, and if any weight or measure shall be found on comparison to differ one half ounce in weight or one twelv'th of an inch in length therefrom then such difference to be considered as a forfeiture of the bond and licence of the person in whose possession it was found.

12th.—That no Indian trader shall credit any Indian for more than thirty pounds weight of leather and the debts above that amount are not to be considerable as recoverable neither shall any trader credit an Indian for more than three pounds weight of powder and twelve pounds of bulletts—

13th.—That no Indian trader by himself substitute or servant shall propagate any false report or reports among the Indians, or convene any meetings with them or deliver any messages to them without the concurrence of the commissary first obtained in writing

14th.—That any Indian trader refuseing or neglecting to appear at any general meeting of the Indians or congress when duly summoned by the governor of the province superintendant or his deputy except in the case of sickness. Then such refusal shall be considered as a forfeiture of their bond and licence

15th.—That all Indian traders clerks factors and packhorsemen shall duly attend the summons of the commissary and conform to such regulations as His Majesty may hereafter be pleased to prescribe with respect to the trade—

16th.—That no Indian trader clerk factor or packhorseman shall beat or abuse any Indians and that they shall pay a proper respect to the medal chiefs and captains bearing commission—

17th.—That no trader by himself substitute or servant shall trade with any of the Indians in the woods under any pretence whatsoever.

18th.—That no Indian trader shall buy or take in barter for his goods any hides in the hair except in the proportion of four to each horse load of dressed skins.

19th.—That no trader by himself substitute or servant shall barter or trade with any of the Indians in any place except at the house or store of such trader neither shall any trader his substitute or servant forcibly take from any Indian any skins on any pretence whatsoever.

[The prices set for trading articles and the signatures of the traders followed.]

APPENDIX B

STUART'S ATTITUDE TOWARD THE DONELSON LINE

PROFESSOR CLARENCE W. ALVORD has set forth a thoroughly untenable thesis to the effect that the Donelson line actually ran from the Holston to the head of the modern Louisa River and down that stream and the Big Sandy to the Ohio; that Donelson and Dunmore so reported to Hillsborough; and that Stuart removed the Cherokee barrier to settlement in the area between the Louisa–Big Sandy watercourse and the Kentucky. Professor Alvord did not have access to Donelson's map; and he labored under the mistaken impression that the name "Louisa" was never applied to the Kentucky except by John Stuart. He thought the superintendent might have erred in giving that name to the Kentucky in his report of February, 1773, but was tempted to believe Stuart deliberately changed the boundary to the Kentucky for the benefit of Virginia land speculators, the Grand Ohio Company, or the speculators headed by Judge Richard Henderson. He states that Stuart must have been on terms of intimacy with the Henderson crowd, although he could locate no proof of financial connection. Nor could he discover any link between Stuart and the Walpole company.[1]

[1] *Mississippi Valley in British Politics* (Cleveland, 1917), II, 84–89, 143, note 257. Astonishingly enough, Archibald Henderson, "A Pre-Revolutionary Revolt in the Old Southwest," *Miss Vall. Hist. Rev.* XVII (1930), 199, asserts that Donelson altered the treaty line to the Kentucky and cites Alvord on the point! Alvord's discussion of the Donelson survey is extremely unsatisfactory. To be sure, he did not have access to Donelson's map. But he failed to heed the report of the Virginia scouts, cited above; and evidence that he adduced to prove his contention actually disproves it. Thus he cites as decisive a letter by Captain Andrew Snape Hammond. Hammond stated that the Cherokees in the surveying party told Donelson and Cameron "that if they went a small distance further west, than was directed by government, they would find a river running toward the north, which would carry them to the exact point of

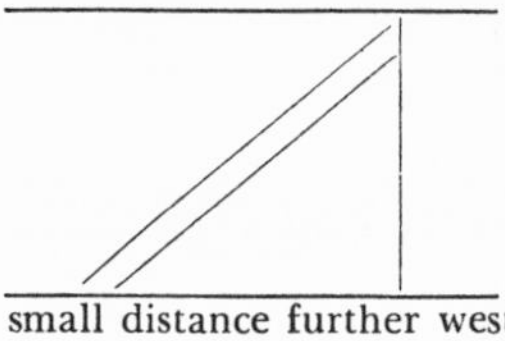

Professor Thomas P. Abernethy, in his *Western Lands and the American Revolution,*[2] pp. 53, 71–77, 125, has given a reasonably accurate account of the course of the Donelson line,[3] but he finds it

the boundary intended to be drawn. This alteration caused a corner in this manner [see the figure] to be added to the colony, which contain many thousand Virginia acres of land." Alvord claims that this figure would describe with some accuracy the lands lying between the Louisa–Big Sandy watercourse and the Lochaber line, but tests made upon maps do not bear out his claim. In fact, Hamond's figure, in spite of its seeming artificiality, is a good description of the area between the Lochaber line, the Kentucky River, and the Ohio as shown on Mitchell's map. That it was intended to portray this area is also indicated by the fact that the hypotenuse of Hamond's right-angled triangle is given as a double line. As a large stream, the Ohio deserved a double line. Again, Alvord attempts to explain away Dartmouth's statement that "A much larger district (several million acres) is taken into Virginia, than was stipulated for by the treaty made in the king's name with the Cherokees," so damaging to his thesis, by arguing that the treaty referred to was that of Hard Labor rather than that of Lochaber. He thinks that the "treaty made in the king's name" must refer to that of Hard Labor rather than to that Lochaber because the former was authorized by the cabinet. But the Treaty of Lochaber was sanctioned by the Board of Trade, Hillsborough, and the king's "confidential servants." Alvord's contention is illogical. If Dartmouth had the Hard Labor line in mind, why should he have ignored the Lochaber line, which had been duly authorized and which was the most recent agreement on the Cherokee boundary? It is significant that there would have been no reason for Dartmouth to bring the addition before the cabinet because it included much territory beyond the Hard Labor line, since that was to be expected. But there was a very definite point in consulting the cabinet because the survey resulted in a large addition beyond the Lochaber line, for that addition was contrary to the orders sent out by Hillsborough.

It should also be noted that, even if the overwhelming evidence is disregarded, Professor Alvord's theory runs directly contrary to the inherent probabilities of the situation. If Stuart had been bribed or otherwise induced to arrange for the Kentucky as the boundary, he could have done so without the clumsy duplicity which Professor Alvord ascribes to him. Why should Stuart have given the lie to Donelson's report in order to achieve what Donelson and Virginia desired, when he could easily have arranged the matter with Donelson before the survey began? Again, if Stuart had changed the boundary to aid the Walpole group or the Henderson crowd, would he not have invited exposure by Donelson?

[2] New York and London, 1937.

[3] It should be stated that Professor Abernethy has offered no very substantial evidence controverting Professor Alvord's thesis regarding the survey. Thus he combats that thesis on the ground that a line following the modern Louisa would, according to the maps of 1771, have given Virginia a less favorable Cherokee boundary than the Lochaber line. But Donelson did not make the survey according to the maps of the time. He went over the ground; and the ignorance of the cartographers would have meant nothing to him. Since he had a good conception of the course of the Big Sandy, as his map demonstrates, he could have run the line down a western tributary of that stream. Professor Abernethy also thinks it significant that Cameron declared that the surveying party had

difficult to explain why Stuart accepted the alteration in the boundary made by Donelson, especially since he believes that prior to 1770 the superintendent had "taken the initiative in the fight to restrict Virginia's western boundary." He indicates Stuart reported to Hillsborough on the Virginia boundary on September 24, 1771, and that the superintendent excused himself from sending a map with that report—"a very suspicious circumstance," he believes. He declares Stuart and Donelson had become good friends at Lochaber and that Stuart may have favored the designs of the Virginia expansionists because of Donelson's influence over him. But a more likely reason for Stuart's complaisance, in his opinion, lies in the fact that the Walpole project was generally expected to succeed in the year 1771 and for some time thereafter. He thinks Stuart knew of the good prospects of the Vandalia scheme in spite of Hillsborough's opposition and that he may have acquiesced in the erasure of Cherokee claims east of the Kentucky because it would benefit the Walpole group rather than Virginia. He is especially inclined toward this view since he suspects that the superintendent turned the prohibitory clause to the advantage of the Walpole crowd. He has unearthed a map sent by Stuart to Ouconnostotah [4] to illustrate the clause, and he notes that the superintendent therein interpreted it to apply to the region between the original western limits of the proposed new colony and the Kentucky River, an interpretation which would have freed the proprietary grant from the restriction. He declares that this map was dispatched to the Cherokee chief more than two months before Stuart sent home the Joseph Purcell map showing the new line and the effect of the prohibition.

Alvord's suspicions of Stuart may be dealt with in summary fashion, since his suggestion that the superintendent may have been influenced by Virginia speculators, the Richard Henderson clique, or the Vandalia group is supported only by the statement of a supposed intimacy between Henderson and Stuart. That intimacy seems completely unreal.[5] That Stuart may have approved Donel-

ceased marking the line at Cedar River. He points out that a stream known by that term flowed into the Kentucky. This fact is hardly conclusive, since the term was used to designate many streams. He states that this information is contained in a "report" by Cameron, and indicates that this "report" was accompanied by a map. However, the information is contained in Cameron's message to the Cherokees of February 5, 1772, cited above. There is no "report" on the matter by Cameron now available. Of course, Cameron made a report to Stuart, but he did not send a map to Stuart. See below.

[4] Cited above. It has been printed by Professor Abernethy.

[5] Alvord's reference on this point is Archibald Henderson, "The Creative

son's work because of his regard for Donelson is also very unlikely. Indeed, Professor Abernethy does not lay much stress on this hypothesis.[6] That Stuart was influenced by the Vandalia group, as the latter authority strongly hints, is equally unlikely. In the first place, Professor Abernethy surely errs in stating that the superintendent exhibited duplicity by excusing himself in a letter to Hillsborough of September 24, 1771, for not sending a map to illustrate the Virginia-Cherokee boundary. Stuart did send such a map at that time, but it dealt with the question prior to the Donelson survey.[7] Since Cameron did not return to South Carolina until October, 1771,[8] and since Stuart was absent from his headquarters at Charleston from May, 1771, to May, 1772, on a mission to West Florida, it seems likely that Stuart then knew little, if anything, regarding the course of the Donelson line. By February, 1772, Stuart knew that the survey had been completed, although he had not

---

Forces in Westward Expansion: Henderson and Boone," *Am. Hist. Rev.*, XX (1914), 86–107. This article shows that Henderson was intimate with one John Stuart. But this John Stuart was in all likelihood the Kentucky pioneer and companion of Daniel Boone, and not the Indian superintendent. I have seen no evidence showing that the superintendent ever met Henderson or that he ever had any correspondence with him. Stuart was hostile to Henderson's project. See Chapter XVI. I have not discovered any substantial evidence connecting Stuart with other land speculators in the South.

[6] It would have been remarkable if the young Virginian had exercised undue influence upon the seasoned and experienced man of the world that Stuart undoubtedly was.

[7] "A Sketch of the Cherakee Boundaries with the Province of Virginia &c. 1771." The original is in the Public Record Office, but there is a freehand copy, together with the letter, in CO, 5/72, Library of Congress transcripts. I had access to a photographic copy of the original, the property of the William L. Clements Library. The map is unsigned, but is dated "Pensacola 24th Septr. 1771." Stuart's excuses for not sending a map had reference to the Joseph Purcell map sent on February 25, 1773, which had its origins as far back as 1769 and which was drawn for the purpose of showing all the Indian boundaries in the southern district. Stuart declared that he hoped to be able to transmit this map to Hillsborough at an early date and that he expected to have a very satisfactory one based on materials already collected and to be collected, "as there will be actual surveys of the lines behind Virginia North and South Carolinas & Georgia accomplished before my return to Charles Town." The Purcell map was not sent until early in 1773 because Stuart was aware that Mitchell's map and others of the interior of North America were unreliable. He tried to secure more authentic information. Finally, in order to satisfy the requests of the colonial secretaries for the map, he temporarily gave up this project and ordered Purcell to do the best he could with Mitchell's map as a basis.

[8] Cameron's return was not announced in the *South-Carolina and American General Gazette* until Dec. 3, 1771.

received from Cameron an account of his proceedings.[9] Before he returned to Charleston he may have received a report from Cameron, but it was not until after he reached his headquarters that he had access to a map of the survey.[10] Probably he also discussed the survey with Cameron some time after his return. Perhaps he reported upon it to the home government during the late summer of 1772.[11] If he did so, there can be no doubt that his account was the same as that which he gave in February, 1773, except that it may have been more complete. He may have neglected to report because he knew that Dunmore had already informed Hillsborough regarding the survey and because he preferred to let Virginia defend Donelson's action.

Professor Abernethy is also surely mistaken when he asserts that Stuart did not transmit his remarks on the survey and his interpretation of the prohibition of settlement to Dartmouth until two months after Ouconnostotah received the map illustrating the prohibition. That map was sent to the Cherokee chief not "late in 1772," but in June, 1773, as a message accompanying it clearly demonstrates. Stuart reported on the line and gave his interpretation of the prohibition to Dartmouth more than three months before he announced the prohibition to Ouconnostotah.[12] To be sure, Stuart did not know at the time of the Congress of Augusta that Dartmouth approved of his interpretation. Nevertheless, there is no evidence in these facts that Stuart was favoring the interests of the

[9] Stuart to Hillsborough, Feb. 9, 1772, CO, 5/72; Stuart to Gage, Feb. 16, 1772, Gage MSS.

[10] Stuart to Hillsborough, June 13, 1772, CO, 5/72; Stuart to Dartmouth, Jan. 4, 1773, CO, 5/74.

[11] In accordance with a custom established by Lord Shelburne, Stuart numbered his letters to the secretaries of state. On July 19, 1772, he wrote no. 44 in the series to Hillsborough, and on September 23 he wrote no. 46. But there is no no. 45 in the Library of Congress transcripts. Furthermore, Dartmouth does not mention receiving no. 45, although he indicates that he received nos. 44 and 46. No. 45 may have contained a report on the survey and may have been lost. This possibility is rendered almost a probability because of the fact that Stuart's remarks on the boundary in his letter of February 25, 1773, were brief, although his reports were usually complete.

[12] An examination of the message convinces one that it was written at the close of the Congress of Augusta, held by Stuart and Wright with the Cherokees and Creeks in June, 1773, to make an important change in the Georgia boundary. Ouconnostotah failed to attend this conference, and Stuart wrote to him giving him a brief account of the proceedings. At the congress Stuart had already informed the Cherokees gathered there of the prohibition. See Stuart to Ouconnostotah, n.d., Papers of the Continental Congress, No. 71, Vol. ii.

Vandalia group or that he was deceiving his superior officers, as Professor Abernethy suggests.

Unless it can be shown that Stuart's interpretation of the prohibitory clause is explainable only on the ground that the superintendent was trying to serve the Walpole speculators, Abernethy's case falls down completely. And there is good reason to believe that Stuart's interpretation was an honest one, although not the correct one. It will be recalled that the prohibition was contained in a letter from Dartmouth of September 2, 1772. When Stuart received this letter at the close of 1772 he knew that the minister had read Dunmore's report and had seen Donelson's map before writing it. Stuart would quite reasonably have assumed that the minister was aware of the change made by Donelson. The superintendent also knew that Donelson on his map mentioned his work as if the Lochaber line and the line as amended by himself were synonymous.[13] Stuart might well therefore have concluded that the Lochaber "treaty line" meant for Dartmouth, as it did for Donelson, the line as amended by Donelson to the Kentucky. It should also be noted that, even if Stuart had made the correct interpretation, he would still have considered almost all the lands within the proposed proprietary grant open to settlement. The reason for this, shown by the map sent by Stuart to Dartmouth and the one sent by him to Ouconnostotah, is that the superintendent believed that the original western boundary of Vandalia lay much farther east than it actually did. In other words, given Stuart's meager knowledge of the geography of the region in question, an interpretation permitting the Vandalia proprietors to settle all, or practically all, of their grant was inevitable.[14]

Not only are the suspicions of Stuart's conduct voiced by Alvord and Abernethy unsupported by valid evidence at this writing, but it is possible to offer some very substantial reasons why Stuart was willing to accept the alteration made by Donelson. In the first place, Stuart was confronted on his return from West Florida with a *fait accompli,* since the Cherokees had already given their consent. Sec-

[13] Donelson declared: "The contents in acres ceded to the crown by the treaty of Lochaber in Oct. 1770 is estimated to 10,000,000 of acres lying between the rivers Louisa Ohio and the Great Kanaway."

[14] This statement may readily be tested by consulting a modern map of the region involved and the map sent by Stuart to Ouconnostotah, printed in Professor Abernethy's work. It should be added that it is difficult to see what Stuart could have gained by intentionally giving a false interpretation to the prohibitory clause, since the home government could have corrected him.

ondly, the superintendent himself was certainly not against the establishment of the Kentucky as the boundary, for he had suggested to Hillsborough in the summer of 1768 and again after Lochaber that the line should follow that stream. The Donelson line no doubt seemed to Stuart a reasonably satisfactory solution of a very troublesome question. Furthermore, the home government, after encouraging Stuart to fight the large private purchase made by Indian traders on the Georgia frontier in spite of the Proclamation of 1763, deserted him early in 1772 and prepared to compel him to ratify the purchase in a formal congress with the Creeks and Cherokees. Indeed, there was every reason why Stuart should not oppose Donelson's alteration; it is difficult to find valid reasons why he should have done so.

APPENDIX C

BRITISH MISSIONARIES TO THE SOUTHERN INDIANS, 1754–75

LITTLE was done by the British to Christianize the southern Indians during the period 1754–75. The Society for the Propagation of the Gospel in Foreign Parts, never very energetic in the work of converting the Indians on the borders of the southern colonies, apparently lost all interest in that field after 1754.[1] But in 1757 the Society in Scotland for Propagating Christian Knowledge, located in Edinburgh and controlled by Scottish Presbyterians, and The Company for Propagation of the Gospel in New England and the parts adjacent in America, housed in London and managed by Anglicans, were eager to do something toward winning the Cherokees and their Indian neighbors to Christianity. At that time they were willing to support two missionaries. The Society in Virginia for managing the Missions and Schools among the Indians, composed chiefly if not wholly of Presbyterians and headed by the Reverend Samuel Davies of Hanover, undertook to choose the missionaries and to direct their labors. In fact, it is not unlikely that the project originated in the mind of Davies, a man of energy and ability who soon afterward became president of Princeton College.

In October, 1757, the Virginia Society employed John Martin, a pupil of Davies and apparently the first Presbyterian minister ordained in Virginia, as a missionary to the Cherokees. At the same time the society tried to secure the immediate ordination of the famous Indian preacher Samson Occom, so that he might assist Martin. But poor Occom, who would have been highly pleased to receive the salary of £70 per annum offered by the British societies, was unable to obtain ordination until 1759; and the onset of the Cherokee War ruined his hopes of employment in the South.[2] Martin was encouraged by the Virginia council and by Governor Lyttelton. He began his labors in the Overhill country in the late spring of 1758. He was the first British missionary to work among the In-

[1] Frank J. Klingberg, "The Indian Frontier in South Carolina as Seen by the S. P. G. Missionary," *Journal of Southern History,* V (1939), 478–500.

[2] Harold Blodgett, *Samson Occom* (Hanover, N. H., 1935), 50–51.

dians in the southern trans-Appalachian region. Martin was able to report that he had preached at Fort Loudoun to the soldiers and the Overhills and that he had had some success. In July, 1758, the Virginia Society appointed the Reverend William Richardson to serve with Martin. Richardson, also a Presbyterian, was a native of Whitehaven, educated in Glasgow and ordained at Cumberland about the time of his appointment. In October, 1758, Richardson accepted employment under the Virginia Society and traveled to the Overhill towns through the back settlements of South Carolina. There he met Martin, who was returning to Virginia to report. In November Richardson set out for his post by way of Fort Prince George. In the following month he reached Fort Loudoun and began his work. But the Overhills, at that time deeply discontented with the conduct of the English, refused to allow him to preach, and he soon became discouraged. Ouconnostotah informed him that he might be able to obtain a hearing through the influence of Attakullakulla when he should return from Virginia. Richardson felt that the chances of success were too slight to warrant the expenditure of the funds of his employers. In February, 1759, he left for South Carolina, where he entered upon a pastorate. The outbreak of the Cherokee War, coupled with the departure of the energetic Davies for Princeton, seems to have put an end to this project for Christianizing the Cherokees.[3]

Although Sir William Johnson displayed much interest in missionary work among the northern Indians, no evidence has been found that Stuart approved or sponsored projects to bring the white man's civilization to his charges. His attitude may have been similar to that taken by a not-too-wise contemporary wag who asserted that a sermon would receive little attention unless accompanied by a keg of rum. Nevertheless, after 1763 other persons thought it possible to do useful work with the southern Indians. In 1766, when Eleazar Wheelock was seeking a new home for his Indian school, one of his followers, Charles Jeffry Smith, urged that the school be reëstablished on the frontier of the Carolinas. Smith pointed out that there were many more Indians on the borders of the Carolinas than near the Hudson. He also indicated that a fertile field existed in the South for useful labor with the backwoods-

[3] Minutes of Va. council, Dec. 14, 1757, Oct. 4, 1758, June 13, 1759, CO, 5/1429; Samuel C. Williams, "An Account of the Presbyterian Mission to the Cherokees, 1757–1759," *Tenn. Hist. Mag.*, Second Series, I (1931), 125–38. The article cited contains the major part of a diary kept by Richardson relating to his mission.

men and the Negroes. In addition, he was inclined to believe that the milder southern climate would prolong Wheelock's life. Johnson, who was not at all eager that Wheelock remain in the North, supported Smith's proposal. About the same time Nathaniel Whitaker suggested that the school be moved to the "southwestward," to a grant that General Phineas Lyman expected to obtain on the banks of the Mississippi. Wheelock eventually chose New Hampshire as a new site,[4] although he did not lose all interest in the southern field. In 1774, no doubt at the suggestion of Lord Dartmouth, he communicated with the New Jersey Board of Correspondents for the Edinburgh Society regarding a plan to send a missionary to the Catawbas. The New Jersey board was willing to grant funds for the purpose,[5] but the project was allowed to drop.

Most promising of plans to civilize the southern Indians after 1763 was one formed by John Daniel Hammerer, a Lutheran and a native of Strasbourg, who fled to England at the mid-century to escape "the civil and religious oppressions which my country is subject to under an arbitrary & Romish government." Hammerer was of middle-class parentage and had studied in the gymnasium at Strasbourg. He hoped both to Christianize and educate the Indians of British North America in the ways of civilization, and to bring about the amalgamation of the Indians with the British to the greater power and glory of Britain. But Hammerer was no idle dreamer. He proposed to begin his work upon a small scale among the Creeks. He made preparations to settle at Coweta town, and in an attempt to secure financial support he published a *Plan for Civilizing the North American Indians.*[6] When Hammerer learned in 1765 that certain Cherokees who had appeared in London under the guidance of Lieutenant Henry Timberlake had urged that missionaries be sent to their nation, he decided to begin his work in the Cherokee country. He asked the Board of Trade to employ him. Lord Hillsborough encouraged him to proceed with his design, though he could offer no financial aid. Charles Witworth, M.P.,

[4] "The Rough Sketch of a Plan for Settling the Indian-Charity-School humbly submitted to Consideration by Charles Jeffry Smith," June 2, 1766, Dartmouth College Library; Nathaniel Whitaker to Wheelock, March 7, 1767, Leon B. Richardson, ed., *An Indian Preacher in England* (Hanover, N. H., 1933), 229; James D. McCallum, *Eleazar Wheelock: Founder of Dartmouth College* (Hanover, N. H., 1939), Chapter VII.

[5] James Caldwell to Wheelock, April 19, 1774, John Brainerd to David McClure, April 22, 1774, Elihu Spencer to Wheelock, May 3, 1774, Dartmouth College Library.

[6] Reprinted and edited by Paul Leicester Ford (Brooklyn, 1890).

Thomas Crowley, and others gave him more substantial assistance; and Hammerer and a companion sailed with the Cherokees on the *Madeira* for Virginia. He had believed that these Cherokees were persons of importance, and that they would help him, but he discovered on arriving at Williamsburg that they had little influence. However, Fauquier and his council gave the missionry £40 and undertook to convey his baggage to Chiswell's Mine. When Attakullakulla appeared at Williamsburg in the summer of 1765, Fauquier persuaded the little chief to escort Hammerer and his companion to the Overhill towns. Attakullakulla and Hammerer reached Chiswell's Mine in August.[7] Shortly afterward they arrived in the Overhill country.

Hammerer enjoyed little success in the Overhill region, partly because the Overhills were engrossed by warfare with the Six Nations and other northern tribes. In the fall of 1765 certain Lower Cherokees invited him to move his headquarters to their towns, promising to do all within their power to assist him. In the following year he accepted their invitation; at the suggestion of Ensign George Price he settled near Fort Prince George. The Lower Cherokees undertook to build quarters for him and for the school, and to provide food for him and his scholars.[8] Observers soon reported that the Lower townsmen were eager to have their children instructed, that Hammerer was an able teacher, and that a number of children entrusted by the chiefs to his care made surprising progress. The pupils learned to write in their own language, although Hammerer declined to attempt the task of compiling a Cherokee grammar.[9] At the close of 1766 the South Carolina assembly, impressed by Hammerer's zeal, voted £100 (provincial currency) for his support.[10] He also received further help from Thomas Crowley, but insufficient funds caused him to remove to Long Canes by 1769, where he continued to instruct a few Cherokee children who remained in his charge. At that time Crowley tried again to secure assistance from the Board of Trade. Hillsborough asked Lord Charles Montagu to persuade the South Carolina assem-

[7] Hammerer to Abraham von Gammern, Aug. —, 1765, Adelaide L. Fries, ed., *Records of the Moravians in North Carolina, Vol. I, 1752–1771* (Raleigh, N. C., 1922), 311–13.

[8] Hammerer to Johann Ettwein, June 13, 1766, Hammerer's brief description of the Cherokee country, Sept. 26, 1766, Archives of the Moravian Church, Bethlehem, Pa.

[9] *South-Carolina Gazette,* Dec. 15, 1766; *South-Carolina and American General Gazette,* April 3, 1767.

[10] *Georgia Gazette,* Jan. 17, 1767.

bly to offer an additional grant to assist the missionary. In the absence of Montagu Lieutenant Governor Bull promised to do what he could to help.[11] No record has been found regarding further teaching activities by Hammerer. The journal of the congress of Lochaber shows that he was present at that gathering. Hammerer later settled in or near Savannah, for he was appointed magistrate and vendue master for Chatham County in 1778 by the revolutionary government of Georgia.[12] However, he probably abandoned the cause of the patriots, since he was named as the publisher of the *Royal Gazette* of January 21, 1780.

The Moravians on the frontier of North Carolina were on friendly terms with Hammerer. They were also interested in proselyting the southern Indians before the Revolution. Apparently, they had little success, although they baptized a Cherokee warrior and his wife in July, 1773.[13]

[11] Memorial by Thomas Crowley to Hillsborough, received at Board of Trade, June 1, 1769, CO, 5/379; Hillsborough to Montagu, July 15, 1769, Bull to Hillsborough, Oct. 4, 1769, CO, 5/392.

[12] Allen D. Candler, ed., *The Revolutionary Records of the State of Georgia* (Atlanta, 1908), II, 64, 86.

[13] George Henry Loskiel, *History of the Mission of the United Brethren among the Indians in North America* (London, 1794), Part III, 90.

BIBLIOGRAPHY

Guides and Calendars

Allison, William H., Inventory of Unpublished Material for American Religious History in Protestant Church Archives and Other Repositories. Washington, 1910.

Andrews, Charles M., Guide to the Materials for American History to 1783, in the Public Record Office of Great Britain. 2 vols. Washington, 1912.

—— and Davenport, Frances C., Guide to the Manuscript Materials for the History of the United States to 1783, in the British Museum, in Minor London Archives, and in the Libraries of Oxford and Cambridge. Washington, 1908.

Atchley, C., Catalogue of the Maps, Plans and Charts in the Library of the Colonial Office. London? 1910.

Brymner, Douglas, Report on Canadian Archives, 1883, 1884, 1885, 1886, 1887, 1888, 1889. Ottawa, 1884–90. Taken collectively, these reports contain a calendar of the Frederick Haldimand MSS. The Report for 1889 also includes a calendar of the Henry Bouquet MSS.

Day, Richard E., Calendar of the Sir William Johnson Manuscripts. Albany, 1909.

Palmer, W. P., McRae, S., and Fleurnoy, W. H., Calendar of Virginia State Papers, 1652–1869. 11 vols. Richmond, 1875–93.

Royal Historical Manuscripts Commission, Eleventh Report; Fourteenth Report; Report on the Laing Manuscripts Preserved in the University of Edinburgh.

Stevens, Benjamin F., Catalogue Index of Manuscripts in the Archives of England, France, and Holland relating to America, 1763–1783. London, 1870–1902. MS, Library of Congress.

Contemporary Sources (Manuscript)

Ann Arbor, Michigan

William L. Clements Library

Manuscripts

Sir Jeffrey Amherst MSS. Contain the papers given by Amherst to Gage for his guidance. A useful collection, including correspondence between Amherst and John Stuart. To be distinguished from the Amherst Papers in Public Record Office, War Office, 34.

Sir Henry Clinton MSS. Contain a few pieces of value on Indian affairs in the South before 1776.

General Thomas Gage MSS. From this collection correspondence between Gage on the one hand, and Stuart, Sir William Johnson, the southern governors, and military officers in the South on the other, has been very informative. Correspondence between Stuart and Gage has been especially valuable. The Gage MSS are of fundamental importance in this study. The most important part, and perhaps the larger part, of Stuart's official correspondence is to be found in the Gage MSS and in the British Colonial Office papers. Taken together, documents from these two collections substantially fill the gap left by the disappearance of Stuart's own papers.

William Knox MSS. Include some useful documents of the period when Knox was provost marshal of Georgia; also some of the period when he served as undersecretary of state for the colonies.

Shelburne MSS. Contain copies of many documents in the British Colonial Office papers, also original documents on Indian policy.

Alexander Wedderburn MSS. Include a few letters of considerable interest by a younger brother of the solicitor general. For a time David Wedderburn was commandant at Mobile.

CHARLESTON, SOUTH CAROLINA

CHARLESTON COUNTY COURTHOUSE

Manuscripts

Probate Court Records

Records of the Court of Common Pleas

Record of Wills, Charleston County.

Miscellaneous Records

CHARLOTTESVILLE, VIRGINIA

UNIVERSITY OF VIRGINIA LIBRARY

Photostatic Copies from Public Record Office of Great Britain

Virginia Council Journals (Executive), 1744–53. Bound in one volume.

Virginia Council Journals (Executive), 1752–74, Colonial Office 5/1429, 1435, 1440.

COLUMBIA, SOUTH CAROLINA

HISTORICAL COMMISSION OF SOUTH CAROLINA

Manuscripts

Indian Books of South Carolina, vols. ii–vi. These papers are a storehouse of information on southern Indian affairs during the period 1750–65.

Journal of the Directors of the Cherokee Trade, 1762–1765. 1 vol.

Council Journals, South Carolina, vols. x–xxxviii. Cover the period 1743–74.

Commons House Journals, South Carolina, vols. xviii–xxxix. Cover the period 1743–75.

Memorial Books

Transcripts and Photostatic Copies from Public Record Office of Great Britain

Sainsbury transcripts of correspondence of the governors, Board of Trade papers, and other official documents concerning the colonial history of South Carolina. Particularly useful for this study were documents from Colonial Office 5/13–20, 211–15, 317–18, 365–80, 385–86, 400–6, 425–27, 658. The old-style Public Record Office classification is followed in the Sainsbury transcripts.

Public Records of South Carolina, vol. iii. Contains journals of the South Carolina council, March 15, 1742—Feb. 19, 1743, Jan. 5, 1761—Dec. 28, 1762, Jan. 3–Dec. 29, 1769. This volume should not be confused with another designated by the same title and included in a series containing the Sainsbury transcripts.

Council Journals, South Carolina, Jan. 8–Nov. 4, 1746, Nov. 29, 1746—May 29, 1747, Dec. 16, 1749—Dec. 14, 1750, Sept. 3, 1754—Jan. 1, 1755, Jan. 6, 1755—Jan. 1, 1756, April 1–Dec. 30, 1760.

NEW YORK CITY

NEW YORK CITY PUBLIC LIBRARY

Transcripts from Public Record Office of Great Britain

American Loyalists: Transcript of the Manuscript Books and Papers of the Commission of Enquiry into the Losses and Services of the American Loyalists held under Acts of Parliament of 23, 25, 26, 28, and 29 of George III. preserved amongst the Audit Office Records at the Public Record Office of England 1783–1790. 60 vols.

PHILADELPHIA, PENNSYLVANIA

HISTORICAL SOCIETY OF PENNSYLVANIA

Transcripts from Public Record Office of Great Britain

Colonial Office 323/13–29. Board of Trade, Plantations General papers, covering the period 1750–80.

RICHMOND, VIRGINIA

VIRGINIA STATE LIBRARY

Manuscripts

Council Journals of Virginia, 1722–1773. One volume of council minutes, scattered over a long period.

WASHINGTON, D.C.

LIBRARY OF CONGRESS

Manuscripts

Papers of the Continental Congress, No. 71, vol ii. A number of documents relating to the Cherokees in the Revolutionary period.

Cherokee Indians, 1760–1774. A volume of documents and newspaper clippings.

Transcripts and Photostatic Copies from Public Record Office of Great Britain and the British Museum

Audit Office 12/51, pp. 146–63. Loyalist papers, containing claims and testimony of John Stuart's heirs.

British Museum, Additional Manuscripts, 21,671 and 21,672. These are a portion of the Frederick Haldimand MSS, containing correspondence between Haldimand, Gage, John Stuart, Charles Stuart, Lieut. Col. William Tayler, Gov. James Wright, Lieutenant John Ritchy, and various other British officials. A very useful collection.

Chatham MSS, 73, British Museum.

Colonial Office 5/6. Valuable papers on British policy and events in 1754–55.

Colonial Office 5/7, 11, 14, 15, 17, 19, 20, 43, 94, 114, 115, 158, 223.

Colonial Office 5/47–50. Letters with enclosures from Loudoun and Abercromby.

Colonial Office 5/54–63. Reports with enclosures from Amherst to secretary of state for the southern department, covering the period 1758–63, and from Forbes to the secretary of state for the southern department.

Colonial Office 5/64–82. Correspondence between John Stuart and the secretaries of state from 1763 to 1779. Similar correspondence between Edmund Atkin, Cameron, Thomas Browne, and the secretaries of state. Indispensable for this study.

Colonial Office 5/225, 227. Correspondence of Shelburne and other ministers with John Stuart and Sir William Johnson, 1766–71.

Colonial Office 5/540–55. East Florida papers, including correspondence of the governors.

Colonial Office 5/574–98. West Florida papers, including correspondence of the governors.

Colonial Office 5/625–31. Minutes of the council and assembly of West Florida.

Colonial Office 5/1328–38, 1345–53. Correspondence and enclosed papers between the governors of Virginia and the secretaries of state.

Colonial Office 5/1367–69. Board of Trade papers regarding Virginia, covering the period 1752–74.

Colonial Office 324/51.

War Office 34/35, 36, 38, 47. A portion of the papers of Amherst, containing correspondence between Loudoun and Amherst on the one hand and southern governors and military officers in the South on the other.

Transcripts from Paris

Archives Nationales, Colonies, B: 93, 95, 97, 99, 101, 103, 105, 107, 109, 111, 114, 116, 119, 121, 123, 126, 129, 132. Letters from the French ministry to Louisiana officials, and other papers, 1751–69.

Archives Nationales, Colonies, C13A: 36–50. Letters of Louisiana officials with enclosures to the ministers of marine and the colonies, 1751–69. Indispensable for French Indian policy in the South during the period indicated. Letters from Kerlérec are especially valuable.

Microfilms and Photostatic Copies

IN POSSESSION OF THE AUTHOR

Edmund Atkin's letters with enclosures to Loudoun. Originals in Henry E. Huntington Library and Art Gallery, San Marino, California.

A few papers, cited in Appendix C, from the Dartmouth College Library and the Archives of the Moravian Church, Bethlehem, Pennsylvania.

PRINTED SOURCES, INCLUDING CONTEMPORARY IMPRINTS, AND ALSO LATER EDITIONS AND COLLECTIONS OF DOCUMENTS

ADAIR, JAMES. *See* Williams, Samuel C.

ALVORD, CLARENCE W., AND CARTER, CLARENCE E., eds., "The Critical Period, 1763–1765," "The New Régime, 1765–1767," "Trade and Politics, 1767–1769," British Series, I, II, III, Collections of the Illinois State Historical Library, X (1915), XI (1916), XVI (1921). Springfield, Ill.

BANNERMAN, W. BRUCE, AND BANNERMAN, MAJOR W. BRUCE, eds., The Registers of St. Stephen's, Walbrook and of St. Benet Sherehog, London. Pt. I. London, 1919.

BARTRAM, WILLIAM, Travels through North and South Carolina, Georgia, East and West Florida, the Cherokee Country, the Extensive Territories of the Muscogulges or Creek Confederacy, and the Country of the Chactaws. London, 1792.

BJÖRK, D. K., ed., "Documents Regarding Indian Affairs in the Lower Mississippi Valley, 1771–1772," Miss. Vall. Hist. Rev., XIII (1926), 398–410. A few documents about John Thomas are given here. The introductory note fails to indicate that Thomas was a member of the southern Indian department.

British Army Lists.

BROCK, R. A., ed., The Official Records of Robert Dinwiddie, Lieutenant-Governor of the Colony of Virginia, 1751–1758 . . . Richmond, 1883–84, 2 vols., designated as Vols. III and IV in Virginia Historical Collections.

BROWNE, W. H., HALL, C. C., STEINER, B. C., AND PLEASANTS, J. H., eds., Archives of Maryland. 55 vols. to date. Baltimore, 1883—.

CANDLER, ALLEN D., ed., Colonial Records of the State of Georgia. Atlanta, 1904–16, Vols. I–XIX, XXI–XXVI. *See* Georgia Colonial Records.

CARTER, CLARENCE E., ed., Correspondence of General Thomas Gage. 2 vols. New Haven, 1931–33. A selection from the correspondence between Gage and the secretaries of state containing many important documents.

—— ed., John Stuart's "Observations on the Plan for the future Management of Indian Affairs . . .," Dec. 1, 1764, Am. Hist. Rev., XX (1915), 817–27.

—— ed., Comments by Governor James Grant on the Plan of 1764, Dec. 1, 1764, *ibid.*, XX (1915), 827–31.

CHAMBERS, ROBERT, ed., Jacobite Memoirs of the Rebellion of 1745. Edinburgh, London, 1834.

CLARK, WALTER, ed., The State Records of North Carolina . . . Goldsboro, N. C. 1895–1905, 16 vols., numbered XI–XXVI to follow Saunders, W. L., ed., The Colonial Records of North Carolina. *See* Weeks, Stephen B.

CLARKE, A. W. HUGHES, ed., The Register of St. Mary the Virgin, Aldermanbury, London. Pt. III. London, 1935.

CLOWES, G. C. LAIRD, ed., A Voyage Round the World In the Years MDCCXL, I, II, III, IV. By George Anson, Esq., Commander in Chief of a Squadron of His Majesty's Ships, sent upon an Expedition to the South-Seas. Compiled From Papers and other Materials of the Right Honourable George Lord Anson, and published under his Direction, By Richard Walter, M. A., Chaplain of his Majesty's Ship the Centurion, in that Expedition. London, Boston, 1928.

Collections of the New-York Historical Society for the Years 1872, 1897, 1899, 1908, 1921. New York, 1873–1922.

COOPER, THOMAS, AND MCCORD, DAVID J., eds., Statutes at Large of South Carolina. 10 vols. Columbia, S. C., 1836–41.

DOVER, LORD, ed., Letters of Horace Walpole, Earl of Oxford, to Sir Thomas Mann, British Envoy at the Court of Tuscany. 2 vols. New York, 1833.

FITZPATRICK, JOHN C., ed., The Writings of George Washington from the Original Sources, 1745–1799. 23 vols. to date. Washington, 1931—.

FORCE, PETER, ed., American Archives, Fourth Series. 6 vols. Washington, 1837–46.

FRASER-MACKINTOSH, CHARLES, ed., Letters of Two Centuries, Chiefly Connected with Inverness and the Highlands from 1616 to 1815. Inverness, 1890.

FRIES, ADELAIDE L., ed., Records of the Moravians in North Carolina, Vol. I, 1752–1771. Raleigh, N. C., 1922.

Gentleman's Magazine, 1731–1876.

Georgia Colonial Records, Vols. XX, XXVII–XXXIX. Typescript copies in Georgia State Department of Archives and History, Atlanta. *See* Candler, Allen D.

Georgia Gazette, The, 1763–70, 1774–75. In Library of Congress. There are considerable gaps in this file.

GRANT, W. L., AND MUNRO, JAMES, eds., Acts of the Privy Council of England, Colonial Series. 5 vols. London, 1908–12.

HAMILTON, STANISLAUS M., ed., Letters to Washington and Accompanying Papers. 5 vols. Boston and New York, 1898–1902.

HAMMERER, JOHN DANIEL, Plan for Civilizing the North American Indians. Paul L. Ford, ed. Brooklyn, 1890.

HAZARD, SAMUEL, ed., Pennsylvania Archives, First Series. 10 vols. Philadelphia, 1852–54.

HEWATT, REV. ALEXANDER, An Historical Account of the Rise and Progress of the Colonies of South Carolina and Georgia. 2 vols. London, 1779.

HUMPHREYS, R. A., ed., "Governor Murray's Views on the Plan of 1764 for the Management of Indian Affairs," Can. Hist. Rev., XVI (1935), 162–69.

HUTCHINSON, PETER O., ed., The Diary and Letters of His Excellency Thomas Hutchinson ... 2 vols. Boston, 1884–86.

JILLSON, WILLARD R., ed., Filson's Kentucke. Filson Club Publications, No. 35 (1930).

Journal of the Commissioners for Trade and Plantations from April 1704 ... to May 1782. London, 1920–38, published in 14 vols., designated by the periods they cover.

Journal of the Congress of the Four Southern Governors, and the Superintendant of That District, with the Five Nations of Indians, at Augusta, 1763, Charles Town, Printed by Peter Timothy [1764]. The official journal.

KENNEDY, JOHN P. *See* McIlwaine, H. R.

KIMBALL, GERTRUDE S., ed., Correspondence of William Pitt, when Secretary of State, with Colonial Governors, and Military and Naval Commissioners in America. 2 vols. New York, 1906.

London Chronicle, The. 1757–75.

McILWAINE, H. R., AND KENNEDY, JOHN P., eds., Journals of the House of Burgesses of Virginia, 1742 ... 1776. 7 vols., designated according to the period covered. Richmond, 1905–9.

MACKAY, WILLIAM. *See* Scottish History Society.

MERENESS, NEWTON D., ed., Travels in the American Colonies. New York, 1916.

MOULTRIE, WILLIAM, Memoirs of the American Revolution, So Far As It Related to the States of North and South Carolina, and Georgia. 2 vols. New York, 1802.

O'CALLAGHAN, E. B., ed., Documents Relating to the Colonial History of the State of New York, Procured in Holland, England, and France by John R. Brodhead. 11 vols. Albany, 1856–61.

——ed., The Documentary History of the State of New York. 4 vols., quarto ed. Albany, 1850.

PARGELLIS, STANLEY M., ed., Military Affairs in North America, 1748–1765: Selected Documents from the Cumberland Papers in Windsor Castle. New York and London, 1936.

PHILIPS, JOHN, An Authentic Journal of the late Expedition under the Command of Commodore Anson .... London, 1744.

PHILLIMORE, ROBERT, ed., Memoirs and Correspondence of George, Lord Lyttelton, From 1734 to 1773. 2 vols. London, 1845.

POWNALL, THOMAS, The Administration of the British Colonies. Second Edition. London, 1765.

REYNELL-UPHAM, W. U., AND TAPLEY-SOPER, H., eds., The Registers of Baptisms, Marriages, & Burials of the City of Exeter. 2 vols. Exeter, 1910–33.

RICHARDSON, LEON B., ed., An Indian Preacher in England. Hanover, N. H., 1933.

ROMANS, BERNARD, A Concise Natural History of East and West Florida. 1 vol., although two were projected. New York, 1775.

ROWLAND, DUNBAR, ed., Mississippi Provincial Archives, 1763–1766: English Dominion, Letters and Inclosures to the Secretary of State from Major Robert Farmar and Governor George Johnstone. 1 vol., although others were projected. Nashville, Tenn., 1911.

—— ed., Publications of the Mississippi Historical Society, Centenary Series, Vols. I, V. Jackson, Miss., 1916, 1925.

Royal Gazette, The. 1779–82. Photostatic copies of a few issues in Library of Congress.

St. Andrew's Society of the City of Charleston, South Carolina. Founded in the Year One Thousand Seven Hundred and Twenty-nine. Incorporated in 1798. Charleston, 1892.

SALLEY, A. S., JR., ed., Marriage Notices in The South-Carolina Gazette; and Country Journal (1765–1775) and in The Charlestown Gazette (1778–1780). Charleston, 1904.

—— ed., Death Notices in The South-Carolina Gazette, 1732–1775. Columbia, S. C., 1917.

—— ed., Register of St. Philip's Parish, Charles Town, South Carolina, 1720–1758. Charleston, 1904.

SAUNDERS, WILLIAM L., ed., The Colonial Records of North Carolina.... 10 vols. Raleigh, N. C., 1886–90. *See* Weeks, Stephen B.

Scottish History Society, First Series, VIII (1890), XXI (1895), LVII (1909). Second Series, IX (1915), William Mackay, ed., "The Letter-Book of Bailie John Steuart of Inverness, 1715–1752." Third Series, XXV (1935).

SHORTT, ADAM, AND DOUGHTY, ARTHUR G., eds., Canadian Archives: Documents Relating to the Constitutional History of Canada, 1759–1791. Second and Revised Edition, in two parts. Ottawa, 1918.

SIEBERT, WILBUR H., The Loyalists in East Florida, 1774–1785. 2 vols. Florida Historical Society, 1929. The first volume is narrative; the second consists of documents.

SMITH, D. E. HUGER, AND SALLEY, A. S., JR., eds., Register of St. Philip's Parish, Charles Town, or Charleston, S. C., 1754–1810. Charleston, 1927.

SMITH, SIR JAMES EDWARD, ed., A Selection of the Correspondence of Linnaeus, and Other Naturalists, from the Original Manuscripts. 2 vols. London, 1821.

SMYTH, ALBERT H., ed., The Writings of Benjamin Franklin. 10 vols. New York and London, 1905–7.

South-Carolina and American General Gazette, The. 1766–72, 1774–75. Photostatic copies and originals in Charleston Library Society.

South-Carolina Gazette, The, 1732–75. Photostatic copies and originals in Charleston Library Society.

SULLIVAN, JAMES, FLICK, ALEXANDER C., LAUBER, ALMON W., AND OTHERS, eds., The Papers of Sir William Johnson. 9 vols. to date. Albany, 1921—.

THOMAS, PASCOE, A True and Impartial Journal of a Voyage to the South Seas and Round the Globe in His Majesty's Ship the Centurion, under the Command of Commodore George Anson.... London, 1745.

THWAITES, REUBEN G., ed., Collections of the State Historical Society of Wisconsin, Vols. XVII, XVIII. Madison, 1906, 1908.

—— AND KELLOGG, LOUISE P., eds., Documentary History of Dunmore's War, 1774. Madison, 1905.

—— —— eds., The Revolution on the Upper Ohio. Madison, 1908.

Virginia Gazette, The (Rind). 1769–71. Photostatic copies in University of Virginia Library.

Virginia Gazette, The (Purdie & Dixon). 1768–72. Photostatic copies in University of Virginia Library.

WEEKS, STEPHEN B., Index to the Colonial and State Records of North Carolina.... 1909–14, 4 vols., numbered XXVII–XXX, to follow the numbers of North Carolina State Records.

WILLIAMS, SAMUEL C., ed., Lieut. Henry Timberlake's Memoirs, 1756–1765. Johnson City, Tenn., 1927.

—— ed., James Adair's History of the American Indians. Johnson City, Tenn. 1930.

SELECTED MAPS

(The maps are listed in chronological order.)

FRY, JOSHUA, AND JEFFERSON, PETER, "A map of the most inhabited part of Virginia.... London, T. Jeffreys, 1755 (WLCL).

MITCHELL, JOHN, "A Map of the British Colonies in North America ...." London, Thos. Kitchin, Sculp., 1755 (WLCL).

BONAR, WILLIAM, "A Draught of the Creek Nation," 1757 (MS, WLCL).

STUART, JOHN, "Map of the Cherokee Country," *c.* 1761. *In* Archer B. Hulbert, ed., The Crown Collection of Photographs of American Maps, Second Series, Plate 34. Shows route of Stuart's escape to Virginia in 1760.

WYLY, SAMUEL, "A Map of the Catawba Indians Land surveyed agreeable to an Agreement made with them by His Majesty's Governors of South Carolina, North Carolina, Georgia and Virginia, and Superintendant of Indian Affairs ...," 1764. *In* Archer B. Hulbert, ed., The Crown Collection of Photographs of American Maps, Third Series, Plate 31.

TIMBERLAKE, LIEUT. HENRY, "A Draught of the Cherokee Country ..., *c.* 1762. *In* Samuel C. Williams, ed., Lieut. Henry Timberlake's Memoirs, 1756–1765.

"Boundary Line between the Province of South Carolina and the Cherokee Indian Country ...," 1766. *In* Archer B. Hulbert, ed., The Crown Collection of Photographs of American Maps, Third Series, Plate 43.

[JOHN STUART? W. G. DE BRAHM?] "A Map of the Indian Nations in the Southern Department, 1766" (MS, WLCL).

Map of the Indian Boundary, Accompanying the Board of Trade Report of March 7, 1768. *In* E. B. O'Callaghan, ed., Documents Relating to the Colonial History of the State of New York ..., VIII, opp. p. 31.

SAVERY, SAMUEL, "Sketch of the Boundary Line as it is now mark'd between the afforesaid Province [of Georgia] and the Creek Indian Nation, 1769" (MS, WLCL).

COLLET, CAPT. JOHN, "A Compleat Map of North Carolina from an actual Survey." London, 1770 (WLCL).

DONELSON, JOHN, [Map of the Virginia-Cherokee boundary as laid down in the Donelson survey]. 1771 (photographic copy, WLCL).

[DURNFORD, ELIAS,] "Field Survey of the River Mobile and part of the Rivers Alabama and Tensa with the different Settlements and Lands marked thereon. . . ." 1770? *In* Archer B. Hulbert, ed., The Crown Collection of Photographs of American Maps, Third Series, Plate 91.

[STUART, JOHN,] Map of proposed colony of Vandalia. 1773. *In* Papers of the Continental Congress, No. 71, Vol. II.

[PURCELL, JOSEPH,] "A Map of West Florida part of ET: Florida Georgia part of So: Carolina including [ye?] Chactaw Chickasaw & Creek Nations with road [from?] Pensacola through ye: Creek Nation to Augusta and Charles Town. Compiled under the direction of . . . John Stuart Esqr: [and presented to the] Honble Thomas Gage" [1773] (MS, WLCL). Very useful for locating Indian boundaries and Indian towns. Identified by Mr. Lloyd Brown, former curator of maps of WLCL, as the work of Purcell, who compiled it from maps and reports by Bernard Romans, David Taitt, and others.

—— "A Map of the Southern Indian District of North America Compiled under the Direction of John Stuart Esqr. His Majesty's Superintendant of Indian Affairs" [1773] (photostatic copy, WLCL).

—— "A Map of the Southern Indian District of North America Compiled under the Direction of John Stuart Esqr. His Majesty's Superintendant of Indian Affairs, and by him Humbly Inscribed to the Earl of Dartmouth . . ." [1776] (photostatic copy, WLCL).

—— "Map of the Boundary Line of the Lands ceded to His Majesty by the Chactaw Indians, from the north boundary of West Florida on the Yazoo River to the River Pasca Ocoola. . . ." 1779. In Archer B. Hulbert. ed., The Crown Collection of Photographs of American Maps, Third Series, Plate 116.

FILSON, JOHN, "This Map of Kentucke, drawn from actual observations. . . ." Philadelphia, 1784 (WLCL).

NON-CONTEMPORARY SOURCES

(A few titles of some importance not cited in the text are included in this classification.)

ABERNETHY, THOMAS P., From Frontier to Plantation in Tennessee: A Study in Frontier Democracy. Chapel Hill, 1932.

—— Western Lands and the American Revolution. New York and London, 1937. Detailed study of Western land speculations, frontier advance, and their ramifications. Unsatisfactory in its treatment of John Stuart. The author has not used all the evidence upon Stuart and the Virginia-Cherokee boundary question. He displays a tendency to put great reliance upon partisan evidence from Virginia sources. Characterized in several places by rather hasty judgments.

ALDEN, JOHN R., "The Albany Congress and the Creation of the Indian Superintendencies," Miss. Vall. Hist. Rev., XXVII (1940), 193–210.

ALVORD, CLARENCE W., "Genesis of the Proclamation of 1763," Mich. Pioneer and Hist. Colls., XXXVI (1908), 20–52. Superseded.

——Mississippi Valley in British Politics, 2 vols. Cleveland, 1917. The first monograph devoted to British Western policy from 1754 to 1775. Useful. Parts of it have been superseded. *See* Crane, V. W., and Humphreys, R. A. Is unsatisfactory in its treatment of John Stuart and of the Virginia-Cherokee boundary line.

BAKER-CROTHERS, HAYES, Virginia and the French and Indian War. Chicago, 1928. A thesis.

BARNES, VIOLA, The Dominion of New England: A Study in British Colonial Policy. New Haven, 1923.

BEER, GEORGE LOUIS, British Colonial Policy, 1754–1765. New York, 1907.

BLODGETT, HAROLD, Samson Occom. Hanover, N. H., 1935.

BROWN, JOHN P., Old Frontiers: The Story of the Cherokee Indians from Earliest Times to the Date of Their Removal to the West. Kingsport, Tenn., 1938.

BURKE, JOHN, A Genealogic and Heraldic History of the Landed Gentry.... 4 vols. London, 1838.

CARTER, CLARENCE E., "British Policy Towards the American Indians in the South, 1763–1768," Eng. Hist. Rev., XXXIII (1918), 37–56. Primarily based on materials in the Colonial Office series. Scholarly, but not complete.

——"Significance of the Military Office in America, 1763–1775," Am. Hist. Rev. XXVIII (1923), 475–88. Attempts to prove that the military commander in America tended to become a viceroy. Overemphasizes the powers and influence of the commander in chief. Unsatisfactory in its treatment of relations between him and the Indian superintendents.

CORRY, JOHN P., Indian Affairs in Georgia, 1732–1756. Philadelphia, 1936. A thesis.

CRANE, VERNER W., ed., "Hints Relative to the Division and Government of the Conquered and Newly Acquired Countries in America," Miss. Vall. Hist. Rev., VIII (1922), 367–73. Professor Crane indicates the significance of this document in the formation of the Proclamation of 1763, overlooked by Professor Alvord.

——The Southern Frontier, 1670–1732. Durham, N. C., 1929. A pioneer work and a definitive one for its period. Useful also for the period after 1732.

Dictionary of American Biography.

Dictionary of National Biography.

DODSON, LEONIDAS, Alexander Spotswood, Governor of Colonial Virginia. Philadelphia, 1932.

EASTERBY, J. H., History of the St. Andrew's Society of Charleston, South Carolina, 1729–1929. Charleston, 1929.

FRANKLIN, W. NEIL, "Virginia and the Cherokee Indian Trade, 1673–1752," The East Tennessee Historical Society's Publications, No. 4 (1932), 3–21.

FRANKLIN, W. NEIL, "Virginia and the Cherokee Indian Trade, 1753–1775," The East Tennessee Historical Society's Publications, No. 5 (1933), 22–38.

GREGORIE, ANNE K., Thomas Sumter. Columbia, S. C., 1931.

HALL, JAMES, The Romance of Western History: or, Manners in the West. Cincinnati, 1885.

HAMER, PHILIP M., "Anglo-French Rivalry in the Cherokee Country, 1754–1757," N. Car. Hist. Rev., II (1925), 303–22.

—— "Fort Loudoun in the Cherokee War, 1758–1761," N. Car. Hist. Rev., II (1925), 442–58.

—— "John Stuart's Indian Policy during the Early Months of the American Revolution," Miss. Vall. Hist. Rev., XVII (1930), 351–66.

[HARRISON, FAIRFAX, AND OTHERS,] The John's Island Stud (South Carolina), 1750–1788. Richmond, 1931.

HENDERSON, ARCHIBALD, "Dr. Thomas Walker and the Loyal Company," Proceedings of the American Antiquarian Society, New Series, XLI (1931), 77–178. Professor Henderson's writings in the field of history should be used with caution.

—— "A Pre-Revolutionary Revolt in the Old Southwest," Miss. Vall. Hist. Rev., XVII (1930), 191–212.

—— "Richard Henderson and the Occupation of Kentucky, 1775," Miss. Vall. Hist. Rev., I (1914), 341–63.

—— "The Creative Forces in Westward Expansion: Henderson and Boone," Am. Hist. Rev., XX (1914), 86–107.

—— The Conquest of the Old Southwest. The Romantic Story of the Early Pioneers into Virginia, the Carolinas, Tennessee, and Kentucky, 1740–1790. New York, 1920.

HUMPHREYS, R. A., "Lord Shelburne and the Proclamation of 1763," Eng. Hist. Rev., XLIX (1934), 241–58.

—— "Lord Shelburne and British Colonial Policy, 1766–1768," Eng. Hist. Rev., L (1935), 257–77. The best account of Shelburne's rôle in the formation of British Western policy before the Revolution is contained in this and the preceding article.

JACKSON, GEORGE B., "John Stuart: Superintendent of Indian Affairs for the Southern District," Tenn. Hist. Mag., III (1917), 165–91. A master's thesis, based on printed documents. Sketchy and inevitably inaccurate.

JONES, E. A., American Members of the Inns of Court. London, 1904.

KLINGBERG, FRANK J., "The Indian Frontier in South Carolina as Seen by the S. P. G. Missionary," Journal of Southern History, V (1939), 478–500.

LONG, J. C., Lord Jeffrey Amherst: A Soldier of the King. New York, 1933.

LOSKIEL, GEORGE HENRY, History of the Mission of the United Brethren among the Indians of North America. London, 1794.

MCCALLUM, JAMES D., Eleazar Wheelock, Founder of Dartmouth College. Hanover, N. H., 1939.

MACKENZIE, ALEXANDER, History of the Macleods, with Genealogies of the Principal Families of the Name. Inverness, 1889.

MERIWETHER, ROBERT L., The Expansion of South Carolina, 1729–1765. Kingsport, Tenn., 1940.

MESERVE, JOHN BARTLETT, "The MacIntoshes," Chronicles of Oklahoma, X (1932) 310–25.

MILLING, CHAPMAN C., Red Carolinians. Chapel Hill, 1940. A careful study by a non-professional. Based largely on South Carolina records and Indian legends.

MOHR, WALTER H., Federal Indian Relations, 1774–1788. Philadelphia, 1933. A thesis.

MORRIS, RICHARD B., ed., The Era of the American Revolution. New York, 1939.

PARGELLIS, STANLEY M., Lord Loudoun in North America. New Haven, 1933.

POUND, ARTHUR, Johnson of the Mohawks. New York, 1930. The best biography of Sir William Johnson.

SHAW, HELEN LOUISE, British Administration of the Southern Indians, 1756–1783. Lancaster, Pa., 1931. A study of the financing and structure of the southern Indian department. Latter part of the volume contains a narrative of the activities of the southern superintendents in the Revolution. Limited in scope, and not devoid of errors.

SIOUSSAT, ST. GEORGE L., "The Breakdown of the Royal Management of Lands in the Southern Provinces, 1773–1775," Agricultural History, III (1929), 67–98.

SOMERVILLE, HENRY B., Commodore Anson's Voyage into the South Seas and around the World. London, Toronto, 1934.

South Carolina Historical and Genealogical Magazine, The (1900—).

STARR, EMMETT, History of the Cherokee Indians and Their Legends and Folk Lore. Oklahoma City, 1921.

STEWART, COL. DAVID, Sketches of the Character, Manners, and Present State of the Highlanders of Scotland: With Details of the Military Service of the Highland Regiments. 2 vols. Edinburgh, 1822.

SWANTON, JOHN R., Indian Tribes of the Lower Mississippi Valley and Adjacent Coast of the Gulf of Mexico. Bulletin No. 43, Bureau of American Ethnology, Smithsonian Institution, Washington, D.C., 1911.

—— Early History of the Creek Indians and Their Neighbors. Bulletin No. 73, Bureau of American Ethnology, Smithsonian Institution, Washington, D.C., 1922.

Virginia Magazine of History and Biography, The (1893—).

VOLWILER, A. T., George Croghan and the Westward Movement, 1741–1782. Cleveland, 1926.

WALLACE, DAVID D., The History of South Carolina. 4 vols. New York, 1934.

—— The Life of Henry Laurens, with a Sketch of the Life of Lieutenant-Colonel John Laurens. New York and London, 1915.

WELLS, WILLIAM CHARLES, Two Essays: One upon Single Vision with Two Eyes; the Other on Dew. London, 1818.

WILLIAMS, SAMUEL C., "An Account of the Presbyterian Mission to the Cherokees, 1757–1759," Tenn. Hist. Mag., Second Series, I (1931), 125–38.

INDEX

UNIVERSITY OF MICHIGAN PUBLICATIONS

HISTORY AND POLITICAL SCIENCE

(The first three volumes of this series were published as "Historical Studies," under the direction of the Department of History. Volumes IV and V were published without numbers.)

VOL. I. A HISTORY OF THE PRESIDENT'S CABINET. By Mary L. Hinsdale *(o.p.)*

VOL. II. ENGLISH RULE IN GASCONY, 1199–1259, WITH SPECIAL REFERENCE TO THE TOWNS. By F. B. Marsh. Pp. xi + 178. $1.25.

VOL. III. THE COLOR LINE IN OHIO: A HISTORY OF RACE PREJUDICE IN A TYPICAL NORTHERN STATE. By F. U. Quillan. Pp. xvi + 178. $1.50.

VOL. IV. THE SENATE AND TREATIES, 1789–1817. THE DEVELOPMENT OF THE TREATY-MAKING FUNCTIONS OF THE UNITED STATES SENATE DURING THEIR FORMATIVE PERIOD. By R. Hayden. Pp. xvi + 237. $1.50.

VOL. V. WILLIAM PLUMER'S MEMORANDUM OF PROCEEDINGS IN THE UNITED STATES SENATE, 1803–1807. Edited by E. S. Brown. Pp. xi + 673. $3.50.

VOL. VI. THE GRAIN SUPPLY OF ENGLAND DURING THE NAPOLEONIC PERIOD. By W. F. Galpin. Pp. xi + 305. $3.00.

VOL. VII. EIGHTEENTH CENTURY DOCUMENTS RELATING TO THE ROYAL FORESTS, THE SHERIFFS AND SMUGGLINGS: SELECTED FROM THE SHELBURNE MANUSCRIPTS IN THE WILLIAM L. CLEMENTS LIBRARY. By Arthur Lyon Cross. Pp. xvii + 328. $3.00.

VOL. VIII. THE LOW COUNTRIES AND THE HUNDRED YEARS' WAR, 1326–1347. By Henry S. Lucas. Pp. xviii + 696. $4.00.

VOL. IX. THE ANGLO-FRENCH TREATY OF COMMERCE OF 1860 AND THE PROGRESS OF THE INDUSTRIAL REVOLUTION IN FRANCE. By A. L. Dunham. Pp. xi + 410. $3.00.

VOL. X. THE YOUTH OF ERASMUS. By Albert Hyma. Pp. xi + 350. $3.00.

VOL. XI. UNIVERSITY OF MICHIGAN HISTORICAL ESSAYS. Edited by A. E. R. Boak. Pp. vii + 182. $2.25.

VOL. XII. THE SIEGE OF CHARLESTON, WITH AN ACCOUNT OF THE PROVINCE OF SOUTH CAROLINA: DIARIES AND LETTERS OF HESSIAN OFFICERS FROM THE VON JUNGKENN PAPERS IN THE WILLIAM L. CLEMENTS LIBRARY. Translated and edited by B. A. Uhlendorf. Pp. xi + 445. $4.00.

VOL. XIII. THE MICHIGAN CONSTITUTIONAL CONVENTIONS OF 1835–36: DEBATES AND PROCEEDINGS. By Harold M. Dorr. Pp. xi + 625. $5.00.

VOL. XIV. FEDERAL COÖPERATION WITH THE STATES UNDER THE COMMERCE CLAUSE. By Joseph E. Kallenbach. Pp. viii + 428. $4.00.

VOL. XV. JOHN STUART AND THE SOUTHERN COLONIAL FRONTIER: A STUDY OF INDIAN RELATIONS, WAR, TRADE, AND LAND PROBLEMS IN THE SOUTHERN WILDERNESS, 1754–75. By John Richard Alden. Pp. xii + 384. $4.00.

Orders and requests for detailed book lists should be directed to the University of Michigan Press, Ann Arbor, Michigan.